Beverly Cassar
2006

ENDORSEMENTS

JOSEPH FARAH

Founder, WorldNetDaily.com

What's going on in our world? Where are we headed? What does it all mean? Dave Hunt has nailed it. This book is a wake up call to a sleep-walking world trying to make sense of events that were foretold in the greatest book ever written, the Bible.

RANDALL PRICE, PH.D.

Founder & President World of the Bible Ministries, Inc.

Holding a Th.M. in Old Testament and Semitic Languages, and a Ph.D. in Middle Eastern Studies, Dr. Price is a prolific author who lectures worldwide about Israel and Islam; he also leads educational tours and directs archaeological excavations in Israel

It has been said that there may be moderate Muslims, but Islam is not moderate. Dave Hunt ably exposes this fact and reminds us that the Islam producing today's terrorism is the Islam of its founder, Mohammed. As such, it is as much a threat to Judaism and Christianity today as it was when it was first spread by the sword in the seventh century A.D. Dave's impassioned warning, however, goes beyond the political to the prophetic, alerting us of the judgment that is about to befall this planet and how to prepare an escape before that day arrives.

HANS KRISTIAN

President of the International Sakharov Committee, Author of 33 Books

This is the most important book on the issues of the Middle East and the Holy Land. Strangely enough, historians, politicians, journalists, and even Christians believe the lies and falsification of "history" conceived by the Muslims and repeated as fact through decades and centuries of propaganda. Dave Hunt goes to the roots and digs up from history...the coming judgment on Israel, Islam, and the nations. Everyone who loves the truth—whether Christian, Muslim, or Jew—should read it. This book can change hearts—and even today's politics.

EARL POYSTI

FOUNDER OF RUSSIAN CHRISTIAN RADIO DURING THE
IRON CURTAIN DAYS, HIS INFLUENCE CONTINUES TODAY
AS PRESIDENT EMERITUS OF RCR

This latest book from Dave Hunt is a must read for everyone everywhere. Well written and heavily documented, Judgment Day makes us realize that we need to wake up to the truth of what is happening in our world. The information it contains is shocking, but the reader will be thankful for the facts. The further one reads, the more compelling it becomes. Especially impressive is the courage of the author to name many of our most highly respected leaders—exposing the truth of where they have stood regarding Islam and Israel.

DAVID SIEGEL

FREELANCE RESEARCHER AND EDITOR OF MEMOIRS
OF HOLOCAUST SURVIVORS; ISRAELI CITIZEN

Dave Hunt's Judgment Day: Israel, Islam and the Nations is clearly written from a Christian Biblical perspective. His treatment of the subject offers no room for political correctness, ecumenical accommodation, or denominational loyalty. Hunt believes that many who claim to be Christians either fail to understand what the Bible says about Israel, or they willfully go against what is written. Whether they are presidents, prime ministers, popes or pivotal Protestant leaders, they risk much by going against what is plainly written in the Bible. The forces arrayed against Israel are well-organized, and quite committed to her destruction. It would be a move of wisdom for Christians to make sure which side they are on. As a Jew of Israel, through the writings of Dave Hunt I have come to appreciate the Biblical imperative for "sola scriptura" Christians to support Israel—spiritually, theologically, and personally.

DEDICATED TO

ALL LOVERS OF TRUTH

AND FREEDOM

UNDER GOD

IN THE HOPE THAT

THE WORLD

(MUSLIM AND NON-MUSLIM)

WILL ESCAPE

THE TYRANNY

OF ISLAM

JUDGMENT DAY!
ISLAM, ISRAEL AND THE NATIONS

DAVE HUNT

The
Berean
Call

BEND • OREGON

JUDGMENT DAY!
ISLAM, ISRAEL AND THE NATIONS

Published by The Berean Call
Copyright © 2005

International Standard Book Number: 1-928660-32-0
Library of Congress Control Number: 2005927651

Unless otherwise indicated, Scripture quotations are from
The Holy Bible, King James Version (KJV)

Printed in the United States of America

The Berean Call
PO Box 7019
Bend, Oregon, 97708-7019

CONTENTS

1—THE STAGE IS SET

THE GOD OF THE BIBLE STATES: "I am God…there is none like me, declaring the end from the beginning, and from ancient times the things that are not yet done…before it came to pass I showed it thee…new things do I declare: before they spring forth I tell you of them."[1] Only the Bible foretells centuries and even thousands of years in advance major events of world history. These numerous prophecies identify beyond question the one true God and the Bible as His unique revelation to mankind.

Some of these prophecies, to which we will turn, are specifically *for our day*. They set the stage for severe judgment from God, for which planet earth is rapidly ripening.

Indisputably, Israel is the major topic of biblical prophecy, just as it is of the daily news. The word "Israel" is found 2,565 times in 2,293 verses in the King James translation of the Bible, while "Jerusalem" is found 811 times in 764 verses. In contrast, the word "Jerusalem" is not found even once in the Qur'an. Yet Muslims insist that Jerusalem is their third holiest city. That this is a false claim we will document beyond dispute, as well as the fact that those who call themselves "Palestinians" and who make the claim that Israel is occupying their land are imposters *(see chapter four)*.

Prophecies concerning Israel and Jerusalem are precise and beyond misinterpretation. We will confine ourselves to several that are clearly being fulfilled in our times. Some of them specifically warn of God's judgment upon those who attempt to bring a "peace" to the Middle East that defies what God has decreed for His people Israel. The methods that the West has adopted in recent decades are denounced in Scripture, including the current "road map to peace."

Remarkably, the prophecies we will focus upon in the following pages could apply only to the present day. Unrecognized by world leaders, who ignore the warnings in the Bible, God is at work behind the scenes, bringing about events that He has foretold in His Word. In the following pages, we will present specific fulfilled prophecies for our day, examples of what God says *He is presently doing on this earth—and the punishment He is about to pour out upon the nations for their mistreatment of His people, the Jews, and Israel.* Hundreds of prophecies fulfilled in the past are the guarantee that biblical warnings are not empty threats.

A CUP OF TREMBLING, A BURDENSOME STONE

Two thousand five hundred years ago, the God of the Bible, through His prophet Zechariah, declared, "Behold, I will make Jerusalem a cup of trembling unto all the people round about, when they shall be in the siege both against Judah and against Jerusalem."[2] This is an amazing declaration—not only that Jerusalem, which was then in complete ruins, would be the focus of world attention one day but also that all of Israel's neighbors would be united against her.

Throughout its history, Israel has had many enemies (Egyptians, Philistines, Syrians, Assyrians, Babylonians, etc.). Never, however, did "all the people round about" (i.e., her neighbors) join together in common cause to destroy her. This is true today, exactly as the Bible foretold, *for the first time* in Israel's history! Moreover, it marks the beginning of the end of anti-Semitism, as we shall see.

God goes on to say, "And in that day will I make Jerusalem a burdensome stone for all people...." The language is very precise:

a "burdensome stone" for "all people," but a "cup of trembling" for Israel's neighbors around her. What is the difference?

For more than fifty years, Israel's neighbors have attacked her repeatedly and she has proved too strong militarily for them, even though they outnumber her fifty to one and have tried to catch her by surprise. Soundly defeated every time, her neighbors tremble and feign a desire for peace with the aim, of course, ultimately to deceive and annihilate her—a strategy established for Muslims by Muhammad himself, the founder and prophet of Islam.

The God of the Bible has promised to protect Israel, while Allah of the Qur'an and Islam has sworn to put an end to her. The real battle is not between Arabs and Jews but between Allah and Yahweh. There is no question of the outcome, but it will be costly for both sides: Israel will be severely disciplined and her enemies will be destroyed.

Precisely as foretold, Jerusalem is a burdensome stone to all people of the world. How much of a burden is she? The United Nations has spent one-third of its time either deliberating and arguing about or denouncing Israel because of its hold upon Jerusalem. A tiny nation that has one one-thousandth of the world's population has occupied one-third of the United Nations' time! More than sixty thousand individual votes have been cast in the UN against Israel. That is a burden indeed, exactly as the Bible foretold! Is this merely a coincidence? We will pile prophecy upon prophecy being fulfilled in our day until "coincidence" is revealed as utter foolishness.

Skeptics have accused evangelicals of trying to fit prophecy to current events, claiming that no one recognized such prophecies in the past but only since Israel was formed in 1948. On the contrary, for centuries before it happened, most evangelical Christians believed and preached from the Bible the return of the Jews to their own land. Even leading Calvinist, John Owen, wrote in the seventeenth century: "The Jews shall be gathered from all parts of the earth...and brought home into their homeland."[3]

Martin Luther recognized some of the prophecies concerning Israel, and because they had not been fulfilled in his day, he wrote off the Jews as God's chosen people: "If the Jews are Abraham's descendants then we would expect to see them back in their own land [with] a state of their own. But what do we see? We see them living scattered and despised."[4] The prophecies concerning Israel were not for Luther's day but for ours. The very fact that the Jews are back in their own land after twenty-five hundred years of being scattered worldwide, and that they speak their original Hebrew just as King David did three thousand years ago, is a remarkable fulfillment of another Bible prophecy for the last days. No other people have returned to establish their own nation once again, having retained their original language, and after being out of their land for such a period of time.

There would seem to be more than enough reasons for this tiny and only recently re-birthed nation to tremble before the enemies surrounding her and before the condemnations of the UN and European Union. Surely such a small country could be easily pushed around. Of course, if that were the case, she would be a burden to no one. But Israel can't be pushed around, either by her neighbors or by anyone else. The Israeli Defense Forces are among the best in the world.

LIKE A FIRE DEVOURING SURROUNDING NATIONS

And that fulfills another prophecy: "In that day will I make the governors of Judah like an hearth of fire among the wood…and they shall devour all the people round about…."[5] This is exactly what has happened, to the surprise and chagrin of the world. Notice the repetition in many last days prophecies of the phrase, *I will.* God is doing something on this earth in preparation for judging the nations. Those who refuse to see God's hand at work will reap the consequences for their unbelief in the face of overwhelming evidence.

In what became known as the Yom Kippur War of October 1973, the attacking Arab forces from Egypt (eighty thousand Egyptians overwhelmed five hundred Israeli defenders along the Suez) and Syria (fourteen hundred tanks swept down the Golan with only *one* Israeli tank in service to oppose them) caught Israel completely by surprise. The Soviets knew exactly when the attack was coming (October 6, 1973) and removed the last of the dependents of their staffs on October 5. America's National Security Administration (NSA) knew that an Arab Pearl Harbor was about to be launched against Israel. Dozens of notices were sent by the NSA to the Nixon White House, which had positive evidence at least two days in advance of the attack. Nixon, however, for his own reasons (he didn't like the Israelis because they knew too much about his past), chose not to notify Israel, probably imagining that this horrible betrayal of our only real ally in the Middle East would not be discovered.

The White House finally gave Israel a reprehensible few hours notice, but insisted that Israel refrain from preemptive strikes and be certain not to fire the first shot. U.S. Secreatry of State Henry Kissinger went incommunicado at the Waldorf Astoria hotel in New York the day of the attack and waited another three days before convening the UN Security Council. He wanted the Israelis to be bloodied up a bit. Instead of rushing military supplies to Israel, the United States gave the excuse that it had to be careful not to upset the Arabs and cause an oil crisis—and that no American airline was willing to fly even the spare parts Israel was pleading for into the war zone. Oil negotiations were underway in Vienna at that very time. Any country that helped Israel in the war faced an oil embargo. Most of Israel's armed forces were off duty, celebrating Judaism's highest holy day. The initial success of the attackers, when Israel was trying to mobilize its military and reservists, so electrified the Arab world that nine other Arab states rushed to get in on the slaughter. "The Soviet Union blocked any UN attempt at a cease-fire and refortified the Arab forces with armaments and supplies from the air and the sea."[6] Israel suffered about three thousand dead—a huge percentage of her population, which would be comparable to one hundred fifty thousand dead for the United States. Except for a series of what could only be called miracles from God, Israel would not have survived.

History Professor David A. Rausch writes, "Jordan's King Hussein sent two of his best armored brigades to Syria. Saudi Arabia and Kuwait financially underwrote the huge cost while sending thousands of troops to fight the Israelis. Kuwait lent her British-made Lightning jets to Egypt. Libya's Muammar Qaddafi turned over forty French-made Mirage III fighters and 100 tanks. Iraqi MiG fighter jets as well as tank and infantry divisions fought on the Golan Heights, while a squadron of Iraqi Hunter jets were utilized by Egypt. Arabs predicted the extermination of the Jewish state and the 'liberation' of Palestine."[7] It was the closest Israel ever came to being defeated. But when the war ended, the Israeli tank columns were on the outskirts of Damascus and Cairo and could have taken those cities had they not been called back for political reasons.

A STERN WARNING TO ALL NATIONS

God goes on to say through His prophet, "All that burden themselves with it [Jerusalem/Israel] shall be cut in pieces, though all the people of the earth be gathered together against it." Obviously Israel, no matter how efficient her armed forces may be, cannot defeat *all* the nations of the world. God does not waste words. A world united in a huge military attack upon Israel is not an idle speculation. Clearly, God is declaring that *all* nations will come against Jerusalem and that He will defend Israel and destroy them. This solemn declaration is made a number of times in the Bible.

But why would God bring all nations against Jerusalem and Israel in order to put an end to them? God gives two very clear reasons: "I will also gather all nations, and will bring them down into the valley of Jehoshaphat, and will plead with [punish] them there for my people and for my heritage Israel, whom they have scattered among the nations, and parted my land."[8]

This is a grim prophecy, precise in its language, and once again it applies only to our day. For twenty-five hundred years all nations have played their role in persecuting and thereby scattering the Jews around the world. Only within the last eighty years, however, has the land been divided. Israel has been conquered by many nations in the past, from the Babylonians to the Romans to the Turks. Always, the conquering power occupied the entire land. Never did they divide the land. That has only recently occurred for the first time in world history—and *all* nations united to do so.

The 1917 Balfour Declaration, 1919 Paris Peace Conference, and 1922 Declaration of Principles of the League of Nations recognized that the ancient land of Israel (which had come to be known as "Palestine") belonged to the Jewish people. It was set apart for them, and Great Britain was given the mandate to see that "Palestine" once again became the national homeland of the Jews who had been scattered worldwide.

Instead, to curry Arab favor because of their oil, Britain divided it, giving more than 70 percent to its protégé, Emir Abdullah Hussein, when he was forced to leave the ancestral Hashemite domain in Arabia. That gift created the Hashemite kingdom of Transjordan, now known as Jordan. The Muslims immediately demolished every Jewish house of worship and expelled all Jews. This was months before the State of Israel was born. (One can count the demise of the British Empire, upon which "the sun never sank," from the time it betrayed the Jews, as God had warned: "I will...curse him that curseth thee."[9]) In UN Resolution 181, November 29, 1947, the nations joined to further divide the land. Israel received only 13 percent of what had been designated for the national Jewish homeland. They were pleased to get anything. The Arabs, however, wanted it all. They rioted and attacked Jewish settlements in a reign of terror.

Every so-called peace proposal that the Western powers have since attempted to force upon Israel has been based upon their demand that she relinquish yet more land to the "Palestinians." Always the cry is, "Just give them a little more!" So it is with President Bush's "road map to peace"—a further dividing of the land. But God has said, "The land shall not be sold [or traded] for ever: for the land is mine...."[10]

God's patience is almost exhausted. His righteous anger is directed against the nations of today's world for dividing His land, and against Israel for ever agreeing to do so. And He is going to punish everyone involved. President Bush, who claims that he is a Christian and that he studies his Bible daily, ought to tremble! So should the other parties to the "road map." They are defying God and planning to do what He says will bring His severest judgment, "a destruction from the Almighty." [11] We will deal with that awesome reality in the last chapter. It is astonishing how many Christians and Jews who claim to believe the Bible remain blind to these prophecies, which are clearly hastening to their fulfillment in our day.

ENTER ISLAM!

The enemies surrounding Israel today have one thing that unites them: they are all Muslims. A basic tenet of Islam is that Israel and all Jews must be destroyed. That qualifies them for special wrath from "the Almighty." Yet this prophecy was recorded in Scripture more than one thousand years before Islam was founded. Muhammad said, as recorded in the Sahih Al-Bukhari *hadith*, "The last day will not come until the Muslims confront the Jews and the Muslims destroy them. In that day Allah will give a voice to the rocks and the trees and they will cry out, 'O Muslim, O Abdullah, there is a Jew hiding behind me. Come and kill him!'" [12]

That every Jew on earth must be killed is not an obscure teaching but part of the very foundation of Islam, taught to Muslims down through the centuries from their earliest years. It is taught in every Muslim school all over the world and in the United States as well.

Why must Israel be destroyed? Why not just leave her where she is and isolate the despised Jews from the rest of the world to be confined there? Why not simply reduce her to poverty by economic boycott?

That would not be enough, because it would leave the Jews in possession of part of the land that the Arabs claim Allah has promised to them as their sole right. The very existence of Israel stands as a rebuke to the declarations of the Prophet Muhammad, the Qur'an, and Islamic tradition, which all declare that the land of Palestine belongs solely to the Arabs—and that they will triumph over the Jews.

The Jewish state of Israel must be crushed! Otherwise, Islam has been proved a false religion. So long as Islam exists, in spite of volumes of rhetoric and mountains of peace negotiations, the Middle

East conflict can be resolved in no other way than by the annihilation of Israel. To imagine otherwise or that the Arabs have any other intention is to be hopelessly deceived.

At a conference of the Islamic Committee for Palestine, in Chicago, Illinois, December 28–31, 1990, Sheikh Abdul Aziz Oudeh, one of the leaders in the Islamic Jihad movement, declared: "Now Allah is bringing the Jews back to Palestine in large groups from all over the world to their big graveyard where the promise will be realized upon them, and what was destined will be carried out."[13] Of course, he was not referring to the many biblical prophecies that God would, in the last days, bring the scattered Jews back into their own land, where the Messiah would return to reign over them and the world from the throne of His father David. He was obviously referring to Muhammad's prophecy (in direct opposition to the Bible) that the Muslims would kill all Jews at the last day.

This was also the prophecy to which Sheikh Yousef al-Kirdawi referred when in 1989 in Kansas City he told a group of Muslim men whom he was recruiting for Holy War, "On the Hour of Judgment, Muslims will fight the Jews and kill them."[14] Clearly, the battle is not so much between Arab and Jew as it is between Allah, the God of Islam and the Qur'an, who hates and has sworn to destroy the Jews, and Yahweh, the God of the Bible, who loves the Jews and has sworn to protect them. There is no question that Allah and Yahweh are not the same!

The consequences for those who follow the wrong "God" will be severe. This is the issue that political, military, and religious leaders are not willing to face. Consequently, they are defying the God of the Bible and will be punished. If that does not occur exactly as prophesied, then all of the Christian seminaries and churches should be shut down as representing an outright fraud. We cannot pick and choose some parts of the Bible and reject others—but this irrational attitude is popularly accepted today.

THIS IS ISLAM!

There is not an Arab/Muslim map in the entire world that shows Israel! The logos of the PLO and similar terrorist groups display "Palestine" without Israel. For Muslims and "Palestinians," Israel does not exist, and they are determined to make that a reality. Apparently, without ever having noticed this damning fact, Israel is also missing from the map of the Middle East on the wall of the apartment of the Christian Peacemaker Team "living in Hebron in solidarity with the Palestinians against 'colonialist' Israel."[15] Until these facts are faced and somehow dealt with, any "peace" plans for the Middle East are a fool's dream.

Although there are Arabs living in all of the Middle Eastern countries, and they are collectively referred to as "the Arab world," these neighboring nations that seek Israel's destruction are not primarily of Arab descent. The Lebanese, Syrians, and Iranians are not Arabs, nor are the Iraqis, the Egyptians, Libyans, Moroccans, Tunisians, Algerians, et al. Only the Saudis are Arabs.

Islam is an Arab religion that originated in the Arabian Peninsula. It was the conquests in the past by Islam's legions of *jihad* warriors that "converted" Israel's neighbors under threat of death: "Submit to Allah, or die!" And it is the religion of Islam to which they were forcefully converted and are now fanatically devoted that unites these otherwise diverse peoples in the passion to annihilate Israel.

Israel's neighbors were not united ethnically, politically, or religiously when Zechariah's remarkable prophecy (it must have seemed impossible in his day) was given twenty-five hundred years ago. Even the popular T. E. Lawrence (Lawrence of Arabia) had found it impossible to unite Arabs in a sense of nationalism. The only unity came "by invoking the deeply rooted religious prejudice of the masses against the Palestinian Jews...." On their part, the British blamed the Jews for provoking the Arabs to hatred and murder "by their very presence."

Were it not for their common hatred of Israel today, these nations would fight one another. One cannot understand the present situation in the Middle East without acknowledging that it is the devotion of Israel's neighbors to the religion of Islam that unites them against her, a fact that western peacemakers refuse to acknowledge, dooming their efforts from the beginning.

This religious unity is not the ancient heritage of these nations. In their early histories they all worshiped different gods and fought one another. It was the Muslim conquest beginning in the seventh century that united these nations by force under Allah and Islam. This was the fastest spreading and largest empire ever seen—and the greatest example of the imperialism of which these Muslim nations accuse Israel!

Arab leaders have declared repeatedly for more than fifty years, "The struggle with the Zionist enemy is not a struggle about Israel's borders, but about Israel's existence." [16] Such statements do not come from a few fanatics but from every true Muslim who knows and practices his religion. This is Islam! Yet these basic facts are avoided by the West in its attempts to establish "peace" in the Middle East.

JERUSALEM: ANOTHER SIGN IN OUR DAY

The possession of a large part of the world's major oil deposits allows Muslim nations to exercise incredible clout for Islam and Allah. Aware of that fact, the European Union continues to remind Israel that it "does not recognize Israel's sovereignty" over Jerusalem. The Vatican, for its own reasons (numerous official documents declare that the Church has replaced Israel as the "people of God"), has opposed Israel consistently, refusing even to recognize its existence until 1994, forty-six years after its declaration of independence. The PLO is in control of Temple Mount, the very heart and soul of Jerusalem. The nations of the world refuse to recognize Jerusalem as Israel's capital.

The United Nations has consistently taken the side of the Arabs against Israel, making the creation of the State of Israel by the UN in 1947—something the UN would not do today—all the more miraculous in fulfillment of Bible prophecy. The UN is adamantly opposed to Israel and everything she does—and is thus defiant of the God of Israel and His pledge to restore His people fully to the land He gave them "from the river of Egypt unto the great river, the river Euphrates."[17] From 1967 through 1989, out of 865 resolutions in the Security Council and General Assembly of the UN, 526 were against Israel. The last anti-Arab vote was fifty-eight years ago, in 1947. Not once has the UN reprimanded those who have without provocation, beginning in 1948, waged five wars against Israel with the openly declared intention of annihilating her. Nor have the terrorists ever been condemned by the UN. In November 2003, Israel introduced its first request for a resolution since 1976, asking for a prohibition against Arab terrorists who deliberately target Israeli women and children. Its request was rejected and the UN instead adopted a resolution demanding protection of Palestinian children from Israel.

On March 25, 2004, the United States blocked a proposed UN Security Council condemnation of Israel's targeted killing of Hamas founder and leader, Sheikh Ahmed Yassin, because the Council refused to include a condemnation of Hamas terrorist attacks on Israeli civilians. The next month, an Israeli missile also killed Yassin's successor, Abdul-Aziz Rantisi. (No wonder Israel's neighbors tremble, considering the technology, precision, and flawless execution required to identify immediately the occupants of a car and destroy it within minutes with a missile!) Hamas has not identified Rantisi's successor for obvious reasons. Again, there was worldwide condemnation for the just execution of a mass murderer and terrorist leader, but no condemnation for the hundreds of suicide bombers Hamas has trained, equipped, and sent into Israel deliberately to kill innocent civilians.

Indeed, suicide bombers (President Bush calls them "homicide bombers," i.e., murderers [18]) are the most honored people in PLO territory. The PLO-controlled newspaper has "wedding announcements" and invitations to join in celebration with families who are rejoicing over the "marriage" of terrorist sons to the "black-eyed" virgins in Paradise through their martyrdom by suicide in Israel, killing innocent women and children in the process.

The very morning of September 11, 2001, in a time zone six hours to the east, an editorial in Arafat's controlled newspaper, *Al-Hayat al-Jadida*, stated, "The suicide bombers of today are the noble successors of the Lebanese suicide bombers who taught the U.S. Marines a tough lesson in Lebanon [243 were killed when a barracks was destroyed]. These suicide bombers are the salt of the earth, the engines of history…the most honorable people among us." Then, down came the Twin Towers, to the glory of Islam and Allah!

JERUSALEM TRODDEN DOWN BY THE GENTILES

We are also witnessing in our day the continuing fulfillment of Christ's remarkable prophecy: "Jerusalem shall be trodden down of the Gentiles, until the times of the Gentiles be fulfilled."[19] Jerusalem has been fought over and occupied by nearly every major power in history. Today, though Israel is militarily in control of Jerusalem, non-Jews continue to reject her legitimacy and to dictate practical policy with regard to Jerusalem. According to Christ, this will continue to be the case until Armageddon. Only then will the "times of the Gentiles" be fulfilled.

When Israel took East Jerusalem in 1967, and her soldiers wept at the Wailing Wall, it seemed that Jerusalem had at last been liberated from Gentile domination. However, acting on his own without official approval, General Moshe Dayan, apparently hoping to prove to the Arab nations Israel's peaceful intentions, turned over Temple Mount (the holiest site in Israel) to the king of Jordan. In 1994, Jordan turned it over to the PLO. This openly terrorist organization through its Waqf (in charge of Muslim sites on Temple Mount) remains in control. It is in the process of building the largest mosque in the world underground (weakening supporting walls holding up the Temple Mount and blaming Israel for their collapse) and at the same time attempting to eliminate every vestige of any historic Israeli presence there. In this construction, the Waqf has destroyed tons of priceless ancient artifacts. The PLO defiantly claims that there never was a Jewish temple on Temple Mount and that this location was never a holy site for Jews—and much of the world believes the lie!

In fact, there are numerous Arab and Muslim statements going back centuries acknowledging Jerusalem and Temple Mount as holy to the Jews. In A.D. 1225, the Arab geographer Yakut, while noting that Mecca was "holy to Muslims," wrote that "the city of Jerusalem was holy to Jews and Christians, as it has been for 3,000 [years]."[20] There are many references in early Arab literature to the fact that the Dome of the Rock was built on the site of the ruins of Solomon's temple. The very fact that, as far back as we can trace, it has always been known as Temple Mount proves that it was the site of a temple—which could only have been Jewish, not Islamic, because Muslims don't have temples but mosques.

The 1978 *Palestinian Encyclopedia* declared, "Ever since the destruction of the Temple, the link with Jews and Christians has been severed."[21] The Palestinian Authority itself has acknowledged that "Umar [in fact, it wasn't Umar but Abd al-Malik] ordered the building of a mosque [Dome of the Rock] on the site of the ruined temple…a revivification of the old Jewish temple…the mosque was not a 'usurper' of a Jewish holy site [but] a legitimate celebration of that site."[22] Yet Muslims today promote the lie of Jerusalem and Temple Mount belonging to them as a major argument against Israel—and that becomes the basis of the world's attitude toward Israel!

Israel considers Jerusalem to be its capital. It became Israel's capital under King David three thousand years ago. Israel's Knesset is located there. The embassies of other nations, however (with the exception of Costa Rica and El Salvador), are located elsewhere. UN Resolution 181, November 29, 1947, which partitioned "Palestine," decreed that "the city of Jerusalem shall be established as a *corpus separatum* under a special international regime, and shall be administered by the United Nations." The UN Security Council, in UN Resolution 478, declared that the 1980 Jerusalem Law designating Jerusalem as Israel's "eternal and indivisible" capital was "null and void and must be rescinded forthwith" (14-0-1, U.S. abstaining). The resolution instructed member states to withdraw their diplomatic representation from the city as a punitive measure. On March 26, 1999, the EU published its "Berlin Declaration" supporting an independent Palestinian state, and the German Ambassador to Israel reiterated that the EU considers the *corpus separatum* declaration of UN Resolution 181 to be "international law." The UN, EU, and the Vatican periodically insist that Israel's "occupation" of Jerusalem is illegal. So the fulfillment of Christ's prophecy continues in our day.

The United States Jerusalem Embassy Act, passed by Congress in 1995, states that "Jerusalem should be recognized as the capital of the State of Israel; and the United States Embassy in Israel should be established in Jerusalem no later than May 31, 1999." Since then, the relocation of the embassy from Tel Aviv has been suspended by the President semi-annually, each time stating that "[the] Administration remains committed to beginning the process of moving our embassy to Jerusalem." As a result of the Embassy Act, official U.S. documents and websites refer to Jerusalem as the capital of Israel. On its part, Israel considers itself not to be bound by Resolution 181 because it was rejected by the Arabs in the UN and in their coordinated attack upon the new state of Israel.

Section 214 of the *Foreign Relations Authorization Act*, 2003, states:

> The Congress maintains its commitment to relocating the United States Embassy in Israel to Jerusalem and urges the President to immediately begin the process of relocating the United States Embassy in Israel to Jerusalem.[23]

STILL TRODDEN DOWN

President Bush dismisses this section as "advisory," stating that it "impermissibly interferes with the President's constitutional authority."[24] Bush is technically correct. The U.S. Constitution reserves the conduct of foreign policy to the President. Therefore, acts of Congress that make foreign policy are invalid. But one wonders why, as a professing Christian, President Bush doesn't take a step that would honor the Bible and the God of Israel, especially since Congress urges him to do so.

Is Bush fearful of offending Muslims because they control most of the world's oil? Surely he is not intimidated by the denunciations they periodically pronounce against the very thought of America moving its embassy to Jerusalem. One of the latest such threats came from Sheik Ibrahim Madiras in his Friday sermon broadcast over Palestinian television on January 7, 2005: "Bush dug a grave the day he invaded Afghanistan, and prepared the grave for burial the day he invaded Iraq. By Allah, America will be buried the day the American embassy will be moved to Jerusalem...."[25] The Sheik acknowledges that the battle for Jerusalem pits Allah against the God of the Bible.

While visiting Jerusalem in 1998, the Vatican's foreign minister likewise called the Israeli presence in East Jerusalem "illegal occupation." In March 1999, Israel was notified again that the European Union "does not recognize Israel's sovereignty" over Jerusalem. In a papal bull on the year 2000 jubilee, John Paul II again rejected Israeli sovereignty over Jerusalem.

In mid-February 2000, the Vatican signed an agreement with the PLO calling for "international guarantees" to preserve "the proper identity and sacred character" of Jerusalem under international control. Waqf director Adnan Husseini, declared, "Israel needs to remember that Jerusalem is not an Israeli city but it is a Palestinian city and we decide what happens here."[26]

Precisely as Christ foretold nearly two thousand years ago, Jerusalem is still being "trodden down by the Gentiles"! That fact is nowhere more thoroughly documented than in the book, *Jerusalem: The Truth*, a compilation of editorials by David Bar-Illan, Executive Editor of *The Jerusalem Post*.

The God of Israel will not allow this desecration of His "holy city,"[27] the "city of God,"[28] to continue beyond the time Christ appointed.

In fact, Jerusalem has been an Israeli city for three thousand years since David established it. Arabs who call themselves "Palestinians" dispute that claim. To whom does Jerusalem and all of the land that once was Israel but is now erroneously called "Palestine" really belong? The truth is a matter of history and the testimony of Scripture, which is easily proved.

1. Isaiah 42:9; 46:9-10; 48:5, etc.
2. Zechariah 12:2.
3. Cited in Bridges for Peace website, May 21, 2004.
4. J. Randall Price, Paper delivered at the Pre-Trib Study Group Conference, December 6, 2004, available at http://www.pre-trib.org/article-view.php?id=218.
5. Zechariah 12:6.
6. David A. Rausch, *The Middle East Maze: Israel and Her Neighbors* (Chicago: Moody Press, 1991), 57.
7. Ibid.
8. Joel 3:2.
9. Genesis 12:3.
10. Leviticus 25:23.
11. Isaiah 13:6.
12. Moshe Ma'oz, *The Image of the Jew in Official Arab Literature and Communications Media* (Hebrew University of Jerusalem, 1976), 14.
13. From the PBS video, *Jihad In America*, narrated by Steven Emerson, first aired in the USA November 22, 1994.
14. Variations of this statement by Muhammad are given in a number of *hadiths* and other authoritative places. Sheikh Nadim Al-Jisr, Member of the Islamic Research Academy, cited several versions in his presentation at the Fourth Conference of the Academy titled, "Good Tidings about the Decisive Battle Between Muslims and Israel, in the Light of the Holy Qur'an, the Prophetic Traditions, and the Fundamental Laws of Nature and History": Muslim's Sahih Bukhari's Sahih, both on the authority of Ibn'Umar; another version on the authority of Abu Huraira, etc.
15. Yossi Klein Halevi, "A pilgrimage to Hebron," *The International Jerusalem Post*, August 15, 2003, 12.
16. Bassam Abu Sharif, a top Arafat aide and PLO spokesman, quoted by the Kuwait News Agency, May 31, 1986.
17. Genesis 15:18.
18. From President Bush's famous June 24, 2002, speech in which he proposed the "Road Map to Peace" and called upon Israel to dismantle Israeli settlement outposts erected since March 2001.
19. Luke 21:24.
20. Eliyahu Tal, *Whose Jerusalem?* (Tel Aviv: International Forum for a United Jerusalem, 1994), 69.
21. *Palestinian Encyclopedia* (Beirut, 1978), 2:667.
22. Sari Nusseibeh, "Islam's Jerusalem," Seminar on Jerusalem—Religious Aspects, Milan, Italy, May 9-11, 1995 (Jerusalem: Academic Society for the Study of International Affairs, May 2001), 4.
23. http://www.mideastweb.orgjeruembassy2002.htm.
24. http://www.state.gov/m/rm/rls/rm/2002/13888.htm.
25. www.worldnetdaily.com/news/article.asp?ARTICLE_ID=42305.
26. *Jerusalem Post*, November 4, 2004.
27. Nehemiah 11:1, 18; Isaiah 48:2; 52:1; Daniel 9:24; Matthew 4:5 ;27:53; Revelation 11:2; 21:2.
28. Psalm 46:4; 48:1, 8; 87:3; Revelation 3:12.

2—HATRED'S "FINAL SOLUTION"

ONE OF THE MOST REMARKABLE prophecies in the Bible is found in the many declarations that Jews would be scattered to all nations, where they would be hated, persecuted, and killed like no other people. These prophecies are specific and vivid, describing in detail the plight of the Jews exactly as it has befallen them through the many centuries of their dispersion.[1] God pronounced this severe judgment because of Israel's disobedience and idolatry after being brought into the Promised Land, and He foretold it in numerous prophecies. This prophesied judgment has been fulfilled consistently throughout Israel's history—and after three thousand years is still being fulfilled today with a vengeance.

What must it be like to be part of a people group that is hated and maligned worldwide with so many lies told about them that it would be impossible to answer them all—and would do little good to try! It would be maddening, frustrating, and, yes, frightening. Hitler did not act alone in the Holocaust by any means, as we shall see, but with the consent and cooperation of other world powers, including the United States.

More than one hundred official anti-Semitic documents have been issued by the Roman Catholic Church throughout its history. The knights and knaves who constituted the First Crusade, inspired by Pope Urban II (who promised heaven to those who died in this cause), slaughtered Jews all across Europe. When they took Jerusalem, they drove the Jews into the synagogue and set it ablaze. Centuries of Jew-hatred inspired by the Roman Catholic Church wherever it was in power helped to prepare the way for Hitler's Holocaust.

Pope John Paul II tried to woo the Jews worldwide by saying nice things about them. He even told them that Catholics "look upon you as our brothers and sisters in the Lord"—hardly compatible with Paul's desire "that they [Jews] might be saved" (Romans 10:1).[2] There was no way, however, that he could undo centuries of his church's hatred and mistreatment of Jews. Such sweet phrases are not only inconsistent with history and official church doctrine, but they were contradicted by his friendship with Arafat. John Paul II had consistently favored the "Palestinians" in their false claims. Nor did he ever affirm the Israelis' biblical right to the land God gave them. In fact, like popes and cardinals before him, he openly denied that right: "The existence of the State of Israel and its political options should be envisaged not in a perspective which is in itself religious, but in their reference to the common principles of international law."[3] So the opinion of secular world leaders overrides God's Word!

Martin Luther never escaped the anti-Semitism of his Roman Catholic past in spite of opposing that church. In his later life, he advocated burning down the Jews' homes and giving them the choice between converting or having their tongues torn out.[4] Luther's anger against the Jews was inexcusable, even though it grew out of a deep-seated frustration that they would not respond to the gospel that he had embraced.

In an interview on September 25, 2001, Israel's former prime minister, Benjamin Netanyahu, claimed that terrorists "don't hate America because of Israel...they hate Israel as an extension of America." As an Israeli, he should be the expert on that subject. Perhaps he had forgotten, however, that Hitler did not hate Jews because of America, nor did the Czars of Russia, nor the popes, nor have Muslims throughout thirteen hundred years of history hated Jews for that reason. A blatant "anti-Semitism" has persisted from Israel's very beginning and is awakening again worldwide.

IRRATIONAL JEW HATRED IS PERVASIVE

The frequent condemnations of Israel by the UN and EU for defending itself against deadly attacks by those determined to exterminate her, and the refusal to condemn the murderers and their backers who attack her, are only one part of a continuing fulfillment of numerous prophecies foretelling worldwide anti-Semitism. This is a major and irrefutable proof of the existence of the one true God and that the Bible is His infallible Word. The hatred did not end with Hitler's Holocaust but is actually escalating once again—in the shadow of six million exterminated Jews.

That escalation has been in progress for many years. Desecration of graves and even bodies of Jews has been going on periodically in France for two decades in a resurgence of anti-Semitism throughout Europe. In Russia in 1990, Pamyat, an anti-Semitic organization, called for a new "final solution to the Jewish problem" and prophesied that "Russia would be the one to eliminate the evil of world Jewry." The rising hatred against Jews in Eastern Europe is especially perverse in view of the fact that out of about 5 million Jews in that area in the 1930s there remain only about 25,000 today. In Poland in 1989, the Catholic primate, Cardinal Joseph Glemp, "accused Jewish survivors of the Holocaust of introducing communism into Poland…and introducing vodka." He is said to speak for the vast majority of Catholics in Poland. In post-Ceausescu Romania it quickly became apparent that it was better for one's political career "to have a Nazi background than a Jewish one."[5]

In September 1993, the body of Nicholas Horthy, Hitler's friend who allied Hungary with Nazi Germany during the war and presided over the deportation of four hundred thirty-seven thousand Jews to Auschwitz, was reburied with high honors in his hometown eighty miles east of Budapest. About fifty thousand people "gathered as the remains of Horthy, his wife and son were placed in a family vault." The prime minister and his ministers honored Horthy in speeches and attended the ceremony, which was broadcast over state television.[6]

A Eurobarometer opinion poll late in 2003 questioned five hundred persons from each European Union nation. Fifty-nine percent overall (74 percent in the Netherlands) considered Israel to be the greatest threat to peace of any country in the world. (In stark contrast, at about the same time, Americans ranked Israel as the tenth greatest threat to world peace.) Outraged at being called by Europeans a greater threat to peace than terrorist nations such as Iran, Syria, and North Korea, Israel's mission to the EU nevertheless did not blame European citizens but "those who are responsible for forming public opinion." It said that "the poll reflected the impact of distorted media coverage of the Middle East conflict."

The Simon Wiesenthal Center in Los Angeles, a Jewish rights group, said the survey "shows that anti-Semitism is deeply embedded within European society…and Israel should exclude the EU from any future Middle East peace process."[7] But how can Israel dictate to Europe?

Not only is media coverage of today's events distorted, but the history being taught in public schools is often deficient by design. A poll in January 2005 revealed that 45 percent of Britons and 60 percent of those under thirty-five years of age had never heard of Auschwitz, while 34 percent polled in Italy believed that "Jews secretly control financial and economic power as well as the media."[8]

In spite of gross ignorance of the facts, people develop firm opinions and prejudices based upon the misinformation they imbibe from the media. It is here that we see the influence of a pervasive and persistent anti-Semitism. More than two thousand adults across Britain were polled in December 2004 concerning their opinions about some two dozen countries. Israel was rated the country most Britons would least like to visit, the least deserving of international respect, and the least democratic (though it is the only democracy in the Middle East).[9]

During December 2004 and January 2005, the official Iranian news agency, MEHR, published a series of anti-Semitic articles. The lies were unbelievably outrageous, yet believed in much of the Muslim world. Two leading Holocaust deniers were quoted: Dr. Fredrick Toben of the Adelaide Institute in Australia, claiming that the state of Israel is "founded on the 'Holocaust lie'…exposing the lie [would help] dismantle the Zionist entity…"; and Professor Robert Faurisson of France, referring to the "alleged Holocaust of the Jews." In a review of the movie, *Exodus*, Mojtaba Habibi accused the Jews, of all things, of "collaboration with the Nazis and of orchestrating a grand scheme of world dominion together with Joseph Stalin." They could just as truthfully claim that about Mickey Mouse! On Iran's TV Channel 1, Professor Heshmatollah Qanbari described Jews as "satanic and anti-human…dangerous to both Christians and Muslims…[the source] of all corrupt traits in humanity…coveting and usurping other nations. Several anti-Semitic TV drama series' were also being aired on Iranian TV."[10] Such lies about Jews are exactly what multitudes love to believe.

HATRED AT THE HIGHEST LEVELS

Unreasonable and persistent animosity toward Jews and Israel is not confined to the ignorant and uneducated. One would expect the United Nations, with its supposed strong stand for the rights of all people, to be a leader in dispelling anti-Semitism. Instead, it has been a bastion of Jew hatred, systematically singling out Israel for punitive treatment while at the same time embracing terrorist nations with never a rebuke. Incredibly, Zionism (the belief that Jews, like the rest of the world, have a right to their national homeland) was condemned as racism by UN General Assembly Resolution 3379 on November 10, 1975. Sixteen long years later (December 16, 1991) that vote was finally reversed over Muslim protests. Zionism, however, continued to be a capital crime in Iraq.

The UN Commission on Human Rights discriminates against Israel before it even votes: that lone democracy in the Middle East is the one UN member excluded from this commission! At its March and April 2004 meeting, about "25 percent of the debates were dedicated to attacking Israel [and] out of the commission's 10 country-specific resolutions, five targeted Israel…. During the six-week session, while 190 countries met for vital consultation within their regional groups, the Israeli representative was—literally—left standing [alone] in the corridor…." There was only one emergency meeting during the 2004 session: "not for the million-plus victims of Darfur, who were virtually ignored, but to condemn Israel for killing Ahmed Yassin, head of the Hamas terrorist group…."[11]

On a leading Russian TV program, *Vremya,* one of Russia's most distinguished mathematicians, Igor R. Shafarevich, expressed support for Saddam Hussein in the Gulf War. In 1990, a group of anti-Semitic Russian writers traveled throughout the U.S., some of whom had signed the infamous "Letter of 74 Writers" (Shafarevich was one of its authors), which expressed support for the "Moslem brothers" in the Gulf War and was widely quoted in the American press. One newspaper covered it with a headline: "Thanks to Iraq for bombarding Israel! The kikes deserve it!!! [emphasis in original]."[12]

Although anti-Semitism is growing in the United States, especially on University campuses, this country remains one of the few in which leaders speak out against it. In July 1992, the U.S. National Academy of Sciences asked Shafarevich, to resign. He refused. G. K. Gunsalus, chairman of the American Association for the Advancement of Science's Committee on Scientific Freedom and Responsibility, wrote to Shafarevich: "We wish to express repugnance at and condemnation of your anti-Semitic writings…. Your prestige as an eminent mathematician gives credence and special weight to your singling out one group for special opprobrium. The committee finds it regrettable that a mathematician of your stature has disseminated such unfounded and vile characterizations in your writings."

At its annual winter meeting, January 12, 1993, the American Mathematical Society passed a resolution condemning "the anti-Semitic writings of I. R. Shafarevich [who] has used his highly respected position as an eminent mathematician to give special weight to his words of hatred, which are contrary to fundamental standards of human decency and to the spirit of mathematics and science."[13] Such protests, however, are rare and, in fulfillment of Bible prophecy, have little effect in stemming the rising tide of anti-Semitism.

A letter dated January 13, 2005, carrying the Russian parliament's letterhead, "called on Russia's prosecutor general to 'officially open a legal investigation into banning all Jewish religious and community groups' on grounds of 'defense of the homeland.' [Using] some of the most profane language against Jews publicly published in the post-Soviet era," the seven-page letter that described Jewish beliefs as "nothing less than satanism," was signed "by 20 members of the 450-seat State Duma lower house of parliament." Andrei Cherkizov, "one of Moscow's most noted Jewish commentators [declared]: 'I can tell you this with absolute certainty.... However you try to cover up anti-Semitism, its naked feet will still be sticking out.'"[14]

A U.S. State Department report to the Senate and House Foreign Relations committees (covering the period July 2003 through December 2004) warned that in Europe, where anti-Semitism is already deeply rooted, "anti-Semitic acts have increased both in frequency and severity since 2000," with the increase in the Muslim population from immigration. There is an increase of anti-Semitic sentiment across the Muslim world even in places like Pakistan, where there are no Jews. This is a new phenomenon, according to the report: "The stereotype of Jews as manipulators of the global economy continues to provide fertile grounds for anti-Semitic aggression."[15]

Although only about one percent of Japanese have ever had any contact with a Jewish person, anti-Semitism in Japan is deeply rooted, is of long standing (anti-Semitic books have been popular in Japan for at least one hundred years), and is growing. Best-selling books in Japan blame Jews for every disaster, from earthquakes to the stock market crash of 1993. Such was the message of an ad covering one-third of a page in the newspaper *Nihon Keizasi* (Japan's equivalent of

The Wall Street Journal). It even claimed that Jews controlled Japan's Finance Ministry and the Bank of Japan. The paper rejected a call for a retraction or apology by the Simon Wiesenthal Center.[16]

There is no rational explanation for this continuous animosity toward a particular people. It cannot be justified by saying that Jews, in contrast to all others, are so despicable that they deserve to be hated. Yet this irrational and implacable anti-Semitism is exactly what biblical prophets foretold. That fact provides another major proof that the Bible is God's word. And there are no Jew-haters as vicious as the Muslims, who didn't even exist when these prophecies were written.

ISLAMIC PERSECUTIONS

Ever since the Muslim conquest of the Middle East in the seventh century, Jews have suffered in Muslim lands from inhumane treatment and periodic bursts of violence. Take only one country, Morocco, as an example of what occurred everywhere under Islam. Jews were forced to live in ghettos called *mellahs*. One historian writes that incidents of rape, looting, burning of synagogues, destruction of Torah scrolls, and murder were "so frequent that it is impossible to list them." In A.D. 1032 in Fez, about six thousand Jews were murdered and many more "robbed of their women and property."[17] In 1066, after Islam took over Spain, the Jews of Granada were massacred. That fate periodically overtook those who would not submit to Allah, even though Islam promises Jews and Christians (described in the Qur'an as "people of the book") protection as *dhimmis* (fifth-class citizens subject to heavy taxation and cultural humiliation).

The *dhimmis* were not to be killed, but often their lives were so unbearable living under "protection" of Muslims, that death would have been preferable. In the early seventeenth century, Christian visitors to "Palestine" declared: "Life here is the poorest and most miserable that one can imagine…[as *dhimmis,* the Jews] pay for the very air they breathe."[18] Yet many thousands of Jews, though periodically wiped out by pogroms, or driven out, managed in desperation somehow to cling to the land God had given them, in Hebron as elsewhere.

The fierce persecution of 1640, in which even women and children were murdered, was called the "al-Khada." Under Muslims, Jews suffered "such repression, restriction, and humiliation as to exceed anything in Europe."[19] Continuing that tradition, although there were no Jews in his country and none are allowed to enter to this day, Saudi Arabia's King Ibn Saud said, "for a Muslim to kill a Jew...ensures him an immediate entry into Heaven...."[20] Diabolical but persuasive motivation indeed! *This is Islam.*

In 1839, a British visitor to Palestine declared, "What the Jew has to endure, at all hands, is not to be told."[21] A Jewish visitor to Palestine in 1847 reported that Jews "do not have any protection and are at the mercy of policemen and the pashas who treat them as they wish...their property is not at their disposal and they dare not complain about an injury for fear of the Arabs' revenge. Their lives are precarious and subject to daily danger of death."[22] Scores of incidents involving anti-Jewish violence, persecution, and extortions filled page after page of documented reports from the British Consulate in Jerusalem.[23] We lack space to give further evidence of continued Islamic persecution of Jews throughout history.

Such persecution has continued against those few thousand Jews who failed to escape Muslim lands. In 1941, hundreds of Jews were viciously tortured and murdered by Iraqi mobs in anti-British, pro-Nazi riots led by Haj Amin Mohammed Effendi al-Husseini, appointed Grand Mufti of Jerusalem by the British, but who had been forced to flee to Syria for his instigation of riots that had killed and wounded hundreds of both Jews, and Arabs who wanted to live peacefully with Jews. Now in Iraq, he was doing more of the same and finding great sympathy among the Muslim masses. Police watched passively as Jewish homes and businesses were looted and synagogues desecrated. When he became a leader in the Ba'ath Party, Saddam Hussein published one of his Jew-hating uncle's pamphlets, *Three Things Allah Should Not Have Created: Persians, Jews, and Flies.*

In a letter dated July 10, 1974, to then UN Secretary General Kurt Waldheim, United States Attorney General Ramsey Clark declared, "Jewish people living in Syria today are subjected to the most pervasive and inhuman persecution.... Young women and children are harassed in the streets. Old people are knocked down. Homes are stoned.... They are forbidden to leave in peace and cannot remain in dignity.... Many have been arrested, detained, tortured and killed." Ironically, in late December 2004, Ramsey Clark signed on as part of the legal team that would defend Saddam Hussein in his trial in Iraq.

Anti-Semitism is not confined to Muslims and Catholics. It is worldwide. The fact that vicious anti-Semitism would pursue the Jews everywhere throughout history is only one—but a very important one—of the many prophecies being fulfilled today concerning Israel that God points to as proof that He is the one true God, that the Bible is His Word, and that the Jews are His chosen people. A pair of researchers (not evangelical Christians by any means), who have probably done more than anyone else to document modern anti-Semitism, write in their "must read" book:

> For more than twenty centuries, the Jewish people, more than any other segment of humanity, have been persecuted, uprooted, and annihilated. It is true that many ethnic and religious groups have suffered grievously at the hands of tyrants, but there is a crucial difference.
>
> More Africans were killed in the era of slavery, but there was no determined intent to eradicate the entire Negro race. A higher percentage of Armenians perished in the Turkish genocide before World War I, but the main intent was to deport them, not extinguish their genetic pool. Stalin, Mao, Pol Pot, and Suharto murdered millions of their own citizens, but the motive for those crimes was political power, not racial animus.
>
> In each of these cases, the genocide was intended to serve a deeper purpose—the conquest of territory, the acquisition of wealth, the enlargement of political power.... In contrast, the genocide of the Jewish people was not intended to be a means to an end. It was not attempted in order to achieve a more fundamental purpose. It was the fundamental purpose. This is what makes the Nazi Holocaust unique in human history.[24]

Brilliant as these researchers are, and as invaluable as the information they have passed along, they have a blind spot when it comes to Islam. Nowhere in their monumental work of more than six hundred and fifty pages do they tell us the vital truth that Islam itself (not some extremists) requires that every Jew in the world must be killed. Nor do they inform us that Islam has been responsible for the slaughter and subjugation of far more people, both Jewish and non-Jewish, than any other evil empire—and that, according to Muhammad, it must take over the entire world. The horrible truth about Islam, which these authors completely overlook, is still being denied by religious and political leaders, educators, and the media today. To fill that vacuum and to expose the truth about Islam before it is too late is a major purpose of this volume.

Why must the Jews, this one very small ethnic group, in contrast to all others, be the universal object of such relentless hatred? Only the Bible gives a satisfactory explanation.

HATRED'S "FINAL SOLUTION"

In fallen creation's long and sordid history of man's inhumanity to man, the Nazi Holocaust was a close second to Islam. Hitler declared that the "final objective [of] rational anti-Semitism...must be the removal of Jews altogether."[25] It is no surprise, then, that to most Muslims, especially those living in Muslim nations, Hitler is one of their greatest heroes.

Mein Kampf in Arabic remains a perpetual bestseller in Muslim countries, especially among "Palestinians." Hitler was, in fact, a partner with Haj Amin Mohammed Effendi al-Husseini (great uncle and mentor of Yasser Arafat and still a hero to Muslims), a murderous terrorist, appointed Grand Mufti of Jerusalem by Britain, and personally responsible for the concentration camp slaughter of hundreds of thousands of Jews.[26] On November 21, 1941, Hitler promised the mufti "a solution to the Jewish problem" in exchange for al-Husseini's recruitment of thousands of Arabs to fight with Hitler.[27] Based on years of careful investigation, Joan Peters writes:

> According to documentary records submitted to the United Nations in 1947, al-Husseini was "responsible for the Arab riots in 1920...[against] Jewish lives and property. Five Jews were killed

and 211 injured" [on Easter Sunday alone]...the Arab police remained passive or in some instances joined the rioting....

British officer R. Meinertzhagen reported later that Haj Amin had been informed by British Colonel Waters-Taylor four days before...that he had a great opportunity at Easter to show the world that the Arabs of Palestine would not tolerate Jewish dominance...that Palestine was unpopular [with the British] and if disturbances of sufficient violence occurred in Jerusalem at Easter, both General Bols and General Allenby would advocate the abandonment of the Jewish home.

Colonel Meinertzhagen, a senior British officer...a non-Jew, was charged with being "pro-Zionist" and sent back to a "desk job" in London, where he later protested British policy against the Jews: "Much has been written about injustice to Arabs. There is nothing in a Jewish State which conflicts with Arab rights... remember that the Arabs are the only nation in the world with at least three kings and several sovereign states. The Jews are a nation without a home."

Hitler and Husseini pledged to work together to exterminate Jews not only in Europe but in the Middle East as well. The mufti tried to set up a Nazi puppet regime in Iraq. When that rebellion failed, he escaped to Teheran, from there to Rome and then to Berlin. "During the three and one-half years (October 1941-May 1945) of serving the Axis, he built up a truly worldwide network of anti-Allied activities, including broadcasting, espionage, and formation of Arab and Moslem military units. After the collapse of the Third Reich, he [escaped] once more to Cairo, where he was greeted by the entire Arab leadership as the greatest Arab patriot and hero."[28]

Egyptian newspaper columnist Ahmad Rajab (echoing Anwar Sadat) wrote, "Thanks to Hitler, blessed memory.... We do have a complaint...his revenge [on the Jews] was not enough."[29] At the same time, much of the Muslim world attempts to deny the Holocaust. Dr. Issam Sissalem of the University of Gaza declared, "They are all lies...no Dachau, no Auschwitz!...[T]he holocaust was against our people...."[30] Sheik Ibrahim Mahdi vowed in a sermon, "Allah willing...Israel will be erased...!"[31]

At the Wannsee Conference in Germany, January 20, 1942, fifteen Nazi officials met to discuss the "Final solution to the Jewish Problem." They enthusiastically and without any conscience plotted the extermination of the eleven million Jews they had identified in Europe and Russia. The conference was convened and chaired by SS General Reinhard Heydrich and followed the protocol written two years earlier by SS Lt. Colonel Adolf Eichmann. About five hundred thousand Jews had already been killed by various means, but the gassing of Jews by mobile vans, which had begun December 8, 1941, had proven too slow and inefficient. Eichman confessed that at Wannsee they "spoke about methods of killing, about liquidation, about extermination."[32]

Hitler and his Nazi henchmen did not act alone. They could not have carried out the Holocaust without the cooperation of the German people as a whole. Nor do Hitler and Germany bear sole responsibility for the Holocaust. Many other governments share in this guilt as well. The world refused to be stirred by the horror of what it knew was happening, much less to do anything significant about it.

A GUILT SHARED BY THE WORLD

The United States government had full knowledge from reliable intelligence of the extermination of the Jews at least as early as August 1942. The State Department (which remains firmly anti-Israel to this day) deliberately suppressed the information and, incredible as it may seem, actively worked to prevent the rescue of Jews. Dated February 10, 1943, State Department telegram 354 shut down the secret channels of communication with informants and indicated that further information about the extermination of Jews was of no interest and should not be accepted in diplomatic channels.

At meetings with British and American leaders (including the British War Cabinet, Foreign Minister Anthony Eden, President Roosevelt, Secretary of State Hull, Secretary of War Stimson, Attorney General Biddle, and Justice Frankfurter), Jan Karski, who had visited the Warsaw ghetto and talked with Jewish resistance leaders, offered shocking statistics of the ongoing efforts to exterminate Europe's Jews. Karski's revelations about the systematic slaughter of Jews by the Nazis appeared in *The New York Times* and other major periodicals. He lectured on the subject diligently all across America, and his book, *Story of a Secret State*, became a Book-of-the-month Club selection and was published simultaneously in Britain, France, Switzerland, and Sweden.

In the end, Karski's disappointed and frustrated comment was, "The Lord assigned me a role to speak and write during the war, when—it seemed to me—it might help. It did not." And sadly, attempts to warn of today's even more destructive Islamic threat to wipe out all Jews in the world and to conquer the world for Allah seem likewise to fall on deaf ears.

It was not until January 16, 1944, at the urging of a minor official who presented to him once more the staggering information already known, that Morganthau persuaded Roosevelt to take action. The motive, however, was not to rescue Jews from Hitler's ovens, but to defer political criticism that could hurt him in the upcoming elections and his bid for an unprecedented fourth term. The War Refugee Board was formed, but its efforts were too little and too late. To the very end of the war, U.S. and British military leaders turned a deaf ear to Jewish pleas to bomb the railroad lines leading in and out of Auschwitz and other death camps.

American journalist Dorothy Thompson wrote in Hitler's day, "It is a fantastic commentary on the inhumanity of our times that for thousands and thousands of people a piece of paper with a stamp on it is the difference between life and death." And even the proper piece of paper proved worthless as the bloodlust reached new heights worldwide.

The ocean liner St. Louis reached Havana, May 27, 1939, with 930 passengers from Nazi Germany who possessed valid permits to land in Cuba. The Cuban government changed its mind, refused to honor the visas and demanded $500,000 per person, then raised the price to $1,000,000 each. Of course, that was impossible. The price was eventually reduced but remained beyond reach of Jewish would-be benefactors by the heartless deadline set. To its everlasting shame, the United States, too, rejected the pleas of Captain Gustav Schroeder to take in his passengers. Eventually, they all found refuge in England, Belgium, France, and Holland; but only the 288 taken in by England and very few of the others escaped the Holocaust.

THE BALD HYPOCRISY OF WORLD POWERS

The die had already been cast a year earlier at the conference held at the luxurious Hotel Royale in Evian, France, on the shores of Lake Geneva, where delegates from thirty-two countries gathered to discuss the worsening plight of the Jews. Though President Roosevelt had called the conference, from the beginning he made it clear that the United States would do nothing. Britain said there was no room in Palestine for Jews beyond the cruel quota its White Paper of 1939 would set of ten thousand per year, to be ended altogether in five years—and insisted that Palestine was not to be discussed. In addition, Britain generously would allow over the same period of five years twenty-five thousand refugees from Nazi Germany to enter. Considering the fact that the Nazis had identified 11 million Jews for extermination, this quota was an insult to common sense, compassion, and conscience.[33]

At the same time, Britain was closing its eyes to and even aiding the influx of many thousands of Arabs who would later claim to be "Palestinians" descended from the original inhabitants and to have been there since "time immemorial." The United Nations would consider Arabs who had been there at least two years to be "original inhabitants," but would not apply the same standard to Jews.

The only purpose of the Evian conference (other than sailing, riding, summer snow skiing at Chamonix on Mont Blanc, mineral baths, and gambling, which the delegates enjoyed to the fullest) seemed to be to give the nations a forum to hypocritically profess their great sympathy for Europe's Jews, who the whole world knew were facing extinction—and then to present the various excuses for their inability to do anything to intervene in their ongoing extermination.

And what an opportunity the conference gave Hitler, like Pilate, to wash his hands of guilt and to show that the entire world was his partner in destroying the Jews! Two days after Roosevelt announced the Evian conference, Hitler shrewdly declared, "I can only hope that the other world which has such deep sympathy for these criminals [Jews] will at least be generous enough to convert this sympathy into practical aid. We on our part are ready to put all these criminals at the disposal of these countries, for all I care, even on luxury ships."

When the conference ended as it began, with nothing for the Jews, Hitler mocked the participants: "Since in many countries it was recently regarded as wholly incomprehensible why Germany did not wish to preserve in its population an element like the Jews...it appears astounding that countries seem in no way anxious to make use of these elements themselves now that the opportunity offers."[34]

No one called Hitler's bluff, if that is what it was. No one can blame Hitler for the Holocaust—not when he offered to let the Jews go and no nation was willing to open its arms and receive them! Later in the war, desperate for cash, he would offer to sell 500,000 Jews for two dollars each, and no one would offer to ransom them from death even at that bargain price! There was no need for millions of Jews to perish in Hitler's ovens; it happened simply because world leaders did not value Jews as human beings enough to accept them.

In April 1943, British and American officials met in Bermuda to discuss the Holocaust, which was grinding out its daily quota of victims, now in the millions. Once again, it was formally decided to do nothing. Finally the reason for the inaction at Evian five years earlier was openly admitted, at least among the delegates. The emerging picture unveils the truth about the evil in the human heart and makes one ashamed to be part of the human race:

> The British Foreign Office and the U.S. State Department were both afraid that the Third Reich would be quite willing, indeed eager, to stop the gas chambers, empty the concentration camps, and let hundreds of thousands, if not millions, of Jewish survivors emigrate to freedom in the West. The Foreign Office "revealed in

confidence" to the State Department its fear that Hitler might permit a mass exodus. If approaches to Germany to release Jews were "pressed too much that is exactly what might happen."[35]

No less callous to the plight of the Jews, two months later Pope Pius XII wrote an urgent letter to President Roosevelt to persuade him that the Jews should not be allowed to return to Palestine. We are able to provide only a small amount of the documentation to demonstrate the evil of anti-Semitism and the fact that the whole world is guilty. This should be enough, however, to reveal the horror of this evil that is still with us and getting uglier. There is no escaping the fact that this is exactly what the Bible prophesied. Just on the basis of prophesied anti-Semitism, no one can deny that the God of Israel exists and that the Bible is His infallible Word.

A RISING TIDE OF JEW HATRED TODAY

Anti-Semitism did not end with the defeat of Nazi Germany and the death of Hitler. In fulfillment of biblical prophecies, not only in Muslim countries but worldwide, it is again on the rise, causing a heightened level of alert in Jewish communities. A brief search of the internet reveals scores of examples. There is an alarming increase in the widespread desecration of Jewish cemeteries. Violence against Jews and Jewish property is rising. In Istanbul, Turkey, in the middle of the fast of Ramadan (a time of "peace" for Arab tribes prior to Islam) car bombs devastated two synagogues, killing or wounding dozens. In Morocco in May 2004, terrorists hit a Jewish community center and hotel, leaving a trail of death. Other incidents are too numerous to mention.

In polls across the EU, most Europeans continue to rate Israel as "the greatest obstacle to peace" in the world, ahead of the United States, which placed second. The EU has repeatedly condemned Israel for using force against Palestinian terrorists who attack her, killing and maiming thousands of innocent women and children. Yet they never condemn the terrorists and have been supporting the

Palestinians at the rate of five hundred thousand Euros a month, much of which has been used to fund terrorism against Israel.

The Jewish synagogue in Vienna, Austria, has suffered attacks in the past. Like others throughout Europe, it must be guarded by heavily armed police twenty-four hours a day. Abraham Foxman, national director of the Anti-Defamation League, recently wrote: "I am convinced that we currently face as great a threat to the safety and security of the Jewish people as the one we faced in the 1930s—if not a greater one."[36] Violent acts against Jews have risen to an alarming level in France, which has a Jewish population of about six hundred thousand, surrounded by six million Muslims worshiping in fifteen hundred mosques. As a result, record numbers of Jews are leaving France for Israel.

The rising tide of anti-Semitism in Germany brought more than four thousand Christians from all over Germany to stage a protest demonstration in front of the Reichstag in Berlin in August 2002. A poll by Germany's University of Bielefeld early in December 2004 revealed that 51 percent of Germans believe that Israel's present-day treatment of the Palestinians is similar to what the Nazis did to the Jews during World War II. The survey also found that 68 percent of Germans believe that Israel is waging a "war of extermination" against the Palestinians. How could they get it exactly backwards? Anti-Semitism prophesied in the Bible blinds to the truth.

Even in Israel, anti-Semitism is on the rise. According to the Information Center for Victims of Anti-Semitism in Israel...there have been some five hundred such incidents in Israel during the past three years. "The Russian-language newspapers in Israel print a story on an anti-Semitic incident every week, and at every police station in the country at least one anti-Semitic case is registered," says Zalman Gilichinsky, director of the information center. [37]

Harvard University's president, Lawrence H. Summers, recently condemned what he termed "growing anti-Semitism" at Harvard and elsewhere. "Nearly 600 professors, students, staff members, and alumni from Harvard and the Massachusetts Institute of Technology, signed a petition urging Harvard and M.I.T. to divest from Israel. Similar efforts have been mounted at about 40 other universities."[38]

According to the Bible, there are two reasons for this universal hatred of Jews and Israel. First of all, the Jews, as God's chosen people, are under His judgment for their rebellion against Him and the rejection of their Messiah.[39] Secondly, anti-Semitism is inspired of Satan. The reason is obvious. It was foretold that the Savior of the world, who would defeat Satan, would be a Jew.[40] Satan's only hope to escape eternal doom, therefore, was to destroy those whom God chose "to be a special people unto himself, above all people that are upon the face of the earth."[41] Had Satan been able to destroy the Jews before the birth of the Messiah, he would have prevented his own defeat and the salvation of mankind through the sacrifice of the Son of God for mankind's sins. Moreover, for promising a Messiah and a salvation that never came, God would have proved Himself a liar and thus could not righteously have punished Satan.

Of course, the Messiah came and defeated Satan, "tast[ing] death for every man"[42] and bearing "our sins in his own body on the tree."[43] Countless multitudes have been redeemed from sin's penalty and will spend eternity in the Father's house of "many mansions"[44] because of having received the Lord Jesus Christ as their Savior. Such is the promise of the gospel.

But the fact that Christ defeated Satan through His death and resurrection did not end the battle between God and His arch-enemy for the hearts, minds, and eternal destiny of mankind. That battle continues to rage—and Israel is at its center. The Bible contains hundreds of prophecies that, although God would severely punish Israel for her sins, He would preserve a remnant and bring the scattered Jews back into their own land. This prophecy, too, is in the process of being fulfilled in our day. Satan must destroy Israel or he is doomed.

ESTABLISHMENT OF THE STATE OF ISRAEL

Nothing aroused Satan's desperate fury and the wrath of Islam as did the birth of the nation of Israel. It must be annihilated or Satan is finished. And to this end, the driving force is not a few "extremists" but Islam itself. Islam promises Muslims victory against the Jews as well as against the entire world. Instead, they taste only humiliation in every attack they launch. Israel, on the other hand, in spite of being under God's judgment, enjoys His protection in many ways, as we have already seen: "In that day will I make the governors of Judah like…a torch of fire in a sheaf; and they shall devour all the people round about."[45]

The wars of 1948, 1956, 1967, and 1973 have borne eloquent testimony to the truth of Scripture: "If it had not been the LORD who was on our side, now may Israel say; If it had not been the LORD who was on our side, when men rose up against us: Then they had swallowed us up quick, when their wrath is kindled against us…Blessed be the LORD, who hath not given us as a prey to their teeth….Our help is in the name of the LORD who made heaven and earth."[46]

The Arabs' repeated defeat at the hands of Israel is both embarrassing and maddening for them. The Imams blame this shame upon the departure from true Islam by the masses of Muslims. They are whipping up a worldwide revival of fundamentalist Islam as the way to regain Allah's blessing and thereby defeat Israel.

As long as Israel retains autonomy over one square yard of land, it is an affront to Islam and declares to the world that Islam is a false religion; Allah, a false god; Muhammad, a false prophet; and the Qur'an, a false revelation. This is the issue—and all the talk of "peace" without recognizing and changing this teaching of Islam is both a fool's dream and a fraud.

It has well been said, if Arabs/Muslims put down their weapons today, that would be the end of Arab-Israeli wars. If Israel put down her weapons, that would be the end of Israel. These are simple facts that no one can deny—and worth thinking about very seriously.

ANOTHER AMAZING PROPHECY

Balaam is one of the most enigmatic figures in the Bible. He was at one time in touch with God and made some genuine prophecies as recorded in Scripture, yet he later turned away from God and is in hell now.[47] For example, he foretold the star in the East[48] that the wise men saw and followed to find Christ at His birth.[49] One of Balaam's prophecies recorded in the Bible that has been and is still being fulfilled in our day is most unusual. He declared that Israel would "not be reckoned among the nations."[50]

This remarkable utterance does not stand alone. God has stated it many times and in other ways. For example, "The LORD thy God hath chosen thee to be a special people unto himself, above all people that are upon the face of the earth";[51] "I am the LORD your God, which have separated you from other people...I the LORD am holy, and have severed you from other people, that ye should be mine."[52]

This is precisely the situation in which Israel finds itself today. Israel has been a member of the United Nations for more than fifty years. Yet she is not allowed to take her two-year turn as one of the ten rotating nations (joining the five permanent ones) on the UN Security Council. Of the 191 current members, 190, including the worst terrorist nations, are allowed to take their turns on the Security Council—but not Israel.

Nor is Israel, as already noted, allowed to take a rotating term on the fifty-three-member UN Commission on Human Rights. All of the other one hundred ninety UN member nations are allowed to do so. These have included Libya, Cuba, Zimbabwe, and other egregious violators of human rights. Incredibly, Sudan, where more than two million blacks in the south have been slaughtered by Muslims, has been voted in for a third consecutive term. But Israel, the only democracy in the Middle East, is excluded, as the Bible foretold.

Nor is Israel allowed to be a member of the International Red Cross. The Red Crescent, representing Muslim countries, among which are many terrorist nations, is part of this international humanitarian organization. But Israel, which signed the 1949 Geneva Conventions (many of the members of the Red Crescent did not), is barred from the International Red Cross.

Whether the rest of the world likes it or not, the Jews are God's chosen people. That fact not only carries blessings and privileges but responsibilities—and penalties for disobedience. Israel has experienced both God's blessing and judgment in the past. Both testify to the integrity of God and His Word. Israel remains in His hands and under His protection today even while she is at the same time experiencing His discipline. Woe to those who oppose God's choice and promised blessing.

TEN LOST TRIBES?

There are other ways to get rid of the Jews than putting them into Hitler's ovens or killing them with Muslim weapons. There is the myth of the "ten lost tribes" that is popularly believed among Christians today. Yes, the ten northern tribes were indeed carried into Assyria in about 740 B.C.: "Therefore the LORD was very angry with Israel, and removed them out of his sight: there was none left but the tribe of Judah...as he had said by all his servants the prophets. So was Israel carried away out of their own land to Assyria unto this day."[53] Of course, "this day" refers to the day in which this was written, not to our day.

Furthermore, it is clear that many if not most of those who were carried away had returned, even at that time. There is specific mention of "a multitude of the people, even many of Ephraim, and Manasseh, Issachar, and Zebulon" who "escaped out of the hand of the kings of Assyria" and kept the Passover in Jerusalem in the days of Hezekiah more than a decade after the carrying away into Assyria.[54] About ninety years later, we read of Israel joining with Judah in keeping the Passover during the great revival under King Josiah. Seven of the "ten lost tribes" are mentioned as being present, and the implication is that all were there.[55] Nearly two hundred years after the ten tribes were carried into Assyria, God gave Ezekiel a vision of the future restoration and referred to the Promised Land being divided "according to the twelve tribes of Israel."[56]

If ten tribes were lost, Christ's promise could not be fulfilled to His disciples: "When the Son of man shall sit in the throne of his glory, ye also shall sit upon twelve thrones, judging the twelve tribes of Israel."[57] Then Christ would be a liar and Satan the victor. Paul didn't think any tribes were lost. In his appeal to King Agrippa, he refers to the "twelve tribes" as in existence at that time.[58] James addressed his epistle "to the twelve tribes which are scattered abroad."[59] Yet the myth of the "ten lost tribes" is still believed by many who call themselves Christians.

MORE ANTI-SEMITISM AMONG CHRISTIANS

Another idea gaining popularity among Christians today is the false teaching that the church has replaced Israel. This is a Roman Catholic doctrine. This form of anti-Semitism is also promoted by evangelicals. It declares that Israel has been cut off because of her sins, and the prophecies concerning her restoration are no longer valid. If that were so, then the "everlasting covenant" promised to Israel eleven times in the Old Testament[60] and the everlasting possession of the land promised twice[61] were not everlasting at all, and God has lied. Again, Satan has won and this world belongs to him.

There are scores of promises that God would in the end restore Israel fully to her land. Yet Christian leaders deny these promises by saying that Israel is finished: "…physical Jews…are in slavery and *will not be heirs of God's promise* because *they are not the children of promise* [author's emphasis]."[62] Another author writes, "The idea that corporate national Israel is still God's chosen people is prevalent in the minds of many today. But…the Word of God shows that… Israel broke the Old Covenant and thereby forfeited any rights to it."[63] This claim, if true, would clearly make God a liar. We will deal with this more fully in Chapter Eleven.

Why did God choose Israel? He had to choose someone through whom the Messiah would come into the world as a man to pay the penalty for our sins. It was not a matter of favoritism, but selection of someone named Abraham who, like Noah, "found grace" in His eyes[64] and would be obedient to Him. He is given the amazing designation in the Bible as "the Friend of God."[65] Abraham was promised a land that would be an "everlasting possession" for his heirs. The present conflict in the Middle East involves the question of who those heirs are today. We will turn to that issue next.

1. Deuteronomy 28:15-62; 2 Chronicles 7:20; Jeremiah 29:18; 44:8, etc.

2. From his address to Australia's Jewish Leaders November 26, 1986, in Sydney.

3. From his Notes on the "Correct Way to Present Jews and Judaism in the Preaching and Catechesis of the Roman Catholic Church," Vatican Commission for Religious Relations with the Jews, May 1985.

4. Will Durant, *The Story of Civilization*, vol. VI, *The Reformation* (Simon and Schuster, 1950), 727.

5. Alan M. Dershowitz, "Resurgence of anti-Semitism in Europe," Seattle Times, May 23, 1990

6. Associated Press, "Former Hitler ally reburied with honors in Hungary," *The Orange County Register*, September 5, 1993, NEWS 30.

7. Robin Pomeroy, "Israel Outraged at 'Peace Threat' EU Poll," World – Reuters, November 3, 2003.

8. *Jerusalem Post*, February 1, 2005.

9. www.jpost.com/servlet/Satellite?pagename=JPost/JPArticle/Printer&cid=1104808686 1/4/2005.

10. www.memri.org/bin/opener_latest.cgi?ID=SD85405.

11. Hillel Neuer, Executive Director of UN Watch, Geneva, Switzerland, "How the UN Can Help Fight Anti-Semitism," *National Post*, January 26, 2005.

12. *Washington Post*, April 17, 1990, p 1.

13. *The Scientist,* Vol 7, No 8, April 19, 1993.

14. Agence France Presse, January 25, 2005.

15. Barry Schweid, AP Diplomatic Writer, http://news.yahoo.com/news?tmpl==story&cid==542&u==/ap/20050104/ap_on_go_ca_st_pe/anti.

16. Leslie Helm, "Japan Newspaper Ad Revives Fears of Anti-Semitism," The Los Angeles Times, July 29, 1993, A8.

17. H.Z. Hirschberg, *A History of the Jews in North Africa* (Leiden, Netherlands, 1974), 108.

18. Samuel Katz, *Battleground: Fact and Fantasy in Palestine* (New York: Bantam Books, 1973).

19. Andre Chouraqui, *Between East and West: A History of the Jews of North Africa* (Philadelphia, 1968), 39.

20. Official British Document, Foreign Office File No. 371/20822 E 7201/33/31.

21. Joan Peters, *From Time Immemorial: The Origins of the Arab-Jewish Conflict Over Palestine* (New York: J. KAP Publishing U.S.A., 1984), 191.

22. Ibid., 154.

23. Ibid., 191.

24. John Loftus and Mark Aarons, *The Secret War Against the Jews: How Western Espionage Betrayed the Jewish People* (New York: St. Martin's Press, 1994), 18.

25. Michael Berenbaum, *The World Must Know: The History of the Holocaust as told in the United States Holocaust Museum* (New York, Little, Brown and Company, 1933), 105.

26. From the Mufti's private diary, cited in *Arab Higher Committee: Its Origins, Personnel and Purposes,* citing captured Nazi records submitted as documentary evidence to the United Nations, May 1947, 6.

27. Ibid.

28. Joseph B. Schechtman, *The Mufti and the Fuehrer: The Story of the Grand Mufti of Jerusalem and His Unholy Alliance with Nazism* (New York: Thomas Yoseloff, 1965), 6.

29. *Al-Akhbar* (Egypt), April 18, 2001.

30. Palestinian Authority TV broadcast, November 29, 2000.

31. Palestinian Television, June 8, 2001.

32. Berenbaum, *World*, 103-108.

33. http://www.yale.edu/lawweb/avalon/mideast/brawh1939.htm.

34. Berenbaum, *World*, 49-50.

35. Loftus and Aarons, *Secret War,* 49; see also David Wyman, *The Abandonment of the Jews* (New York: Pantheon, 1984), 342.

36. http://www.today.ucla.edu/2004/040413.voices.

37. www.jewishaz.com/jewishnews/030725/rise.shtml.

38. *The New York Times*, September 21, 2002; see also http://www.president.harvard.edu/speeches/2002/morning prayers.html.

39. Deuteronomy 28:15-68; 29:24-28; 30:17-20, etc.

40. Genesis 12:3; 2 Samuel 7:8-16; Isaiah 9:6-7; Micah 5:2, etc.

41. Deuteronomy 7:6.

42. Hebrews 2:9

43. 1 Peter 2:24.

44. John 14:2-6.

45. Zechariah 12:6.

46. Psalm 124:1-8.

47. 2 Peter 2:15; Jude 11; Revelation 2:14.

48. Numbers 24:17.

49. Matthew 2:1-2.

50. Numbers 23:9.

51. Deuteronomy 7:6.

52. Leviticus 20:24-26.

53. 2 Kings 17:17-23.

54. 2 Chronicles 30:6, 18, etc.

55. 2 Chronicles 34, 35.

56. Ezekiel 47:13.

57. Matthew 19:28; Luke 22:30.

58. Acts 26:7.

59. James 1:1.

60. Genesis 17:7, 13, 19; Leviticus 24:8; 2 Samuel 23:5; 1 Chronicles 16:17; Psalm 105:8-11, etc.

61. Genesis 17:8; 48:4.

62. Brian Godawa, "The Promise to Abraham: Yesterday, Today and Forever," *SCP Journal*, 27: 2-27:3, 53-70.

63. Alan Morrison, "The Two Jerusalems: A Biblical look at the Modern State of Israel, Judaism & the Church," *SCP Journal*, 27:2-27:3, 14-51.

64. Genesis 6:8.

65. James 2:23.

3—WHO INHERITS THE PROMISED LAND?

THE PROBLEMS IN THE MIDDLE EAST all center upon a dispute over a land that was promised to Abraham and to his heirs. On that promise, Jews, Muslims, and Christians basically agree. The dispute concerns the identity of the heirs. We know from the Bible that Abraham had at least eight sons: Ishmael, the firstborn, by Hagar, his wife Sarah's maid;[1] Isaac, the second born, by his wife Sarah;[2] and six other sons by Keturah, whom he married after Sarah's death.[3] Which of these sons' descendants qualify? Or do they all get a share? The Bible gives a clear answer, as we shall see.

When reading the Bible, one is immediately impressed with the fact that this is not the fiction of the Bhagavad Gita, Hindu Vedas, Qur'an, or Book of Mormon. The Bible presents real people, real places, and real events that actually happened in space, time, and history on this earth. That evaluation must apply as well to the Garden of Eden, the flood, and the Tower of Babel, all of which we learn about in the first eleven chapters of Genesis—but those are not our subject.

As we have already seen, the numerous prophecies found in the Bible (in contrast to the scriptures of the world's religions, which contain none) prove beyond question that there is one almighty God, infinite in knowledge, wisdom, love, and holiness, who created this universe, and that the Bible is His infallible Word to mankind. Therefore, no matter what any other book says (whether religious or scientific), if it contradicts the Bible it is wrong.

In the last two verses of Genesis 11, we meet a man named Abram. At the age of seventy-five, in obedience to God, he leaves his homeland in Ur of the Chaldees and by faith takes his wife, servants, and flocks on a long journey to a strange land of which God had said, "I will show thee."[4] God's purpose, reaching into our own day, goes far beyond anything Abram imagines, but he believes what God has said: "I will make of thee a great nation, and I will bless thee.... And I will bless them that bless thee, and curse him that curseth thee: and in thee shall all families of the earth be blessed."[5] Because he believes implicitly what God has said, God credits Abram with righteousness.[6]

CANAAN, NOT "PALESTINE"!

Surprise! The land into which God led Abram was *not* "Palestine." There was no such place. Nor was there such a people as "Palestinians." In all of history, there never were a Palestinian people, nation, government, language, culture, religion, or economy. There are those today who call themselves "Palestinians" and claim that they descended from a Palestinian people who lived for thousands of years in a land called Palestine. In fact, that claim is an outright hoax. Yet the world accepts this lie as the basis of a false peace that they have been attempting for years to force upon Israel.

God's Word declares, "Into the land of Canaan they [Abram et al.] came...the Canaanite was then in the land.... Abram dwelled in the land of Canaan.... And the LORD said unto Abram...all the land which thou seest, to thee will I give it, and to thy seed for ever...walk through the land...for I will give it unto thee. Then Abram removed his tent...and dwelt...in Hebron, and built there an altar unto the LORD [and] the LORD made a covenant with Abram...unto thy seed have I given this land, from the river of Egypt unto the great river, the river Euphrates."[7] The land is further defined by the nations then living in it, which Israel was to destroy and displace. It is far larger than that tiny piece of it that the world has allotted to Israel.

Abram settled in Hebron in the land of Canaan.[8] Everyone knows that Hebron and Canaan are nowhere near Saudi Arabia. Yet the Qur'an and Islam claim that Abraham and his firstborn son, Ishmael, together built the Ka'aba in Mecca. This is pure fabrication, of which the Qur'an has many more. For example, the Qur'an claims that Noah had another son, who refused to enter the ark and died in the flood,[9] that Mary the mother of Jesus was the sister of Moses[10] and gave birth to Jesus under a palm tree,[11] that the golden calf was built by a Samaritan seven hundred years before Samaritans even existed,[12] etc. Nevertheless, Pope John Paul II, on May 14, 1999, at a ceremony in the Vatican, bowed to and kissed a copy of the Qur'an presented to him by Shi'ite and Sunni leaders from Iraq, even though it contradicts the Bible, rejects the Trinity, denies Christ's deity, says He didn't die on the Cross,[13] and offers no way that God could justly forgive sins. Tragically, Muslims are continuously being pacified in an unconscionable disregard for truth.

ISHMAEL AND ISAAC

As the years went by, both Abraham and his wife Sarah began to doubt God's promise that He would give them a son. Sarah was sure she could never bear a child and told Abraham that God would give him the son He had promised through Hagar, her maid. He accepted the idea (even though God had promised him a son through Sarah) and Hagar gave birth to Abraham's first son, Ishmael, after Abraham had lived in Hebron for ten years.

There are few things on which the Bible and Qur'an are in complete agreement. One of them is the fact that God gave the entire Promised Land of Canaan to Abraham and to his heirs. There is agreement also that Abraham's firstborn was Ishmael and that Isaac was born next. Disagreement comes with Islam's insistence that the

Arabs, who claim to be descended from Ishmael, are the rightful heirs to the Promised Land, whereas the Bible clearly states that the legitimate heirs to the promise are the descendants of Abraham, Isaac, and Jacob. In fact, God declares: "I AM...the God of Abraham, the God of Isaac, and the God of Jacob: this is my name for ever, and this is my memorial unto all generations."[14] Twelve times He is referred to in this way. Both Jesus [15] and Peter [16] honor God with this title. Never is He called the God of Ishmael or of the Arabs—or of any people group except Israel.

Islam claims that as the firstborn Ishmael had the right of inheritance to the Promised Land. Ordinarily that would have been true—but God had promised Abraham that his wife, Sarah, would bear him a son who would be his heir. Ishmael was not the son of God's promise but of Abraham's and Sarah's unbelief. Nevertheless, Abraham loved Ishmael (now thirteen years of age) and told God that he didn't want another son. Here is the fascinating story that authoritatively settles forever any dispute between the descendants of Ishmael and Isaac concerning the land God gave to Abraham and his heirs forever:

> And God said unto Abraham, As for Sarai thy wife...Sarah shall her name be...I will bless her, and give thee a son also of her....
> Then Abraham fell upon his face, and laughed.... And Abraham said unto God, O that Ishmael might live before thee!
> And God said, Sarah thy wife shall bear thee a son indeed; and thou shalt call his name Isaac: and I will establish my covenant with him for an everlasting covenant, and with his seed after him. And as for Ishmael...I have blessed him.... But my covenant will I establish with Isaac, which Sarah shall bear unto thee.[17]

The following year, fourteen years after Ishmael's birth by Hagar, Isaac was born in Hebron to Abraham and Sarah, his wife. Ishmael mocked his half-brother, Isaac. In anger, Sarah banished him and his mother from the land God had given to Abraham and to his heirs.[18] From that time onward, Ishmael was no longer part of Abraham's household but lived far away "in the wilderness of Paran."[19]

THE ULTIMATE TEST OF ABRAHAM'S FAITH

Distinguishing Isaac beyond dispute from the other sons born to Abraham, God called Isaac Abraham's "only son." As a test of Abraham's obedience and faith, God commanded him to sacrifice Isaac on Mount Moriah: "Take now thy son, thine *only son* Isaac, whom thou lovest...and offer him [as] a burnt-offering...."[20] In submission to God's command, Isaac willingly allowed his father to bind him upon the altar.

Confident now of God's promises, Abraham believed that God would raise Isaac from the dead.[21] God tested Abraham to the very point where he had raised his knife to slay Isaac. At that moment, God intervened and provided a ram to be offered in Isaac's place, having proved the complete obedience of both father and son.[22] This is the testimony of Scripture from the God who "cannot lie"[23] and whose "gifts and calling...are without repentance."[24]

The fact that Isaac, miraculously born to both Abraham and Sarah, was the one through whom God's promises of the land and of the Messiah would be fulfilled, and that Ishmael *was not* the son whose descendants would possess the Promised Land, is so clearly and repeatedly declared in Scripture that it cannot be honestly disputed. Yet the Arabs, who say they are descended from Ishmael, lay claim to the promises given by God to Isaac and through him to the Jews. Islam's assertion that Ishmael was the son of promise not only contradicts Scripture but irrationally gives an illegitimate son priority over the legitimate son, whom God designated to be the true heir.

IMPORTANCE OF HEBRON TO ISRAEL

Thirty-seven years after giving birth to Isaac, Sarah died at the age of 127.[25] Abraham was still residing in Hebron of Canaan, where he had lived more than seventy years. He purchased the cave of Machpelah from Ephron the Hittite[26] and there he buried Sarah. Thirty-eight years later, at the age of 175, Abraham died and was buried in Machpelah next to Sarah. After Abraham's death, Isaac continued to live in Hebron in the land of Canaan another one hundred and ten years. Ishmael never lived there as an adult. One by one, Isaac, Rebekah, Jacob, and Leah all died and were buried beside Abraham and Sarah in the family tomb, the cave of Machpelah— but not Ishmael. No Arab or Muslim was ever buried there.

David was first crowned king in Hebron and ruled there over Judah 7½ years before moving his throne to Jerusalem. Hebron is of great significance to the Jews. Yet Muslims built a mosque at Machpelah, claim the burial place of Jewish patriarchs as their own, forbid access to Jews (Israeli soldiers in full battle gear are required to keep it open to Jews), have periodically slaughtered and expelled Jews from Hebron, and are determined to make it as Jew-free as Nazi Germany. They also persist in the preposterous claim that Jerusalem and the entire land of Israel have always belonged to them, that no Jews ever lived there, and that the Israelis are occupying Arab land! And the world accepts such outright lies as the basis for forcing upon Israel an unjust "peace" in the Middle East.

Abraham, Isaac, and Jacob and their families lived for more than three hundred years in Hebron in the land of Canaan, which God had promised to them and to their descendants. (Arabs never lived there in any numbers until after the seventh-century-A.D. Muslim invasion of Israel). Jacob and his family temporarily moved to Egypt because of a famine in Canaan. Their descendants remained there four hundred years and became the slaves of the Egyptians, and then were brought back to conquer Canaan as God had foretold, establishing them as the heirs of God's promises to Abraham.[27]

The PLO claims that Hebron, a city with no connection to Islam, belongs to Muslims and insists that every Jewish resident be removed. In fact, Hebron is one of the most revered places to every Jew. No "Palestinian" ancestor was buried there. Ishmael is buried hundreds of miles away.

THE BATTLE FOR HEBRON

On February 25, 1994, a deranged American-born Israeli, Dr. Baruch Goldstein, acting on his own, walked into the Il Ibrahimi mosque in Hebron and sprayed praying Muslims with an automatic weapon, killing twenty-nine and wounding many others. It was a brutal act, headlined and regurgitated in the media around the world for days as proof that Israel is the evil aggressor who has stolen a country from the Palestinians and is continually abusing them in its "occupation." Goldstein was overwhelmed and killed by survivors.

In fact, unlike the terrorism Israel has endured for fifty years, which is carefully planned and continues with the full knowledge and blessing of the Arab world, this was an isolated act by one Israeli—and it was condemned by Israel. That Israelis have been murdered by the thousands in continuous assaults for more than fifty years, and that the murderers of Israelis are praised as heroes, was somehow overlooked as unimportant. One might be justified in wondering why, for example, the slaughter of sixty-one Israelis and the maiming of hundreds in two bus bombings in Jerusalem just two months earlier was not referred to as a comparison—but the headlines and multi-page criticisms world-wide blaming Goldstein's act on Israel failed to mention it.

Nor did any of the reports in the Western media refer to the rumors of an imminent pogrom by the Arabs that had been cir-culating in Hebron for days, or that the evening before, Muslims had threatened Jewish residents, nearby settlers, and worshipers at the Tomb of the Patriarchs. At Purim services that evening, as Jewish worshipers, including Goldstein, were reading the Scroll of Esther, local Muslims loudly disrupted the ceremony with chants of "It-bakh al Yahud" (slaughter the Jews), a cry frequently heard in Hebron. Though not an excuse for his actions, these facts reveal the situation Dr. Goldstein, an IDF medical officer, had lived with in Hebron, where he had treated victims of Muslim violence.

A pacifist group called the Christian Peacemakers moved into Hebron in June 1995 at the invitation of its mayor to monitor vio-lence and to document Israeli aggression against Palestinians. Seemingly blind to Palestinian aggression against Israelis, the Peacemakers concluded that "to the Jewish settlers, Palestinians are inferior and murderous by nature, and killing those who refuse to leave [Hebron] is justifiable self-defense."[28] A full page was devoted to the Goldstein story in the *National Catholic Reporter*. It declared that "problems began some 20 years ago when Jewish settlers, claiming an exclusive right not only to the city, but to all of Palestine, began moving into Hebron." How can these "unbiased observers and peacemakers" get it so wrong?

Began moving into Hebron twenty years ago? On the contrary, the Jews, though chased out periodically by invaders, had been there for three thousand years. Arabs only arrived after the seventh-century Muslim conquest of Palestine and immediately began to brutalize the Jewish residents for failing to convert to Islam. That mistreatment has continued to a greater or lesser degree ever since—for more than thirteen hundred years. Reading this full-page *National Catholic Reporter* truth-defying diatribe (typical of so many others) condemning the Jews for their alleged brutal mistreatment of innocent and helpless Palestinians, and praising the latter for patiently enduring such suffering, one's blood begins to boil!

In the vicious pogrom of 1929, sixty-seven Jews were murdered in Hebron alone, and the rest forced to flee. Based on deliberate lies that he had invented about Jews raping Muslim women and murdering widows and babies, the Grand Mufti of Jerusalem, Haj Amin al-Husseini, fomented riots against Jews throughout the entire country in order to convince the British that stopping Jewish immigration would prevent violence. "Hebron was attacked. Unarmed yeshiva students were murdered, Jewish homes were attacked, and their occupants were slaughtered. The synagogues were desecrated.... The grand mufti's policy of ethnic cleansing of Jewish inhabitants was being implemented with a vengeance. The British police chief of Hebron later gave the following testimony:

> On hearing screams...I went up a sort of tunnel passage and saw an Arab in the act of cutting off a child's head with a sword. Seeing me, he tried to aim the stroke at me but missed.... I shot him.... Behind him was a Jewish woman smothered in blood with a man I recognized as an Arab police constable named Issa Sheril from Jaffa...standing over the woman with a dagger in his hand. He saw me and bolted into a room close by and tried to shut me out—shouting in Arabic, "Your Honor, I am a policeman." I got into the room and shot him.[29]

As a result of that pogrom, Hebron, which had been the exclusive home of Jews for centuries, became for the first time in its history an Arabs only city. Years later, cautiously and fearfully some Jews began moving back into one of their most sacred cities, where their patriarchs are buried. Then came the war of 1948, when Israel, accepting the partition under UN Resolution 181, declared its independence and was attacked by the regular armed forces of six Arab nations. Jordan captured the West Bank and with it Hebron. It was a further disaster for Jewish residents, who were trying to reestablish themselves in Hebron. All were summarily expelled.

BLINDED BY PREJUDICE?

In its zeal to depict the four hundred Israelis in Hebron as the aggressors brutally mistreating the one hundred twenty thousand Arab residents, the *National Catholic Reporter* forgot to explain why there are so few Jews and why they have only recently begun to return to Hebron. During the Jordanian occupation from 1948 to 1967, Jews were not allowed to live in Hebron or even to visit the Jewish holy sites there—though that prohibition was a blatant violation of the terms of the 1948 Armistice Agreement. In East Jerusalem and throughout the West Bank, which they had captured, Jordanian authorities and Arab residents undertook systematic destruction of all evidence of any Jewish presence in the past in order to bolster their preposterous claim that Jews never lived in Israel! They razed the Jewish Quarter of Hebron, desecrated the Jewish cemetery, and built an animal pen on the ruins of the Avraham Avinu synagogue. Of course, that means nothing in view of the horrible way today's Israeli settlers treat the Muslims! It is maddening how eagerly the world accepts bald-faced Arab lies and revisionist history, and repeats it all with pomp and authority as though it were really true! Indeed, these lies become the basis for "peace"!

The "Peacemakers" seem to be completely ignorant of the history of Hebron and unwilling to consider anything that puts the "Palestinians" in a bad light. The truth is that Jews in Hebron have through the centuries been subjected there, as elsewhere, to indescribable cruelty and murder at the hands of Muslim Arabs. Jumping quickly over a few instances: In 1518, Hebron's prosperous Jewish community was "plundered [by Muslims], many Jews killed, and the survivors forced to flee." By 1540, however, the Jewish community had recovered,[30] though still plundered periodically by traveling Arab marauders. In 1775, lies about Jews killing non-Jews for their blood to make matzo balls (still a popular myth among Muslims today) caused riots against the Jews. In 1834, the Jews of Hebron were massacred by Egyptian soldiers. Some converted to Islam to escape persecution.[31]

In 1851, the British Consulate in Jerusalem reported that "the Jews in Hebron have been greatly alarmed by threats of the Moslems there at the commencement of Ramadan...." In May 1852, the Consul General came to Hebron because of reports of the mistreatment of the Jews. He reported that "the Jews were all so alarmed...that they would tell me nothing...one of the leading Rabbis implored me not to inform [governor] Abderrahhman... that I had come to protect the Jews, as he would inevitably punish them the more for it after my departure." In July 1858, he reported, "During my stay [in Hebron] a Jewish house was forcibly entered by night [and] heavy stones thrown from invisible hands at every person approaching the place to offer help."

Under the influence of the Grand Mufti of Jerusalem, Haj Amin al-Husseini (whose terrorist followers killed Jews and Arabs alike that stood in his way), "The mayor of Hebron, Nasr el Din Nasr, was murdered August 4, 1936; the wife and daughter of the mayor of Bethlehem were wounded July 1937; the mayor of Nablus, Suleiman Bey Toukan, who publicly warned the government of chaos if terrorism was not squelched, fled after an attempted assassination in December of 1937. No fewer than eleven mukhtars [heads of villages] were slain [for living peacefully with Jews], along with family members, between February 1937 and November 1938."[32] The same is true today. The number of "Palestinian" Arabs killed for political reasons by Palestinian death squads far exceeds the number killed in clashes with Israeli troops.

The misinformation today is nothing new, and just as maddening as it has always been. In 1937, angry at the pro-Arab lies being reported in British newspapers, one British Foreign Office correspondent complained that terrorists "were viewed by an increasing number of British officials and observers as 'sincere Arab patriots' whose violence was 'justified.'" He went on to report:

> The Arabs [Muslims] hate civilization and would like to keep the country in its present backward state…. The goats are allowed to eat off all the young plants and the women take what is left for fuel. Fortunately, the Jews are enclosing their land and they are the one hope…. The Arabs…talk big about *their* country but what have they done for it? *They tread down the poor and take backshish [bribes] and that is all they care for."* [Emphasis in original][33]

AMAZING AGREEMENT IN THE QUR'AN!

Thoroughly established history along with the verses cited above from the Bible prove beyond question that the land God promised to Abraham and his heirs belongs to the Israelis. Their title deed was signed by God four thousand years ago. How can today's Arabs reject biblical passages supported by prophecy, a multitude of ancient manuscripts, and indisputable history? Muhammad's early "revelations" in the Qur'an called Jews and Christians the "people of the book"[34] and honored the Books of Moses as inspired of the true God. But when they refused to accept him as a prophet of God, and Muhammad turned against them, the tone of the Qur'an changed. Muslims claim that between the early parts of the Qur'an, which honored the Bible, and later parts that contradict it, the Bible was perverted in order to make it seem that the Jews were the rightful heirs to the Promised Land.

However, there are manuscripts of the Old Testament dating back nearly nine hundred years before the Qur'an, and they are identical to the Bible we have today. The Bible wasn't "changed"! The Greek Septuagint of the Old Testament, for example, was translated in about 275 B.C. from even earlier Hebrew manuscripts and is identical to what we have today. Furthermore, the Qur'an itself agrees with the Bible that the Jews are the rightful heirs to the land:

> We made a covenant of old with the Children of Israel (Surah 5:70); We brought the Children of Israel across the [Red] sea, and Pharaoh with his hosts pursued them...and we verily did allot unto the Children of Israel a fixed abode (10:91, 94); [Pharaoh] wished to scare them from the land, but we drowned him and those with him [in the Red Sea] all together. And we said unto the Children of Israel...dwell in the land..." (17:103-104); we delivered the Children of Israel...from Pharaoh.... We chose them, purposely, above all creatures (44:30-32); we favored them above all peoples (45:16); Remember Allah's favor to you.... He...gave you what he gave no other of his creatures. O my people, go into the Holy Land which Allah hath ordained for you (95:20-21), etc.

In spite of the undeniable fact that the Qur'an declares repeatedly and in the clearest language that the Jews are God's chosen people, unique among all nations, and that the Promised Land was given by God to them alone, Muslims insist that the land belongs to Arab "Palestinians." This is only one of many similar contradictions found in Islam. For example, the Qur'an even declares that the God of the Jews is the true God and the one Muslims should worship: "Pharoah...when the fate of drowning overtook him [in pursuing the Israelites through the Red Sea]...exclaimed: I believe that there is no God save him in whom the Children of Israel believe, and I am of those who surrender unto him."[35]

Despite such passages scattered throughout the Qur'an, and a profusion of other proofs, Islam declares that "Palestine" belongs to the Arab descendants of Ishmael. This is the basis for the hatred Muslims have toward Israel and for their determination to exterminate its people and to possess all of Israel for themselves. In fact, the word "Palestine" is not found once in the Qur'an—very strange, considering the importance Muslims attach to it today.

FURTHER PROOF THAT THE LAND IS ISRAEL'S

Though it is hardly needed, we are given additional conclusive evidence that the Jews and Israelis are the heirs of Abraham, to whom God gave the land. God made an everlasting covenant with Abraham, saying, "Unto thy seed have I given this land, from the river of Egypt unto...the river Euphrates...."[36] At that very time, before either Ishmael or Isaac had been born, God identified which descendants of Abraham would inherit the land: "Know of a surety that thy seed shall be a stranger in a land that is not theirs, and shall serve them [i.e., as slaves]; and they shall afflict them 400 years... and afterward shall they come out with great substance [and] shall come hither [to Canaan, the Promised Land] again."

God could not have stated the fact more clearly that the true heirs were to be slaves in a foreign land for four hundred years before being led back into the Promised Land. Never did this happen to the Arabs. In fact, they were not even an identifiable people at this time but scattered nomads, who would only take on their identify centuries later—and not in Canaan but in the Arabian Peninsula.

There were two reasons why the children of Israel had to remain for four hundred years in Egypt. First of all, during that time as slaves they did not intermarry with the Egyptians under whom they served—or with any other non-Jews. Thus they became an identifiable, ethnic people who were led *en masse* into the Promised Land, and we know who they are today.

Ishmael's descendants, on the other hand, intermarried with those of Abraham's son Midian (by his second wife, Keturah) so that the term "Midianite" was used interchangeably with "Ishmaelite."[37] The Ishmaelites also intermarried with the Edomites (descendants of Esau),[38] who intermarried with the Hittites.[39] The Arabs were a nomadic people, who tended to intermarry among the nations with whom they traveled and traded and later conquered.

Secondly, God told Abraham, "the iniquity of the Amorites is not yet full."[40] God was not going to wipe out the Canaanites simply to give their land to the Jews. He would do so only because of the wickedness of these people. In four hundred years, they would be so evil that the Lord would righteously be forced to destroy them as He had the people of Sodom and Gomorrah—and He would use His chosen people, delivered from Egyptian slavery, to execute His judgment. And so it happened.

Thereafter, Canaan was known as the land of Israel, which it is called thirty-one times in Scripture. Its kings ruled from Jerusalem over a vast empire stretching from the Sinai to the Euphrates. In fact, Israel was the only united, sovereign nation-state that ever existed in what today is called "Palestine." Thus, for three hundred years before they were enslaved in Egypt and about one thousand years thereafter (a total of thirteen hundred years), the Jews dwelled in their own land, the land of Israel, before Jerusalem was destroyed by the Babylonians. It is an insult to the God of Israel and to His chosen people to call the promised land of Israel "Palestine"!

A FINAL PROOF

As an important part of their deliverance from Egypt, the Israelites were commanded to kill a lamb for each household, sprinkle its blood on the house frame around the door, roast it, and eat it in readiness to leave Egypt on the night that God delivered them. Thereafter, as a memorial of this miraculous event, they were to keep the feast of the Passover each year forever. The Passover is not like the *hajj* and Ramadan, both of which had been practiced by pagan Arab tribes for centuries before the Muslims began to claim them as their own. The Passover is unique to the Jews, and it began the day they were delivered from slavery in Egypt.[41]

Furthermore, in another amazing and confirming prophecy, God declared that, in spite of breaking the Ten Commandments, and in spite of breaking and even abandoning the many other ordinances that He would give them, they would keep the Passover forever: "Ye shall keep it a feast to the LORD…by an ordinance for ever."[42] Only one people on earth, the Jews, keep the Passover. And they continue to do so exactly as God foretold. Here is the final proof that they are the heirs whose ancestors were slaves in Egypt, were miraculously delivered by God, and as a result brought back to conquer Canaan, where their patriarchs had already lived for three hundred years.

More than 90 percent of Jews worldwide keep the Passover every year. This same percentage holds true among those living in Israel, even though very few believe the Bible and about 30 percent claim to be atheists. This is an undeniable fulfillment of a specific prophecy. To see how remarkable this is, note two well-known comparisons. The "prophets" in Rome declared that the sacred fires of the goddess Vesta tended by the Vestal Virgins would never go out. They went out. The Zoroastrian prophets swore that their sacred fires would never go out. They were extinguished in the Muslim invasion of Persia in the seventh century. God said Israel would keep the Passover forever, and Jews worldwide still keep it today.

But how do we know that the Passover story is true? The proof is contained in the Passover itself and the fact that the Jews still keep it and have done so continuously. When an event is witnessed by many people and is immediately commemorated by some special rite, which then continues ever after, we have absolute proof that the event actually occurred.

No one could invent such a story and start the tradition of keeping the Passover if it had never really happened. Jews would immediately protest, "But we didn't do this last year!" The very fact that it was done last year, and the year before, and the year before—as far back as one can trace—is proof that an original Passover marked Israel's deliverance from Egypt and passage into the Promised Land. It also marks the Jews as those to whom the Promised Land was given. In fact, such proof was God's intent. He commanded Moses to tell the Israelites:

> And it shall come to pass, when your children shall say unto you, What mean ye by this service? That ye shall say, It is the sacrifice of the LORD's passover, who passed over the houses of the children of Israel in Egypt, when he smote the Egyptians.... [43]

ISRAEL'S RIGHT TO HER LAND IS BY GOD'S GRACE

The promise of the land and of the Messiah was renewed by God to Isaac: "Unto thee, and unto thy seed, I will give all these countries, and I will perform the oath which I sware unto Abraham thy father...in thy seed shall all the nations of the earth be blessed."[44] God confirmed the same promise to Isaac's son Jacob (Israel) as well: "The land whereon thou liest, to thee will I give it, and to thy seed...and in thy seed shall all the families of the earth be blessed."[45]

Islam can produce no evidence (either from the Qur'an or from history) that the land was ever promised to Ishmael, that all of his descendants together were ever slaves for four hundred years anywhere, or that upon their deliverance they were led *en masse* into the Promised Land. In fact, Ishmael's descendants never lived in Canaan. Furthermore, Arabs certainly don't keep the Passover, but follow the same pagan rituals that their ancestors observed for centuries before Muhammad was born!

Sadly, the Israelites eventually came under God's judgment for practicing the idolatrous ways of the nations they had displaced. Pleading with them to repent, God had warned, "[Y]e shall be plucked from off the land...and the LORD shall scatter thee among all people, from the one end of the earth even unto the other."[46] Stubbornly, Israel continued in idolatry and rebellion and was put out of the land. Around 600 B.C. they were conquered by the Babylonians and scattered to many nations—but not forever.

In spite of their disobedience and being under divine judgment, the Jews are consistently identified as the chosen people belonging to the God of the Bible. He is called "the God of Israel" 203 times. *Never* is He called the God of any other people—and certainly never is He called the God of Ishmael or of the Arabs. It is not because of Israel's obedience that God promised that after her dispersal under His judgment He would restore her fully to her land in the last days. Far from meriting restoration, she has been disobedient and rebellious and has forsaken the Lord throughout her history. Nevertheless, numerous times God has made such promises as the following:

> Therefore say unto the house of Israel, Thus saith the Lord GOD; I do not this for your sakes, O house of Israel, but for mine holy name's sake, which ye have profaned among the heathen, whither ye went. And I will sanctify my great name…and the heathen shall know that I am the LORD, saith the Lord GOD, when I shall be sanctified in you before their eyes. For I will take you from among the heathen, and gather you out of all countries, and will bring you into your own land.[47]

THE "GOD OF ISRAEL" IS ANGRY!

Chased out of their land under God's judgment in the Babylonian dispersion, and later twice by the Romans, Jews always returned to their ancient homeland. This despised people have lived in Israel continuously for twenty-five hundred years since returning from Babylon. Thus, for nearly four thousand years, beginning with Abraham and Isaac, Israelis have lived in the land God gave them—though during most of that time they suffered under the oppressive heel of various conquerors.

God is angry with the nations of today's world for having robbed Israel of most of the land that He gave as an everlasting inheritance to Abraham's descendants. They have confined Israel to a small fraction thereof, and are demanding that she give up even more to the "Palestinians." The "Palestinians" claim that all of the land belongs to them and that Israel is therefore occupying *their* land and must be removed. This defiance of God cannot continue without His righteous judgment falling upon the perpetrators!

God is also angry with present-day Israel for going along with this fraud, even though under heavy pressure from the United Nations, European Union, and the United States. God's judgment will come upon Israel for her disobedience and unbelief—but He will not forsake her. Tragically, modern Israel has repeatedly agreed to give away ever more of the Promised Land for one transparently false promise of "peace" after another. They have violated what David Ben-Gurion, her first prime minister, relying upon the Bible, correctly declared at Israel's modern beginning:

> Our right to this land in its entirety is steadfast, inalienable and eternal.... This right...cannot be forfeited under any circumstance...[Israelis] have neither the power nor the jurisdiction to negate it for future generations.... And until the coming of the Great Redemption, we shall never yield this historic right.[48]

Yes, but the land *is* called "Palestine," and there *are* millions of people whom the whole world recognizes as "Palestinians" who have lived there for generations. After all, Muslims conquered that land in the mid-seventh century A.D and held it until 1917. Even after that, Arabs continued to live there. Why are not their claims of prior occupation of that land valid? We turn to that question in the next chapter.

---

1. Genesis 16:1-16.
2. Genesis 17:15-21; 21:1-12.
3. Genesis 25:1-2.
4. Genesis 12:1.
5. Genesis 12:2-3.
6. Romans 4:5.
7. Genesis 12:5-6; 13:12, 14-18; 15:18.
8. Genesis 13:18; 23:2, 19; 35:27; 37:14, etc.
9. Surah 11:42-43.
10. Surah 19:28.
11. Surah 19:21-27.
12. Surah 20:85-87, 95-97.
13. Surah 4:157.
14. Exodus 3:13-16.
15. Matthew 22:32; Mark 12:26; Luke 20:37.
16. Acts 3:13.
17. Genesis 17:15-21.
18. Genesis 21:10-20.
19. Genesis 21:21.
20. Genesis 22:1-2.
21. Hebrews 11:17-19.
22. Genesis 22:3-14.
23. 1 Samuel 15:29; Psalm 89:35; Titus 1:2, etc.
24. Romans 11:29.
25. Genesis 23:1.
26. Genesis 23:1-20.
27. Genesis 15:13-14.

28. Rosemary Radford Ruether, "Jewish settlers as pushy 'chosen people' – Christian Peacemakers have thankless task," *National Catholic Reporter*, April 26, 1996, 12.

29. Joan Peters, *From Time Immemorial: The Origins of the Arab-Jewish Conflict Over Palestine* (New York: J. KAP Publishing U.S.A., 1984), 315.

30. Ruether, "Peacemakers," 21.

31. Moshe Ma'oz, ed., *Studies on Palestine During the Ottoman Period* (Jerusalem: The Magnes Press, 1975), 147-148.

32. Peters, *Immemorial.*, 314.

33. Cited in Alan Dershowitz, *The Case for Israel* (Hoboken, NJ: John Wiley & Sons, Inc., 2003), 43.

34. Surah 3:18-20, 64-71, 72-80; 4:171; 5:15-19, 59, 77-80; etc.

35. Surah 10:91.

36. Genesis 15:18.

37. Judges 8:8, 12, 22, 24.

38. Genesis 28:9.

39. Genesis 26:34.

40. Genesis 15:16.

41. Exodus 12:1-13.

42. Exodus 12:14.

43. Exodus 12:26-27.

44. Genesis 26:3-4.

45. Genesis 28:13-14.

46. Deuteronomy 28:63-64.

47. Ezekiel 36:22-24.

48. "BETRAYAL," American Friends of Women For Israel's Tomorrow, Norfolk, VA, ad in *The International Jerusalem Post*, November 30, 2001, 11.

4—THE TRUTH ABOUT "PALESTINE"

THE CLAIM THAT "PALESTINE" belongs to Arabs (as Islam insists) is a *cause célèbre* for the entire Arab world. It is vigorously pursued on behalf of certain Arabs (both inside and outside of Israel) who call themselves "Palestinians." As far as Arabs are concerned, Israel does not exist. For example, "Israel is not recognized as a sovereign state in Saudi Arabian textbooks and its name does not appear on any map. All maps in Saudi schoolbooks [and those of other Muslim nations] bear only the name Palestine...presented as a Muslim country occupied by foreigners who defile its Muslim holy places, especially the Al-Aqsa Mosque in Jerusalem. The occupation of Palestine is portrayed as the most crucial problem of the Arabs and the Muslims who should all join forces for the total liberation of Palestine."[1]

About four million "Palestinians" are registered as refugees with the United Nations Relief Works Agency (UNRWA), of which 33 percent live inside UNRWA's fifty-nine refugee camps throughout the West Bank, Gaza Strip, Jordan, Syria, and Lebanon. They claim to be the children and grandchildren of Palestinians who were descended from the "original Palestinians" and who were allegedly driven from their homes, businesses, and farms by the Israelis in the 1948 War of Independence. Backed by world opinion, the United Nations, the EU, and most world leaders, they demand a return to their native Palestine.

In that 1948 war, Transjordan (which England had created in 1946 out of land that the 1922 Declaration of Principles of the League of Nations had recognized belonged to the Jewish people) took East Jerusalem. Some units of Jordan's Arab Legion were actually led by British commanders in the assault on Jerusalem. Jordan had launched an air attack against Israel even before it declared itself an independent state. Their heavy artillery and air bombardments were too much for the Jewish defenders, who had no artillery or war planes. They surrendered the Jewish quarter of the Old City on May 28, 1948, losing their precious Wailing Wall two weeks after declaring themselves a nation. The Arabs had pounded the city with more than ten thousand shells, killing twelve hundred civilians and destroying more than two thousand homes. The poorly equipped Israelis bravely managed somehow to hang on to West Jerusalem.

Transjordan (now known as Jordan) had been given more than five times as much of "Palestine" as Israel eventually was allotted. Greedy for more, its Arab legions took the West Bank, and Egypt took the Gaza Strip. All Jews were expelled and all Jewish property was demolished or confiscated. This is standard procedure for Muslims whenever possible. Yet the Arabs hypocritically demand that Jerusalem must continue as an international city for fear that Israel will eradicate Muslim holy sites. Incredibly, the UN and world leaders make policy on this basis.

The 1993 Oslo Accords left Nablus (ancient Shechem) under Israeli jurisdiction. Located there was the traditional site of Joseph's tomb, a place dear not only to the heart of Israelis and of all Jews worldwide, but to Christians as well. On October 7, 2000, then Prime Minister Ehud Barak, relying upon a Palestinian agreement to protect the site, ordered Israeli troops to leave Nablus. Within hours, smoke was seen billowing from the tomb as a joyful mob, celebrating Israeli withdrawal, burned Jewish prayer books and other articles. With pickaxes and hammers, they began to tear apart the stone building. Two days later, bulldozers were clearing the area.[2] The UN and EU were silent at this desecration—but they continually thunder their denunciations of Israel for defending itself.

After the IDF vacated Ramallah on January 3, 1996, Arafat, addressing the assembled mob of cheering Palestinians from the roof of the former IDF Headquarters, declared that Ramallah and Al-Bira "have become liberated forever.... Today we begin our path towards an independent Palestinian state with Jerusalem as its capital!"[3] This is what the "peace process" was all about for Arafat, and still is for Mahmoud Abbas (Abu Mazen), Arafat's successor as Palestinian Authority Chairman and long-time partner in terrorism. Nothing has changed except that the rhetoric will be much smoother and more deceptive.

The manner in which Israeli Defense Forces (IDF) have departed each position that they have in good faith relinquished under signed agreements to their "partner in peace," and the manner in which the Palestinians have taken over, unmasks the delusion of any desire for real peace. Consider the spectacle at the transfer of Nablus into the hands of Arafat's Palestinian Authority (PA):

> The scenes on television showed [departing] Israeli soldiers cowering in their vehicles, being stoned, spat upon, and cursed.... The raging mob, gleeful and power-intoxicated, burnt Israeli flags.... It is difficult to imagine a more humiliating sight [for Israel]....
>
> The Nablus evacuation scenes reinforce the impression that it was only Arab force [not Israeli good will]...which has compelled Israel to withdraw. Fatah [Arafat's own terrorist group] leaflets in Nablus hailed the Palestinian victory over "the Nazi occupation army," boasting that it was the Palestinian fire "which scorched the ground under the feet of the monkeys and pigs." The obvious conclusion is that the same fire can make Israel flee from the rest of Palestine.[4]

The West Bank and Gaza, so much in the news today, were held by Jordan and Egypt for nineteen years and used as terrorist launching pads against Israel until the latter was forced—for its own protection—to occupy them in the Six-Day War in 1967. It was the Arabs, not Israel, who put the "refugees" in the camps and have kept them there ever since. The world that remained predictably silent when Jordan and Egypt confined the "Palestinian refugees" to camps, and had no word of rebuke during the nineteen years of terrorist attacks launched against Israel from these areas, now blames Israel for "oppressing" these peoples and clamors for Israel to end its "unlawful occupation of Palestinian territory."

In spite of the Palestine Liberation Organization's (PLO's) obvious duplicity, Israel has continued to turn over territory to them, literally staging its own destruction, as the Hebrew prophet Ezekiel foretold: "Have ye not seen a vain vision...[the leaders] have seduced my people, saying, Peace; and there was no peace...the prophets...prophesy concerning Jerusalem...see visions of peace for her, and there is no peace, saith the Lord God."[5]

IS ISRAEL COMMITTING SUICIDE?

In a news conference on December 27, 2004, PLO Chairman Mahmoud Abbas stressed "the inalienable rights of the Palestinian people, mainly the rights of refugees to return back to Israel and to establish an independent Palestinian state with Jerusalem as its capital."[6] Of course, no such state ever existed, so how could they return to it? Nor did the Arabs ever suggest forming such a state when they had control of this area from 1948 to 1967. Why not? That is not their objective, but the destruction of Israel.

It would be tantamount to national suicide for the small country of Israel, with less than eight million citizens (more than one million of them Arab Muslims who would love to see her destroyed), to allow within its borders another four million Arabs who have sworn her annihilation. This is the Arab goal in demanding a return of all "refugees." And this is why President Bush has gone on record that the only right these "refugees" have is to be received within their own independent Palestinian state formed out of present Palestinian territory, which his road map to peace is designed to create.

Although the "Palestinians" pretend to be interested in negotiations brokered by Western powers to make "peace" in exchange for Israel giving up additional land, their ultimate aim is to possess *all* of Israel. That remains their unwavering determination today. Nor could they be satisfied with anything less without renouncing Islam and its founding prophet, Muhammad.

The willful persistence in this illegitimate claim, and its support by the rest of the world in the demand for a "Palestinian State," constitutes an inexcusable rejection of the clear testimony both of history and of Scripture. It is a flagrant rebellion against the God of Israel. This triple crime has created the Mideast crisis facing us today. Not only the Muslims but the entire world of politics continues to defy the God of Israel. His patience is bound to wear thin—and that is a terrifying thought.

ARAB INTENTIONS

Under the assertion that they are descended from the "original Palestinians" who lived in the land of "Palestine" before the Israelites, led by Joshua, invaded and conquered it, the Arab refugees claim the entire land as theirs. The Jews, they insist, are unlawfully occupying their hereditary land and must leave.

One repeatedly hears the complaint that the obstacle to peace is Israeli "occupation" of the West Bank and Gaza Strip. If that is the case, why was the Palestine Liberation Organization created in 1964, when Israel had nothing to do with those territories, which were then under Arab control? What did they intend to "liberate" when Jordan and Egypt held the "Palestinians" in their grip, whom they (not the Israelis) had put in squalid camps in these areas? Why did the PLO and her coterie of terrorists attack Israel from these territories, and Hizballah (Party of Allah) attack from Lebanon? There is only one answer: talk of a Palestinian state is a smokescreen to cover the real intention of annihilating Israel. The "Palestinians" are mere pawns of the Arabs.

The Arab armies that had attacked the new state of Israel in May 1948 were soundly defeated. They reluctantly signed temporary "cease-fire" agreements (allowed by Muhammad's example at Hudaybiya in 628): Egypt on February 24, 1949, Lebanon on March 23, Transjordan on April 3, and Syria on July 20. The borders of Israel agreed upon at that time have been known ever since as the "Green Line."

The victory had been costly. Israeli deaths had mounted to 6,373 (2,400 civilians), about 1 percent of her entire population (which would compare to a loss of nearly 3 million Americans today). Estimates of Arab losses vary from 5,000 to 15,000—about 1/40 of 1 percent.

On October 11, 1949, Egyptian Minister of Foreign Affairs, Muhammad Saleh el-Din, declared that "the Arabs intend that they [refugees] shall return as masters.... More explicitly: they intend to annihilate the state of Israel.... The Arab people will not be embarrassed to declare: 'We shall not be satisfied except by the final obliteration of Israel.'"[7] Even Nazi Germany didn't intend to "obliterate" France or England—but this is what the Muslims intend for Israel. And the world blames Israel for not making peace with such enemies!

"PALESTINE"?

We have already seen that the land into which God brought Abraham some four thousand years ago, which He promised by everlasting covenant to him and to his heirs, and in which he and his descendants through Isaac and Jacob lived for centuries thereafter, was not a non-existent place called "Palestine," as those who erroneously call themselves "Palestinians" today insist. It was the historic land of Canaan: "And I will give unto thee, and to thy seed after thee...all the land of Canaan, for an everlasting possession; and I will be their God....[8] Be ye mindful always of his covenant...which he made with Abraham, and of his oath unto Isaac; and hath confirmed the same to Jacob for a law, and to Israel for an everlasting covenant, saying, Unto thee will I give the land of Canaan...."[9]

The ancient land of Canaan and its inhabitants are unmistakably identified both in the Bible and by archaeology. Canaan was never promised to the Arabs, nor did they ever live there in any numbers until modern times. Canaan's early inhabitants were Kenites, Kenizites, Kadmonites, Hittites, Perizites, Rephaims, Amorites, Canaanites, Girgashites, and Jebusites—not "Palestinians."[10] When the Israelites returned after four hundred years as slaves in Egypt (marking them as the promised heirs), they conquered Canaan at God's command: "For the wickedness of these nations the LORD thy God doth drive them out from before thee. Not for thy righteousness...."[11] Canaan became Israel and was so known for more than fifteen hundred years.

But most of the world, and even most Israelis, call that land Palestine today. That has been its designation for centuries. If this was the land of Israel, when and how did it become known as "Palestine"?

Around A.D. 132, the Romans, who had decimated Jerusalem in A.D. 70, began to rebuild it for Roman Emperor Hadrian as a pagan city dedicated to himself and to Jupiter. They started construction of a temple to Jupiter on Temple Mount at the site of the ancient Jewish temples. Understandably, there was an uprising of the Jews to prevent such desecration. It was led by Simon Bar Kochba, whom many considered to be the Messiah.

At first the revolt was remarkably successful. But more legions were brought in, and the Romans eventually destroyed nearly one thousand villages, killed about five hundred thousand Jews, and sold thousands into slavery. When the revolt was finally crushed in A.D. 135, the Roman conquerors angrily renamed the land of Israel, *Provincia Syria-Palestina,* after Israel's ancient enemies, the Philistines. From that time forward, all those living there were known as "Palestinians."

JEWS, THE "PALESTINIANS"

Who lived in the newly designated Palestine and were thus known as "Palestinians"? Jews, of course. Chase them out and they return to the land God gave to their forebears. At that time, Arabs hadn't even dreamed that "Palestine" was their land. That ambition would not take hold for another five hundred years until the advent of Islam—and even then Arabs would not call themselves Palestinians.

In World War II, Britain had a volunteer brigade known as "The Palestinian Brigade." It was made up entirely of Jews. The Arabs were fighting on Hitler's side. (Hitler had promised, in addition to the destruction of Israel, freedom and self-rule to all the Arab states in return for their assistance. One entire SS Division was made up of Bosnian Muslims.) There was the Palestinian Symphony Orchestra, a Jewish orchestra, and the *Palestinian Post,* a Jewish newspaper. As late as the 1950s, Arabs refused to be called Palestinians and declared that if there were such a people, they were Jews.

To the British Peel Commission in 1937, a local Arab leader testified, "There is no such country as Palestine. 'Palestine' is a term the Zionists invented...." Professor Philip Hitti, Arab historian, testified to an Anglo-American Committee of inquiry in 1946, "There is no such thing as Palestine in history—absolutely not!"[12] To the UN Security Council on May 31, 1956, Ahmed Shukairy declared, "It is common knowledge that Palestine is nothing but southern Syria." Eight years later, in 1964, Shukairy became the founding chairman of the Palestine Liberation Organization and coined the infamous slogan, "[W]e'll drive the Jews into the sea." And he wasn't even a "Palestinian"! Like Arafat, he was born in Cairo. The Palestine Liberation Organization was not founded by Palestinians but has been used to exploit these abused people in Islam's war against Israel.

DEBUNKING THE MYTH OF ARAB "PALESTINIANS"

Today's Arab "Palestinians" are close relatives of the Arabs living in neighboring countries, from which most of them—or their immediate ancestors—came. They make a number of conflicting claims, which by their very absurdity betray their illegitimacy. Even had there been a land of Palestine occupied by Palestinians, the Arabs could not have descended from them. Arabs claim that they are descended from Ishmael, Abraham's first son, and that they are therefore the legitimate heirs to the land that God gave to Abraham. They do have much Ishmaelite blood in them, but there is no direct genealogy tracing today's Arabs back to Ishmael. They are a mixed race.

We've already seen that Isaac was the son of promise. Even if the Arabs were 100 percent Ishmaelites, they would still not be descended from the land's original inhabitants. God promised the land to Abraham before Ishmael was born. It already had many inhabitants. So how could Arab descendants of Ishmael (born to immigrants centuries after Canaan had been settled) be at the same time descendants of the "original inhabitants" of the Promised Land? Impossible!

Ishmael himself was not descended from Canaan's original inhabitants. His father, Abraham, was from Ur of the Chaldees, and his mother, Hagar, was an Egyptian. Neither of them was among the "original inhabitants of Canaan," nor even remotely related to such a people—nor could any of Ishmael's descendants be so related. Today's "Palestinians" are simply lying! But it is a lie that the world loves and gladly uses as a club against Israel.

Canaan was already settled when Abraham with his wife, Sarah, and her maid, Hagar, arrived there. At the age of fourteen, Ishmael (with his mother), banished by Sarah from Abraham's household, left Hebron and Canaan and lived ever after in the "wilderness of Paran."[13] Ishmael's descendants never lived in Canaan but settled in the Arabian Peninsula. It would not be until the seventh century A.D., through the Islamic *jihad* invasions, that Arabs would come in any significant numbers into the land of Israel, which by that time was erroneously called Palestine.

How could the descendants of Ishmael, who didn't even live in "Palestine," claim descent from the "original Palestinians"? They couldn't. Clearly, Arabs could not possibly be descendants of the original inhabitants of Canaan. Such contradictions do not provide a good foundation for the claims of today's "Palestinians." Yet the world accepts these fantasies as the basis of a settlement they intend to impose upon Israel, whose legitimate ancestral claims to that land go back four thousand years!

NO RELATIONSHIP TO PHILISTINES

If "Palestine" is so important to the Arabs, why is it not mentioned *once* in their holy book, the Qur'an? The word is used four times in the Bible,[14] but never refers either to the land of Canaan or to Israel. The Hebrew word from which it is translated is *pelensheth*. It referred to a small region also known as Philistia,[15] the land of the *Pelishtee,* or Philistines. Philistia was in the same location but a bit larger than the Gaza Strip of today, named after the Philistine city of Gaza. Their other cities were Ashdod, Gath (home of Goliath), Gerar, and Ekron. This is the true history, of which the Qur'an knows nothing.

The Philistines were not a Semitic people like the Arabs but had invaded Canaan by sea from across the Mediterranean and occupied that particular area before the Israelites arrived. They were not the "original inhabitants of the land" (as today's "Palestinians" claim their ancestors were), but displaced certain Canaanites just as they were themselves eventually displaced by Israel. Arab "Palestinians" (who are Semites) living there today can claim neither ethnic, linguistic, nor historical relationship to the Philistines, nor can they justify on any other basis calling themselves Palestinians.

Those who today claim to be Palestinians are Arabs by birth, language, Islamic religion, and culture. Their "Palestinian" parents and grandparents immigrated from surrounding Arab countries, attracted by the prosperity being created by Jews returning to their ancient Promised Land. In most cases, this influx occurred only a few months or years before Israel declared independence. The United Nations defined a "Palestinian" as one who had lived there at least two years. Even that loose qualification was not strictly followed. Of course, this rule was generously applied to Arabs but not to Jews, though they lived in "Palestine" as well.

WHAT ABOUT JERUSALEM?

Jerusalem was established as the capital of Israel by King David three thousand years ago. It is not mentioned once in the Qur'an. Even when Muslim empires controlled all of the Middle East, Jerusalem was given no importance and was largely neglected. In the late 1800s, out of a population in Jerusalem of about forty thousand, most were Jews, the rest Christians of various shades, and only a few were Arabs.

Nor is there any reference to Jerusalem in the Palestine National Covenant of 1964. It was a new invention and complete turnabout when the Muslim world began to insist that the West Bank, the Gaza Strip, and Jerusalem itself had always belonged to "Palestinians."

Muslim writers recently began to laud Jerusalem as "comparable in holiness" to Mecca and Medina, or even "our most sacred place."[16] But this was another fabrication and never the case historically. The Islamic terrorist organization Hizballah (Party of Allah), headquartered in Syria, displays the Dome of the Rock on its promotional materials to inflame its followers against Israel. Arafat declared that "Al-Quds [Jerusalem] is in the innermost of our feeling, the feeling of our people and the feeling of all Arabs, Muslims, and Christians in the world."[17] Not surprisingly, he left out the Jews, to whom Jerusalem means more than to anyone!

The PLO mentions Jerusalem in its 1968 constitution as "the seat of the Palestine Liberation Organization." It attempted to implement that fraudulent claim by establishing Palestinian Authority offices in Jerusalem's venerable Orient House (in violation of the Oslo Accords), where it conducted business and welcomed international delegates and "peace" activists. Finally, the Israelis had enough of the PLO's attempts to establish precedents legitimizing its claims to Jerusalem as the capital of a Palestinian state. They ousted the PLO and took over Orient house and other PA offices in Jerusalem on August 10, 2001.[18]

At the very beginning, Muhammad made the *qiblah* (direction of prayer) toward Jerusalem, apparently to attract the Jews. But when that did not work, he once again had Muslims pray facing the idol-filled Ka'aba in Mecca, as they must today. Thus the Qur'an not only does not mention Jerusalem but by implication demeans it as the wrong *qiblah*: "And even if thou broughtest unto those who have received the Scripture [i.e., Jews and Christians], they would not follow thy *qiblah*, nor canst thou be a follower of their *qiblah*...then surely wert thou of the evil-doers."[19] Of course, Christians have no *qiblah*, unless it is to lift up their eyes to heaven in prayer as Jesus did.[20]

Yet Palestinians demand the *return* of Jerusalem as their capital. In furtherance of the Palestinian myth, King Fahd of Saudi Arabia calls on Muslim states to protect "the holy city [that] belongs to all Muslims across the world!"[21] In fact, during the many centuries when one Muslim regime or another controlled Jerusalem, and even with the Dome of the Rock located there, it was never given any special significance in Islam. To do so is part of the recent effort to displace the Israelis, which would shock Muslims from centuries past.

A TANGLED WEB

There are many other problems with "Palestinian" claims. Of course, no one can unscramble eggs, but this is pretty much the situation. It was the UN that partitioned the land. Israel was content with what they received, although it was so narrow in some places as to be indefensible. They did not attack the Arabs; it was the Arabs who attacked Israel and with the publicly stated and oft-repeated intention of annihilating her. Any territory Arabs lost from what the UN had allotted to them was taken by Israel in the process of defending itself from an enemy that had attacked with *extermination* in mind.

Time magazine pointed out[22] that had the Arabs not attacked but accepted the UN partition, as Israel did, the "Palestinians" would have been living in their own State all these years. Of course, they never intended to accept any co-existence with Israel, as their leaders repeatedly vowed. And now, after five failed wars, they demand what the UN originally gave them. Surely Israel has no obligation to hand the original UN boundaries back to the Arabs, who violently rejected them and made them the basis of attempts to exterminate her. That would be a suicidal reward of aggression.

It would be absurd for Israel to give back to her attackers the strategic territory she had to take in order to defend herself. Nevertheless, in a gesture unheard of in the history of war, victorious Israel has given back more than 95 percent of the land she took in self-defense—and the Palestinians have used that territory for launching terrorist attacks against their benefactor.

PALESTINIANS AND TERRORISM

There is no reasoning with terrorists. Force is all they understand. Without question, the premier terrorist of recent years was Yasser Arafat, not Osama Bin Laden. Born Abd al-Rahman Abd al-Rauf Arafat al-Qudwa al-Husseini on August 27, 1929, he shortened his name to omit the telltale al-Husseini. His main purpose was to hide his relationship to his grandfather's cousin, Haj Amin Mohammed al-Husseini, appointed Grand Mufti of Jerusalem by the British in 1921, Jew-killing partner of Hitler (Hitler gave him $500,000 to fight the Allies and Jews), a terrorist in his own right, and Arafat's "mentor and guide."[23] Arafat called himself "Yasser" in memory of Yasser al-Birah, "a leader of the Grand Mufti's reign of terror in the 1930s."[24] Arafat committed his first murder at age twenty—of an innocent Palestinian, Rork Hamid.[25]

The Palestine Liberation Organization was founded in 1964, not in Palestine but in Cairo, by Gamel Abdel Nasser, Egypt's President,[26] supposedly to represent the "oppressed Palestinian people." Yasser Arafat, already the head of the terrorist group known as *Fatah*, became chairman of the PLO in 1969. Under Arafat, it became the wealthiest (with an annual income exceeding $1.2 billion,[27] of which Arafat hid billions in his own personal Swiss accounts) and most vicious international terrorist organization on record, involved in hundreds of "bombings, shootings, hijackings, rocket attacks, and kidnappings in twenty-six countries." Most of the victims and more than 90 percent of the thousands of hostages were not Israelis.[28]

Negotiating with Arafat and the PLO was and is meaningless, yet Israel has been forced into that role by world opinion. The Palestinian National Charter of the PLO spells out their goals very clearly. These people are Muslims, so their goals are not merely that of their organization but of their religion. Unless the religion changes, the goals cannot possibly change. In the process of negotiating with Israel for "peace," they may pretend that they have changed—but that is simply not the case.

Arafat ran (and so will his successor, Abu Mazen) the territories the PLO has taken over from Israel like the Royal family runs Saudi

Arabia. There is no freedom. No one dared to disagree or even to question Arafat and his Palestinian Authority (PA). Voting has been a joke. The press is controlled. An experienced Arab journalist wrote, "Every journalist who wishes to interview a senior Palestinian official must be equipped with the following items: a casket, a burial plot for himself and his family, and a will prepared well in advance."[29]

Truth meant nothing to Arafat or his partners in crime, who (like Communists have always done) invent "history" as they need it. Soviet dissidents had a saying that applies equally to the Palestinians: "The Soviet Union is the only country with an unpredictable past." The PLO National Charter reveals a perverse mindset. In the face of reams of history to the contrary, it dares to declare (and the world gladly believes such lies):

> Claims of historical or religious ties of Jews with Palestine are incompatible with the facts of history.... Nor do Jews constitute a single nation with an identity of its own; they are citizens of the states to which they belong.
>
> Zionism is a political movement...racist and fanatic in its nature, aggressive, expansionist and colonial in its aims, and fascist in its methods. Israel is...a geographical base for world imperialism placed strategically in the midst of the Arab homeland to combat the hopes of the Arab nation for liberation, unity and progress. Israel is a constant source of threat *vis-a-vis* peace in the Middle East and the whole world.[30]

This is even worse than the pot calling the kettle black! Arafat died November 11, 2004. Palestinians wanted to bury him at the Al-Aqsa Mosque on Temple Mount, but Israel refused, careful to avoid giving their enemies any further claim to Israel's holiest site. As a compromise, amid a frenzied mob clamoring to touch the coffin, he was buried with high honor in Ramallah, where the PLO is headquartered. His body, however, was placed in a concrete coffin so that it could be moved to Al-Aqsa when Israel shall be finally ousted from the land. Almost immediately, world leaders came to pay their respects at this arch criminal's grave. British

Prime Minister Tony Blair did so in late December 2004, standing at a respectful distance. Among those laying wreaths at the tomb have been Italian Foreign Minister Giancarlo Fini and World Bank President James Wolfensohn.[31]

THIS IS "PEACE"?

Are the UN, EU, and world leaders such as Bush and Blair, blind to the real intentions of the Arabs? That seems impossible, considering how blatantly and often the Arabs state that their true aim is not to live in peace with Israel but to do away with Israel altogether. That Israel's destruction is what is meant by "peace" could not be stated more clearly than the following from the PLO Charter:

> Since the liberation of Palestine will destroy the Zionist and imperialist presence and will contribute to the establishment of peace in the Middle East, the Palestinian people look for the support of all the progressive and peaceful forces, and urge them all, irrespective of their affiliations and beliefs, to offer the Palestinian people all the aid and support in their just struggle for the liberation of their homeland.[32]

When the PA took possession of Bethlehem just before Christmas 1995, Arafat helicoptered in and triumphantly addressed a wildly cheering mob of tens of thousands: "This is the birthplace of our Lord the Messiah, the Palestinian, the Palestinian!" His speech made it appear that Jesus was a Palestinian freedom fighter against Israel. There was certainly no acknowledgment that Jesus was a Jew and the founder and head of the Christian church, which has irreconcilable differences with Islam. Instead of rebuking Arafat for his passion to annihilate Israel and for his anti-Christian Islamic beliefs, the Pope accepted Arafat's invitation to join him in Bethlehem to celebrate "our Jesus Christ." *Our* Jesus Christ?

Arafat was a Muslim. The "Palestinian Jesus" to whom he referred ("Isa" in the Qur'an) is not the Son of God, co-equal with the Father, who died for man's sins. Islam teaches that a look-alike disciple died in Isa's place. Isa was taken to heaven alive, from whence He must return and marry, have children, and die a natural death. Surely the Pope did not believe *that* for a moment—yet Arafat's total misrepresentation of Jesus was greeted by smiles from the Pope and his blessing on the "Palestinian fight for freedom"!

Islam and its Allah (by his many statements in the Qur'an) are notorious for their hatred of Israel and all Jews. That fact alone is enough to distinguish Allah from Yahweh, the God of the Bible. Sadly, the Arabs, persisting in the false claim that Ishmael was the legitimate son of promise, have rebelled against the true God and His Word. As a result, their jealous hatred of the descendants of Isaac (exacerbated by the teachings and example of Muhammad and Islam) has left a blot on the history of mankind unequaled even by Hitler.

---

1. Excerpted from The Statement of David A. Harris, Executive Director, the American Jewish Committee, before the Senate Appropriations Committee, Subcommittee Labor, Health and Human Services, and Education; Hearing on "Palestinian Education—Teaching Peace or War?", October 30, 2003. Based on an analysis of 93 school textbooks published by the Saudi Ministry of Education and in circulation between 1999 and 2002 [showing] contempt toward Western civilization and followers of other religions.

2. http://www.worldnetdaily.com/news/article.asp?ARTICLE_ID=31203.

3. *The Jerusalem Post International Edition,* Week Ending January 6, 1996, p. 3.

4. *The Jerusalem Post International Edition*, Week Ending December 23, 1995, p. 10.

5. Ezekiel 13:6-16.

6. http://www.ipc.gov.ps/ipc_new/english/details.asp?name=1707.

7. *Al-Misri*, October 11, 1949.

8. Genesis 17:8.

9. 1 Chronicles 16:15-18.

10. Genesis 15:19-21.

11. Deuteronomy 9:4-5.

12. Cited in Eliyahu Tal, *Whose Jerusalem?* (Tel Aviv: International Forum for a United Jerusalem, 1994), 93.

13. Genesis 21:21.

14. Exodus 15:14; Isaiah 14:29, 31; Joel 3:4.

15. Psalms 60:8; 87:4; 108:9.

16. PA Mufti 'Ikrama Sabri quoted in Khalid Amayreh, "Mufti of Palestine: Alqods is the Sister

of Mecca and Madina," Islamic Association for Palestine, August 6, 2000; Hasan Abu `Ali, a stone throwing teenager, quoted in Associated Press, September 30, 2000.

17. *The Jerusalem Post*, August 29, 2000.

18. www.pna.gov.ps/subject_details2.asp?Docld+263.

19. Surah 2:145.

20. John 17:1.

21. Reuters, Aug. 12, 2000.

22. Time, April 4, 1988.

23. Benjamin Netanyahu, *A Place Among the Nations: Israel and the World* (New York: Bantam Books, 1993), 188.

24. Ibid.

25. Thomas Kierman, *Yasir Arafat* (London: Sphere Books, 1976), 138.

26. Jill Becker, *The PLO: The Rise and Fall of the Palestine Liberation Organization* (New York: St. Martin's, 1984), 14.

27. John Laffin, *The PLO Connections* (London: Transworld, 1982), 18.

28. Ibid.

29. "Arafat's plan for democracy: Freedom from the press," *Jerusalem Post International Edition*, December 3, 1993.

30. PLO Charter, paragraphs 20, 22.

31. http://www.mmorning.com/articleC.asp?Article=2036&CategoryID=6.

32. PLO Charter, paragraph 22.

5—THE TRUTH ABOUT "REFUGEES"

IN ALL OF THE CONCERN for Arab refugees who fled Israel, mostly in late 1947 and early 1948, the Jews who had hoped to become refugees from Nazi Germany but could find nowhere in the world that would receive them have been forgotten. Millions of them perished in the Holocaust. In 1939, when Jews longing to escape Nazi Germany most desperately needed a homeland to flee to, the British tried to suspend all Jewish immigration into, and land purchase by Jews in, Palestine. Jewish underground organizations were appalled. Great Britain was attempting to seal off the only escape route the European refugees had."[1] In spite of its mandate to see that "Palestine" became a national home for the Jews, Britain was adamantly opposed to the fleeing Jews returning there and was doing everything it could to stop them. Frustrated and angry, a Jewish extreme right-wing underground group founded in Palestine in 1931, Irgun Zvai Leumi, blew up the British embassy in Rome and the King David Hotel in Jerusalem in retaliation. Though headed by Menachem Begin (later prime minister), its terrorist actions were condemned by David Ben-Gurion. Hitler offered to sell for two dollars each, 500,000 Hungarian Jews still untouched in 1944. The Allies refused to take the offer seriously. Britain said there was "no room in Palestine for them."

If anyone deserved to be called refugees, surely it was the survivors of Hitler's attempt at their extermination. Yet when they came, in half-sinking ships, within sight of the Promised Land they had been longing to reach, they were driven back by the British navy and put into detainee camps! Many of those few who had managed to get ashore in hope of starting a new life in the land God had given their ancestors were rounded up by the ever-alert British and deported to the same camps—all in violation of the mandate Britain had received to resettle the Jews in their rightful homeland. And all in violation of common decency, of human compassion, and of the conscience God has implanted in each of us. Britain's actions toward the Jews were, in a word, unconscionable!

Britain, in exercising its mandate, had given the Arabs many independent states, from Egypt (1922) to Saudi Arabia (1931) to Transjordan (1946). The latter was taken from the land that the League of Nations had set apart for the Jewish homeland and for which Britain had the mandate to see that Jews were settled there. It was given to the Hashemite Emir Abdullah I (Ibn Hussein), as a compromise when Ibn Saud was given Saudi Arabia. Hussein was the brother of King Faisal I of Syria, who had been ejected from Damascus in July 1920 by the French. Britain's motive was to keep peace between feuding Muslim families and to establish relations for future oil exploitation.

The Jews were still waiting for their promised state while Muslim terrorists daily attacked and murdered them. Without settling the Jews in their own homeland as promised, and claiming that the situation had gotten beyond its control, Britain turned its mandate over to the United Nations in February 1947. UN debate began over what to do about the Jews in Palestine—a problem that is still the overwhelming burden to the nations of the world, which the Bible said it would be. The families of some of them have been living for a hundred generations in the land that God gave to their ancestors as an *everlasting* heritage.

In a 1964 interview, Nasser had stated that Egypt "still pledged allegiance to the old Nazi cause: 'Our sympathy was with the Germans.'"[2]

Indeed, the entire Arab world had sided with the Nazis against the Allies, while Jewish volunteers had fought in the British army—which makes it all the more perplexing that the British would side with the Arabs against the Jews. Of course, Israel has almost no oil—at least, not by discoveries to date.

On November 29, 1947, UN Resolution 181 partitioned the remaining 23 percent of Palestine that was left after 77 percent had been carved out to create Jordan. Of that reduced territory, 56 percent (13 percent of the original mandate) was allocated to a Jewish state, 42 percent to an Arab state, and 2 percent was set aside in an international zone for the holy sites in and around Jerusalem. Though they had been literally robbed of the land they had been promised, Jewish settlers accepted what they had been allotted. At least they had a national home recognized by the world. Furious, the Arabs demanded all of "Palestine," and the six Arab delegates from Iraq, Syria, Lebanon, Egypt, Saudi Arabia, and Yemen stormed out of the UN, threatening a war that would annihilate the Jews.

ARAB REACTION

Muslims intensified their rioting in Jerusalem and elsewhere. Attacks against Jewish settlers were launched by armed Arab invaders, with the supposedly watchdog British turning a blind eye and in some cases aiding the belligerents. Speaking in Cairo, Iraqi Foreign Minister, Fadel al-Jamali declared: "I can assure you that the British forces in Palestine would not try to oppose or fight the Arabs, because Britain is a real friend of the Arabs."[3] It was a friendship carefully cultivated for selfish reasons at the expense of suffering Jews. Robert Macatee, American Consul General in Jerusalem, reported on a typical incident among many being repeated almost daily:

> It is tragic that many of the present casualties comprise innocent and harmless people.... They are picked off while riding in buses, walking along the streets, and stray shots even find them while sleeping in their beds. A Jewish woman, mother of five children, was shot in Jerusalem while hanging out clothes on the roof. The ambulance rushing her to the hospital was machine gunned and

finally the mourners following her to the funeral were attacked and one of them was stabbed to death.[4]

Haj Amin al-Husseini, with the demise of Hitler and his Nazi regime and a price still on his head if he reappeared in Palestine (but admired by most Arabs as "Mr. Palestine"), was directing much of the terrorism from Damascus (which is still the headquarters for terrorist organizations today). On November 24, Jamal el-Husseini, vice-chairman of the Mufti's Arab Higher Committee, had warned the United Nations: "By imposing partition on Palestine you will precipitate the country into a virtual blood bath.... The boundary line proposed, if ever decided upon, shall be nothing but a line of fire and blood." He declared a three-day general strike from December 2-4, 1947. Even prior, his followers had "launched a campaign of indiscriminate violence against the Jewish community. Within the first 24 hours—on November 30, 1947—eight Jews had already been killed near Nathanya. Ambushes, arson, bombings became the order of the day."[5]

Between November 29, 1947, and March 3, 1948, more than five thousand Arabs invaded Palestine while British authorities looked the other way. They were largely bank rolled by the mufti, who was "'lavishly financed' by Saudi Arabia's Ibn Saud and Egypt's King Farouk." Supplying the funds for the destruction of Israel, the mufti was setting himself up to be the future ruler of a Palestine Arab state. From his years in Germany working with Hitler, he had "managed to get a large proportion of his Nazi financial backing out of Germany even while the war was still on." He had "a large cache of gold in Iraq, and a considerable fortune in Switzerland, largely in the form of easily negotiable Swiss watches."[6]

History puts today's terrorism in perspective—its methods, goals and financing are nothing new but have been the *modus operandi* of Arab/Muslims against Israel from the very beginning as their means of bringing about its intended and vowed demise. Infiltration of foreign terrorists such as is occurring in Iraq and Afghanistan today is nothing new: the mufti used the same tactic seventy years ago.

Within a week after the UN partitioned Palestine, Arab guerillas and terrorists had killed more than one hundred Jews. John Bagot Glubb, British commander of Transjordan's Arab Legion, admitted: "Early in January [1948], the first detachments of the Arab Liberation Army began to infiltrate into Palestine from Syria. Some came through Jordan and even through Amman…. They were in reality to strike the first blow in the ruin of the Arabs of Palestine."

Unashamedly, the Arabs boasted to the entire world of their intentions. Jamal Husseini, speaking for the Arab Higher Committee, had told the Security Council on April 16, 1948: "The…Jewish Agency [said] that the Arabs had begun the fighting. We did not deny this. We told the whole world that we were going to fight." This was a month before Israel declared itself a nation. The vow to exterminate Israel is a foundational doctrine of Islam. That fact obviously requires unusual measures to ensure real peace in the Middle East—but political correctness remains in denial of this awful truth.

ISRAELI OVERTURES OF PEACE AND THE ARAB RESPONSE

On May 14, 1948, re-born Israel declared itself an independent nation. Within minutes, at 5:16 p.m., in swift reaction that astounded the United Nations and flew in the face of objections of his government ministers, President Truman authorized recognition of Israel by the United States. The Soviet Union was next. Other nations followed. Impossible in today's world, it was a miracle that could have taken place only in the shadow of the Holocaust. That horror had aroused a momentary worldwide guilt for having stood by while millions of Jews were exterminated like vermin.

The world was unwittingly participating in the fulfillment of another remarkable prophecy. Looking forward to Israel's rebirth in the last days, the prophet Isaiah had written, "Who hath heard such a thing? who hath seen such things? Shall…a nation be born at once? for as soon as Zion travailed, she brought forth her children."[7] Surely "Zion travailed" was an eloquent description of Zion's loss of six million of her children.

Truman's brave recognition of Israel came over the stern objections of Secretary of State George C. Marshall. Reflecting an anti-Semitic/anti-Israel attitude that permeates the State Department to this day (Secretary of State James Baker, for example, was very anti-Israel), the Secretary threatened angrily, "They don't deserve a state; they have stolen that country. If you give this recognition, Mr. President, I may not vote for you in the next election." *Stolen that country?* In fact, as we have shown, most of that country had been stolen from the Jews by Britain and the UN, leaving Israel with very little of what rightfully belonged to her. Marshall was expressing a willing blindness to the truth that still frames the thinking of political leaders worldwide.

Israel's Proclamation of Independence stated: "We extend...to all neighboring States...an offer of peace...and appeal to them to establish bonds of cooperation and mutual help with the sovereign Jewish people settled in its own land...placing our trust in the Almighty...." That olive branch held out by Israel in good faith was trampled by the regular armies of at least five Arab nations.

The next morning, the fledgling State of Israel found itself at war in earnest, under heavy attack on several fronts. The Arab armies had begun their coordinated invasion: the Lebanese from the north, the Syrian armies down the Golan from the northeast, the Arab Legion and the Iraqi forces attacking in the center, and the Egyptians from the south assisted by bombers—in what they unashamedly announced to the world would be a war of extermination.

Yes, annihilation was their avowed intention, but by God's grace it was an empty boast. Israelis who have defended their country have told this author, "I was an atheist. But in the war [it could be any one of the five] I saw things happen that could only be described as miracles, and I came to believe that the God of Abraham, Isaac, and Jacob was fulfilling His promises to His ancient people." One retired general, who carries the Bible with him everywhere he goes, claims that at least 30 percent of Israel's top military officers believe in the "God of Abraham, Isaac, and Jacob" and trust His care over Israel, without which she could not have survived.

THE FIRST CEASE-FIRE

Fearing that the Arabs, with their overwhelming superiority numerically and in weaponry, could make good their boast, the United States demanded a UN Security Council resolution creating a cease-fire and sanctions to enforce it. Soviet delegate Andrei Gromyko told the Security Council on May 29, 1948, "This is not the first time that the Arab states, which organized the invasion of Palestine, have ignored a decision of the Security Council or of the General Assembly."

Consistent with their history of favoring Arabs and opposing Jews, Britain rejected the cease-fire resolution, confident that the Arabs would destroy Israel. Arab delegates demanded, as a condition for peace, that Israel's independence be rescinded. Israel's response was blunt and to the point: "If the Arab states want peace, they can have it. If they want war, they can have that too. But whether they want peace or war, they can have it only with the State of Israel."

The first truce with a cease-fire went into effect on June 11, 1948. It left the Arabs in control of about one-third of the minimal territory that had been allotted to Israel. Fighting broke out again, and by this time Israel had procured some tanks, artillery, and sufficient small arms to equip all of its fighters. In the next ten days of fighting, Israel made important gains, causing Britain to plead for haste in establishing another cease-fire.

THE REFUGEE PROBLEM

War is cruel and costly in every way. The five full-scale wars that Israel has been forced to fight during its brief modern existence were not of her choosing. She didn't start any of them but has had to finish them, defending herself against an enemy determined to destroy her. In the 1948 War of Independence, instead of Arabs driving the Jews into the Mediterranean as they had sworn they would do, about five hundred thousand Arab civilians fled the war zone. From that time to the present, they and their descendants, whose numbers have multiplied into the millions, have been classified as "Palestinian refugees."

The most tragic part about these abused and misused people is that most of them didn't need to flee. Such a necessity (though imaginary) was a direct result of the Arab nations' refusal to accept the UN partition plan. As already noted, the Arabs now want to go back to the borders set by UN Resolution 181. Israel, however, considers that resolution to be null and void because the Arabs sternly rejected it and attacked Israel in an attempt to exterminate her at that time. Furthermore, the Israelis tried to persuade them all to remain to build a new country together. Israel's Proclamation of Independence, issued on May 14, 1948, had offered:

> In the midst of wanton aggression [Arab military units, with the tacit approval and sometimes help of the British "peace keepers," had been attacking Israeli settlements for months], we yet call upon the Arab inhabitants of the State of Israel to preserve the ways of peace and play their part in the development of the State, on the basis of full and equal citizenship and due representation in all its bodies and institutions. We extend our hand in peace and neighborliness to all the neighboring states and their peoples....

The Arabs who remained in Israel learned that Israel kept its word. They now make up more than 20 percent of Israel's voters with full citizenship rights. Some Arabs are even members of the Knesset. In fact,

> Every Knesset, since the founding of the State in 1948, has had Arab and Druze members. All transactions in the Knesset are simultaneously translated into Arabic, and Arab members may address the Knesset in Arabic.... Arabic is an official language in Israel, together with Hebrew. Israel's Arabic press [more than twenty periodicals] is the most vibrant and independent of any country in the region.... There are daily TV and radio programs in Arabic. Arabic is taught in Jewish secondary schools.... There are nearly 1,000 Arab educational institutions in Israel, with about 300,000 students.... Israeli universities and technical institutions are freely available to the Arabs. About 5,000 Arab students attend such schools.... Israeli Arabs...are free

to exercise their faiths, to observe their own weekly day of rest and holidays…. In contrast to the non-Israeli Arab world, Arab women in Israel enjoy the same status as men. Israeli law grants women equal rights…to vote and to be elected to public office, prohibits polygamy, child marriage, and the barbarity of female sexual mutilation [practiced under Islam]…. Arabs are exempted from military duty…to spare them conflicts of loyalty and con-science…. In a recent poll, 70 percent of Israel's Arabs…declared that they would much prefer to live in Israel than in any other country in the area.[8]

In contrast, no Jew has such rights in any Arab or Muslim country. In fact, a Jew isn't allowed to set foot in Saudi Arabia. Contrary to the claims that put the blame on Israel, the truth is that it was the Arab military command who told the Arabs to get out.

ENEMIES OF TRUTH

Truth is not easy to find. One must be careful of the source of information and check it out, especially when it comes to the subject of Palestinian refugees and their alleged mistreatment at the hands of Israelis. Professor David A. Rausch has said it well in his excellent book:

Hatred by Christian Arabs for Jews and the Jewish state runs as deep as it does among Muslim Arabs. Periodicals and analysts who believe they are receiving an unbiased "Christian" perspective on the problems of the Middle East because they are in touch with Christian Arabs of their denomination or theological persuasion need to use extreme caution. Missionaries from the West who work among Arabs often become unwitting accomplices in spreading anti-Israel propaganda and deceit. Lest one seem to be too harsh toward such missionaries, consider that even hardened news reporters working the beat in an Arab country soon learn that their sources dry up if their reports appear to be too harsh on the Arabs or too lenient toward the Israelis.[9]

A number of books have been written expressly to whitewash the Arabs, Palestinians, and Islam, and to paint Israel as the villain.

Among these, we would put at the head of the list a large and impressive volume, *Fateful Triangle: The United States, Israel & the Palestinians* by Noam Chomsky.[10] Many of its stories of the plight of the Palestinians are tragic. One would surely side with them against Israel—were it not for suspicions aroused by its total one-sidedness. In its nearly six hundred pages, there is not a single reference to Islam or Muhammad, not a word of Arab/Muslims' sworn vows to annihilate Israel, of their years of military build-up and attacks against Israel for that express purpose, not a word of Israelis suffering from Arab terrorism (terrorism isn't even listed in the index!).

There are even books written by Jews that are in the same category. For example, *Image and Reality of the Israel-Palestine Conflict* by Norman G. Finkelstein,[11] whose parents are survivors of the Warsaw Ghetto and Auschwitz and Maidanek extermination camps. The endorsements are impressive, coming from *Le Monde Diplomatique* and *The London Review of Books*—and one of them, of course, by Noam Chomsky. The Royal Institute of International Affairs says it "will challenge the most cherished beliefs of Israel's supporters." The *Middle East Journal* says it "calls into question many of the accepted 'truths' associated with the Israel-Palestine conflict." Yet there is not the slightest hint in the entire volume of any culpability at all on the part of Arabs, no mention of anti-Semitism or of sworn vows to annihilate Israel. Finkelstein likens Israeli soldiers to the Nazis, as though it was the European Jews who attacked, and the SS had to put them in extermination camps in self-defense!

WHO DROVE THE ARABS OUT OF ISRAEL?

The accusation has been widely publicized and believed that the Israelis drove nearly a million Arabs out of Palestine during the 1948 war. This is the foundation for the demands that the "Palestinians" make for the right of return to their former villages. There were some instances where Arab civilians who were sheltering, helping, or hiding attacking Arab soldiers were forced to leave. But most of the Arabs who fled did so in spite of Israeli promises of safety and pleas to stay, and without ever seeing an Israeli soldier. Many left before Israel declared its independence and the war had really begun.

It was the Arab military that warned Arab civilians to "get out" and declared that those who remained would be considered traitors to the Arab cause. Nevertheless, they are the only "refugees" in the Middle East, as far as the world is concerned, and to whom all the sympathy is given. No thought is given to the Jewish refugees who, in far larger numbers, were either expelled or managed to flee Muslim countries in 1948.

On April 22, 1948 (three weeks before Israel declared itself a nation), Aubrey Lippincott, U.S. Consul-General in Haifa, stated that "local mufti-dominated Arab leaders [were urging] all Arabs to leave the city, and large numbers did so."[12] About the same time, Haifa's British police chief, A. J. Bridmead, reported, "Every effort is being made by the Jews to persuade the Arab population to remain." A foreign visitor reported: "In Tiberias I saw a placard affixed to a sealed Arab Mosque that read, 'We did not dispossess them [and] the day will come when the Arabs will return to their homes and property in this town...let no citizen touch their property.' It was signed by the Jewish Town Council of Tiberias."[13]

Unquestionably, "...the Arab Higher Committee encouraged the refugees' flight from their homes in Jaffa, Haifa, and Jerusalem."[14] A Jordanian newspaper reported, "The Arab States encouraged the Palestine Arabs to leave their homes temporarily in order to be out of the way of the Arab invasion armies."[15] Another Jordanian newspaper quoted a complaining refugee: "The Arab government told us: 'Get out so that we can get in. So we got out, but they did not get in.'"[16] A New York Lebanese paper reported: "The Secretary-General of the Arab League, Azzam Pasha, [gave] brotherly advice to the Arabs of Palestine to leave their land, homes and property and to stay temporarily in neighboring fraternal states, lest the guns of the invading Arab armies mow them down."[17]

Iraqi Prime Minister Nuri Said declared: "We will smash the country with our guns and obliterate every place where the Jews seek shelter. The Arabs should conduct their wives and children to safe areas until the fighting has died down."[18] Syrian Prime Minister, Haled al Azm, later admitted, "Since 1948 we have been demanding the return of the refugees.... But we ourselves are the ones who encouraged them to leave."[19] Jordan's King Hussein stated in 1960: "Since 1948, Arab leaders have approached the Palestine problem in an irresponsible manner. They have used the Palestine people for selfish political purposes. This is ridiculous and I could say even criminal."

In his 1972 memoirs, Syria's Prime Minister after the 1948 war, Khaled al-Azem, deplored what Arab leaders had done:

> Since 1948 it is we who demanded the return of the refugees... while it is we who made them leave.... We brought disaster upon...Arab refugees, by inviting them and bringing pressure to bear upon them to leave.... We have rendered them dispossessed.... We have accustomed them to begging.... We have participated in lowering their moral and social level,...then we exploited them in executing crimes of murder, arson, and throwing bombs upon...men, women and children—and this in the service of political purposes.... [20]

OVERWHELMING TESTIMONY

The New York Times reported that "The mass evacuation, prompted partly by fear, partly by orders of Arab leaders, left the Arab quarter of Haifa a ghost city...."[21] The Arab National Committee in Jerusalem, following instructions of the Arab Higher Committee, ordered women, children, and the elderly in various parts of Jerusalem to leave their homes and warned, "Any opposition to this order...is an obstacle to the holy war...and will hamper the operations of the fighters in these districts."[22]

Emil Ghory, secretary of the Palestine Arab Higher Committee, admitted, "The fact that there are those refugees is the direct consequence of the action of the Arab states in opposing partition and the Jewish state. The Arab states agreed upon this policy unanimously...."[23] Arafat's successor, the Palestinian Authority's current prime minister, Mahmoud Abbas, admitted in writing, "The Arab armies, who invaded the country in '48, forced the Palestinians to emigrate and leave their homeland and forced a political and ideological siege on them."[24] According to a British report, "Of the 62,000 Arabs who formerly lived in Haifa not more than 5,000 or 6,000 remained...the most potent [factors in the Arab flight]...were the announcements made over the air by the Higher Arab Executive urging all Arabs to leave...[and] that those Arabs who remained in Haifa and accepted Jewish protection would be regarded as renegades."[25]

While visiting Palestinian Arab refugee camps in Lebanon and Jordan, Carl Hermann Voss was told by the refugees themselves that "the Arab High Command ordered them out of Palestine during the 1948 war...told [them] that the Jews in Palestine would be annihilated within a few weeks and that the Arab Liberation Army did not want to worry about any fellow Arabs getting in the way of such a devastating Arab *jihad*. Those Palestinian refugees were bitter at their Arab compatriots who had left them homeless.... [But] four decades later he would be reading about the intense hatred harbored toward the Jewish people by the grandchildren and great-grandchildren of those refugees.... Accounts of Arab negligence and Arab miscalculation during the 1948 war had been forgotten, having been replaced with stories of Jewish 'atrocities.'"[26]

Having failed to exterminate Israelis by military attack, the Arabs are now trying to do it by playing on world sympathy for "abused refugees." In the summer of 2000, Palestinian negotiators submitted an official document at Camp David demanding that the refugees automatically be granted Israeli citizenship and that the right of return should have no time limit. Additionally, the PA demanded that Israel provide compensation amounting to $500 billion. Abu Mazen said that compensation payments should be made by Israel alone and not from any international funds. Such unconscionable demands can come only from minds badly twisted by Islam.

The PLO continues its attempt to rewrite history. In spite of the Arabs' outright rejection of UN Resolution 181 and their failed attempts to destroy Israel ever since, Muslim nations and the "Palestinians" demand that Israel be held to that resolution's terms.

Israel, as already noted, rightly considers UN Resolution 181 null and void because the Arabs rejected it and would only pretend to agree to it now in order to recover their losses due to that rejection and the aggression that followed.

ISLAM'S RECORD OF OPPRESSION AND SLAUGHTER

The hatred against all Jews, which comes not from being an Arab but specifically from Islamic teaching, was reflected in the inhumane treatment of Jews in Arab countries ever since Islam took over. Prior to the seventh century and the advent of the prophet Muhammad and Islam, as investigative reporter Joan Peters (in her monumental book, *From Time Immemorial*), points out from her exhaustive research, "Jews and Arabs did have harmonious relations, and words of praise regarding the noble virtues of the Jews may be found in ancient Arab literature. Indeed, Muhammad himself in the early years, as he was seeking recognition as a prophet, looked with favor upon both Jews and Christians and cultivated their friendship." But that turned to hatred when they rejected him as "the prophet of Allah."

Though he continued to call Christians and Jews "the people of the book," that fierce hatred that had begun when they rejected him continued to grow. The Qur'an declares, "O ye who believe! Take not the Jews and the Christians for friends."[27] Muhammad's dying words were, "May Allah curse the Christians and Jews!" What a contrast to Christ's teaching that we are to love all mankind as ourselves,[28] and to His dying words spoken specifically of those who had tortured and crucified Him—but also of all mankind: "Father, forgive them; for they know not what they do."[29]

As we noted in Chapter Two, the oppression of Jews and Christians in Arab countries throughout the centuries after the birth of Islam was at times almost beyond description. Hundreds of books have been written about this evil, but thousands could not contain the full record. The following is a sample of what Bat Ye'or reports in a fully documented volume:

The religious oppression…in the period…regarded as the "Golden Age"…began under Abd al-Malik (685-705)…. The destruction of churches and convents [and synagogues] was perpetrated on such a scale in the whole Arab Empire that in 830 Ma'mun forbade further destruction without his permission. Yet during the Caliphate of al-Mutawakkil (847-61) a wave of religious persecution, forced conversions, and the elimination of churches and synagogues plagued the whole Abbasid Empire….

During their 1268 expedition, the Mamluks put all the men of Antioch to the sword and seized all the women and youngsters. The town became a pile of uninhabited ruins. During the 1275 expedition…sixty thousand people were killed [in just one city] and an incalculable number of women, youngsters and children deported as slaves. Jean-Baptiste Tavernier…in 1651, recounts that all the churches [on Cyprus] had been converted into mosques….[30]

In 1012 A.D., one Caliph in Egypt, al-Hakim of the Fatimids, furious at failing to convert Jews and Christians to Allah despite threats and humiliation, destroyed Cairo's Jewish quarters along with its residents.[31] A new community eventually grew in its place. They had no country of their own. There was never a way of escape and nowhere to go. Treatment of Jews varied from country to country and from generation to generation. Under the Ottoman Turkish Empire, it was recognized that the Jews in Egypt were less oppressed than elsewhere. There was a relatively flourishing Jewish community for a time.

Nevertheless, in early nineteenth-century Egypt, Jews were "held in the utmost contempt and abhorrence by the Muslims in general…detested by the Muslims far more than Christians… jostled in the streets of Cairo…beaten merely for passing on the right hand of a Muslim…dared not utter a word of abuse when reviled or beaten unjustly by the meanest Arab or Turk; for many a Jew has been put to death upon a false and malicious accusation of uttering disrespectful words against the Qur'an or the Prophet…[or] sacrificed to save a Muslim….[32] In 1926, it was made a national law that immigrants desiring to become citizens had to belong "racially to the majority of the population of a country whose language is Arabic or whose religion is Islam."[33]

In the 1940s, organized anti-Jewish riots injured or killed many Jews in Egypt. Egypt passed a law that made it nearly impossible for a Jew to find employment, the government confiscated much Jewish property, and within a few months Jews were reduced to financial ruin. After the UN partitioned Palestine November 29, 1947, "Jews in Cairo and Alexandria were threatened with death, their houses were looted, and synagogues were attacked."[34]

THE FORGOTTEN JEWISH REFUGEES

In 1948, as soon as a national Jewish homeland was created, more than eight hundred and fifty thousand Jews fled (most of them to Israel for refuge) from Muslim lands, where they had lived for two thousand or more years, leaving behind virtually everything they had possessed. This was more than the number of Arab refugees who fled from Israel during the War of Independence. Beginning in 1947 and accelerating in 1948 and thereafter, there has been an aggressive effort on the part of the international community to assist the "Palestinian" refugees. Many programs have been put into action and billions of dollars expended for their assistance. During the same period, no concern has been expressed by the United Nations for the plight of some eight hundred fifty-six thousand Jewish refugees who fled severe persecution in (or were forcibly expelled from) Arab lands. There have been more than six hundred eighty UN General Assembly resolutions dealing with every aspect of the Middle East Arab-Israeli conflict. More than one hundred have dealt specifically with the "plight of Palestinian refugees." In none of these, nor in any others, has the slightest concern been expressed for the even larger number of Jewish refugees from Arab lands.

This has not been due to ignorance. On many occasions, the Israeli government, the World Organization of Jews from Arab Countries (WOJAC), and other agencies, have brought to the attention of the UN and its affiliates the numbers of and circumstances creating the far larger number of Jewish refugees, and appealed for help. Numerous times, the gross violations of the UN Charter and its Declaration of

Human Rights against Jews in Arab countries have been brought to the attention of the UN: by Golda Meir on November 27 and 30, 1956; on December 21, 1956 by Henry Cabot Lodge, Jr., as U.S. Representative to the UN; on December 2, 1968, to then UN Secretary General U-Thant by the International League for the Rights of Man (non-Jewish), and on many other occasions. The appeals fell on deaf ears.

UN Resolution 237, adopted during the 1967 Six-Day War, called upon all parties to "respect scrupulously the humanitarian principles governing the protection of civilian persons in time of War" as set forth in the fourth Geneva Convention of 1949. Though there was no specific mention of Jewish refugees, one could by implication include them. Yet a year later, the UN passed Resolution 259 clarifying the intent of 237 and expressing concern for "the safety, welfare and security of the inhabitants of the Arab territories under military occupation by Israel." Any mention of Jewish refugees was specifically excluded.

Here are a few examples revealing the origins of the Jewish refugees whose existence the UN and world community refuse to acknowledge. In 1948, there were about two hundred sixty-five thousand Jews in Morocco; today there are about five thousand. There were about one hundred forty thousand Jews in Algeria, while today there are none. There were about one hundred thirty-five thousand in Iraq, seventy-five thousand in Egypt, and thirty thousand in Syria, with only about one hundred remaining in each of these countries. In all the Muslim countries in the Middle East, there were more than nine hundred thousand Jews in 1948, while today there are less than twenty thousand. The rest managed to flee from the brutal totalitarian regimes of Syria, Transjordan, Egypt, Lebanon, Yemen, Iran, Iraq, Algeria, Tunisia, and Morocco.

How could more than *eight hundred fifty thousand* refugees be overlooked by the United Nations and the world? Yet these Jewish refugees who fled the unbelievably inhumane persecution and slaughter they and their forebears had endured for centuries are ignored at the UN and in the media. In her report, after investigating the refugee problem, Joan Peters writes:

> Though I read through stacks of documents concerning the
> refugees, looking for official consideration of these "other" Jewish
> "Middle East refugees," I found little or none. But in the process,
> some other key beliefs in the popular (and my personal) under-
> standing of the Arab-Israeli conflict were shaken.[35]

One would think that the larger number of Jewish refugees from
Muslim countries who were given refuge in Israel would be more
than a fair exchange for the Arabs who fled from Israel. Arab leaders
have cautiously expressed concern that Israelis would raise this argument—but for some unknown reason, they never have. Perhaps it is
because they realize that these eight hundred fifty thousand Jewish
refugees would count for nothing as far as the UN is concerned, so
why raise the point?

An Arab researcher, author, and member of the Palestinian
National Council admitted that "The Jews of the Arab states were
driven out of their ancient homes…shamefully deported after their
property had been commandeered or taken over at the lowest possible valuation…. This is true for the majority of the Jews in question."
He was concerned that Israel would argue, "Israel is absorbing the
Jews…*the Arab states for their part must settle the Palestinians in their
own midst and solve their problems* [author's emphasis]."[36] Indeed, in
1977, Lebanese Arabs demanded that "the Palestinian refugees be
relocated to all Arab nations…."[37]

TREATMENT OF "PALESTINIAN" AND JEWISH REFUGEES CONTRASTED

On June 7–8, 2004, delegates from more than ninety countries,
"addressing the humanitarian needs of the Palestinian refugees…made
a solemn declaration on behalf of the international community— 'you
will not be abandoned….' They committed the international community, UNRWA, and the host countries to the continuing support
of the four million refugees scattered across the Middle East." The
conference was hosted by the Swiss Agency for Development and

Cooperation and chaired by its director, Swiss Ambassador Walter Fust. Conspicuous by its absence was any mention of, or concern about, the more than eight hundred fifty thousand Jewish refugees who fled from Muslim lands in 1948.

Israel's six hundred fifty thousand settlers absorbed nearly seven hundred thousand refugees into normal life. Yet Arab nations with seven hundred times the land, and huge oil revenues, refused to absorb five hundred thousand refugees. In December of 1948, supposedly to deal equitably with the refugee problem created by the war that had raged that year over Israel, the UN General Assembly adopted Resolution 194. It declared (among other provisions) that "refugees wishing to return to their homes and live in peace with their neighbors should be permitted to do so." It also provided that "compensation should be paid for the property of those choosing not to return."

Of course, by "refugees" the UN meant "Palestinian"—but not Jewish. Sadly, "live in peace" in Islam's vocabulary does not exclude terrorist attacks against neighbors. Surely the United Nations would not accept such a definition—or would it? During the years of continual international pressure upon Israel to receive the Muslim "refugees" into its midst as peace-loving citizens, the UN has steadfastly refused to condemn the terrorists.

PRETENSE AND ROAD BLOCKS

Officially, the UN covers up the axiomatic fact (acknowledged in rare instances at lower levels) that Jewish refugees from Arab lands must be taken into account in any equation dealing with the Middle East conflict. "Refugees and Displaced Persons" is the title of Article 8, Paragraph 1, of the 1994 Israel-Jordan Peace Treaty. It recognized "the massive human problems caused to both parties by the conflict" and was clearly not limited to Palestinian refugees but must have been intended to include Jewish refugees as well. In Article 24, the parties agreed to establish a claims commission for settlement of all financial claims. However, this commission was never created.

At Camp David II in July 2000, President Clinton declared that the rights of Jewish refugees would have to be taken into account. On July 28, 2000, in an interview on Israeli television, Clinton said,

> There will have to be some sort of international fund set up for the refugees. There is, I think, some interest…on both sides, in also having a fund which compensates the Israelis who were made refugees by the war, which occurred after the birth of the State of Israel. Israel is full of…Jewish people who lived in predominantly Arab countries who came to Israel [as] refugees.

Other leaders (with the exception of President George W. Bush) have not echoed Clinton's concern. The UN did appoint a "High Commissioner for Refugees" (UNHCR). Mr. Auguste Lindt, in his first statement after being elected to this office, declared at the January 29, 1957, meeting of the United Nations Refugee Fund Executive Committee, "There is no doubt in my mind that those [Jewish] refugees [from Egypt] fall under the mandate of my office." On July 6, 1967, representing the office of the High Commissioner, Dr. E. Jahn declared in a letter that "Jews [who fled] from Middle Eastern and North African countries…may be considered *prima facie* within the mandate of this office."

The High Commissioner has attempted to obtain permission from Arab governments for Jewish refugees to transfer the assets they left behind when they fled from Arab countries. Such efforts have met with no cooperation from the Arabs. Although the UNHCR has gone on record that Jewish refugees fled from Arab lands because they were suffering serious human rights violations, nothing has happened to redress that wrong. In spite of such efforts at lower levels, at the higher levels Jewish refugees are treated as though they never existed.

NEEDLESS SUFFERING, HATRED, AND HYPOCRISY

It is almost maddening to anyone with even a minimal sense of fairness that in the continual concern expressed in repeated international conferences that discuss the plight of the Palestinian refugees, no concern is expressed, nor is any mention made, regarding the far greater number of Jewish refugees from Muslim lands. Of course, they are no longer refugees, having been absorbed into normal life in Israel. Nor would there be any "Palestinians" remaining in that category had the Arab nations, with their vast wealth and resources, accepted them—but they refused.

From 1967 to 1985, income from oil for Kuwait and Saudi Arabia was nearly $1 trillion, yet, in spite of the billions of dollars that they provide for terrorism, they contributed a pitiful $84 million to Palestinian refugees. By comparison, since 1950 the United States has contributed $1.5 billion to the United Nations Relief and Welfare Agency (UNRWA) for Palestinian refugees. Much of that, of course, was diverted by Arafat for terrorism against Israel. At the same time, Palestinian refugees were kept in the refugee camps when they could have been absorbed many times over by the Arab nations who desperately needed workers. Joan Peters reports:

> In June 1977, during interviews in Damascus, Syrian officials expressed the wish that Syria might get American technological assistance to develop the arable Syrian land.... The Syrian Minister of Trade and Economy asked that a message be given to the American government. Syria hadn't the population to develop that land...[they] needed people as well as technology. They would give plots of valuable land in Syria to anyone who would come to work it....
>
> I asked various Syrian officials, "Why not give the land to those Palestinian Arabs who would choose to accept your offer?" The answer was always the same...: "We will give the land to anyone—the Ibos, the Koreans, Americans...anyone who comes—anyone but the Palestinians! We must keep their hatred directed against Israel.[38]

Popularly accepted propaganda gives the average person the impression that it was the Israelis who forced these exploited people into refugee camps. On the contrary, as we have seen, it was not Israel but the Arabs who did so, but that fact is suppressed. One author writes that, in the course of investigating the refugee problem, he found it impossible to get an interview with the head of the

Palestinian delegation in Washington, D.C., and that "his assistant sidestepped the one question I put to him: 'With so much money in the Arab world, why are the Palestinians still living in refugee camps?'" Another investigative reporter writes:

> In 1951 Syria was anxious for additional workers who would settle on the land. An Egyptian paper reported, "The Syrian government has officially requested that half a million Egyptian agricultural workers...be permitted to emigrate to Syria in order to help develop Syrian land which would be transferred to them as their property. The responsible Egyptian authorities have rejected this request on the gounds that Egyptian agriculture is in need of labor."
>
> Near East Arabic Radio reported that Syria was offering land rent free to anyone willing to settle there. It even announced a committee to study would-be settlers' applications. [Yet] the Arab world has assiduously worked to build the myth that no jobs were available in Arab lands for Arab refugees in 1948 or since.... At about the same time, the Egyptian Minister for Foreign Affairs, Muhammad Saleh el-Din...demanded the *return* [to Israel] of the refugees," even admitting that in returning, "they intend to annihilate the state of Israel...."[39]
>
> United Nations Secretary-General Dag Hammerskjold reiterated that there were ample means for absorbing the Arab refugees into the economy of the Arab region [and] that the refugees would be beneficial to their host countries, by adding needed manpower to assists in [their] development....[40]

Thousands of Arab refugees did return to their homes and businesses in Israel. The Jewish refugees would much rather stay in Israel. But they have received no compensation for what they were forced to leave behind. Indeed, they are ignored as though they never existed.

THE ONE EXCEPTION!

In the last one hundred years, there have been about one hundred million displaced persons who have fled from violence in their former homelands to be taken in as refugees by neighboring countries. For example, when India and Pakistan were given independence by Britain, more than eight million Hindus and Sikhs fled from what had become East and West Pakistan, while nearly seven million Muslims fled from what had just become independent India. About fifteen million refugees were created in that exchange. No one has called for their return to the homes from which they fled—nor for a return of any of the other eighty-five million. This is the rule and practice.

Ah, but there is *one* exception—the "Palestinians." In March 1976, Matthew Mitchell, then director of the United States Committee for Refugees, declared in an interview that in contrast to "the world situation…Arab refugees are a special case."[41] These exploited victims of Arab hatred against Israel, deliberately kept on display in squalid camps, must be received back to Israel in order to destroy her. As John McCarthy, one of the world's leading experts on refugees, admitted in a December 19, 1978, interview, the Arab world demands that these people go "back to Israel, right or wrong. You must remember—well—these people are simply pawns."[42] The tragedy is all the more disturbing in light of the editorial in a Damascus newspaper in 1949: "Syria needs not only one hundred thousand refugees, but five million to work the lands and make them fruitful."[43]

If justice demands that the "Palestinians" return to Israel, why isn't there an equal cry of justice for the even larger number of Jews to be allowed back into Muslim lands? The answer to that question is just one more proof of the pervasive anti-Semitism that the Bible prophesied the Jews would suffer until the Messiah returns at Armageddon to rescue them.

1. David A Rausch, *The Middle East Maze: Israel and her Neighbors* (Chicago: Moody Press, 1991), 35.

2. Interview published in *Deutsche National Zeitung,* April 1, 1964.

3. Cited in Joan Peters, *From Time Immemorial: The Origins of the Arab-Jewish Conflict over Palestine* (New York: J KAP Publishing USA, 1984), 360.

4. *Foreign Relations of the United States*, 1947.

5. Joseph B. Schechtman, *The Mufti and The Fuehrer* (New York: Thomas Yoseloff, 1965), 220.

6. Schechtman, *The Mufti*, 221.

7. Isaiah 66:8.

8. "The Arabs of Israel: Are they a 'persecuted minority?'" FLAME, Facts and Logic About the Middle East, P.O. Box 590359, San Francisco, CA 94159, *WORLD*, December 30, 2000/ January 6, 2001.

9. Rausch, *Middle East*, 79-80.

10. Noam Chomsky, *Fateful Triangle: The United States, Israel & the Palestinians* (Cambridge: South End Press, 1999).

11. Norman G. Finkelstein, *Image and Reality of the Israel-Palestine Conflict* (London: Verso, 1995).

12. *Foreign Relations of the U.S. 1948*, Vol. V. (GPO, 1976), 838.

13. *The New York Times,* 4/23/48.

14. Near East Broadcasting Station of Cyprus, April 3, 1949; Samuel Katz, *Battleground-Fact and Fantasy in Palestine* (Bantam Books, 1985), 15.

15. *Filastin,* February 19, 1949.

16. *Ad Diofaa*, September 6, 1954.

17. *Al Hoda*, June 8, 1951.

18. Myron Kaufman, *The Coming Destruction of Israel* (The American Library Inc., 1970), 26-27.

19. *The Memoirs of Haled al Azm* (Beirut, 1973), Part 1, 386-387.

20. Khaled Al-Azm, *Memoirs [Arabic], 3 volumes* (Al-Dar al Muttahida lil-Nashr, 1972), vol. 1, 386-87, cited in Peters, *Immemorial*, 16.

21. *The New York Times*, May 3, 1948.

22. *Middle Eastern Studies*, January 1986.

23. *The Beirut Daily Telegraph*, September 6, 1948.

24. PLO journal *Palestine a-Thaura,* March 1976.

25. *The Economist*, October 2, 1948.

26. Rausch, *Middle East,* 75-76.

27. Surah 5:51.

28. Matthew 22:39.

29. Luke 23:34.

30. Bat Ye'or, *The Decline of Eastern Christianity under Islam: From Jihad to Dhimmitude* (London: Associated University Presses, 1996), 84, 85, 110, etc.

31. Saul Friedman, "The Myth of Arab Toleration," *Midstream*, January 1970, 58.

32. Edward William Lane, *Manners and Customs of the Modern Egyptians 1833-1835* (London, 1890), 512-517.

33. Article 10 (4) of Egyptian Nationality Code.

34. Peters, *Immemorial*, 48, see comments in footnotes 120 and 121.

35. Ibid., 4.
36. Sabri Jiryis, *Al Nahor* (Beirut), May 15, 1975.
37. *Chicago Sun-Times*, January 24, 1977; *The New York Times*, August 27, 1977.
38. Peters, *Immemorial*, 406.
39. *Al-Misri*, October 1 1949.
40. Peters, *Immemorial*, 23.
41. Ibid., 27.
42. Ibid., 29.
43. *Al-Qubs*, January 1949, quoted in *az-Sameer* (New York), March 28, 1949.

6—TERRORISM'S PAGAN ISLAMIC FOUNDATION

MUHAMMAD, the founder of Islam, was born in Mecca into the Quraish tribe around A.D. 570. There are no known non-Muslim sources for his biography and only two main Islamic sources: *The Life History of Muhammad*, by Ibn-Ishaq (A.D. 768), edited by Ibn-Hisham (A.D. 833); and *The Expeditions of Muhammad*, by Al-Waqidi (A.D. 822). The various *hadith* (the sayings and deeds of Muhammad as recited by his closest companions) also give insights into the life of the Prophet of Islam.

The Quraish of Mecca had a lucrative business as the guardians of the Ka'aba, an idol temple filled with some three hundred sixty images representing the various tribal deities worshiped by anyone who might be traveling with one of the huge commercial caravans passing through Mecca. Allah (a contraction of *Al-ilah*, literally, "the chief god") was recognized as the chief of the idols in the Ka'aba. It had been the official god of Muhammad's tribe for centuries before he was born.

Muhammad began receiving "revelations" under circumstances so strange and terrifying that he feared he was being deceived by

Satan. According to Islamic sources, he thought he had become demon possessed and at times acted as though he were. His wife Khadija consoled him, assuring him that Allah was speaking to him. Ibn Ishaq recorded that when the spirit came another time, Khadija tested it:

> She said to the apostle of Allah, "O son of my uncle, are you able to tell me about your visitant, when he comes to you?" He replied that he could, and she asked him to tell her when he came.
>
> So when Gabriel came to him, as he was wont, the apostle said to Khadija, "This is Gabriel who has just come to me."
>
> "Get up, O son of my uncle," she said, "and sit by my left thigh." The apostle did so, and she said, "Can you see him?"
>
> "Yes," he said.
>
> She said, "Then turn around and sit on my right thigh."
>
> He did so, and she said, "Can you see him?" When he said that he could, she asked him to move and sit in her lap. When he had done this she again asked if he could see him, and when he said yes, she disclosed her form [i.e., removed her clothes] and cast aside her veil. With the apostle sitting in her lap, she said, "Can you see him?"
>
> He replied, "No."
>
> She said, "O son of my uncle, rejoice and be of good heart, by Allah he is an angel and not a satan."[1]

Muhammad then agreed that his inspiration was from Allah through "the angel Gabriel." These revelations (except for those that were lost—and some were) make up the Qur'an today.

Doubts continued to plague Muhammad, however, and he attempted suicide a number of times over the next few years.[2] After he received the ninety-sixth Surah, "inspiration" was suspended for a number of months. Depressed by that, Muhammad again contemplated suicide. His suicidal tendencies, acknowledged by all Islamic authorities, hardly seem to be the mark of a great spiritual leader under divine inspiration.

These alleged revelations (there were eventually one hundred fourteen Surahs) presented a revolutionary idea: that Allah was not merely the *chief* god in the Ka'aba, but the *only* god anywhere; that

Muhammad was Allah's exclusive prophet; and that the whole world must be brought into submission (Islam) to Allah. This new doctrine was, naturally, opposed by the Meccans. It didn't seem to be a good idea to them to do away with all gods except Allah—it could seriously diminish their lucrative Ka'aba business.

Faced with growing opposition to his "revelations," and having only a handful of followers, Muhammad fled Mecca in A.D. 622 in what is known as the *Hijrah*, from which the Muslim calendar dates. A.H. (*anno Hijrah*, in the year of the Hijrah) is like A.D. (*anno Domini*, in the year of the Lord). He settled in the town of Yathrib, now known as Medina. That became his headquarters until he returned in triumph as the conqueror of Mecca eight years later.

After fleeing to Yathrib, and as he gained power and the number of his followers grew, Muhammad's revelations from Allah became increasingly belligerent. Not only must the entire world submit to Allah (Islam means "submission"), but it must be forced to do so with the sword under threat of death to those who refused to acknowledge Allah alone and Muhammad as his prophet. Challenged to do miracles like Christ, he could do none—but he was a clever military strategist.

BEGINNING A "RELIGION OF PEACE"

On March 16, 624, as the prophet of Allah and to the glory of Allah, Muhammad led three hundred warriors in a vicious attack near Badr upon a large Meccan caravan laden with riches and protected by a force of eight hundred. Some forty Meccans were killed and sixty taken prisoner, to a loss of only fourteen Muslims. This victory against a superior force was seen as the attesting miracle from Allah that Muhammad needed. From that time, the ranks of Muslims swelled with those eager to share in the plunder Allah promised in this life and in Paradise. A timely revelation declared, "Whoso fighteth in the way of Allah, be he slain or be he victorious, on him We shall bestow a vast reward."[3]

Having proved his military prowess, Muhammad solidified his power through the murder of more than twenty-five of those who opposed him. The first had been al-Nadr, an old enemy from Mecca. Taken captive in the battle at Badr, he reminded Muhammad that the Quraish didn't kill captives. Showing no mercy, Muhammad had him beheaded on the spot, setting the example for his followers of what would become the ruthless slaughter of millions. He justified the deed with another shocking "revelation": "It is not for any Prophet to have captives until he hath made slaughter in the land."[4] Timely "revelations" came from Allah just when Muhammad needed them, often for his own personal benefit.

For example, Muhammad went to visit his adopted son, Zaid. His wife, Zaynab, Muhammad's cousin, came to the door to say that Zaid was not there and invited the prophet inside. She was rather scantily clad and Muhammad was overwhelmed with her beauty and passionately desired her. He declined to enter, but exclaimed aloud to Allah, "How you do turn the hearts of men!" Zaynab later repeated the prophet's words to Zaid, who dutifully offered to divorce his wife so Muhammad could have her. Zaynab was thrilled with the chance to be married to the prophet of Allah. At first, Muhammad declined, but he could not quench his passion for her. Sitting next to Aisha, his favorite wife, whom he had married when she was nine years old, an inspiration to be added to the Qur'an suddenly came upon Muhammad that Allah required him to marry Zaynab—supposedly to show Muslims that it is not sin to marry one's adopted son's wife even if she is his cousin.[5] Zaid, of course, was obedient to the revelation. It was not for him or anyone else to question the will of Allah. Thus Zaynab was added to Muhammad's growing number of wives.

Many of Muhammad's murder victims were poets who had mocked him in verse. The first was the poetess Asma bint Marwan, silenced by being stabbed to death as she nursed her youngest child. The poet Abu Afak (reportedly more than one hundred years old) was murdered next. Justifying these killings, another revelation added to the Qur'an explained that all poets were inspired of Satan.[6] As one former Muslim writes, "Assassinations, murder, cruelty, and torture must all be taken into consideration in any judgment on the moral character of Muhammad."[7]

Far from trying to hide what a normal conscience would recognize as unspeakable evil, Muslims speak openly of such savagery as normal to Islam—the commendable example set by Muhammad himself and worthy of repeating today. In October 2004, Magdi Ahmad Hussein, Egyptian Labor Party General Secretary, spoke on Al-Jazeera TV in defense of terrorism. He praised both the suicide bombers, who target women and children, and the beheading of prisoners. In defensive response to what we hope and pray is a growing embarrassment among at least some Muslims for the many barbaric practices committed in the name of Islam, Hussein argued:

> So how come some voices in the Islamic movement and official clerics tell us that killing prisoners is un-Islamic? No, both the Qur'an and the Prophet's biography permit the killing of prisoners. This exists in our Islamic law.... Why do the government clerics ignore the killing of the prisoners during the time of the Prophet? Some 600-700 [actually 900, who surrendered and were promised safety, were beheaded] prisoners were killed in the raid on the Qurayza tribe [of Jews]. Why do they conceal this? Why do they hide the fact that the Prophet gave the order to assassinate some poets—to assassinate! Not in military operations, but rather by individual assassination?[8]

Among those assassinated was the Jewish poet Ka'b bin al-Ashraf. Far from being an embarrassment to Muslims today, Ka'b's murder is still justified as foundational to Islam. (No wonder one author titled his book on Islamic terrorism, *Muhammad's Monsters*![9]) Painting the account in the best light possible with fictitious details, a popular Muslim website reveals Islam's peculiar definition of "peace" and "justice":

> Ka'b had become a real danger to the state of peace and mutual trust which the Prophet was struggling to achieve in Madinah.... The Prophet was quite exasperated with him.... This was all part of the great process...which helped to make Islam spread and establish it on foundations of justice and piety.[10]

There would be no freedom of speech in Islam. Those who opposed the prophet had to be eliminated. And so it is today. To raise a legitimate question about the Qur'an or Muhammad in any country where Muslims are in power brings the sentence of death. In the days when Pakistan had only one television channel, it always began the day warning viewers that Islam was not to be questioned. Nor would anyone dare to raise a question today.

For writing a book in 1988 that Muslim clerics deemed to be an attack upon Islam and its prophet, author Salman Rushdie (and all sympathizers) was given a death sentence. Rushdie is still in hiding in fear of his life with a reward on his head. It does not speak well of any religion that must maintain itself by threats and killing rather than by voluntary belief and willing loyalty in response to facts.

It takes little research to learn that Muslims have their own peculiar meaning of words that enable them to sound peaceful when in fact they are not. For example, to "prove" that Islam is opposed to terrorism, the following quote attributed to Muhammad in both the *Bukhari* and Muslim *hadiths* is used: "By Allah, he is not a true believer, from whose mischief his neighbors do not feel secure."[11] Yet Muhammad's neighbors couldn't feel secure—he might have them murdered at any time, especially if they were poets or Jews. Nor could the neighboring villages or passing caravans feel safe from his attacks, not even during Ramadan, a time of peace for pagans! Muhammad's words sound assuring, but they clearly have a special meaning. Neighbors could only feel confident of peace if they submitted to Islam and didn't antagonize Muhammad.

EARLIEST ROOTS OF TODAY'S ISLAMIC TERRORISM

The way in which Muhammad established his new religion in Arabia—by attacking caravans and villages, putting the defeated to the sword to bring fear and to impose his will on other Arabs—was nothing short of terrorism. There is no other word in today's vocabulary to describe it. In his *Pensées*, Blaise Pascal made a comparison: "Mohamet established a religion by putting his enemies to death; Jesus Christ by commanding his followers to lay down their lives." As another author put it, "*Jihad* was...accepted [from] the Koran as the direct word of God [Allah]. No one had any difficulty in reconciling religiosity and rapacity. Muhammad had not only made it easy for them to do so, he had made it a virtue by presenting plunder and war as righteous paths to Paradise."[12]

Terrorism is endemic to Islam because for centuries it had been an integral part of the pagan Arab society into which Muhammad was born and from which Islam sprang. A former professor of Islamic history at Al-Azhar University in Cairo, Egypt (built around the al-Azhar mosque and the most authoritative center of Islamic doctrine in the world), describes that society in seventh-century Arabia:

> Only the strongest survived…these tribes fought constantly as a way of existence. This mentality was manifested into a basic lifestyle: Plunder the possessions of those you defeat…invade others to gain position and wealth.…When invading an enemy country, they killed all the males and took the women and children as slaves.
>
> Islam did not change any of these characteristics or influence the behavior of Arabs. Instead, Islam embraced the Arab mentality and used it to accomplish its agenda. *Jihad* (fighting the enemy of Allah to death) as a core belief of Islam came to the Arabic mentality not as a new behavior but as one with which they were very familiar.… Muhammad was born into a culture where conquest and bloodshed were the norm [and] were incorporated into Islam through the concept of *jihad*.[13]

The average Westerner imagines that terrorism is something new that began in the 1990s with the Intifada in Israel and has been getting worse ever since, spreading around the globe. Many believe that it is justified against Israelis because of their alleged mistreatment of Palestinians, but it is viewed as a horrible crime when perpetrated anywhere else. Muslims have practiced terrorism, especially against Jews (and even against themselves), for centuries, but with increasing intensity as soon as the United Nations partitioned Palestine in November 1947.

In the anti-Jewish riots of December 1947, mobs burned down most of the synagogues in Aleppo, Syria, destroyed one hundred fifty Jewish homes, five Jewish schools, fifty shops and offices, an orphanage, and a youth club. Scrolls were destroyed and a priceless ancient manuscript of the Old Testament was burned while firemen watched passively and police "actively helped the attackers."[14] A letter from several Aleppo rabbis, dated April 28, 1948 (two weeks before Israel declared its independence), delivered to the Mogen David congregation in Brooklyn, New York, pleaded, "This is the third day we are in hiding. The Arab mobs are raging and threatening our lives. Pray for us. Act on our behalf before your government. Our lives are in total danger…help us!"

JUSTIFYING MURDER IN THE QUR'AN

Does it bother today's Muslims that murder, rape, plunder, and slavery of innocent people was the accepted way of life into which Muhammad led his followers and upon which Islam was founded and still operates? Most Muslims are not aware of Islam's history; and most of those who do know the brutal truth seem to be proud of it. Like all oppressive systems, Islam established itself on the principle that "might makes right." And this is the way it maintains itself today whenever possible, killing all who refuse to submit.

Yathrib had been founded by Jews. Muhammad shared his "revelations" with them and also with the Christians living in the vicinity. When they would neither accept Allah as God (whom they knew was the chief idol in the Ka'aba), nor Muhammad as His prophet, he turned against the Christians and Jews, killing all who refused to become Muslims and were unable to escape. After surrendering to the superior Muslim force in exchange for a pledge of safety, every male Jew of fighting age in Yathrib was nevertheless slaughtered and their bodies buried under the marketplace. Women and children were taken as "wives" or slaves. The name of the town was changed to Medina, which means "city of the prophet." Here Muhammad himself was buried and his tomb remains to this day.

Eventually, every Jew in Arabia was either slain or escaped. The law remains today that no Jew may set foot in Saudi Arabia—nor would any Jew dare to enter. (Secretary of State Henry Kissinger and

Senator Joseph Lieberman were the two lone exceptions.) It would mean their death, a penalty that the Saudis would exact in Riyadh's "chop-chop square" without any sense of shame before today's world. This is the official penalty decreed by Muhammad, which is still meted out to any Muslim who converts to any other religion. By Muhammad's command, only Islam may be practiced in Saudi Arabia—and so it would be everywhere in the world if Islam could fulfill the mission Allah has given it.

When Saudi Arabia asked the Americans to protect them from Saddam Hussein's armies ("might makes right" again), which had raped Kuwait and intended to conquer the rest of the Gulf States, they stipulated that no Jew could enter Arabia. The Americans replied that Jews were an integral part of their armed forces and would come whether the Saudis liked it or not. Then it was realized that if Iraqi troops captured an American soldier whose dog tags identified him as a Jew, they would literally skin him alive. So a new category was invented: "Protestant B." That designation was thereafter stamped on the dog tags of the Jewish military personnel assigned to Muslim areas.

That Islam is a violent religion, which requires putting to death all Jews to bring about its consummation, is of no concern to world leaders. Politics does not pretend to be moral. Many PLO agents continue working today for the British secret service. Still favoring Muslims at the expense of Israel, and covertly playing both sides, Britain was brazenly supplying Saddam Hussein with shells a full six weeks after his invasion of Kuwait.

FIGHTING TERRORISM IN A STATE OF DENIAL

All non-Muslims are viewed as pagans. One is puzzled as to why pagans who have not yet submitted to Islam, the peaceful religion, should be asked to bring peace between warring Muslim countries. We might believe that Islam is a religion of peace, as President Bush and other political and religious leaders in the West insist, if they would stop fighting among themselves and killing us. The Muslim is enjoined by Allah and the Qur'an to declare to non-Muslims, in effect: "This is a religion of peace! And if you refuse to admit that 'Islam is peace,' I'll kill you to prove it!"

In 1990, in order to allow pagan American troops to enter Saudi Arabia so that they could protect it from the invading Islamic armies of Iraq, Sheikh Abdul Aziz bin Baz, top Saudi religious authority, issued this fatwa: "Even though the Americans…are not Muslims, they deserve support because they are here to defend Islam."[15] Defending Islam, the religion of peace, against Muslims who are practicing the religion of peace, seems rather odd. It is no less unbelievable that those whom Islam looks upon as enemies to be killed should defend Islam. American troops surely didn't understand that to be their mission. Yet their leaders continue to praise this violent religion as peaceful.

No world leader expresses an understanding of terrorism and a determination to stamp it out more clearly and with more earnestness than President Bush. At the same time, however, he naïvely (or purposely for the sake of "political correctness") persists in calling Islam a religion of peace and carefully avoids mentioning it in the same breath with terrorism. The contradictory omission is glaring as in the following from his January 29, 2002, State of the Union Address:

> Our discoveries in Afghanistan…showed us the true scope of the task ahead…[that] the depth of our enemies' hatred…is equaled by the madness of the destruction they design. We have found diagrams of American nuclear power plants and public water facilities, detailed instructions for making chemical weapons, surveillance maps of American cities, and thorough descriptions of landmarks in America and throughout the world.
>
> What we have found in Afghanistan confirms that…our war against terror is only beginning…. Thousands of dangerous killers, schooled in the methods of murder, often supported by outlaw regimes, are now spread throughout the world like ticking time bombs, set to go off without warning.
>
> Hundreds of terrorists have been arrested. Yet, tens of thousands…are still at large. These enemies view the entire world as a battlefield, and we must pursue them wherever they are. So long as training camps operate, so long as nations harbor terrorists, freedom is at risk. And America and our allies must not, and will not, allow it.

> Our nation will continue to be steadfast and patient and persistent in the pursuit of two great objectives. First, we will shut down terrorist camps, disrupt terrorist plans, and bring terrorists to justice. And, second, we must prevent the terrorists and regimes who seek chemical, biological or nuclear weapons from threatening the United States and the world.
>
> Our military has put the terror training camps of Afghanistan out of business, yet camps still exist in at least a dozen countries. A terrorist underworld—including groups like Hamas, Hezbollah, Islamic Jihad, Jaish-i-Mohammed—operates in remote jungles and deserts, and hides in the centers of large cities....
>
> States [that sponsor terrorism] and their terrorist allies, constitute an axis of evil, arming to threaten the peace of the world. By seeking weapons of mass destruction, these regimes pose a grave and growing danger. They could provide these arms to terrorists, giving them the means to match their hatred. They could attack our allies or attempt to blackmail the United States. In any of these cases, the price of indifference would be catastrophic.
>
> We will work closely with our coalition to deny terrorists and their state sponsors the materials, technology, and expertise to make and deliver weapons of mass destruction. We will develop and deploy effective missile defenses to protect America and our allies from sudden attack. And all nations should know: America will do what is necessary to ensure our nation's security.

It hardly makes sense, however, to pursue terrorists, yet at the same time to ignore the very root from which terrorism sprang and which gives it life. Its roots are not hidden but are there for all to see in an Arab pagan religion known as Islam.

MUSLIMS AND PAGANS TOGETHER

In A.D. 628 (A.H. 6), Muhammad approached Mecca with some of his followers—all recent converts to this new religion of Islam. They longed to join in the *hajj*, the annual pilgrimage to the idol-filled Ka'aba where Allah was still honored as the chief god among hundreds. Muhammad and his Muslim followers desired to renew the same superstitious rituals they had practiced before becoming Muslims and which their ancestors had followed for centuries. It would be the first time that Muhammad had attempted to join in the *hajj* since he had fled Mecca.

The Meccans were still too strong for Muhammad and turned him away. Anxious to make peace, however, with this powerful and violent enemy, they entered into one of the most important agreements in Islamic history, the Treaty of Hudaybiya, a ten-year cease-fire, called a *Hudna*. That document established Islam's law of war and peace and set the precedent for future Islamic policy that remains to this day. No Muslim leader has the authority to go over Muhammad's head to make genuine peace with non-Muslims. Only a *Hudna* can be entered into, and that for no longer than ten years. The purpose, following Muhammad's example, is not to achieve a sincere end to hostilities, but to deceive the enemy with the promise of peace in order to gain time and advantage to eventually conquer the unsuspecting "peace partner." This was always Arafat's intent and, since his death, continues to be the PLO's purpose in the so-called "peace process" with Israel.

This treaty allowed Muhammad and his Muslim followers to join the *hajj* the following year on the condition that Muhammad acknowledge that he was not the prophet of Allah. Muhammad swallowed his pride and signed. Thus, in 629 with his fellow Muslims he entered Mecca and joined with the pagan Arabs in going seven times around the idol-filled Ka'aba, kissing the dark stone in one corner and touching another stone in the Yamani corner each time around. The new Muslims, with Muhammad at their head, joined in all of the other traditional pagan rituals, climbing nearby Mount as-Safa, then running from there back and forth seven times to the summit of as-Marwah, supposedly commemorating Hagar's search for water. They climbed Mount Arafat, then hurried to Muzdalifah, a place between Mina and Arafat, in time for sunset prayer.

The next day, the new Muslims, along with crowds of pagans, proceeded to Wadi Mina, where each threw seven stones at each of three pillars representing Satan. And so it went (the full details are too long to include here). These ancient pagan rituals were all carried over into Islam and are practiced to this day in the *hajj*, which most people, both Muslims and non-Muslims, naïvely imagine was initiated by Muhammad as part of Islam. Nothing could be further from the truth.

WHAT DID MUHAMMAD CHANGE?

In A.D. 630, two years after signing the Treaty of Hudaybiya, Muhammad's army was strong enough to take over Mecca, which he did, destroying the idols, including Allah, in the Ka'aba. For a time, he allowed the pagans to continue to practice the *hajj*, joining with the new Muslims in its rituals. Then he gave the pagans four months to convert to Islam or be killed. Thereafter, only Muslims could approach Mecca and the Ka'aba, which remains the rule today. Muhammad's last official public act shortly before his death was to lead forty thousand of his followers in these very same rituals, establishing this traditional pagan practice in perpetuity as the most important part of Islam.

The Qur'an claims that the Ka'aba was "the first Sanctuary appointed to mankind...where Abraham stood up to pray; and...pilgrimage [*hajj*] to the House is a duty unto Allah for [all] mankind, for him who can find a way thither."[16] It also claims that Abraham and Ishmael together built the Ka'aba.[17] In fact, Abraham (Ishmael was no longer with him, having been banished together with his mother, Hagar) lived in Hebron in Canaan. The idea that he would make the arduous journey across hundreds of miles of Arabian desert to Mecca—and to build an idol temple to be used by pagan Arabs—is an outrageous fabrication contrary to common sense, to everything the Bible says about Abraham, and without any history to support it.

Family loyalty had long been the rule among the Arabs, who fought rival tribes and plundered passing caravans as a way of life. Muhammad changed tribal loyalty into devotion to Islam. The Qur'an commanded Muslims to force submission to Allah upon the entire world and required that those who refused to submit must be killed. The usual fighting and plunder long practiced by Arab tribes was carried on as before but now in the name of Allah and to spread the "new" religion that all must embrace or die.

Appropriately, there is a sword on Saudi Arabia's flag. The most sacred mosque for Sunni Muslims is the Grand Mosque in Mecca. Its Imam, appointed by the Saudi government, is "the closest thing in Islam to the Pope." His sermons "call for Jews to be 'annihilated' and urge the overthrow of Western civilization." The home page of the Islamic Affairs Department of Saudi Arabia's embassy in Washington, D.C., unabashedly declares, "The Muslims are required to raise the banner of jihad in order to make the World of Allah supreme in this world."[18]

A ONE-WAY STREET TO SURRENDER

Such bold declarations that Islam must conquer the world, thundered almost daily by Muslim leaders in their denunciations of the West, seem to pass unnoticed as the West continues to praise Islam—and even to welcome into its halls of government outspoken enemies who are determined to destroy us. On March 19, 2004, the United States Institute of Peace (funded by Congress) hosted a panel discussion about reforming Islam. One of the invited panelists was Muzammil Siddiqi, past president of the Islamic Society of North America. Yet Siddiqi, at an anti-Israel rally outside the White House on October 28, 2000, had openly threatened the U.S. for its support of Israel: "America has to learn...if you remain on the side of injustice [i.e. in support of Israel], the wrath of Allah will come." He has called for *sharia* law in the United States, and has praised suicide bombers, whom he considers to be messengers of justice. Incredibly, Siddiqi has been an invited guest at administration events with President Bush present and was invited to lead in prayer at the national prayer breakfast following the September 11, 2001, attacks.[19]

For many years, the United States has gone out of its way to make overtures of peace to Muslims. On June 21, 1979, the United States Congress and Senate made a concurrent resolution recognizing "the rich religious, scientific, cultural, and artistic contribution [Islam] has made to mankind since its founding." U.S. Senate Resolution 43 stated in part:

> Whereas November 21, 1979, marks the fourteen hundredth anniversary of the founding of Islam [wrong date—Muhammad was only nine years old]...; and

> Whereas Islam is one of mankind's great religions...encompassing every major region of the world; and

> Whereas the word "Islam" derives from Abraham's willingness to accept all God's commands...; and

> Whereas Islam strives for a worldwide community which...does not recognize the superficial differences of race....

> *Resolved by the Senate (the House of Representatives concurring),* The Congress takes note of the contribution of Islam and wishes success to the fourteenth centennial commemoration...[and] pledges its efforts to achieve better understanding, reductions of tensions, and the pursuit of improved relations with all nations of the world [and] requests that the President forward a copy of this resolution to the Chief of State of each country where Islam has a significant following....

By now, the reader has enough information to know how grossly this declaration misled Americans and the world at large. The "worldwide community" that Islam aims to achieve is by force, under threat of terrorism and death. It is true that it does not recognize "superficial differences of race"—but only among Muslims. It will not tolerate the religions of different races. It is unconscionable to praise Islam for its contributions without also acknowledging its slaughter, enslavement, and oppression of millions. Political correctness is the enemy of truth and fairness.

WHAT ABOUT RAMADAN?

Like the *hajj*, Ramadan was also carried over into Islam almost unchanged from the manner in which idol-worshiping Arab tribes had practiced it for centuries. Ramadan always began (as it still does for Muslims) with the first sighting of the new moon in the ninth month of the Muslim lunar calendar. The crescent moon, so prominent on minarets and flags of Muslim countries, harks back to the early Arab worship of Allah as the moon god. Although Allah has no son, as the Qur'an declares, this god was traditionally believed to have three daughters: al-Lat, Manat, and al-Uzza.

The pagans had long agreed not to fight during Ramadan (a time of fasting from sunrise to sunset), but to set it apart as thirty days during the year that was to be free from tribal warfare. After three failed attacks against caravans, another timely "revelation" added to the Qur'an gave Muslims permission from Allah to fight during that "holy month."[20] This gave the advantage of surprise and brought Muhammad's first successful robbing of a rich caravan (near Badr), to which we have earlier referred. From that time, Islam began to grow as others joined to share in the booty Allah promised to those who fought in its cause.

Today, Ramadan is celebrated as a holiday that began with the advent of Islam. But this is no more true of Ramadan than of the *hajj*. It had been observed by Arab tribes for centuries before Muhammad was born and is practiced by Muslims in virtually the same manner today. As the Qur'an itself says, "The month of Ramadan in which was revealed the Qur'an...."[21]

HONORING PAGANISM

The celebratory feast at the end of Ramadan is known as Eid al-Fitr. On Sept. 1, 2001, the U.S. Postal Service issued a 34-cent Eid stamp at the annual Islamic Society of North America's convention in Des Plaines, Illinois. Such gestures of good will and appeasement only encourage Muslims in their determined conquest of the world for Allah. The Eid stamp commemorates the two most important festivals, or Eids, in the Islamic calendar: Eid al-Fitr, the feast of Ramadan, and Eid al-Adha, the Feast of Sacrifice. The latter is celebrated in memory of Abraham allegedly offering Ishmael on the altar—rather than Isaac, as the Bible declares.

In his speech at the Islamic Center of Washington, D.C., on

December 10, 2002, President Bush said, "I am pleased to join you today in the celebration of Eid, the culmination of the Holy Month of Ramadan.... Islam traces its origins back to God's call on Abraham. And Ramadan commemorates the revelation of God's word in the Holy Koran to the prophet Muhammad."

How could President Bush, a professing Christian, honor Muhammad as a prophet of God and call the Qur'an God's holy word? The Qur'an is completely anti-Christian, contradicting the Bible on almost every major point, including denying the deity of Christ, denying His death upon the cross for our sins, denying His resurrection, and declaring that those who believe in the Trinity go to hell. Isn't this quite a stretch for Bush in order to achieve "political correctness"? To avoid offending Muslims by keeping the truth to oneself is one thing; to blaspheme the true God by associating Him with paganism is far worse and inexcusable.

United States presidents have long honored Ramadan as a holy Islamic month, hosting a special Iftaar dinner in the White House for American and foreign political leaders, along with Muslim religious leaders, at the end of Ramadan's thirty-day fast. On October 14, 2004, President Bush sent "warm greetings to Muslims in the United States and around the world as they begin observance of Ramadan, the holiest season in their faith [commemorating] the revelation of the Qur'an to Muhammed." Likewise, in 1967, the Vatican invited Christians to offer their best wishes to Muslims at the end of the fast of Ramadan "with genuine religious worth."

President Bush's speech at the Iftaar dinner on November 10, 2004, included the following: "As we gather during this holy month...we honor the traditions of a great faith.... In recent years, Americans...have come to learn more about our Muslim brothers and sisters.... We share a belief in God's justice, and man's moral responsibility. We share the same hope for a future of peace. We have so much in common, and so much to learn from one another. Once again, I wish you a blessed Ramadan. I want to thank you for joining us at the White House for this Iftaar, and may God bless you all."[22]

THIS IS GOD'S WORD?

Surely, Bush must know that the Allah of Islam is not the Yahweh of the Bible. Nor does Islam have any relationship to "God's call on Abraham." That call brought him into the land that "the God of Israel"[23] promised to his descendants through Isaac and Jacob. Muhammad hated and killed these descendants, whom God calls His chosen people—"the apple of his eye."[24] The Bible warns, "[H]e that toucheth you toucheth the apple of his eye."[25] It is Islam that causes the Muslims to seek the destruction of Israel and the possession of that land by the descendants of Ishmael! We are supposed to honor this denial of biblical teaching?

The Qur'an, allegedly inspired by Allah through Gabriel, is God's Word? In contrast to the thousands of ancient manuscripts we have for the Bible, the Qur'an was taken down on palm leaves, sticks, stones, bark, bones, and anything available when Muhammad began to recite. Some revelations were recalled by memory with nothing in writing to support them. Muhammad's favorite wife, Aisha, said that more than one hundred verses were missing from one chapter alone, having been eaten by domestic animals while in her possession.

The four Caliphs who immediately succeeded Muhammad are called the "rightly guided Caliphs." The Qur'an (which was "revealed" over a period of sixteen years) was not compiled in Muhammad's lifetime, but many years later under Uthman Ibn Affan, the third of these four. When it was proposed to Abu Bakr, Muhammad's father-in-law and first successor, that he put together an official version of the Qur'an, he objected, because Muhammad had said nothing about doing so. Some who had memorized the Qur'an during Muhammad's lifetime protested that Uthman's version was not correct. He answered these sincere concerns by having all rival copies destroyed.

A number of Surahs in the Qur'an[26] have titles so strange that not even Muslim scholars know what they mean: "Taha," "Yasin," "Sad," "Qaf," "Nun," etc. Others have meaningless names such as "The Ant."[27] This section describes a battle between Solomon's army of Jinn (spirit beings, possibly good, but usually evil), men, and birds, and an army of ants. Solomon hears an ant named Tahina speaking three miles away. There is a "hoopoe" bird that is late showing up because it has been with the Queen of Sheba. Solomon sends it back to preach the "gospel."

Much of the Qur'an reads like children's Arabian fairy tales. "The Elephant" is about a battle between elephants and vultures. "The Cow" tells of Jews who were transformed into apes for breaking the Sabbath (this is why Muslims often call Jews "apes"), of two angels who seduce people in Babylon with magic, and of a Jew murdered by a cousin. God tells Moses to kill a cow and hit the dead man with part of it. The dead man revives, identifies his killer, then dies again.

Muhammad, under inspiration from Allah, said that upon awakening one must blow his nose three times to rid himself of the Devil, who spends the night in a man's nostrils.[28] This is God's Holy Word, the foundation of the one true religion? In fact, falling asleep can be very dangerous for a Muslim. Muhammad said that "Yawning is from Satan."[29] As for Muslims who fall asleep while praying, the prophet said Satan urinates in their ears.[30] Furthermore, one must be very careful not to turn one's eyes upward when praying. Abu Huraira heard the prophet say, "People should avoid lifting their eyes towards the sky while supplicating in prayer, otherwise their eyes would be snatched away."[31] Moreover, apparently Allah does not accept prayer from those who have bad breath from eating raw onions or garlic. We have the word of the prophet for that, who said on more than one occasion, "Whoever has eaten garlic or onion…should not come near our mosque."[32]

On the positive side, Muhammad had a remedy even for those in hell. Passing by two graves one day, Islam's founding prophet stopped, took a green date-palm leaf, split it, and put half on each grave. "'O Allah's Apostle! Why have you done so?' people asked. Muhammad replied, 'I hope that their punishment [in hell] may be lessened until they [i.e., the palm leaves] become dry.'"[33] Women should be especially concerned, however, because Muhammad claimed that he had been given a look into hell, and most of its inhabitants were women.[34]

CHRISTIANS HONOR ALLAH AND ISLAM

Most Christians are ignorant of what Islam is like, yet many recommend it. Billy Graham has naïvely said, "Islam is misunderstood.... Muhammad had a great respect for Jesus, called Jesus the greatest of the prophets except himself. [Isn't that kind!] I think we're closer to Islam than we really think we are...." Yes, as close as the distance between hell and heaven—and Muslims would agree! As we have already seen, Islam is thoroughly anti-Christian. Belief in the Trinity sends one to hell.

Graham's long-time friend, Robert Schuller, has sponsored at his Crystal Cathedral in Garden Grove, California, a joint Christian-Muslim Institute for Peace. He told the Imam, Alfred Mohammed, that if all of his (Schuller's) descendants became Muslims, it wouldn't bother him as long as they weren't atheists. Two months after 9/11, Schuller, who on Sunday mornings has the largest religious TV show in the world, basked in the acclaim of Muslims at a Villa Park, Illinois, mosque. Schuller co-hosted this "Evening of Religious Solidarity" with Imam W. D. Mohammed. One of the honored guests, pseudo-Muslim Louis Farrakhan, praised Schuller as a "mighty spiritual giant," whose *Hour of Power* television program he had watched with approval for about thirty years.[35]

Farrakhan succeeded Elijah Muhammad, who had been the head, until his death, of black America's Nation of Islam (NOI). In spite of its name, NOI has little relationship to Islam. Malcolm X, who founded several NOI temples, became a minister and was second only to Elijah Muhammad, realized that fact and converted to orthodox Islam. In April of 1964, he went to Mecca in Saudi Arabia, made his first *hajj*, and changed his name to El-Hajj Malik El-Shebazz. He exposed NOI as far from true Islam and was marked for death. He and his family survived a firebombing of his New York home on February 14, 1965. Then, a week later, as he was just beginning a speech at Manhattan's Audubon Ballroom, he was shot to death by three NOI members. The assassins were arrested and convicted of first-degree murder. Of course, it was rumored that

Farrakhan was responsible, but that was never proved.

Farrakhan claims to have spent time consulting his predecessor, Elijah Muhammad, in a giant space ship circling earth (the precursor of a fleet of UFOs coming to earth to destroy the white man). That obvious fiction makes no difference to Schuller, who has generously declared that "asking people to change their faith was utterly ridiculous." Coming to the defense of history's most cruel and violent religion, Schuller insists: "This is a time to guard against attacking religion.... It has been my honor to become acquainted with the power leaders of positive Islam. And there is and has been a strong anti-Islam propaganda loose in this world."[36] *Positive* Islam? Muhammad never heard of it! "Anti-Islam propaganda"? No one could give Islam a worse name than Muhammad, the Qur'an, and centuries of slaughter have done from the beginning!

AN ANTI-CHRISTIAN RELIGION

In contrast, Jerry Falwell (who has publicly spoken out in support of Israel many times [37]) declared on *60 Minutes* that Muhammad was a terrorist,[38] and, as Franklin Graham has also said, that Islam is "evil and wicked."[39] For those remarks, *Christianity Today* rebuked them, saying that "Islam would not have become the second largest world religion if it were...as thoroughly evil as these comments suggest."[40] So evil can't grow and prosper as Islam has done with the sword? Jesus said something about the "broad way"[41] and Solomon, about "a way that seemeth right unto a man,"[42] both of which lead to destruction.

In an article titled "Allah Does Not Belong to Islam," Hank Hanegraaff's Christian Research Journal declared: "Allah is the God Arab-speaking Christians worship. The Arabic Bible is replete with the word Allah, beginning with Genesis and ending with Revelation. Jesus Christ is even called the son of Allah in the Arabic Scriptures.... Allah is simply the word or term for God in another language [Arabic]...equivalent to...English God...French Dieu... Spanish Dios.... We can join our Arab brothers and sisters in Christ who often say, 'Allah be praised!'"[43]

Some Christian leaders, in their eagerness to placate Muslims, mouth the most outrageous platitudes under the umbrella of "scholarship." In fact, "Allah" is not a generic term but the *name*, as we have seen, of a particular pagan deity—the chief of the idols in the ancient Ka'aba. The generic word for "God" is *ilah*, found throughout the Qur'an, as in: "Allah! There is no Ilah save him…. Allah is only one Ilah."[44] The confession one must make or die—"La ilaha i' Allah, Muhammadan Rasoulu Allah"—declares that there is "No ilah but Allah."[45]

Of Allah, the Qur'an says, "So believe in Allah…and say not 'Three'—cease! Allah is only one God. Far is it removed from his transcendent majesty that he should have a son."[46] Then how can the Arabic Bible call Jesus the "Son of Allah"? That Allah has a son is denied sixteen times in the Qur'an. How blasphemous, then, to use "Allah" for "God" in the Arabic Bible! What could, "For Allah so loved the world that he gave his only begotten Son…the Father sent the Son to be the Savior of the world"[47] possibly mean?

Furthermore, Allah has none of the characteristics of Yahweh, the God of the Bible. Allah is unknowable, whereas the God of the Bible reveals Himself to His own. Christ even stated that life eternal is only for those who know Him and the Father. Allah changes his mind and his revelations,[48] whereas the God of the Bible never changes,[49] nor does His Word.[50] Allah requires that Muslims die for him, but the God of the Bible came to this earth through a virgin birth and died for us, paying the full penalty for our sins on the Cross. Allah has no just basis for forgiveness of man's sins, but the God of the Bible does. He forgives sins righteously, because the full penalty for all of mankind's sins was paid by Christ.

Of course, this grievous heresy that Allah and Yahweh are one and the same has been promoted for years by the Roman Catholic Church. The Second Vatican Council declared: "But the plan of salvation also includes those who acknowledge the Creator, in the first place amongst whom are the Moslems…together with us they adore the one, merciful God…."[51] Somehow, the Jews were left out. In 1969 at the Muslim University of Al-Azhar, Cairo, Cardinal Koenig proclaimed that Muslims and Christians believe in the same God. On April 24, 1974, Cardinal Pignedoli, President of the Vatican Office of Non-Christian Affairs, paid an official visit to Saudi Arabia, conveying "to His Majesty King Faisal as supreme head of the Islamic world...the regards of His Holiness [Pope Paul VI], moved by a profound belief in the unification of Islamic and Christian worlds in the worship of a single God."[52]

It is a blasphemous insult to the God of the Bible to equate Him with the pagan deity Allah. Yet this is typical of the willingness of professing Christians to trample on truth in their eagerness to placate Muslims. Such fawning flattery will not appease Islam but only encourage its terrorism and violent conquest. Nor will such compromising confusion help Muslims to know the true God, which is essential for salvation. We have already quoted the Qur'an's statement that the true God is the God of the Jews—and He is surely not Allah!

1. Ibn Ishaq, The Life of Muhammad, tr. Guillaume, 1967, 107.
2. *Sahih Al Bukhari*, Vol. 9, number 111, and other Muslim sources such as Ibn Ishaq, Ibn Sa'd, Tabari, etc.
3. Surah 4:74.
4. Surah 8:67.
5. Surah 33:36-38.
6. Surah 26:221-27.
7. Ibn Warraq, *Why I Am Not A Muslim* (Amherst, NY: Prometheus Books, 1995), 99.
8. Middle East Media Research Institute, October 18, 2004.
9. David Bukay, ed., *Muhammad's Monsters: A Comprehensive Guide to Radical Islam for Western Audiences* (Green Forest, AR: Balfour Books, 2004).
10. www.islam101.com/people/companions/maslamah.htm.
11. http://www.islamfortoday.com/terrorism.htm.
12. Paul Fregosi, *Jihad in the West: Muslim Conquests from 7th to 21st Centuries* (Amherst, NY: Prometheus Books, 1998), 61.
13. Mark A. Gabriel, *Islam and Terrorism: What the Quran really teaches about Christianity, violence and the goals of the Islamic jihad* (Lake Mary Florida: Charisma House, 2002), 67, 75.
14. *Jewish Agency Digest of Press and Events*, December 28, 1947.
15. Dore Gold, *Hatred's Kingdom: How Saudi Arabia Supports the New Global Terrorism* (Washington, D.C.: Regnery Publishing, Inc., 2003), 159.
16. Surah 2:125; 3:96-99; 5:97.
17. Surah 2:127.
18. Anthony Browne, "The triumph of the East," *The Sunday Mail* (Brisbane, Australia), September 5, 2004, 54.

19. Worldnetdaily.com/news/asp?ARTICLE_ID=37660.

20. Surah 2:217.

21. Surah 2:185.

22. http://whitehouse.gov/news/releases/2004/11/20041110-9.html.

23. Exodus 5:1; 24:10; 32:27; 34:23; Joshua 7:13; Judges 4:6; 1 Samuel 1:17; Ezra 6:22; Psalm 69:6; Isaiah 37:21; Matthew 15:31; Luke 1:68; and 191 other references.

24. Deuteronomy 32:10.

25. Zechariah 2:8.

26. Surahs 36; 38;50; 68, etc.

27. Surah 27.

28. Sahih Bukhari, IV, 516; Muslim I, 462.

29. Bukhari IV, 509.

30. Ibid., II:245.

31. Muslim I, 863.

32. Bukhari, 1:812-15; VII:362-63.

33. Ibid., II:443.

34. Ibid., I:28, 301; II:161.

35. FinalCall.com, 11/14/2001.

36. Ibid.

37. Merrill Simon, *Jerry Falwell and the Jews* (Middle Village, NY: Jonathan David Publisher, Inc., 1984).

38. CBS, *60 Minutes*, October 6, 2002.

39. MSNBC Nightly News www.msnbc.com/news/65907.asp.

40. "Muslim Phobic No More," Editorial, *Christianity Today*, December 9, 2002, p 28.

41. Matthew 7:13-14.

42. Proverbs 16:25.

43. Helen Louise Herndon, *Christian Research Journal*, vol. 25, no. 1 (2002).

44. Surahs 2:255; 4:171; 6:102; 10:69-70, etc.

45. Surah 5:73.

46. Surah 4:171, etc.

47. John 3:16-17.

48. Surah 2:106; 16:101.

49. Malachi 3:6, etc.

50. Psalm 119:89, etc.

51. Austin Flannery, O.P., Gen. Ed., V*atican Council II: The Conciliar and Post Conciliar Documents* (Northport, NY: Costello Publishing Company, 1988), Vol 1, 367.

52. *Le Monde,* April 25, 1974.

7—HATRED'S PEACE

WHEN MUHAMMAD DIED in A.D. 632 (poisoned in revenge by the widow of a man he had murdered), much of Arabia, having been forced into this new "faith" by the sword, tried to defect, thinking they could abandon Islam. The prophet responsible for their subjugation was dead, and with his passing had died any loyalty they had been forced to profess to this oppressive religion. They had either forgotten or no longer feared the decree Muhammad had passed on from Allah: "Whoever relinquishes his faith, kill him!"

During the next two years (A.D. 630-32), in obedience to Allah's command to behead apostates, Muhammad's successor and father-in-law, Abu Bakr, and loyal Muslim warriors, killed about seventy thousand former Muslims. Obedient to Muhammad's command and example, Abu Bakr sent forth his troops: "Command them [apostates] to re-embrace Islam; but if they refuse, do not spare any one of them. Burn them with fire and kill them with force and take the women as prisoners."[1]

These were all Arabs killed by Arabs, former Muslims killed by Muslims, and their slaughter has come down in history as the "Wars of Apostasy." Thus Arabia was forced back into Islam and remains its bulwark today.

Muhammad's decree that apostates must be killed is still foundational to Islam. And even if one was never a Muslim, the Qur'an declares that pagans (the label attached to all non-Muslims except Christians and Jews, who are "people of the book") who refuse the opportunity offered them to submit to Islam must be killed. Though certainly not adhered to in most cases of terrorism (nor in Islam's long, violent history), the offer of conversion or death is supposed to be followed whenever possible, even in the West.

The Armanious family—father, mother, and two young daughters, were stabbed and their throats slit in mid-January 2005 in their home in New Jersey. The father, a Coptic Christian immigrant from Egypt, had debated with Muslims on a Middle East internet chat room and had not backed down from their threats: "You'd better stop this, or we're going to track you down…and kill you!" Yes, it can happen even here in the United States. Doubt has been cast upon whether this was a Muslim revenge killing—but that all four throats were slit in the same manner is hard to ignore.

A DELIBERATE COVER-UP

The police refused to see any "religious motive" in the murders, in spite of the repeated threats from Muslims and the fact that Jersey City has a history of Islamic violence against American citizens. As in this instance, so in many similar cases across the country, the authorities have seemed to be more concerned that they avoid offending Muslims than in finding the murderers.

The 1990 murder of Israeli Knesset member Rabbi Meir Kahane in Manhattan by Egyptian terrorist El Sayyid A. Nosair was at first attributed by police to a prescription drug that Nosair was taking for depression. Although Nosair shot Kahane in the head, he was acquitted of murder and was found guilty only of illegal possession of a firearm. The 2002 deliberate crash of a small plane into a Tampa high-rise by a bin Laden sympathizer was blamed on the acne drug Accutane. In the 2003 murder and near-beheading of an Israeli by a Saudi Arabian, Houston police were unable to find "any evidence" of a religious motive. Similarly, the 1990 deliberate crash of EgyptAir flight 990 (killing 217) by a co-pilot who wrenched the controls and dove it into the ocean while praising Allah was left unexplained by the U.S. National Transportation Safety Board. Canadian police refused to rate as a "hate crime" the murder of a Hasidic Jew by a cursing skinhead outside a kosher pizzeria in Toronto. Twin Towers included, the popular delusion must not be disturbed that "Islam is peace."

Serge Trifkovic reminds us of the complicity of Western governments in Islam's evil for the sake of avoiding offense:

> American citizens can be detained indefinitely [in Saudi Arabia] at the pleasure of their Saudi Muslim father who kidnapped them from their American mother. [As an example], this happened to Patricia Roush, whose daughters Alia and Aisha are now clad from head to toe in the black abaya.[3]

The Western world, oblivious to the seriousness of the challenge it faces, must awaken. To allow Muslims freedoms in the West that are denied to Westerners and even to their own citizens in Muslim nations is to encourage Islam in its goal of world domination. Avoiding offending the Muslim world at all cost is not the road to peace but to subjugation.

Within Saudi Arabia, "the practice of any religion besides Islam is as strictly prohibited now as it was in Muhammad's lifetime. While the Saudis continue to build mosques all over the world, thousands of Christians among the hundreds of thousands of foreign workers [in Saudi Arabia] from India, Europe, America and the Philippines must worship in secret, if at all. They are arrested, lashed, or deported for public display of their beliefs."[4] Yet the policy of suppressing truth continues. For example:

> In July 1977, an Englishman with a miniature camera was able to take photographs that shocked the world…the public execution in Jeddah of Princess Mishael bint Fahd bin Mohammed…and her boyfriend, Khalid Muhallah. She was shot six times in the head, he was beheaded. The photographs became part of Anthony Thomas' TV documentary, "Death of a Princess." This news threw the Saudis into a fit of rage, and Western governments hurried to suppress the showing of the film. In 1980, the Carter Administration strenuously opposed the program being shown on PBS.[5]

Truth is only a threat to those who hide behind lies—and truth *is* a threat to Islam. Tragically, Western religious and political leaders assist Muslims in their deceit and cover-up. And to what end? Surely closing our eyes and burying our heads in the sand of denial will not bring peace with an enemy for whom lies are a major weapon!

As it was at the beginning, so it is now: no retreat is allowed from Islam. It remains Islamic law that any Muslim who turns to any other religion must be beheaded. That penalty is still meted out unashamedly in public executions—or privately by one's family, where the primary responsibility lies. In Saudi Arabia, the executions take place before huge crowds in Riyadh's infamous "chop-chop square." For the Taliban, it was the new sport in unused soccer stadiums, which even the unwilling were forced to witness and to hide their disapproval for fear of their own lives. The Taliban were not fanatics but true Muslims, who attempted, like Muhammad, to force Islam on the unwilling.

Flogging (the record is four thousand lashes administered publicly in Saudi Arabia to an Egyptian) and amputation of limbs are used extensively as judicial punishments. Prisoners often receive no warning that they are about to be executed. They are taken to a public square, blindfolded, forced to kneel, and beheaded before the cheering onlookers.[6] This penalty was meted out recently to a father and son who had become followers of Christ. The number of beheadings in Saudi Arabia tripled from 59 in 1994 to 191 in 1995.[7]

Beheadings dropped off to between fifty and one hundred in 2002, and were about the same in 2003, although the exact number is difficult to obtain. Saudi Arabia is the only country that officially practices beheadings for apostasy, which marks it as the most Islamic country in the world. The Western world is shocked when Muslim terrorists behead their victims, yet pays no attention to the same thing being practiced by the Saudi government. In fact, both practices are in obedience to the teachings of Islam and the example of Muhammad. Defending the practice, Tarik Allagany, information supervisor at the Saudi Arabian embassy in Washington, D.C., explained that the beheadings of three men early in January 2002 were "not because of their homosexuality but because they had practiced it upon young boys. 'I would guess there's sodomy going on daily in Saudi Arabia…but we don't have executions for it all the time,' he said."[8]

ISLAMIC CULTIVATION OF HATRED

By decree from Muhammad, still honored as Islamic law, no Jew may enter Saudi Arabia. That oppressive state has accomplished what Hitler only dreamed of—a Jew-free society—carrying on what Muhammad created thirteen centuries earlier. Is this Nazism resurrected? No, this is Islam as it was long before Hitler. Remember, Muhammad decreed that all Jews in the entire world must be killed before any Muslims who have died can be resurrected and before anyone except *jihad* martyrs can enter Paradise.

To that end, from earliest childhood, Muslims in Saudi Arabia, as in other Muslim countries, are taught to hate Jews with a passion. On October 1, 2004, Saudi Arabia's IQRA TV Channel conducted "man on the street" interviews. Here are some of the questions and answers proudly televised. They clearly reveal the effect of foundational Islamic beliefs passed down from Muhammad and of supporting anti-Jewish propaganda that constantly bombards Muslims worldwide, especially in the Middle East, day and night:

> *Interviewer:* "Would you, as a human being, be willing to shake hands with a Jew?"
>
> *Respondent 2*: "No, because the Jews are eternal enemies. The murderous Jews violate all agreements [and are] full of hatred towards me."
>
> *Interviewer:* "Would you refuse to shake hands with a Jew?"
>
> *Respondent 4:* "Of course, so I wouldn't have to consider amputating my hand afterwards."
>
> *Interviewer:* "If a child asks you, 'who are the Jews?' what would you answer?"

Respondent 5: "The enemies of Allah and his prophet."

Respondent 6: "The Jew is the occupier of our lands."

Respondent 7: "The murderers of prophets—our eternal enemies, of course."

Respondent 8: "If only [the Muslims] declared Jihad…they would turn them [the Jews] into rotten carcasses under their feet."[9]

On January 7, 2005, Sheik Ibrahim Madiras declared in his weekly sermon, which is broadcast over Palestinian Authority television: "The Jews are Jews. Their character and custom are the corruption and destruction of this land. We keep warning you: Jews are a cancer that spreads inside the body of the Islamic and Arab nation…. We want to return to the 1948 [pre-Israel] borders…we can't forget and will never forgive…Britain and all governments who assisted that state [Israel] to be established on this land…a false state…." He went on to declare that America and Israel were to blame for the tsunami that killed more than two hundred sixty-five thousand in South East Asia and that "America, today, is the sponsor of terror on this land [Palestine]. America…is on the way to the abyss [hell]."[10] Al-Jazeera television news, popular in Muslim countries, seriously offered several theories including the charge that the U.S. government knew of the tsunami disaster ahead of time but deliberately warned no one, or that an atomic bomb was detonated underwater by Israel and/or the United States.[11]

SAUDI ARABIA: MODEL OF TRUE ISLAM

There is no need to question or debate the true nature of Islam. One need only look to Saudi Arabia's feudal kingdom, where daily life reveals the truth about this vicious and hateful religion. This is where Islam began, where its holiest sites are, and where it is still practiced in accordance with the Qur'an and Muhammad's example as recorded in the *hadith*. Any Muslim may have four wives, beat them for disobeying his demands, and divorce them by simply repeating three times, "I divorce you." Ibn Saud, founder of Saudi Arabia (who had been sponsored by Britain in the creation of this new state), had between two hundred and three hundred wives, but in obedience to Islam, he never, so far as we know, had more than four at a time. No wonder the extended royal family now consists of many thousands who live like princes and princesses!

Saleh al-Sayeri, a sixty-four-year-old Saudi businessman who lives in the desert five hundred miles west of Riyadh and was forced into his first marriage at age fourteen, has married fifty-eight women in fifty years and has forgotten the names of most of them. He remembers ten sons and twenty-five daughters. He has paid out in wedding expenses and divorce settlements more than $1.6 million. He keeps each wife in a separate villa and sometimes even in a different town to keep the peace, and he assures each that she's his favorite. Al-Sayeri has married women from about thirty tribes. "As a leader of a tribe, I can't marry just anybody," he said. His latest marriage was to a fourteen-year-old girl, which he calls "the perfect age." There were ten thousand guests. Each divorce is documented with court-issued papers that follow a simple declaration to a wife: "You are divorced." Al-Sayeri intends to keep on marrying until the number of wives he has acquired equals the number of years he has lived—all perfectly acceptable in Islam.[12]

Only Muslims may be citizens of Saudi Arabia. There is no distinction between church and state. Religious law rules the entire country. No non-Muslim place of worship may be built. The practice of any religion except Islam is forbidden. No one would dare to carry a Bible openly on the street. Even a secret Bible study in one's home could mean prison or expulsion from the country for any foreigner. For a Muslim who had converted, it would mean death.

There are none of the freedoms Western democracies hold dear: freedom of speech, of the media, of the press, of conscience, of religion, of genuine vote, etc. And so it would be in America, Europe, and every other country if Muslims could accomplish Allah's command to take over the world by force. Then there would be "peace" everywhere—Islam's peace.

This is not fanaticism, but genuine Islam as Muhammad and his successors established and practiced it and from which no Muslim has the authority to diverge. Do not be deceived: this would be life in every country in the world if Muslim fundamentalists could impose *sharia* (Islamic law according to the Qur'an and the teachings and example of Muhammad) as they have been able to do in Iran, Saudi Arabia, Sudan, in parts of Nigeria, and Indonesia, and as the Taliban did when it was in power in Afghanistan—and as it is practiced by Muslim terrorists wherever they are able.

Islam cannot thrive where there is true freedom. Therefore, Muslim regimes have been adamantly opposed to the United States establishing democracy in Afghanistan and Iraq. Freedom might spread and put an end to their tyranny—and to Islam as well. The hatred of democracy is seen in the fierceness with which the terrorists attempted to prevent Iraqi citizens from voting in the first free elections in that country and have continued their murders since. Most terrorists in Iraq are foreigners who have infiltrated from other Muslim countries. These are Muslims killing fellow Muslims for cooperating with the hated West in establishing democracy. Yet Muslim leaders had no complaints against Saddam Hussein's murderous regime, and the masses outside of Iraq (not within) praised him.

A VERY SERIOUS PROBLEM

Democratic elections, however, do not guarantee democracy for Iraq indefinitely into the future. They do not change Iraq into a secular country—and here we face a very serious problem for which there may be no solution if America is to give the Iraqis the promised autonomy, which she must. Sixty percent of Iraqis are Shi'ite Muslims. Iraq's leading Shi'a cleric, Grand Ayatollah Ali al-Sistani's United Iraqi Alliance (UIA) won 140 seats in the 275-member National Assembly—but still far short of the two-thirds majority needed to elect a president. The Kurds from the north won 75 seats, which gives them a powerful position. Thankfully, the UIA will have to cooperate with the Kurds to form a coalition and elect a president, who will then give a mandate to the prime minister.

It is not clear whether other measures can be decided by a simple majority vote, in which case the UIA would have almost a free hand in running the country. While Sistani (as almost every other Iraqi politician) has gone on record saying that he does not favor *sharia*, people say lots of things for political reasons at a particular time and then change their minds.

One of the most powerful groups within the UIA is the Supreme Council for the Islamic Revolution in Iraq (SCIRI), an Iran-backed resistance group that was formed in Tehran, Iran, in 1982. It is now Iraq's largest and best-organized political organization. They have called for *sharia* law to be imposed. It would be a severe blow to discover that American blood had been shed to replace Saddam Hussein with a religious dictator who could be as bad or worse.

British army officers have reports of illegal *sharia* law courts operating in mosques and claim that groups of militia men turned politicians are attempting to enforce strict religious codes. It is a dangerous situation!

A university student who was beaten for holding his girlfriend's hand in public said, "I don't want a radical system to rule Iraq like in Iran; it would be a disaster. We would have ended up with different faces of the same coin, from dictatorship to religious rule."

WITH FRIENDS LIKE THIS...

It is considered honorable for a Muslim to lie to non-Muslims in order to promote or defend his faith. The Saudi embassy in Washington, D.C., has repeatedly assured the United States that its country is not funding any suspected terrorist groups. Yet in documents captured by Israeli forces, Saudi officials promise that they will continue to support Palestinian terrorism against Israel.[13] Western intelligence has verified that the Saudi government has funded terrorist organizations such as Osama bin Laden's Al Qaeda, the PLO, Hamas, Hizballah, and others. Palestinian terrorism alone was supported with more than $4 billion between 1998 and 2003.

In January 2002, Prince Naif, Saudi Minister of the Interior, declared that Saudi Arabia would pay $5,333 to each member of a martyr's family. King Fahd Ibn Abd Al-Aziz has promised to support one thousand families of Palestinian "martyrs." There was certainly no expected reduction in Palestinian terrorism against Israel as the "peace process" progressed! Every Saudi citizen is encouraged to help in this effort with donations to the Al-Quds Intifada Fund.[14] Sheik Saad Al-Buraik, prominent Saudi government cleric, hosted a two-day telethon that raised $109 million from Saudi viewers for the families of Palestinian "martyrs." In a Riyadh government mosque in April 2002, Al-Buraik declared:

> I am against America until this life ends.... She is the root of all evils and wickedness on earth.... Muslim brothers in Palestine, do not have any mercy, neither compassion on the Jews.... Their women are yours to take.... Allah made them yours...wage jihad...pillage them.[15]

Yet Saudi Arabia poses as our partner in the fight against terrorism! After a yearlong study of more than two hundred original documents published in Saudi Arabia and distributed through mosques in the United States, the human rights group, Freedom House, in an eighty-nine-page report declared that Saudi Arabia is spreading "hate propaganda." The literature incites ordinary Muslims attending mosques "to hate Christians and Jews and to kill any Muslim who converts to another religion...to behave [in the United States] as if one is on a mission behind enemy lines."

In a classic case of speaking out of both sides of its mouth, Saudi Arabia through Abdulmohsen Alyas, spokesperson for the Saudi embassy in Washington, D.C., declared, "Saudi Arabia condemns extremism or hateful expression among people anywhere in the world." Apparently, hating and killing Christians and Jews in the name of Allah is not viewed as extremism or hateful. In fact, it is the obligation Islam lays upon every true Muslim.[16]

HUMAN RIGHTS?

The Western world is genuinely concerned about individual freedom. Reflecting that concern, on December 10, 1948, after the defeat of Fascist regimes in Nazi Germany and Japan, and in the face of Arab threats to annihilate Israel, "The Universal Declaration of Human Rights" was adopted as UN Resolution 217. The basic freedoms it advocated, however, are diametrically opposed by Islam. Yet Saudi Arabia and other Muslim countries remain in the United Nations, professing freedoms that Muslims enjoy in the West but won't allow in their own countries. Thirty-two years later, while accusing democratic Israel of being "a Fascist regime," Muslims showed the world the "freedoms" they advocate by adopting their own declaration.

"The Universal Islamic Declaration of Human Rights" was proudly announced at the International Conference on the Prophet Muhammad and his Message held in London in April of 1980 and adopted by Muslim nations on September 19, 1981. Incredibly, it declares, "Islam gave to mankind an ideal code of human rights fourteen centuries ago...based on the Qur'an and the Sunnah [the teachings and example of Muhammad]...." It held up *sharia* (Islamic law) as the ideal guarantee of human freedom! True Muslims really mean this and intend to force this "freedom" on the rest of the world!

How can a meaningful and equitable peace, or even a basic understanding, be arrived at with those who equate *sharia* with freedom? Islam and the West speak different languages. Some of the words sound the same, but the meaning is obviously completely foreign.

Fifteen of the nineteen northern states of Nigeria have adopted *sharia*. As a result, thousands of Christians have been killed and hundreds of Christian churches destroyed. In 1983, the government of Sudan in Khartoum in the north imposed *sharia* on the entire country. As a result primarily of imposing Islam (and the fact that oil and gas are found in the south), more than two million non-Muslims in the south have been killed and thousands tortured or sold into slavery. There is an active slave market in the Muslim world today on which Qaddafi buys slaves for fifteen dollars each.

Most of this death and oppression is an attempt to force all of Sudan into Islam—as one more step toward the goal of taking the entire world for Allah.

More than five thousand churches have been burned down in Indonesia (the largest Muslim nation in the world), about three thousand in the last three years, and thousands of Christians have been killed and many forced into Islam under threat of death. Legislation enacted in 2002, called "Letter of Decision No. 137," allows churches in West Jakarta to be closed down at the whim of the local community, a rule designed for Muslims to exploit. This is "Islamic Human Rights."

Muslims call "human rights" and "personal freedom" as advocated in the West "the most perilous [and] repugnant" threat facing the world. They justify Islam as the true guardian of human rights by ignoring the oppression and terror created by enforcing Islam and pointing to the evils produced by Western "freedom":

> America…as the leading superpower and the sole power broker in the world…is leading…this onslaught [against Islam] under the slogans of Democracy, Pluralism, Human Rights and Market Economy. The most perilous of these slogans is that of Human Rights…one of the cornerstones of her foreign policy. She utilizes this slogan as a pretext to interfere in other countries' affairs [and] deems Human Rights as a law that must be abided by….
>
> Personal freedom is the most repugnant aspect of these freedoms, for according to them, it means that man is free to choose the behavior he likes, such as being homosexual or fornicating or taking intoxicants…thus debauchery is a moral constitution amongst the followers of this ideology.[17]

In contrast to Allah and the Qur'an, the God of the Bible, who calls Himself "the God of Israel," gave man moral freedom to act responsibly without coercion. There is no way that man could truly love, trust, and believe in God and receive the free gift of salvation He provides and offers in Christ, without the freedom to reject Him and the love and salvation He desires for all mankind to receive. The God of the Bible does not force anyone to do His will. He desires willing obedience that comes from the heart—not hypocrisy that has been forced by threats to deny in visible life what one practices in secret or in the imagination.

The God of the Bible, in giving man freedom of choice, does not encourage men to sin, much less is that freedom a license for evil. On the contrary, He prohibits all sin in the moral law that He has written in every human conscience.[18] He has also ordained that governments should be His ministers of righteousness enforcing morality to keep order in the world.[19] Yet God himself cannot force man to love in his heart what His laws require in outward behavior. He wants our hearts, but we must willingly give them to Him. When Christ is acknowledged as Lord and believed on and received as Savior, that transformation takes place *within,* out of gratitude and love for the One who paid the full penalty for our sins and delivered us from the judgment we deserve.

Jesus declared that to lust in the heart is the same as committing the sin.[20] That condemnation applies to wealthy Muslim businessmen or members of the royal family who, when visiting the West from Saudi Arabia or other strict Muslim countries, enjoy all the sins that they profess to shun and condemn when at home. Christ's words equally condemn the immorality of Westerners, including those who call themselves Christians with their lips but deny Christ in their behavior.

ISLAM'S VICIOUS RECORD

One need only look at the record of Islam to see the fruit of "forced morality." There are more revolutions, assassinations, and terrorist acts in Muslim countries, Muslim against Muslim, than in all the rest of the world combined. During the 1940s, a young Yasser Arafat, getting his training in terrorism, was a zealous member of Amin al-Husseini's Qassamite group, which fought the rival Arab Nashashibi family (all "good" Muslims) in a blood feud. Even in their unified effort to destroy Israel in 1947 and 1948, before it could be born, Muslims were at odds with one another. Islam's "peace" was unable to unite them. "The Mufti…wished to maintain in his own hands effective control over all forces in Palestine and their activities. The Arab League was by no means inclined to recognize the Mufti as 'the sole authority.' As soon as the Mufti realized that, he began to act independently, appointing his own men as commanders in various areas of the country, who competed with commanders appointed by the Arab League."[21]

Syria attacked its Muslim neighbor, Jordan, on April 13, 1957. On June 10, 1958, at Jordan's request, two thousand British paratroopers (non-Muslim "pagans" to the rescue again!) landed in Amman to protect King Hussein from threats by Iraq and Egypt. In 1960, Jordan's prime minister and ten other officials were killed by a bomb planted by Nasser's agents and intended for the King. The president of Tunisia accused Nasser (at that time considered to be the leader of the Arab world) of sending secret agents to assassinate him. In 1979, Hussein's forces killed some two thousand PLO guerrillas and thousands of Palestinian civilians in driving the PLO into Lebanon. Ayatollah Khomeini, who took over Iran in a bloody coup, was known to have plotted the overthrow of other Muslim nations, including the Persian Gulf states.

From 1948 to 1973 there were eighty revolutions in the Islamic world, thirty of them successful, including the murder of twenty-two heads of state. King Abdullah Ibn Hussein bin Talal was assassinated in Jerusalem in 1951 by a Palestinian. His grandson, King Hussein I, who succeeded him, escaped a number of assassination attempts. Saudi Arabia's King Faisal was shot to death by his nephew. Muslims attempted to kill Egypt's Nasser, and the Muslim Brotherhood succeeded in assassinating his successor, Anwar Sadat—a deed that received Arafat's public applause. In his turn, Sadat's successor, Hosni Mubarak (commander of the Egyptian Air Force during the 1973 Yom Kippur War), has narrowly escaped a number of attempted assassinations.

In 1971, East Pakistan rebelled against West Pakistan (both Muslim states) and became Bangladesh. In 1979, a dissident group of Muslims seized the Holy Mosque in Mecca with the Ka'aba in its center. The Saudi National guard was unable to cope with the situation, so the Saudis turned to the West for help. Of course, only Muslims are allowed in Mecca, necessitating the disguise of the non-Muslim rescue team, who were all dressed in Saudi uniforms. Once again it was Muslim fighting and killing Muslim in the promotion of this peaceful religion—with "pagans" having to come to the rescue.

In February 1982, Syrian president Hafez Assad sent tanks and troops into the beautiful Syrian city of Hama, leveling it to rubble and killing as many as twenty-five thousand civilians while at the same time criticizing alleged Israeli mistreatment of Palestinians. In 1983, Arafat was almost unseated by a rebellion against him (supported by Syrian president Assad and Libyan leader Muammar Qaddafi) within his own Fatah organization, which actually ran the PLO. Further examples could be multiplied, and some will be given. This is the "peace" Islam has produced from the beginning!

SPREADING ISLAM'S "PEACE"

Having reestablished Islam in Arabia through the Wars of Apostasy, Abu Bakr and succeeding Caliphs spread it swiftly by brutal conquest. Millions were killed by the conquering *jihadists*. With stunning swiftness and overwhelming ferocity, Islam's insatiable sword created an unprecedented empire— "…more rapid than the Roman, more lasting than the Mongol, [in] the most amazing feat in military history,"[22] conquering country after country. From France all the way to China, they compelled the unwilling to submit to the new paganism or death. Muslims assure us that they only fight "defensive" wars. Really? All the way to China?

That deceit is exposed by the Qur'an's more than one hundred verses commanding Muslims to spread Islam with the sword. The following are a small sample:

> To him who fighteth in the cause of Allah—whether he is slain or gets victory—soon shall We give him a reward of [great] value. (Surah 4:74)
> Then, when the sacred months have passed, slay the idolaters wherever ye find them…. But if they repent and establish worship

[of Allah] and pay the poor-due [tax], then leave their way free [in brutal, humiliating submission under Muslim rule]. (Surah 9:5)

Fight against such of those who have been given the Scripture [Bible] as believe not in Allah nor the Last Day…until they pay the tribute readily, being brought low. (Surah 9:29)

Therefore, when ye meet the Unbelievers [in battle], smite at their necks…when ye have thoroughly subdued them, bind a bond firmly [on them]…those who are slain in the way of Allah, He will never let their deeds be lost. (47:4)

Truly Allah loves those who fight in His Cause in battle array….(61:4)

He it is Who sent His Messenger with the guidance and the true religion, that He may make it overcome the religions, all of them, though the polytheists may be averse. (61:9)

Giving early notice of the mayhem and murder that Islam would create on this troubled earth—i.e., hatred's "peace"—three of the four "rightly guided Caliphs" were assassinated by fellow Muslims. Only Abu Bakr was not. (Try to imagine Christ's apostles murdering one another!)

Abu Bakr was succeeded as Caliph by Umar Abu Hafsa. His armies secured all of Arabia. Fearless in battle, Muslim warriors struck terror into their enemies. Their reckless bravery was the secret of their unparalleled success. These devout Muslims actually wanted to die. Archaeologists have uncovered inscriptions dating back to this time that say, "Please, Allah, let me die in battle!" To die as a "martyr" in *jihad* is the only way a Muslim may be certain of Paradise. And this is the motive that drives today's suicide bombers.

Yet neither the ancient "martyrs" nor today's "suicide bombers" realize that, in fact, they cannot be certain of Paradise and reward. Abu Bakr, Muhammad's first successor, fought loyally in *jihad*, but he to whom the Prophet had personally promised Paradise lamented, "I have no trust concerning Allah's schemes, even if one of my feet is inside paradise, who can determine which deed is acceptable and which is not. You do all you can do, and the accountability is with Allah. You ask him for acceptance."[23]

A verse in the Qur'an refers to those who are "afraid because they are about to return to their Lord [i.e., to Allah in death or on the last day].[24] His favorite wife, Aisha, asked Muhammad to explain this verse: "O, apostle of God, is the one who is afraid of Allah the one who commits adultery, steals, drinks wine, thus he is afraid of punishment?" Muhammad gave her an answer that explains why Abu Bakr, her father, had no assurance of getting to Paradise: "No...he is the one who prays, fasts, and gives alms, thus he is afraid that Allah may not accept these things from him."[25]

In contrast, Christ promised, "He that heareth [i.e., believes and acts upon] my word, and believeth on him that sent me, hath everlasting life, and shall not come into condemnation; but is passed from death unto life."[26] "I am the good shepherd...[that] giveth his life for the sheep...and I give unto them [my sheep] eternal life; and they shall never perish."[27] John the Apostle declared to all Christians, "These things have I written unto you that believe on the name of the Son of God; that ye may know that ye have eternal life...."[28] The Christian's salvation is not dependent upon whether God would accept his good deeds (none of which are acceptable to salvation), but is assured by Christ's payment in His death and resurrection of the full penalty for the sins of the world.

Hoping to buy their way into Paradise, Islam's *jihad* warriors took Damascus in 635, Antioch in 636, in 638, Syria in 640, and Egypt and Persia in 641. Thousands were massacred. Entire cities were put to the sword, among them Behnesa, Fayum, Nikiu and Aboit in Egypt, Tripoli in North Africa, and Euchaita in Armenia. Carthage was razed to the ground. This was the story of Islam's peace as it progressed and spread!

CHAMPIONS OF "PEACE" KILL ONE ANOTHER

In 644, Umar, Abu Bakr's successor, was murdered by a Muslim and succeeded by Uthman ibn Affan. This third Caliph, a son-in-law of Muhammad (Abu Bakr had been Muhammad's father-in-law), consolidated and expanded the growing Islamic empire. As already noted, he standardized the Qur'an, burning all rival copies over protests of those still alive who remembered different readings and verses that were missing. The protesters included Aisha (Abu Bakr's daughter), one of perhaps fifteen wives the prophet had simultaneously by special dispensation of Allah and now his widow, forbidden (as a special favor of Allah to Muhammad) to remarry. Betrothed to her when she was six years of age, Muhammad had consummated the marriage when Aisha was only nine and still playing with dolls.

Uthman, too, was murdered by a rival Muslim faction. Prevented from being buried in a Muslim cemetery, he was, ironically, buried at night by friends in a *Jewish* cemetery.

The fourth and last of the "rightly guided" Caliphs was Ali ibn Abi Talib, Muhammad's cousin and another son-in-law, who, the prophet had asserted, was "preserved from error and sin in his actions and sayings." Accused of complicity in Uthman's murder (if not one of the killers, he at least protected and joined forces with them), he never fully established his rule from Damascus. Aisha supported a rebellion against him, resulting in the Battle of the Camel, in which twelve thousand Muslims were killed by other Muslims. Ali won, but his troubles only increased.

Within a very few years after Muhammad's murder, more than one hundred thousand Muslims had been killed in battle or were likewise murdered by fellow Muslims. Muhammad's closest companions and staunchest disciples (some of whom he had praised as perfect Muslims and to whom he had promised Paradise without martyrdom) fought each other for his wealth and power. Battles raged over who would be the next leader of the growing but fiercely divided "peaceful" religion of Islam.

Muhammad's chief enemy from Mecca, Abu Sufyan, had "converted" to Islam to keep from being beheaded. He had never, however, become a true believer, as everyone well knew—mere confession with the lips to save one's life was accepted by Muhammad as sufficient to make one a Muslim. His son, Mu'awiyah, was Ali's mortal enemy in a bitter rivalry for leadership. After Ali had taken the caliphate, a number of skirmishes between their forces, in which many died, led to the battle of Siffin.

Ali had hated Abu Bakr and had demanded his share of Muhammad's wealth and property, but Abu Bakr had refused. Eventually Abu Bakr's successor, Umar, gave in to Ali's demands and went against Muhammad's command not to distribute his wealth to family members. When Ali finally succeeded Uthman to become the fourth "rightly guided" Caliph, he found himself besieged by Muslims who resented his leadership because of his part in Uthman's murder.

If he was to keep control of Islam, Ali had to deal with the growing opposition. Eventually, from his strongholds in Basra and Kufa, Iraq, Ali and his men moved against Mu'awiyah. Before a truce was finally called, in the battle at Siffin, according to some estimates, tens of thousands of Muslims were slaughtered by fellow Muslims.

Ali, the last of the "rightly guided Caliphs," was murdered during morning prayers in 661 in a mosque in Kufa, Iraq, and was buried in Najaf, Iraq. The location of Ali's mausoleum and shrine there (destroyed several times by rival Muslims, then rebuilt each time) makes Najaf the center of wealth (its treasures are worth an estimated $1 billion) and religious power in Iraq.

DIVISION BETWEEN SHI'ITES AND SUNNIS

Muslims who regard the murdered Ali and his sons as the rightful successors to Muhammad are known as Shi'ites (the majority in Iran and Iraq); the others are called Sunnis and comprise the far greater majority elsewhere. Saddam Hussein and his fellow Sunnis, though the minority in Iraq, ruled and oppressed the Shi'ite majority, murdering untold hundreds of thousands, until his ouster by coalition forces in 2003. These two Muslim factions have long demonstrated that "Islam is peace" by fighting one another, as in the eight-year war (1980-1988) between Iran and Iraq, when more than one million combatants were killed. The Imam Ali mosque in Najaf (the scene of fierce fighting during the Iraq war in 2004) is the holiest shrine to the world's one hundred fifty million Shi'ite Muslims.

Fierce wars between rival Muslims were fought from the very beginning: Quraish against Bedouin Muslims, Umayyads of Medina against the Hashemite followers of Ali, etc. One of Ali's sons, Husayn ibn-Ali, intended to establish "true Islam" from Kufah in Iraq, but he and most of his family were killed by rival Muslims in 680. Mecca was besieged by troops of Yezid, an Umayyad; the Ka'aba (later restored) was burned to the ground, its Black Stone split into three pieces. Mecca was finally retaken in 692 by Abd al-Malik (who in 691 had built the Dome of the Rock in Jerusalem to replace the Ka'aba). He united Muslims once again by force, and Islam continued its conquests.

The Umayyad Caliphate ruled the Muslim world from 661 to 749, when all of the Umayyads were murdered by the rival Abbasids except for one survivor, Abd-al-Rahman, who fled to Spain, where he established an independent Caliphate. Thus began the Abbasid Caliphate, which lasted, in spite of intrigue, assassinations, and uprisings, until 1058.

The betrayal and murder of Muslims at the hands of their fellows continues to this day. Scarcely a Muslim regime is not ruled by a dictator who seized power from other Muslims, as in Syria and Iraq. The twelve-year revolution in Algeria has cost one hundred thousand lives. In Afghanistan, rival Muslim warlords still fight one another. "Infidels" had to intervene there, as in the Gulf. This is Allah's peace in the world of Islam! The God of the Bible alone can deliver us—but the Western world has thrown Him out of its schools and public institutions and will not allow Him any voice in its politics. That is a choice that the true God allows in this life—but after death comes judgment.[29]

THE BLOODIEST EMPIRE IN HISTORY

In 712, Muslim raiders under Muhammad Qasun began the invasion of India, demolishing temples and palaces and massacring entire cities. As in Constantinople, where the streets ran with blood, the slaughter went on for three days in India's port city of Debal. "The massacres perpetrated by Muslims in India are unparalleled in history, bigger in sheer numbers than the Holocaust...."[30] Everyone has heard of the Taj Mahal, but few remember that it was built by a Muslim mogul with twenty thousand slave laborers. And thus Islam spread the "peace" that today's Muslim terrorists dream of bringing to the entire world!

Muslim conquests, involving multiple massacres of literally millions, continued for more than thirteen hundred years. The Abbasid dynasty ruled until 1258, and under them the Islamic empire reached its zenith of power, prosperity, and learning. Caesarea surrendered under agreement that its two thousand knights would be spared. Once disarmed, they were massacred like the Jews of Yathrib. Antioch fell, with sixteen thousand Christians killed and one hundred thousand sold into slavery.

In Spain (where Islam was said to be the most humane), the garrison of Muez was slaughtered in 920; Pamplona was put to the sword in 923; then followed Cordova, Zaragoza, and Mereda, with all adult males killed and women and children enslaved. The Jews of Granada were butchered in 1066, thirty-four years after six thousand Jews had been slaughtered in Fez, Morocco. In 1146, Islamic Fez was decimated by another faction of Muslims, the Almohads, who conquered much of North Africa after annihilating the Almoravides (also Muslims), with about one hundred thousand massacred there and another one hundred twenty thousand killed in Marrakesh. Similar bloodbaths of Muslim against Muslim continued to occur. (We have been able to cite only the tip of the iceberg.) Such violence is the inevitable fruit of Islam, as its thirteen-hundred-year history has repeatedly and consistently demonstrated. *Not one example can be given where Islam ever brought peace!*

The four-hundred-year rule of the Ottoman Turks, which ended in 1917, included kidnappings of young non-Muslim boys, who were forced to "convert" and serve for life as slave warriors in Muslim armed forces. Many desperate parents mutilated their children to make them undesirable. Being Greek, Armenian, Serbian, or any other non-Muslim under Ottoman rule, was to live in daily fear of murder, rape, torture, and general genocide. To this day, Serbs and Bulgarians loathe Turks and Bosnian Muslims.

When Sultan Murad III died, his son Muhammad had all nineteen of his brothers murdered and the seven of his father's concubines who were pregnant sewn into sacks and thrown into the Bosphorus. All three hundred women in Murad IV's harem met the same fate at the hands of his successor when he, like so many other Muslim leaders, was murdered by fellow Muslims—all in the interest of establishing "peace" the Muslim way.

SLAUGHTER OF CHRISTIANS

Several volumes would be required even to begin to recite the brutality of the Islamic conquests that provide an essential background to today's claims that "Islam is peace." However, we can cite only a few examples. "The Christians of Damascus were killed or sold into slavery, and their churches burned to the ground. The Sultan Baibars...had all the population decapitated when they did surrender.... He sent a troop to destroy the Christian village of Qara [near] Damascus.... The adult inhabitants were massacred and the children enslaved. When the Christians from Acre sent a deputation to ask to be allowed to bury the dead, he roughly refused, saying that if they wished for martyrs' corpses they would find them at home. To carry out his threat he marched down to the coast and slaughtered every Christian that fell into his hands."[31]

In 1400, the infamous Tamerlane (Timur the Lame) "devastated the country in and around Tifflis. In 1403 he...destroyed 700 large villages and minor towns, massacring the inhabitants and razing to the ground all the Christian churches.... Under the pretext that the hundred thousand Hindu prisoners presented a grave risk to his army, Tamerlane ordered their execution in cold blood...and had victory pillars built from the severed heads....Tamerlane systematically destroyed the Christians, and as a result the Nestorians and Jacobites of Mesopotamia have never recovered. At Sivas, 4,000 Christians were buried alive; at Tus there were 10,000 victims. Historians estimate the number of dead at Saray to be 100,000; at Baghdad 90,000; at Isfahan 70,000."[32] This is hardly a tiny fraction of the slaughter.

As horrible as it was, the persecution of Jews in Roman Catholic Europe was mild compared with what Ottoman Christians and Jews endured for four centuries. The slaughter included more than one million Armenians in the last decades of the nineteenth and first of the twentieth centuries, as well as many thousands of Jews, Greeks, Syrians, Lebanese, and others. Tragically, the oppression and bloodshed were often condoned and even encouraged by Western powers, particularly England and at times America. In the great 1915 massacre, "Turkish women were given the dagger to give the final stab to dying Armenians in order to gain credit [with] Allah for having killed a Christian."[33]

The destruction of Christian Smyrna (leaving nothing but the Turkish/Muslim suburb) in September of 1922, with Mustapha Khemal's (Ataturk's) deliberate massacre of some two hundred thousand Armenian and Greek inhabitants, becomes even more despicable when we realize that English, American, Italian, and French battleships anchored in the harbor repelled fleeing victims who swam out to them for help.[34] As with today's appeasement of Islam, the Western powers didn't want to offend Turkey! In his "must-read" book, *The Blight of Asia,* George Horton, U.S. Consul in that doomed city and eyewitness to the unspeakable cruelty of Islam and of Western complicity, writes, "One of the keenest impressions which I brought away with me from Smyrna was a feeling of shame that I belonged to the human race."[35]

In its foreword, James W. Gerard, former U.S. Ambassador to Germany, describes Horton's book as "the whole story of the savage extermination of Christian civilization [by Muslims] throughout the length and breadth of the old Byzantine Empire...." Horton himself writes, "This process of extermination was carried on over a considerable period of time, with fixed purpose, with system, and with painstaking minute details; and it was accomplished with unspeakable cruelties, causing the destruction of a greater number of human beings than have suffered in any similar persecution since the coming of Christ."[36] Yet Islam continues to masquerade as a divine religion with peaceful intentions—and Western political and religious leaders, educators, and media, help to promote this deception to their own eventual destruction!

A NEW KIND OF THREAT

To our shame, this horror of Islamic brutality and intended world conquest to which the West has deliberately closed its eyes, is being swept under the carpet of political and religious appeasement. Those few who know the truth and the imminent danger, speak of it urgently and with passion. To their deep sorrow and frustration, they find it almost impossible to awaken Westerners to the historic facts and to the unchanging and present threat of Islam. It has invaded the West in seemingly benign form, professing "peace" for all. Most perplexing is the persistent claim of President Bush and other Western political and religious leaders that "Islam is peace"!

Confident that Nazi crimes, too, would soon slip from the world's memory, Hitler reportedly told his generals, "Go! Kill without mercy! Who today remembers the annihilation of the Armenians?" As the Western world refuses to acknowledge the victims of Islamic slaughter through the centuries, and either denies the Holocaust or is fed up with being reminded of it, so it continues to pretend that Islam is peace amid the ongoing butchery of our day.

The imams boldly preach *jihad* in the mosques, while the followers of Islam are determined to conquer under cover of the popular lie that Islam is as peaceful as any other religion—as though Baptists or Presbyterians might just as well be behind the spreading worldwide terrorism as Muslims! Late in 2002, Sheikh Muhammad bin Abdul Rahman al-Arifi, imam of the mosque of King Fahd Defense Academy in Saudi Arabia, declared: "We will control the land of the Vatican; we will control Rome and introduce Islam in it. Yes, the Christians…will pay us *jiziya* [poll tax paid by non-Muslims as *dhimmis*, under Muslim rule] in humiliation, or they will convert to Islam."[37]

This time the invasion is not with armies but with immigrants. As avowed Muslims, building their mosques and keeping themselves aloof from neighbors through Arabic/Islamic customs and religion that date back to the days of Muhammad, this new breed of Islamic "invaders" know in their hearts that Islam must inevitably conquer the world. If they fail in this quest, Muhammad was a false prophet and Allah a false deity—which no Muslim can admit without being marked for the death penalty prescribed for apostasy.

This new invasion army will use democratic processes to gain control in communities where immigration creates Muslim majorities. And when they are strong enough, inevitably *sharia* must follow. The very human rights that are denied in Muslim countries are being used to destroy the Western world that grants them.

Examples such as the following news report dated January 25, 2005, could be multiplied into thousands throughout the non-Islamic world:

> Sheik Omar Bakri Muhammad, a 46-year-old Syrian-born cleric [granted political asylum years ago by Britain], has urged young Muslim men all over the world to support the Iraq insurgency on the front line of "the global jihad," investigators say. He struck a similarly defiant tone this month at a rally attended by 500 people at a central London meeting hall, where a giant screen behind him showed images of the World Trade Center falling. "Allahu akbar!"—"Allah is the greatest"—some audience members shouted at the images.
>
> After eavesdropping for months on his nightly praise of the September 11 hijackers and of suicide bombings, Scotland Yard said last week that it was investigating Sheik Omar, the leader of Al Muhajiroun [which, interestingly, is Arabic for "the immigrants"] Britain's largest Muslim group, and officials are exploring whether they can deport him....
>
> On Sunday [January 23, 2005], the German police arrested a man suspected of being a member of Al Qaeda and charged him with recruiting men to carry out suicide bombings in Iraq. These arrests were part of an ongoing investigation in cooperation with the United States of recruitment and other terrorist activities in Europe....
>
> Italian investigators say several recruits from Italy carried out bombing attacks in Baghdad. Swiss officials say they are concerned that several militant clerics have openly urged men to become terrorists....
>
> Bohre Eddine Benvahia, the 33-year-old imam recently deported by France to Algeria, had urged young men in a working-class neighbourhood of L'Ariane, outside Nice, to join jihad, French intelligence officials said....

In raids in several German cities on January 12, the German police arrested 22 people suspected of being militant Muslims while recovering dozens of forged passports and boxes of militant propaganda....

British officials say that if they want to deport an imam who they fear is inciting violence, the proceedings can often take months or even years. In Britain, where 1.8 million Muslims live, elected officials are demanding that the police move quickly against several imams who they say have become far more vocal in recent weeks. Sheik Omar, who has lived here since 1985... warned that Britain must scale back its antiterrorism laws or it would face a "horrendous" response from angry Muslims....

In the months after September 11, diplomatic pressure built for Britain to move against outspoken imams. But it was not until last May that British officials arrested the most high-profile militant cleric, Abu Hamza al-Masri of the Finsbury Park mosque in north London. He was charged with soliciting or encouraging others to murder people who did not believe in the Islamic faith. Mr. Masri also faces extradition to the United States, where he is charged with 11 terrorist counts, including trying to establish a terrorist training camp in Oregon....

Now leading the [Finsbury] mosque...imam Abu Abdullah... said in an interview, "People see us as extremists because we don't compromise the religion of Allah."[38]

THIS IS "THE RELIGION OF ALLAH"

So terrorists are not "extremists" after all, but real Muslims—exactly what we are documenting to be true. Muslims in England threaten an "angry" response if Britain doesn't soften its attitude toward terrorism? And they become angriest of all if we reject the slogan "Islam is peace"! Yet how many Westerners are willing to face the truth?

Sheik Omar Bakri justifies violence and murder against all Americans (those who voted for them are equally guilty with the leaders they elected) because "After World War II, America effectively declared war on Muslims and Islam...by giving military, financial, and diplomatic support to the Israelis." He justifies 9-11 because "Americans had no 'Covenant of Security with the Muslims...only qualified scholars in *fiqh* [Islamic jurisprudence] could have planned this—because the 19 used non-Muslim aliases to enter the county (which legally allowed them to act in *jihad*).'

"After Al-Queda admitted responsibility, it was obvious that qualifed *ulema* [Islamic scholars] were behind it. Thus, Al-Queda has revived the culture of terrorism in Islam after 200 years.... In terms of Islamic jurisprudence, only Muslims are innocent...all non-Muslims are rebel criminals against Allah. Muslims who engage in interfaith [dialogue] are apostate [subject to the death penalty].... Muslims did not attack the USA...9/11 was an act of retaliation...to force America out of the Muslim world [even though they came there in response to Saudi Arabia's pleas for help]."[39] The brazen double standard and special meaning of common words is evident and alarming. Are any political leaders and their advisors paying attention?

THE WEST DREAMS ON!

Episcopal bishop Bullen Dolli from Sudan was stunned at the attitude he encountered in the United States. He came to Washington, D.C., in October 2001, seeking sympathy for the two million of his countrymen murdered by Muslims from the north and for those who would without substantial Western intervention likewise become victims. The World Trade Center had just come down, the Pentagon had been attacked, but he could scarcely arouse any interest at poorly attended press conferences where he warned that Islam "is a militant religion." In vain,

> ...he pointed out that Sudan's death toll is larger than the combined fatalities suffered in Bosnia, Kosovo, Afghanistan, Chechnya, Somalia, and Algeria. Twice as many Sudanese have perished in the past two decades as in all the war-related deaths suffered by Americans in the past 200 years. But hardly anyone listened. The bishop's hosts could not get him a slot on NPR, on the networks, or any other high-profile venue previously so eager to accommodate any itinerant mullah praising the "Religion of Peace and Tolerance."
>
> To Bishop Dolli, it may seem incomprehensible that the U.S. has intervened militarily and politically to "save" the Muslims in

Bosnia and Kosovo from alleged genocides perpetrated by their Christian neighbors while it remains indifferent to the very real genocide of Christians that has been perpetrated by the ruling Muslims in Sudan for two decades. He does not understand that his flock's very Christianity barred them from certified victimhood in the eyes of the ruling Western elites.[40]

It is frustrating and puzzling that there is "a consistent American bias in favor of the Muslim party in virtually every conflict with a Christian nation."[41] Will the West ever gain the moral conviction to face the truth and act upon it? If not, we are willfully, and in spite of much warning, contributing to our own eventual subjugation to the horror of Islamic rule.

The height of American leaders' naiveté—or willful blindness to the truth about Islam—is seen in the appointment by New York Mayor Michael Bloomberg of Omar Mohammedi to his city's Human Rights Commission October 15, 2002. This was little more than a year after 19 Muslims destroyed New York's Trade Center and attacked the Pentagon. Mohammedi is general counsel to the New York chapter of the Council on American-Islamic Relations (CAIR). To understand not just the irony but the insanity of this appointment, see Appendix B on page 341.

1. Chronicles of Tabari, II, 258, 272.

2. http://www.jihadwatch.org/archives/004660.php; http://www.jihadwatch.org/archives/005241.php.

3. SergeTrifkovic, *The Sword of the Prophet: Islam, history, theology, impact on the world* (Boston: Regina Orthodox Press, 2002), 242.

4. Ibid., 242.

5. Ibid., 243.

6. www.cbc.ca/fifth/saudi/justice.html.

7. Dore Gold, *Hatred's Kingdom: How Saudi Arabia Supports the New Global Terrorism* (Washington, D.C.: Regnery Publishing, Inc., 2003), 167.

8. http://www.sodomylaws.org/world/saudi_arabia/saudinews17.htm.

9. "Voices of Hate," *The Wall Street Journal*, October 1, 2004.

10. www.worldnetdaily.com/news/article.asp?ARTICLE_ID=42305.

11. "Al-Jazeera's tsunami conspiracy theories," www.worldnetdaily.com/news/article.asp?ARTICLE_ID=42271.

12. http://www.foxnews.com/story/0,2933,143074,00.html.

13. Gold, *Hatred's*, 247.

14. http://worldnetdaily.com/news/article.asp?ARTICLE_ID=33482.

15. Quoted by Cal Thomas, *Star Ledger*, April 30, 2002.

16. *The Washington Times*, January 29, 2005; www.washingtontimes.com.

17. www.tzemachdovid.org/Facts/claim.shtml. www.middleeastinfo.org/modules.php?op=modload& name=XForum&file=viewthread&tid=1276.

18. Romans 2:11-16.

19. Romans 13:1-7.

20. Matthew 5:27-28.

21. Lt. Colonel Netanel Lorch, *Israel's War of Independence*, 1947-1949; cited in Schechtman, *Mufti*, 222.

22. Will Durant, *The Story of Civilization*, vol. VI, *The Reformation* (Simon and Schuster, 1950), 188.

23. Abd El Schafi, *Behind the Veil* (n.p., 2000), 274.

24. Surah 23:60.

25. Baydawi, 457; Jalalan, 288; Zamakh-shari, III:192; cited in Abd El Schafi, *Behind the Veil: Unmasking Islam* (n.p., for obvious reasons), 273.

26. John 5:24.

27. John 10:11, 28.

28. 1 John 5:13.

29. Hebrews 9:27.

30. Trifkovic, *Sword*, 112.

31. S. Runciman, *A History of the Crusades* (Cambridge, 1954), III, 321.

32. Ibn Warraq, *Why I Am Not A Muslim* (Amherst, NY: Prometheus Books, 1995), 234-35.

33. Michael J. Arlen, *Passage to Ararat* (Ballentine Books, 1975).

34. Nicholas Gage, *Greek Fire* (Alfred A. Knopf, 2000), cited in Trifkovic, 125.

35. George Horton, *The Blight of Asia: An Account of the Systematic Extermination of Christian Populations by Mohammedans and of the Culpability of Certain Great Powers; with the True Story of the Burning of Smyrna* (Indianapolis: Bobbs-Merrill Company, 1926).

36. http://members.fortunecity.com/fstav1/horton/horton.html.

37. MEMRI *Special Dispatch Series*, No. 447, December 6, 2002.

38. Don Van Natta, Jr. and Lowell Bergman, "Militant Imams Under Scrutiny Across Europe," *The New York Times*, January 25, 2005.

39. Anthony McRoy, "There Can Be No End to Jihad," interview with Sheikh Omar Bakri Muhammad in late January 2005, *Christianity Today*.

40. Trifkovic, *Sword*, 255.

41. James Jatras, "Pravoslavophobia," *Chronicles*, February 1997, 43.

8—FACING HARD FACTS

MIDDLE EAST ANALYSTS and authors A. J. Abraham and George M. Haddad have stated the Islamic view very clearly: "Islam is God's plan for the world, every inch of it, not only the Islamic regions. Islam is for everyone, whether one wants it or not. It is the duty of every Muslim to help expand the borders of Islam until every being on this planet acknowledges that 'There is no God but Allah and Muhammad is his Messenger.'"[1] No honest Muslim would deny this.

As Omar Bakri declares:

> The aim of the Khilifah [Caliphate]—the ideal Islamic State, which does not presently exist—is to conquer the world, either militarily or intellectually through people converting to Islam.... There can be no end to jihad.... The final hour will not come until the Muslims conquer the White House....[2]

Compromisers (both Muslim and non-Muslim) call Bakri an extremist. On the contrary, he represents true Islam, which is gaining strength. Nothing less can be justified by the Qur'an, by Muhammad's words and deeds as recorded in the *hadith*, and by the history of Islam as practiced consistently by Muhammad's immediate successors and through the centuries that followed.

Although Egypt has a secular government, Islam is nevertheless strong and presents a perpetual problem for Egypt's rulers, who are Muslims—at least in name. In this "works religion," Egypt's Western ways are criticized by those who believe that the only way to dress, eat, and behave is the way Muhammad and his followers did in the seventh century and as the Taliban enforced. The power of Islam even in this secular state is evident in the fact that Cairo is the location of the Al-Azhar University, recognized as the authoritative center of Islamic thought and theology for the entire Muslim world.

Muslims insist (apparently in all sincerity) that the only true freedom comes through submission to Islam. How is that possible? Could it merely be a semantic problem that centers upon differing interpretations of the meaning of words? Or must it go deeper?

In the previous chapter, we noted that on December 10, 1948, The Universal Declaration of Human Rights was adopted by the General Assembly of the United Nations at its third session after coming into existence on October 24, 1945. There were fifty-six members at that time and fifty-four present. The vote for the Declaration as a whole was forty-eight in favor (including, surprisingly, a number of Muslim countries: Afghanistan, Egypt, Iran, Iraq, Pakistan, Syria, and Turkey), with eight abstentions. Those abstaining were the Soviet block of nations (USSR, Byelorus, Czechoslovakia, Poland, Ukraine, and Yugoslavia), Saudi Arabia, and South Africa.

This Declaration remains one of the most important ever adopted by the UN. Article One of the Charter, upon which the UN was founded, declares that one of the principal purposes of the United Nations is: "To achieve international co-operation in promoting and encouraging respect for human rights and for fundamental freedoms for all without distinction as to race, sex, language or religion."[3]

In the process of composing the entire Declaration, votes were cast by the members for and against each proposed article. Of particular interest is the fact that Article 18 was adopted by all fifty-six members. It reads:

Everyone has the right to freedom of thought, conscience and religion; this right includes freedom to change his religion or belief, and freedom, either alone or in community with others and in public or private, to manifest his religion or belief in teaching, practice, worship and observance.

WHAT DID YOU SAY?

Although it abstained from voting for or against the Declaration as a whole, Saudi Arabia, along with every other member state, approved Article 18. Even the Soviet Union and China agreed to abide by Article 18, although any child living in either of those countries knew that these freedoms were no more permitted there than under Islam. Saudi Arabia was pledging to the world that every person in that country would have the right to "change his religion or belief" and "in public or private, to manifest his religion or belief...." Yet as we have seen, Saudi Arabia beheads any Muslim who changes from Islam to any other belief, no non-Islamic religion may be practiced, and these Islamic laws came into being by decree of Muhammad himself and are therefore unchangeable. Could the contradiction between Islam and Article 18 be any more plain?

How can the undeniable difference between what Saudi Arabia professes to the world and what it does in practice be explained? Of course, the same question could be asked not only of other Muslim countries but of communist countries as well. We would rather not believe that they are deliberately lying. Then what is the explanation?

The Bible provides the uncomfortable answer: "The heart is deceitful above all things, and desperately wicked: who can know it? I the LORD search the heart...."[4] Quoting Isaiah 29:13, Christ rebuked the rabbis of His day with these words: "Ye hypocrites, well did Esaias prophesy of you, saying, This people draweth nigh unto me with their mouth, and honoureth me with their lips; but their heart is far from me. But in vain they do worship me, teaching for doctrines the commandments of men."[5] It is a common human failing to profess one thing with the lips while denying it in practice.

Those who call themselves Christians are as prone to such hypocrisy as anyone else. The Bible declares that the hearts of all people are the same. But some cultures encourage the natural evil and dishonesty of the heart. Such was the situation in the pagan Arab culture from which Islam sprang and in which it is still deeply rooted. It is one thing for an individual Christian to profess to love Christ and neighbor as oneself and yet to fail to live up to this in daily life. It is something else altogether, however, for one's religion itself to teach its followers to lie, commit violence, plunder, and murder, in order to advance its cause in the world. As we have seen, this is the case with Islam—and the hypocritical denial of the truth is practiced daily throughout the Muslim world and in its dealings with the West. And Western leaders seem content to go along uncomplainingly with the deception.

A POLICY BASED UPON DENIAL

It has too long been politically correct to overlook the past and present persecution and slaughter of Jews and Christians by Muslims worldwide and to persist in defining Islam as peace. As one historian states: "Thirteen centuries of religious discrimination, causing suffering and death of countless millions, have been covered by the myth of Islamic 'tolerance'...."[6] The West overlooks the outright denial of basic human rights and support of terrorism by Saudi Arabia and other Muslim countries—and, incredibly, favors and sometimes even arms Islamic terrorists, as in Afghanistan, Chechnya, Cyprus, Bosnia, Kashmir, Kosovo, Macedonia, Sudan, and East Timor.

Repeatedly, Israel has been taken to task for "overreacting" to suicide bombings, for pursuing terrorists into PA territory, and for destroying the houses from which terrorists have operated. How could someone who acts in self-defense to save himself from someone who is intent upon murdering him possibly be accused of overreacting? America and Britain and their few allies in Iraq and Afghanistan are finally learning what Israel has faced alone and under heavy criticism for the past fifty years. It is a shocking discovery to finally realize that we are confronted by an enemy that is *eager* to kill or be killed in order either to conquer the world for Allah or be martyred in that battle and thus hopefully gain the Paradise promised by his religion.

The world court has condemned Israel for building a fence and wall. This barrier is not like the Berlin wall, designed to keep the oppressed from escaping communism's paradise. This one is put up in self-defense to keep out terrorists intent upon murdering Israelis. It has, in fact, reduced the death rate in those areas where it has been completed. But without sympathy for the murder victims, the UN and EU censure Israel for defending itself, while never expressing any disapproval of the murderers.

WHY THIS DOUBLE STANDARD?

We have quoted statements from many Muslim leaders declaring in the clearest language possible that Israel must be annihilated and that they intend to do it no matter what the cost in human lives on both sides. Typical of hundreds of such threats was this statement by Farouk Kaddoumi, head of the PLO political department at the time: "This Zionist ghetto of Israel must be destroyed."[7] It couldn't be said any more brazenly because he knew, as Muslims today are confident is still the case, that no matter what murderous intent they declare and effect against Israel, Western political leaders will continue to pressure Israelis as though they are the aggressors.

If Israel made such threats against those who are determined to destroy her, Muslims would go berserk and the UN, EU, and United States would condemn her soundly. Has the world gone completely mad?

The Iron Curtain was rightly condemned by the non-Communist world. Stiff pressure in the form of world opinion and various sanctions was laid upon the Soviet Union. That pressure eventually brought down the wall and helped to bring about at least some of the desired changes. Yet the United States, UN, and EU remain silent concerning the Islamic Curtain, even though it is more vicious and impenetrable than the Iron or Bamboo Curtains ever were.

Even during the most oppressive times under Stalin and Mao, at least a few churches were allowed to remain open. In today's China there are many Christian churches as well as other places of worship for Buddhists, Muslims, and those of other faiths. But in Saudi Arabia, not one non-Muslim place of worship is tolerated! In other Muslim countries where, under secular governments, *sharia* is not officially practiced, churches are nevertheless being destroyed and Christians killed by Muslims because this is what Islam requires.

Is it not time for the United States to bring serious pressure to bear upon Saudi Arabia and other Islamic countries for their violations of human rights professed by UN members, just as it did with the Soviet Union and continues to do with China? How can the United States be a party to the hypocrisy of the United Nations professing to stand for human rights while its own members flaunt their violations with impunity? How can we ignore any longer the hundreds of millions of Muslims held in bondage behind the Islamic Curtain without raising an anguished cry of protest in their defense?

Although the EU, UN, and Western powers have been slow to put public pressure on Muslim countries, there has been behind-the-scenes arm-twisting, especially by the United States during the Bush administration. Through greater understanding and boldness on the part of some in the Western media to report the truth (such as Mortimer B. Zuckerman, editor-in-chief of *U.S. News & World Report*), the pressure of public opinion is beginning to have its effect. Saudi Arabia, for example, "will make all possible efforts to improve its international image...Higher Education Minister Dr. Khaled Al-Anqari said" in Riyadh, October 2, 2004. Much of the effort will be deceptive window dressing and pure public relations. Nevertheless, incremental changes are being forced upon the Saudis, who are feeling the heat of what Anqari defensively called "strident media campaigns [attempting] to tarnish the Kingdom's international image and...discredit its values and institutions...since the Sept. 11 events...."[8]

The Saudis have begun by attempting to cover up the truth, as Anqari's speech revealed: "We will work with our friends in the world to highlight the true picture of Saudi Arabia, the qiblah of Islam and Muslims and the heart of the Arab world." Anqari said the Higher Education Ministry was making contacts with educational agencies and institutions in other countries "to correct the distorted picture of Saudi Arabia." Obviously, their intent is not to receive correction, but to polish their false image, which hasn't been distorted at all except by the Saudis themselves in covering up the horrible truth of what Islam really is.

Nevertheless, the door has been opened, albeit a tiny crack. In trying to protect what it calls its "true image," Saudi Arabia will have to face frank criticism. For example, a four-day forum (the second annual communication forum titled "The image of Saudi Arabia in the world") was held in early October 2004 involving more than one hundred prominent personalities from within and without Saudi Arabia. The Saudis will have to make real changes. Hopefully, the scholars they have called in for help from around the world will not be satisfied with smoke and mirrors.

REMEMBER, THIS IS ISLAM!

Most of today's Muslims (whatever their origin, including Saudi Arabia) have forgotten, if they ever knew, that their ancestors were unwillingly forced into Islam under threat of death. This is Islam as it was at the beginning, always has been whenever possible, and still is. If Western religious and political leaders do not awaken from their delusion and stop mouthing the lie that "Islam is peace," it will soon be too late to defend our freedoms!

In the early centuries of Islam, its forces nearly conquered Europe. Had they not been turned back at Tours, France, and Vienna, Austria, we might all be speaking Arabic right now. It must be understood that such aggression was not a mistaken zeal or a holy resolve applicable only to the past; it is the very heart of Islam as Muhammad and his immediate successors taught and practiced it and as it remains today. The conquest of the world is demanded by Islam as its unchangeable goal.

Foundational to Islam is the declaration Muhammad made: "Allah has commanded me to fight against all people until all people confess that Allah is the true God and Muhammad is his prophet." Islam divides the entire world into Dar al-Islam (the house of peace) and Dar al-Harb (the house of war) and demands perpetual *jihad* everywhere against Dar al-Harb, i.e., non-Muslims. There can never be "peace" until Islam has subjected the entire world to Allah—and that includes America. Islam marches on!

Islamic fundamentalists are playing out their special role in that conquest through terrorism. It is universally recognized that Islam is behind most terrorism. Yet in spite of that fact, the spread of Islam's mosques is allowed throughout the Western world and accelerates even while Islam denies the same liberty for other religions in territories it controls. Most mosques are funded by Saudi Arabia with oil profits from money we pay at the pump. Many mosques in the West are centers for terrorist cells and training, an indisputable fact consistent with Islam (thoroughly documented in the video, *Jihad In America*).[9]

In July 2002, "a RAND Corporation analyst told the Pentagon's Defense Policy Board that Saudi Arabia was an enemy of the United States, [that]…Saudis were active 'at every level of the terror chain.'"[10] It is clear that Saudi Arabia now "exports two products around the globe—oil and religious fanaticism."[11] Dore Gold, former Israeli ambassador to the UN, documents the uncomfortable truth about Saudi Arabia in his excellent book that everyone in the West ought to read—especially our leaders.[12]

There is no way to explain away today's suicide bombers and other Muslim terrorists as a handful of "extremists." In Muslim countries, terrorists are treated with the same hero worship that matadors receive in Spain and that NFL and NBA stars receive in America. Their faces appear on posters everywhere, with slogans of praise and admiration.

A NEW AND MORE SUBTLE JIHAD

But side-by-side with terrorism is a new, more subtle, and very effective kind of *jihad* today. In one of the most important battles in European history, in A.D. 732, Prince Charles Martel, at Tours/Poitiers, France, defeated an invading Muslim army of several hundred thousand *jihad* warriors, killing their commander, Abd el-Rahman.

That was nearly thirteen hundred years ago. And now, through another and more successful invasion, Islam has become the second largest religion in France, with about six million Muslims and fifteen hundred mosques. Jean-Louis Bruguiere, France's top anti-terror judge, recently said, "The threat is before us, not behind us. And we are quite concerned.... I think that the terrorist threat today is more globalized...[and] more powerful...than it was before September 11. Rabei Osman El Sayed Ahmed, known as Mohammed the Egyptian [alleged mastermind behind the Madrid train bombing in 2004 that killed 191 and injured 1,400], is an example of this new generation of jihadi operatives who apparently operate independently of the old Al Qaeda network...an example of the next generation of Islamist terrorist that Europe must now contend with."[13]

An eye-opening documentary aired on PBS in late January 2005 explained, "It might come as a surprise to many Americans, but the most pressing threat to the United States is not the suspected Al Qaeda cells at home, but rather the cells operating overseas, especially in Western Europe. Home to an estimated 18 million Muslims, Western Europe has become the new and deadly battleground in the war on terror."[14]

In England, more Muslims meet in mosques each week than Christians in churches. Islam is not capable of launching a military frontal assault against Europe, but it is accomplishing more than earlier *jihad* warriors ever did, by the "peaceful" invasion of immigrants and propaganda about its benevolent intentions. Sir David Veness, assistant commissioner for specialist operations with London's Metropolitan Police, recently said, "This country has seen

terrorism since the end of the 1960s, both domestic…and international terrorism here on the streets of London. What is different
about this form of terrorism is the unequivocal intention to cause
mass murder…without warning in any form to the public. [The
new terrorists hide inside the mosques and Muslim communities.]

"European police have thwarted dozens of Islamist terrorist
plots set to be launched following the U.S. attacks of September 11.
Reda Seyam, an Egyptian-born German citizen who reportedly had
been under investigation in connection with the Bali bombings, has
said: 'Any observer can see that this war in Iraq [has created] a school
to train graduates on acts of terrorism and fighting…. It revives the
spirit of jihad in the Muslim nation.'"[15]

Areas in England, Germany, and elsewhere in Europe, already
have concentrations of Muslims that are able to vote in their own
local candidates. By 2009, the three largest cities in the Netherlands
will have a Muslim majority. Yet Europe is very slow to awaken to
the threat of Islam in its midst. Incredibly, in spite of the fact that
constant pressure to accept Islam is exerted by Muslim terrorists
worldwide, the lie that Islam is a benevolent, peaceful religion like
any other continues to be accepted.

AN IMPASSABLE BARRIER?

It is nearly impossible for Muslims to be integrated into society
like other immigrants because Islam does not allow any distinction
between religion and the state. Islam must rule not only in the
mosque but in daily life and commerce, in the legal system, courts,
and government. Thus, for genuine democracy to be established in
Afghanistan, Iraq, and PLO territory would be the death of Islam.
Muslim countries will do all they can to prevent this disaster for
their religion. Furthermore, even in secular Islamic countries, such
as Egypt and Pakistan, the Islamists rule to a large extent.

In contrast, Western civilization follows the clear distinction
Jesus made between church and state when He said, "Render therefore unto Caesar the things which are Caesar's; and unto God the

things that are God's." (Matthew 22:21; Luke 20:25). This fundamental difference in political philosophy (recognizing that Muslims will attempt to use lawful democratic means in order to establish *sharia*) must be confronted if the West is to survive the internal threat posed by the flood of immigrants. Omar Ahmad of CAIR (Council of American Islamic Relations) has bluntly said:

> Islam isn't in America to be equal to any faiths but to become dominant.... The Koran should be the highest authority in America, and Islam the only accepted religion on earth.

Texans used to cry, "Remember the Alamo!" Jews still remind themselves, "Remember the Holocaust—never again!" So Westerners had better repeat to one another in earnest, "Remember the conquest of India ('the bloodiest story in history'); remember the slaughter of a million Armenians; remember what Islam has done for centuries and is still doing in Sudan, Indonesia, Nigeria, and elsewhere—stop it now!"

Instead, many leading Christians promote "peaceful" opposition to terrorism, as though terrorists would be impressed. The liberal Christian (allegedly evangelical) organization, Sojourners, placed a full-page ad in a national newspaper that naïvely assumed that violence could be stopped by non-violence. [16] By implication, blame for terrorism that operates by force was placed upon Israel and the United States for opposing it with force. Particular blame was placed upon Christian leaders who encouraged the president to pursue terrorists. It critically quoted Jerry Falwell: "But you've got to kill the terrorists before the killing stops. And I'm for the president to chase them all over the world. If it takes 10 years, blow them all away in the name of the Lord."[17]

Although most Christians might be uncomfortable with Falwell's rhetoric, the ad criticizing him made no criticism of the terrorists, much less of Islam's promotion of murder in the name of Allah. We have documented Islam's role. As Israel's former ambassador to the UN succinctly declared, "Without an unshakable conviction in the merits of martyrdom and in its rewards in the afterlife, terrorists would never have undertaken the suicidal attacks of the past decade."[18] Such teaching comes from Islam alone. No other religion even comes close to promoting murder and mayhem, much less offers heavenly reward for such deeds. Islam itself is the root of the terrorist problem that plagues the world. Western leaders must begin there if we are to win the war against terror!

TERRORISM IS ISLAM'S PATH TO "PEACE"

To bring "peace," Allah commands, "I shall cast terror into the hearts of the infidels. Strike off their heads!;[19] Slay the idolaters wherever you find them...;[20] O Prophet, struggle with the unbelievers and hypocrites and be thou harsh with them...;[21] Believers, make war on the infidels that dwell around you...."[22] More than one hundred other verses in the Qur'an advocate fighting to bring Islam's peace to the world.[23]

Muhammad's dying words were, "May Allah curse the Christians and Jews!" Muhammad Atta, Egyptian leader of the 9/11 terrorists attended a mosque in Hamburg, Germany, where the imam preached that "Christians and Jews should have their throats slit."[24] The same violence is preached in many other mosques worldwide. This is real Islam.

Throughout its history, Islam unquestionably has been responsible for the slaughter of many millions of innocent victims, including Muslims themselves by rival factions. Islam doesn't bring peace even among its most devoted followers. In the last chapter, we made brief mention of the eight-year war between Iran and Iraq, both Muslim countries. They used one thousand tons of poison gas on one another. Many thousands of young boys were sacrificed to clear mine fields for the troops following them (and were promised Paradise with unnumbered dark-eyed virgins for doing so).

We have seen the slaughter of Muslim citizens by Muslim rulers, such as the murder of thousands by Saddam Hussein in Iraq. Muslim leaders of Iran and Syria have committed similar atrocities against their citizens. The destruction and rape of Kuwait (a Muslim country) by Iraq (another Muslim country) shocked the world—while Arafat and the "Palestinians" were cheering Saddam as a great hero because he was raining Scud missiles on Israel. In twelve years of civil war in Algeria, Muslims have killed more than one hundred thousand of their fellows. In Afghanistan, where Islam has been the official religion for centuries, there has been perpetual war between rival factions. The Taliban, who claimed to be true Muslims, slaughtered and enslaved their own people. Today, Muslim warlords would fight one another in a bloody civil war if American and British troops should withdraw from Afghanistan.

The vast Al Qaeda terrorist network began in the early 1990s. It was composed of a loose amalgam of groups in Algeria, Egypt, and Saudi Arabia, who sought to overthrow their respective governments for not being true to fundamentalist Islam. Unsuccessful in this enterprise, they turned their attention to America, seen as the evil "Satan" representing a democratic and stabilizing presence in the Middle East [25]—and worst of all, the supporter of Israel.

ARAFAT AND THE PLO

Dangerous as Al Qaeda is, it ranks far below Arafat's Islamic PLO networks, which still hold the record for the largest number of hostages taken at one time (three hundred), the largest number of people shot at an airport, the largest ransom collected ($5 million paid by Lufthansa), the greatest number and variety of targets (forty civilian passenger aircraft, five passenger ships, thirty embassies or diplomatic missions plus innumerable fuel depots and factories), plus assassinations by the thousands, etc.[26] Jordan had given these fellow Muslims shelter. But their heinous crimes against his people, and Arafat's attempt to take over the country, became so unbearable that King Hussein I finally turned his Bedouin troops on them and, with the help of the Israelis, drove them out of his country and into Lebanon.

There the PLO (all devout Muslims sincerely believing they were acting in the name of and to the greater glory of Allah in obedience to the Qur'an) created an unequaled legacy of mayhem and murder, killing tens of thousands and leaving about one hundred thousand young girls pregnant when they were driven out. Often the bodies of PLO victims, some of them small children, were mutilated and dismembered. With increased weaponry and the blessing of Syria, Lebanon became a huge PLO base for terrorist attacks upon Israel.

Life for Israelis became intolerable in Galilee, where there were constant massive artillery and mortar attacks launched by the PLO from within Lebanon. Thousands of residents either fled their homes or were forced to spend much time in bomb shelters. Israeli air strikes and commando raids failed to stop or even lessen the PLO attacks, forcing Israel to take more decisive action. As Former U.S. Secretary of State Henry Kissinger said, "No sovereign state can tolerate indefinitely the buildup along its borders of a military force dedicated to its destruction and implementing its objectives by periodic shellings and raids."[27]

On June 6, 1982, under the direction of then Defense Minister Ariel Sharon, Israel invaded Lebanon, determined to drive the PLO out of that country as King Hussein I had driven them out of Jordan. There was a further reason: to remove huge hidden caches of arms known to be stashed in Lebanon—enough to equip a million-man army, much of it too sophisticated for the PLO to operate. It was obviously intended for a planned major Soviet invasion of Israel. Thousands of truckloads were required to haul it all into Israel.

As the battle raged and the Israelis tightened the noose, the PLO retreated toward Beirut. Arafat's men would take people off the street, strap them into hospital beds, command the nurses to drain every drop of blood for transfusions for their wounded, and stack the dead bodies like cordwood in the halls. Sharon would have destroyed the PLO murderers and killed Arafat, but President Reagan insisted that the worst terrorist of our day be allowed to leave Lebanon alive. He was given shelter in Tunisia, where he set up PLO headquarters in Borj Cedria. Arafat was still directing world-wide terrorist operations from Tunisia when, incredibly, Israel took him on as its partner for peace and recognized the PLO as the official representative of the Palestinian people. He was allowed to leave Tunisia and set up his new headquarters in Ramallah in the West Bank, where he received a hero's welcome.

Instead of being tried by an international tribunal and treated like the Nazi, Serbian, Taliban, and Iraqi leadership, as justice would require, Arafat was given the status of a highly honored world statesman. His bloody exploits gained for him international acceptance as a leader for peace and the Nobel Peace Prize! The United Nations, European Union, and countless world political and religious leaders sided with Arafat in his unjust demands and terrorism against Israel—and every indication is that his equally terrorist successors will receive the same favoritism. Arafat was treated at a French military hospital during his last days, and after his death French President Jacques Chirac eulogized him as "a man of courage and conviction."[28] Tunisia has named a major avenue in Arafat's honor.

Arafat was cheered by the United Nations general assembly, received at the Clinton White House, Camp David, warmly at least ten times by Pope John Paul II—and the Pope visited him in his palace in PLO-occupied Israel and supported Arafat's opposition to Israel. In spite of murdering eleven members of Israel's team at the 1972 Munich Olympics (for which Libya's Qaddafi awarded Arafat $5 million), the PLO was invited to send its own team to the Olympic Games! In 1973, the PLO was granted observer status in the United Nations, and in 1974, Yasser Arafat was invited to address the UN General Assembly, where he received a standing ovation though he called for Israel's destruction. At the 2004 Olympics in Greece, the "Palestinians" received the most applause as all of the teams made their entrance. The West encouraged terrorism by rewarding Arafat. He became proof that terrorism can pay big dividends.

TRAINING THE NEXT GENERATION FOR "PEACE"

That every Jew on earth must be killed and the entire world subjected to Islam to the glory of Allah is not an obscure teaching. One does not have to search in dark corners of a library to find it.

This ambition is taught in today's textbooks in Islamic schools worldwide, including, for example, the Muslim Academy outside Washington D.C. It is devoutly preached in Mosques, presented as the heroic ideal in schools, and blared forth on radio and TV and over loudspeakers in the streets. Textbooks in Syria today lead pupils to the "inevitable conclusion...that all Jews must be annihilated."[29] The Egyptian textbook, *Studies in Theology: Traditions and Morals*, explains that the Qur'an encourages the faithful "to perform jihad...[and] behead the infidels...."[30] The beheading of hostages in Iraq simply marks the terrorists as Muslims who are following the example of Muhammad and the teaching of the Qur'an and *hadith*.

Captured documents have revealed that "at the graduation ceremonies for the [Hamas] Islamic Society's network of kindergartens [funded by Saudi Arabia], Palestinian children enacted the attacks of suicide bombers. Children wore military uniforms and mock explosive belts, wielded imitation Kalashnikov rifles, and burned the Israeli flag."[31] Palestinian TV carries a children's program modeled after *Sesame Street* called *The Children's Club*. It features children singing songs about wanting to become suicide bombers against Israel. Sheik `Ikrima Sabri, appointed Mufti (highest Islamic authority) of Jerusalem by Arafat, told the Egyptian weekly *Al-Ahram Al-Arabi*, "The younger the martyr, the greater and the more I respect him...a new generation will carry on the mission with determination."[32] What a tragedy!

Could the innocence of such children ever be restored? Can that generation ever be convinced of what a normal conscience knows for sure—that the true God would never condone murder, much less give murderers a special reward in Paradise? If so, millions of lives might be saved.

To die as a martyr in *jihad* was always the only sure way (maybe) to Paradise for the Muslim. However, committing suicide in the process was never considered honorable until fairly recently. Perhaps as a result of having attempted suicide himself a number of times, Muhammad condemned suicide. He reportedly said, "Whoever kills himself in any way in this world will be tormented with it on the day of resurrection."[33] If Muhammad's condemnation of suicide as part of *jihad* could be widely communicated, it might turn the Islamic world against this practice. However, most imams justify suicide bombings as *jihad* martyrdom operations and claim that suicide in such instances is justified and rewarded.

Hatred for and destruction of Israel is a prominent theme in publications officially distributed by Ministries of Education in Muslim lands. For example, in Jordan a book used in the first year of high school declares, "Israel was born to die. Prove it." A book for the second year of junior high in Damascus declares, "The Jews are vile, greedy enemies of mankind." In Syria, a fifth-grade book boasts, "We shall expel all Jews from all Arab countries." In Egypt, a textbook for the first year of junior high urges students, "The Arabs do not cease to act for the extermination of Israel." A ninth-grade textbook declares, "Israel shall not live if the Arabs stand fast in their hatred.... Even if all the human race and the devil in hell conspire to aid her, she shall not exist." One finds this underlying and perpetual hatred for Jews and the accompanying resolve to annihilate them in the writings of Muslim fundamentalists everywhere.

In his testimony before the Senate subcommittee referred to earlier, David A. Harris pointed out that "Saudi Arabian schoolbooks, even grammar books, are full of phrases exalting war, *jihad*, and martyrdom. And though all forms of terror are rejected by the Saudi Arabian schoolbooks, it appears that such prohibitions do not apply to cases that fall in the categories of *jihad* and martyrdom."[34] Harris elaborated further in a newsletter:

> Saudi schoolbooks are a hate-filled portrait of a bizarre and fictitious world—a place where the *Protocols of the [Learned] Elders of Zion* is a history text...where Israel does not exist on a map...where organizations such as the Freemasons, the Lions, and Rotary clubs are bound together in a global Zionist conspiracy.
>
> The textbooks are not the product of renegade religious fanatics. They are official publications of the Saudi Education Ministry—the work of a monarchy that passes itself off as a moderate regime and American ally....

Recently we joined with the Center for Monitoring the Impact of Peace to conduct an investigation into Saudi schoolbooks. What we found was—to put it plainly—chilling. Practically every lesson—from grammar, to geography, to history—was bent and twisted to transform it into a vehicle for teaching hate....

"You will hardly find any sedition without the Jews having a part in it," one schoolbook says...blaming Jews for...World War I and the French and Russian Revolutions.

Students are challenged to fill in this blank: "Those who have incurred Allah's wrath are _____." You will not be surprised to learn the correct answer: 'the Jews.'"

Nor is bigotry confined to Jews alone. Saudi textbooks teach youth to despise all that is Western as well....

Our work on this report was instrumental in the introduction of a resolution in the U.S. House and Senate condemning the bigotry in Saudi textbooks, calling on the Saudi monarchy to change its curricula and expressing "extreme disappointment" with the slow pace of education reform....[35]

AN IMPORTANT DISTINCTION

This is not to criticize fundamentalism or fundamentalists. Every person who stands firmly upon his convictions is a fundamentalist. All Christians ought to be fundamentalists. That simply means teaching and practicing the fundamentals of the faith as set forth in the Bible and as taught and exemplified by Jesus Christ. All Muslims, too, ought to be fundamentalists. The problem is that the fundamentals set forth in the Qur'an and as taught and exemplified by Muhammad involve force, violence, and murder in order to spread Islam. But a true Christian is supposed to spread his faith by love, by charitable example, and by appealing to reason—helping people face the fact that the penalty of sin was paid in full by Jesus Christ on the Cross and salvation is offered as a free gift to "whosoever will." There is a vast distinction in the various fundamentals—a distinction that any honest person ought to recognize and not deny.

Everyone is free to make up his own religion if he so desires. But no one is free to make up a religion and call it "Islam," because that religion is already established, with its founder, scriptures, traditions, and lengthy history of those who have practiced it. So it is with those who make up their own religion, then call it "Christianity" and claim to be "Christians." They have no right to do so. Christianity, like Islam, has its founder, scriptures, and lengthy history of those who practiced it biblically. It is deceitful for anyone to call himself a Christian who does not follow the teachings and example of Jesus Christ—just as it is deceitful for anyone to call himself a Muslim who doesn't follow the teachings of the Qur'an and the example of Muhammad as recorded in the *hadith*. That much is axiomatic.

No one can excuse Islamic violence and murder by saying that the same thing (though on a much smaller scale) was practiced by the crusaders. Though they waved crosses and obeyed the Roman Catholic Church and her popes in doing so, their slaughter of Jews and Muslims was in violation of the teachings of the Bible and of the life and teachings of Jesus Christ, proving that they were not Christians at all. But what the Muslims did in slaughtering millions in spreading Islam from France to China, and what terrorists do today, is in obedience to the Qur'an and the life and teachings of Muhammad. Thus they demonstrate that they are true Muslims. Those who claim that Islam is peace and that they are not in favor of violence in spreading Islam have no right to call themselves Muslims, and they are deceiving Westerners when they make that claim.

FACING THE AWFUL TRUTH

Every child in the Palestinian Authority's schools reads the textbook, *Our Country Palestine*. Its title page declares, "There is no alternative to destroying Israel!" What a bald-faced deception, then, for the Palestinian Authority to pretend it wants peace with Israel and at the same time to teach its citizens that Israel must be destroyed! And yet the West encourages this fraud.

Bosnian Muslim leader Alija Izetbegovic declared, "There can be no peace or coexistence between the Islamic faith and non-Islamic societies...." Could he have explained Islam more plainly—and doesn't that statement include the entire non-Muslim world? How can anyone who denies this basic Islamic teaching honestly call himself a Muslim? And isn't it dishonest in view of such foundational Islamic teaching for Islamic diplomats from Saudi Arabia or elsewhere to pretend otherwise?

Islam has created a culture of hatred and murder that has devalued human life. On March 22, 2004, eleven-year-old Abdullah Quran was stopped at an IDF checkpoint outside Nablus. When soldiers opened his schoolbag, they found inside, along with his Spiderman doll, a ten-kilo bomb that his dispatcher, who was obviously following and watching him from a distance (not having told the boy he was blessing him with a free ride to "Paradise"), had rigged to be detonated by cell phone. As the sappers worked to disarm the bomb, the cell-phone trigger was dialed. Only a technical failure saved the lives of the boy and many around him. In this case, Abdullah (his name means "servant of Allah") did not know his true mission. He said he had been offered "a lot of money" to take a package into Israel.[36]

Speaking at the United Nations on September 23, 2003, President Bush said that the Palestinian Arab cause "is being betrayed by leaders who cling to power but are feeding old hatreds and destroying the good will of others." The necessity of being politically correct prevents Bush from stating the truth: that not only certain of today's leaders but Islam itself is the direct cause of Palestinian hatred of Israel and provides the motivation for terrorism and suicide attacks. Morton A. Klein, National President of the Zionist Organization of America (ZOA), stated that truth clearly: "In fact, the central obstacle to peace between Israel and the Palestinian Arabs is the fact that a culture of anti-Jewish hatred and violence envelops the entire Palestinian Arab society, including its educational system, summer camps, its media, and the Palestinian Authority's cabinet ministers and parliament members."[37] And that culture is created by Islam.

As noted in Chapter Two, after more than sixty years, Hitler's *Mein Kampf* is still a bestseller in Muslim countries. Egyptian columnist,

Ahmad Rajab, wrote: "Thanks to Hitler, blessed memory, who on behalf of the Palestinians, revenged in advance, against the most vile criminals on the face of the earth. But we do have a complaint against him—his revenge was not enough."[38] The Palestinian Peace Prize for Culture was awarded to Abu Daoud for his book telling how he planned and carried out the murder of eleven Israeli athletes at the 1972 Munich Olympics. Imagine a self-confessed mass murderer in the West, instead of being imprisoned or executed for his crime, boasting of it in a best-selling book, for which he is lauded and honored with a special prize!

Islam destroys the normal sense of right and wrong that God has implanted in every human conscience so that murder is rewarded with paradise, and murderers are lauded as the most highly honored heroes!

This is the atmosphere Islam has created and in which not a few fanatics but the average follower of Islam is immersed from earliest childhood. Muslims in the West may attempt to be aloof from such evil, but in the long run they cannot be. Is it not time for them to admit the truth about the religion to which they still cling in denial of its established teachings and many centuries of history? But even Western governments reward these murderers. Arrested by the French police in 1977, Daoud was released from custody for fear of PLO reprisals against France. If we continue out of fear to give in to terrorist demands, we have surrendered our moral sense of right and wrong—and lost the war.

When I present such undeniable facts to audiences around the world, I see reactions ranging from discomfort to outright disbelief. It is extremely difficult for a normal person to acknowledge that a religion in our day literally calls for the extermination of an entire people. Islam itself is Israel's chief and most determined enemy—and it is the enemy of Muslims, too, as well as of all non-Muslims. Though many Muslims living in the West do not reflect the passion of world dominion in the cause of Allah which is their duty—and may not even be aware of this aspect of Islam—they would soon learn the awful truth if they resettled in a Muslim country. Instead of enjoying their former Western freedoms, they would have to conform to real Islam!

Why is there such a migration of Muslims to the West? Obviously, they prefer living in freedom under a democracy than under the totalitarian regimes in Muslim countries. Speaking frankly, with rare courage, and calling upon Muslims living in the United States to face the awful truth of what Islam does to a country, Dr. M. A. Muqtedar Khan, Director of International Studies, Adrian College, Michigan, put it succinctly: "It is time that we Muslims acknowledge that the freedoms we enjoy in the U.S. are more desirable to us than superficial solidarity with the Muslim World. If you disagree, then prove it by packing your bags and going to whichever Muslim country you identify with." He is among a growing number of Muslim scholars who are raising their voices against terrorism in the name of Islam.

A WAKE-UP CALL

The Western world prides itself on freedom, democracy, and liberality. There is no better proof of the genuineness of this boast than the openness, generosity, and opportunities with which it greets emigrants, and especially Muslims. That the latter are particularly favored above all others, including Christians, apparently reflects the fact that Muslims control most of the world's oil deposits, and the West is afraid to offend them. They are allowed to build their mosques by the thousands, to have special prayer rooms in public places such as schools and airports. They are given equal freedom to become citizens and to express their opinions, desires, and complaints with their votes in elections and in every forum offered in an open and free society that practices the human rights denied in Muslim countries: freedom of conscience, of speech, of the press, and of religion.

Nor do we deny that such freedoms ought to be granted equally to all without regard to race or religion. But there is no justification for suppressing (and even denying) the truth about Islam's aggressiveness unto the death of all who oppose it. As a result, tens of thousands of deluded Westerners have converted to Islam, which they have been assured is "peace"—and its influence is steadily increasing so that both political parties in the United States wooed Muslims in the 2004 elections.

In stark and shameful contrast, no such freedoms are offered in Muslim countries to non-Muslims—and generally not even to Muslims themselves. Yet no voice is raised at the UN in objection, nor do Western political leaders speak out. Israel, the lone democracy in the Middle East, is criticized for every misstep. Yet the Muslim world, in virtual slavery to a religion that threatens with death any who dare question, much less oppose it, is never criticized for its continual denial of basic human rights. This is not pleasing to God, and it is only one of the sins for which He will shortly punish the world.

The West has stood up for civil rights in the face of communism, bringing pressure upon Russia and China that has born fruit. On what basis can it any longer be justified that Muslim countries are in a class of their own—untouchables when it comes to basic human rights? Continuing to give Muslims in the West freedoms that are denied in Muslim countries supports a gross unfairness that encourages the continuation of a double standard that denies everything the West holds dear. It can only lead to the discovery one day that we have gone so far along this shameful one-way road (supported by the so-called "road map to peace") leading to the destruction of the rights we advocate that there is no turning back.

Would it not be best, instead of deluding ourselves further, to insist right now upon a just and fair equality with Muslims—an equality without which no lasting peace can ever be established among free peoples? Rather than continuing to promote the grossest of inequities that can only lead ultimately to a loss of basic liberties, should not the same pressures that brought down the Iron Curtain be applied to Muslim countries to bring down the even more vicious and impenetrable Islamic Curtain?

WHAT SHOULD THE WEST DO?

The "World Islamic Front for Jihad Against the Jews and the Crusaders," over the signatures of Osama bin Laden and various leaders of militant Islamic groups in Egypt, Pakistan, and Bangladesh, declared: "...the United States has been occupying the lands of Islam in the holiest of its territories, Arabia...and using its bases [there] to fight against the neighboring Islamic peoples.... To kill Americans and their allies, both civil and military, is an individual duty of every Muslim who is able.... By Allah's leave, we call on every Muslim...to obey Allah's command to kill the Americans and plunder their possessions wherever he finds them and whenever he can."[39] This infamous organization was co-founded by bin Laden and his personal physician, Dr. Ayman Zawahiri, in February 1998. Zawahiri comes from one of the most aristocratic families in Egypt. He and bin Laden met in Afghanistan in 1987 and have been partners in terrorism ever since. Zawahiri is, in fact, the mastermind behind Al Qaeda. He has declared his willingness on Al-Jazeera television to die in *jihad* for Allah.

This talented physician, raised among the wealthy in a luxurious villa in Cairo, proves the lie of the insistent excuse that it is poverty among the Muslim masses that drives them in desperation to desire to die in *jihad*. None of the nineteen September 11 hijackers was from a deprived background. *Islam itself* is the catalyst for terrorism. As journalist Stephen Schwartz has pointed out concerning fifteen of the nineteen September 11 hijackers:

> These were not poor people from refugee camps on the West Bank or in Gaza. These were not people who had grown up feeling some grievance against Israel and the United States because they lived in difficult conditions. These were not people from the crowded and disrupted communities of Egypt or Pakistan, or people who had experienced anti-Islamic violence in the last 20 years and had therefore turned against the United States. These people had grown up in the country that Americans often think of as our most solid and dependable ally in the Arab world—the kingdom of Saudi Arabia.... Al-Qaeda is essentially a Saudi political movement...twenty-five percent of those detained in Guantanamo are Saudis.[40]

A LONG OVERDUE AWAKENING IN WESTERN EUROPE?

Nor are the many acts of terrorism occurring in Europe the work of poverty-stricken men who have sneaked in from downtrodden parts of the Muslim world. These are devoted Muslims who are for the most part well educated, have lived in the West for years, have enjoyed its freedoms and opportunities, and in gratitude have carefully plotted its destruction to the glory of Allah. Only recently have there been signs that Europeans are slowly awakening to the truth and preparing to fight back. It is high time.

In Holland, the shooting and stabbing to death on November 2, 2004, of Dutch filmmaker Theo van Gogh in revenge for his having made a documentary showing the abuse of women under Islam has aroused angry reactions. Geert Wilders, one of the most popular politicians in the Netherlands has warned that "the country's democracy is under threat and [has] called for a five-year halt to non-Western immigration." The man arrested for Van Gogh's murder is a twenty-six-year-old Muslim activist who holds both Dutch and Moroccan passports.

Wilders's own life has been threatened many times for speaking out about the danger that Islam poses to his country and to all of Europe. The latest threat broadcast on the internet (in Dutch with a background of Arabic music) "condemns Wilders for insulting Islam and offers the reward of paradise for his beheading." Citing a recent report by Dutch intelligence that "recruitment for jihad…is taking place in as many as 20 mosques in the Netherlands," with a sense of urgency Wilders declares:

> If in a mosque there is recruitment for jihad, it's not a house of prayer, it's a house of war [and] should be closed down…its imams, or preachers, arrested and deported. Without swift, bold action, Islamic fundamentalism will topple the country's democratic system.
>
> The Netherlands has been too tolerant toward intolerant people for too long. We should not import a retarded political Islamic society to our country…closing borders isn't enough. Newcomers should be forced to integrate.

> If we don't do anything…we will lose the country that we
> have known for centuries…this is something that I get angry
> about and I am going to fight for, to keep the country Dutch! [41]

In Belgium in mid-November 2004, "authorities arrested a suspect accused of sending death threats to a senator of Moroccan heritage who criticized radical Muslims." In a meeting on November 19, 2004, European Union justice and interior ministers agreed that "immigrants to the 25-nation bloc should be required to learn local languages, and to adhere to general 'European values' that will guide them toward better integration…. EU justice and home affairs commissioner Franco Frattini told reporters in Rome that integration had to be an essential part of an EU policy." Pointing to the fact that five hundred thousand Turkish and Moroccan immigrants in the Netherlands don't speak Dutch, immigration minister Rita Verdonk declared, "If you want to live in the Netherlands, you have to adhere to our rules…learn our language."[42]

This is a good start, but the awakening will have to go much further than blaming terrorism on extremists. Even Wilders still imagines that the problem is radical Muslims. Those who have begun to speak out and call for action against the growing terrorism in Europe must be willing to admit that Islam itself is the problem. Until then, they will be tilting with windmills and missing entirely the real culprit.

MUSLIMS DESPERATELY NEED TO BE FREED FROM ISLAM

Ernest Renan once praised Islam. After further study, which revealed its evil, he declared, "Muslims are the first victims of Islam…to liberate the Muslim from his religion is the best service that one can render him." The words of Serge Trifkovic may sound harsh, but they are the truth—and the sooner the West faces that uncomfortable reality the better:

> Islam is a collective psychosis seeking to become global, and any
> attempt to compromise with such madness is to become part of

the madness oneself. No one who believes that jihad is the right or duty of all Muslims, or who promotes adoption of Shari'a law or reestablishment of the Caliphate, should be allowed to settle in any Western country, and every applicant should be asked. The passport of anyone preaching jihad should be revoked. This may be called discrimination but the quarrel is not of our choosing.

Islam, in Muhammad's texts and its codification, discriminates against us. It is extremely offensive. Those who submit to that faith must solve the problem they set themselves. Islam discriminates against all "unbelievers." Until the petrodollars support a Kuranic revisionism that does not, we should go for it with whips and scorpions, hammer and tongs. Secularists and believers of all other faiths must act together before it is too late.[43]

We need a series of international debates to expose Islam to the world—to show what it really believes and advocates. We need to convince the entire world, and Muslims themselves (especially the jihad warriors and those who are being recruited as suicide bombers), that terrorism exposes Islam as a bully without any valid claim upon the minds, hearts, and souls of would-be converts. If the entire world could be intimidated into accepting Islam, that would only prove that it takes threats of death to maintain it and that Islam has no appeal to truth, honesty, and love from the heart.

The God of the Bible calls to mankind, "Come now and let us reason together...." Allah never calls for that. It is submission without any reason, except that to refuse means that you will be killed. The fact that Muslims from the very beginning had to use the threat of death to enlist and keep converts proves that it has nothing to offer to the person of goodwill. As Netanyahu has well said, "It is the terrorists who are in fact weak, resorting to bombs only because they can get no one to listen to them in any other fashion."[44]

1. A. J. Abraham and George Haddad, *The Warriors of God* (Bristol, IN: Wyndham Hall Press, 1989).

2. Anthony McRoy, "There Can Be No End to Jihad," interview with Sheikh Omar Bakri Muhammad in late January 2005, *Christianity Today*, January 31, 2005.

3. The United Nations Yearbook Summary, 1948. http://www.udhr.org/history/yearbook.htm#(2)%20Provisions%20of%20the%20United%20Nations%20Charter.

4. Jeremiah 17:9-10.

5. Matthew 15:7-9.

6. SergeTrifkovic, *The Sword of the Prophet: Islam, history, theology, impact on the world* (Boston: Regina Orthodox Press, 2002), 127.

7. *Newsweek*, November 17, 1975 and March 14, 1977.

8. http://www.arabnews.com/?page=1&section=0&article=52314&d=3&m=10&y=2004.

9. Available at www.amazon.com.

10. Dore Gold, *Hatred's Kingdom: How Saudi Arabia Supports the New Global Terrorism* (Washington, D.C.: Regnery Publishing, Inc., 2003), 2.

11. Fareed Zakaria, "The Allies Who Made Our Foes—How Arab states we call our friends sow seeds of terror—and what we should do about it," *Newsweek*, October 1, 2001, 34.

12. Gold, *Hatred's*.

13. "Al Qaeda's New Front," produced by FRONTLINE and aired January 24-25, 2005 on PBS.

14. http://www.freerepublic.com/focus/f-news/1327711/posts.

15. New Front…," PBS.

16. *USA TODAY* , November 1, 2004.

17. *CNN Late Edition*, 10/24/04.

18. Gold, *Hatred's*, 6.

19. Surah 8:12.

20. Surah 9:5.

21. Surah 9:73.

22. Surah 9:123.

23. Surahs 2:190-193, 210, 224; 4:74-76, 89, 101; 5:36, 54; 8:12, 17, 59-60, 65; 9:5, 14, 29, 41, 123; 47:4, etc.

24. *The New York Times,* July 16, 2002.

25. Zakaria, *Newsweek*, October 1, 2001, 34.

26. John Laffin, *The PLO Connections* (Transworld, 1982), 18.

27. *Washington Post*, June 16, 1982.

28. *USA Today*, November 22, 2004.

29. Meyrav Wurmser, *The Schools of Ba'athism: a Study of Syrian Textbooks* (MEMRI, 2000), xii.

30. Anthony Browne, "The triumph of the East," *The Sunday Mail* (Brisbane, Australia), September 5, 2004, 54.

31. Gold, *Hatred's,* 246.

32. *World Net Daily*, January 14, 2003.

33. Bernard Lewis, *A Middle East Mosaic* (New York: Random House, 2000), 273.

34. From testimony of David A. Harris before Senate subcommittee hearing.

35. http://www.ajcadvocacy.net/saudi.htm.

36. *International Jerusalem Post*, March 26, 2004.

37. www.middleeastinfo.org/modules.php?op=modload& name=XForum&file=viewthread&tid= 1276.

38. *Al-Akbar,* April 18, 2001.

39. *Al-Quds-al-Arabi*, February 23, 1998; quoted in The Bulletin (Bend, Oregon), September 16, 2001, A1, 9.

40. Stephen Schwartz, "Radical Islam in America," *Imprimis*, May 2004, available at www.hillsdale.edu.

41. Anthony Deutsch, "Popular Dutch lawmaker urges halt to non-Western immigrants, shutting down radical mosques," November 19, 2004.

42. Constant Brand, "EU officials implore new immigrants to learn 'European values,'" Associated Press, Brussels, November 19, 2004.

43. Trifkovic, *Sword,* 173.

44. Benjamin Netanyahu, *Fighting Terrorism: How Democracies Can Defeat the International Terrorists Network* (New York: Farrar, Straus and Giroux, 2001), 49.

9—APPEACEMENT IN OUR DAY

DEMOCRATIC WORLD POWERS seem at their wits' end in the futile effort to bring real peace to the Middle East. As we have documented beyond question, a major reason for failed peace efforts is the refusal of Western leaders to admit the truth: that the heart of the problem is Islam itself and what Muslim leaders are doing in the name of Allah to foment unrest and hatred of Israel and of the West. Time and again, Israel is pressured to live at peace with and to give "back" yet more land to the "Palestinians." But appeasement works no better now than it ever has: there is no appeasing or appealing to a mass murderer once he has the upper hand! Until we are willing to admit the truth and to state clearly to ourselves and to the world—including the Muslim world—that terrorism will not be rewarded with further concessions, the slide down the slippery slope to destruction will only gather momentum.

Watching this abortive "peace process," which has been going on for many years with one American president after another trying to "bring peace at last," one is reminded of Neville Chamberlain's efforts to do the same in the late 1930s in Europe. Must we learn the bitter and costly lesson again and again that appeasement (of which Chamberlain, with his umbrella and winged collars, has become the pitiful, mocking symbol) doesn't work? Chamberlain was sympathetic to Hitler's complaints that Germany had been badly treated, as indeed nearly everyone later agreed was true. In this case, however, with some exceptions, "Palestinians'" complaints about "Israeli aggression" are false—and even if true, would not justify murderous terrorist attacks against Israel's civilian population.

Chamberlain was confident that Hitler was a reasonable man, a trustworthy man of his word. The world treated Arafat the same way, as though he, too, in spite of being the world's leading terrorist and murderer, were a man of his word to be reasoned with and trusted. Getting Arafat to sign yet another agreement was the hopeful goal when the latest arrangement wasn't working because the Palestinians were violating every provision they had promised to keep. Predictably, however, failure to achieve peace was always Israel's fault, though she attempted to abide by every new revision. Giving in to Hitler's and Mussolini's demands for "a little more land" to avert war in that day has a familiar ring to what has been going on in our time, chipping away at Israel to bring a supposed peace.

After visiting Germany, Lord Halifax (who became foreign secretary upon Anthony Eden's resignation in protest against appeasing Hitler) said that he was much impressed by the Nazi leaders and confident there would be peace after all. But the continued appeasement by Britain and France only encouraged Hitler to become bolder. As the crisis worsened and war seemed inevitable, Chamberlain announced in the House of Commons that he would make a "sudden and dramatic move." He would tell Hitler he was coming to Germany to talk with him personally. All Britain cheered "such courage." We've had a lot of talk in the Middle East—one bold "peace initiative" after another by American presidents and other Western leaders, while the situation only worsened.

In the midst of this lengthy speech, Chamberlain was handed a note that had just arrived from Hitler, inviting him to come to Munich to meet with him, Mussolini, and French president Daladier. Hearing that marvelous news, the members of the House of Commons jumped to their feet, stood on their seats, and shouted, "Peace must now be saved, and with it the world!"[1]

How many times has fresh optimism been aroused by another "peace" proposal brokered by the West between Israel and the "Palestinians"? And what has ever been achieved except Arafat's signature on another worthless piece of paper setting forth promising agreements he never intended to keep? No better will be the signature of Arafat's successor and long-time terrorist partner, Mahmoud Abbas, who received his Ph.D. in history from the Oriental College in Moscow on the thesis that the Holocaust never took place!

Chamberlain returned in triumph to England from Munich after giving to Germany the industrial and fortified region of Sudetenland, all but wiping out her major defenses against the Nazis. Bravely announcing "peace in our time," he was cheered for his courage and genius in achieving such a favorable agreement. As anyone with a modicum of moral courage and not blinded by his own selfish interests should have known, Hitler was not appeased, nor would he be. Nor was Britain saved from what would turn out to be the costliest war in its history. Germany completed its intended takeover of all of Czechoslovakia in March of 1939.

It was only the beginning. "Peace in our time" turned out to be a fool's nightmare. And the history of every attempt at peace between Israel and her Muslim neighbors has been no different, from the first "cease-fire" in 1948 until the present.

PEACE AT ANY PRICE?

Anthony Eden warned that Britain was allowing "the impression to gain currency abroad that we yield to constant pressure." Of course he was right, and Hitler hadn't needed to exert much pressure to discover this weak lack of moral resolve. Likewise, Arafat quickly learned that in the interest of a supposed peace, the West was also willing to pay almost any price at Israel's expense when new pressure was applied. A great propaganda advantage and other rewards were reaped from the Intifada, suicide bombers, and false accusations about Israeli atrocities, such as the alleged massacre in Jenin that the media eagerly passed on, only to learn that the PLO had lied to them—again.

After reporting in headlines and sensational stories of "eyewitness accounts" that hundreds of civilians had been massacred by Israeli troops in Jenin, the media was forced to admit that they had been deceived by the Palestinian propaganda machine. Reports that Israel had bombed Jenin into rubble brought protests worldwide and calls for intervention by the United Nations. The truth that was finally admitted was far different. In an attempt to minimize civilian casualties, instead of using available planes and artillery, Israeli troops risked their lives taking control of Jenin by fighting door to door. Colonel Gal Hirsh, head of operations in the Central Command, declared:

> Most of the Palestinians that were killed were armed terrorists; many had explosive devices strapped to their bodies [when they pretended to surrender]. I regret that some Palestinian civilians were injured and some were killed. We were fighting against armed terrorists. We asked the Palestinian civilians to evacuate their homes so they would not get hurt; some chose not to.

One of many newspapers that trumpeted the bogus accounts in order to cast Israel in the worst possible light, the *Minneapolis Star Tribune,* finally was forced to admit that its handling of the alleged "Jenin massacre" had been "awful…an editorial disaster…egregious stumble…." *The New York Times* and Associated Press at last admitted that Human Rights Watch had found "no evidence" of a massacre. The final count for the ten days of fierce fighting was forty-five Palestinians (most of them terrorists) killed and twenty-three Israeli soldiers.

Yet much of the Western media continues to wait hungrily for another juicy and tantalizing story to show that the Palestinians are killing, maiming, and purposely targeting thousands of innocent civilians only because they are forced to defend themselves from Israeli terrorism. Brigadier-General Eyal Shlein, head of army operations in the Jenin campaign, said, "It is important to emphasize that whoever uses [civilians] as defensive shields would pay a price for doing so. We uncovered large quantities of arms, ammunition, explosives, bombs, as well as dozens of laboratories where bombs were made." All were in residential areas, many in private homes.

SO MANY SIMILARITIES!

Hugh Christie, an M16 agent based in Berlin, had reported to Britain the fact that in a private conversation Hermann Goerring had frankly admitted that Germany intended to annex all of Czechoslovakia and Austria and "wanted a free hand in Eastern Europe." And did not Arafat declare plainly many times, not just in private conversation but publicly to the entire world (and have not a host of other Arab leaders said the same for more than fifty years), that the "Palestinians" intended to have their own state, stretching from the Jordan to the Mediterranean with Jerusalem as its capital? How many more times do Arafat's terrorist successors have to tell us this before we believe they really mean it and that they will be satisfied with nothing less than Israel's avowed destruction? Is it any less reprehensible to hand Israel over to the Arabs piece-by-piece than all at once?

Hitler flaunted his violations of the Versailles Treaty in Europe's face by increasing his armed forces three times beyond the agreed amount. Following an almost identical pattern, Arafat did the same, turning what was supposed to be a domestic police force into a modern army inside Israel capable of waging war against her from within her borders. Through Chamberlain's appeasement, Germany made a peace pact with England that gave the enemy time to build up its forces and only slightly delayed the inevitable war. Have not the results of appeasement in the Middle East been the same? The aggressor's promises are never kept and his appetite is never satisfied. Each concession opens the door to more demands, for which Israel is always blamed. Will we never learn?

As condition after condition of Versailles was broken, there were merely feeble complaints from the League of Nations, while England seemed only interested in "peace" for herself at any price, since others were paying the outrageous cost. The parallels to the current situation in the Middle East cannot be denied. For decades now, Western powers have fruitlessly attempted to appease Arafat and the Arab world, and are ready to do the same for his successor, Mahmoud Abbas—always at the expense of Israel's security and at the cost of thousands of Israeli lives. Unwilling to believe the plain statements by Arafat and the entire Muslim world that the goal is annihilation of Israel, appeasement has been stepped up notch after notch in the fool's dream that eventually the "Palestinians" would be satisfied and make no more demands. The current road map to peace, which was supposed to be completed in 2005 but hasn't even gotten started, is one more misstep in the wrong direction.

Other similarities between now and then cannot be denied. As Hitler moved boldly, with well-publicized intentions of taking over all of Czechoslovakia, Germany's calculated and wanton aggression was excused as justified reaction to violence and atrocities against Germans in Sudetenland by brutal Czech police. The reports were false, but the Nazis didn't care, nor apparently did the world that accepted them—all in the interest of "peace in our time." So today, Israel, acting in self-defense, is accused of using violence against those who harbor, train, and send suicide bombers to kill her civilians. Incredibly, terrorists are believed when they charge Israel with unprovoked aggression against them, but Israel is accused of lying no matter what she says.

Under heavy pressure from world opinion, Israel has been forced to negotiate with a mass murderer and to look the other way while he violated every provision of every agreement that he had so solemnly signed. Arafat consistently flaunted his violations in the faces of Israeli leaders. Intimidated by pressure from the UN and EU, which could bankrupt it by refusing to buy its products, Israel has excused its "peace partner's" bad faith and continued to attempt in good faith to negotiate "cease-fires" in defiance of common sense. Again and again, Israel failed to hold Arafat to his word and instead appeased his greedy demands. They have permitted lies and aggression to continue without adequate response in order to "make peace" with those who only mouth words about peace to cover their true intentions.

HITLER ANNOUNCED HIS INTENTIONS PLAINLY

Jews were not the only people targeted for death. In 1938, Hitler said he would send his troops forth in the East with "the command to send every man, woman and child of Polish origin and language to death, ruthlessly and mercilessly. This is the only way to win the living space we need. Poland will be depopulated and settled by Germans."[2] Jews, however, were his main target everywhere that he could find them.

Germans knew very well what was happening—and so did the rest of the world. *Mein Kampf* earned Hitler one million dollars a year in royalties, because all municipalities were required to purchase it to give *gratis* to all newly married couples. Its Chapter Eleven is an unabashed diatribe against the Jew, who is described thus: "He will stop at nothing. His utterly low-down conduct is so appalling that one really cannot be surprised if in the imagination of our people the Jew is pictured as the incarnation of Satan and the symbol of evil." Again there is a familiar ring that resounds in the same anti-Semitic hate propaganda emanating from Saudi Arabia and the entire Muslim world, whether in textbooks and other official publications, sermons in mosques, news reports on radio and television, etc.—all somehow excused as justified by the provocation of Israel's very existence in the heart of the "Arab nation."

In *Mein Kampf*, Hitler argues that "the Jewish peril will be stamped out the moment the general public come into possession of...*The Protocols of the Learned Elders of Zion* [an acknowledged fraud but still popular in Muslim circles today]...and understand it."[3] He couldn't wait for that to happen, so he planned and efficiently organized the mass extermination of Europe's Jews in special camps designed for that purpose.

In Hitler's January 30, 1939, Reichstag speech, he plainly declared that the outbreak of war would result in the annihilation of Europe's Jews. His passion to exterminate all Jews, though expressed so often and so clearly, was either not believed, or it was tolerated because no one cared enough to do anything about it. Of course, after the fact, it was universally condemned in the West with the excuse that the truth about the Holocaust hadn't really been known—but that was a lie, and the professed good intentions came too late to help any of the six million victims.

And now what is to be done with regard to Muhammad's even clearer declaration that every Jew in the world must be killed? When will that be believed as current and irrevocable Islamic doctrine and denounced by the media and world leaders? And when will our foreign policy be based on the truth instead of cover-up and excuses for Muslim lies?

As in Hitler's time, so today, no voice is raised in the United Nations or in Europe against the clearly pronounced vows of Muslim leaders that an entire people must be exterminated. Naïvely, Muhammad's unequivocal statement is treated as though it no longer applies to our day, when indeed it does. No Muslim leader has the authority to abrogate anything in the Qur'an or anything that Muhammad taught and practiced as recorded in the *hadith.*

Nor are the repeated threats and efforts of the PLO and Arab leaders to annihilate Israel met with the international outrage they deserve. Instead, the persistent demands of Arabs for the destruction of Israel are honored as a legitimate cry on behalf of aggrieved "Palestinians" who must be appeased through the "peace" plans that the West intends to impose upon Israel.

PEACE IS NOT ALLOWED

Those Arabs who recognize that Israel isn't going to be defeated and who want to normalize relations with her for the good of the entire Middle East find it difficult and extremely dangerous to express that opinion and virtually impossible to implement it. The visit of Anwar Sadat to Jerusalem in 1977 was only one of a number of perceived offenses against fundamentalist Islam that would bring about his assassination. A devout Muslim, he went to the Al-Aqsa mosque to pray—another unforgivable offense. The Saudi royal family has pledged not to do so until Jerusalem is "liberated" and under Muslim control. Old Saudi-Egyptian rivalries were resurrected.

It was the last straw when Sadat made "peace." The Grand Mufti of Jerusalem, Sheik Saadeddin Alami, issued a *fatwa* ordering Sadat to be killed, promising his assassins a place in Paradise. What other "god" or religion incites and rewards cold-blooded murderers?

To negotiate in good faith with Israel under any pretext is, in the Muslim mind, the unpardonable sin. Arafat was criticized and had to walk a fine line. Even to pretend to make peace with Israel, though it was a ruse to gain her trust in order to destroy her, was deemed an outrage. Consider what Egypt's *Al-Da'wa*, the magazine of the Muslim Brotherhood, had to say:

> Because of the essential nature of the Jew, it was futile to seek to establish relations with Israeli progressive forces, as Yasser Arafat, the chairman of the PLO, had proposed. In fact all Jews, like Menachem Begin, had spilled the blood of the Arabs and usurped their lands and homes. The inclination to betrayal and belligerence is deeply implanted in the soul of every Jew.[4]

The sentiment expressed by the Muslim Brotherhood cannot be ignored as merely the view of an extremist fundamentalist faction. This is Islam. Any Arab raised in PLO territory or in any other Muslim country will testify that he has been taught to hate Jews and to work for their annihilation from the time he was old enough to understand the slogans and raise his tiny fist in affirmation.

After losing the 1967 Six-Day War that had been intended to annihilate Israel, Arab heads of state met in Khartoum, Sudan, August 29–September 1, 1967. Under Nasser's leadership they adopted the "three no's": "No peace with Israel; No negotiations with Israel; No recognition of Israel." These express the very heart of Islam and have never been rescinded, making even the pretence of negotiations toward peace with Israel a complete fraud.

As the "peace process" continues, Palestinians murder and torch the homes of fellow Arabs suspected of cooperating with Israel. Again we hear echoes from the past. The same thing was being done in the 1920s, '30s, and '40s to any Arabs who did not join al-Husseini in his riots against the Jews and who favored peaceful coexistence. In fact, at that time more Arabs were being killed by the Mufti's terrorist followers than either Jews or British soldiers: "Mayor, affiliated official, sheikh, village *mukhtar* (headman), rival Arab notable, and even prominent Muslim religious figures—all were victims" of the Mufti's henchmen. From April 1936, "the Mufti's 'systematic extermination' caused the murder or flight from the country of any Arab suspected of less than total loyalty" to the ongoing persecution and murder of British and Jews.[5]

Now, as then, Muslim terrorists who kill Jews are honored with streets and holidays named after them. This is the glorious foundation for "peaceful coexistence"? Yet an ad in *The Jerusalem Post* boasted that "The Jerusalem Heights Penthouses" were "As close to heaven as you can ever get." In fact, they are close enough to the enemy to be destroyed with a few mortar rounds. Will Israel awaken to the grim reality before it is too late?

Speaking for God, the prophet Ezekiel condemns the leaders of Israel who "have seduced my people, saying, Peace; and there was no peace...which prophesy concerning Jerusalem...visions of peace for her, and there is no peace."[6] Ezekiel's rebuke, so apropos at that time, is also a prophecy that surely describes Israel and her leaders today.

THE REWARDS OF "PEACE"

With high hopes, the Gaza-Jericho Autonomy Agreement (Cairo Agreement) was signed April 5, 1994, by Yitzhak Rabin and Yasser Arafat and witnessed by The United States of America, The Russian Federation, and The Arab Republic of Egypt. It is stated to be an "implementation of UN resolutions 242 and 338" within the framework of the "Middle East peace process initiated in Madrid in October 1991." It explicitly requires Israel and the Palestinian Authority (PA) mutually to "cooperate in combating criminal activity which may affect both sides"[7] and to "take all measures necessary in order to prevent acts of terrorism, crime and hostilities directed against each other, against individuals falling under the other's authority and against their property, and shall take legal measures against offenders...."[8]

Arafat never intended, nor has the Palestinian Authority even pretended, to keep one provision. It will be no different with his successors. The PA audaciously violates every promise, and the UN turns a blind eye. Instead of demanding compliance (which it could through its superior military power), Israel helplessly accepts the fact (even as terrorism increases) that the PA will never extradite even car thieves, let alone terrorists. The PA police all drive cars stolen in Israel.

When Israel attempts to pursue terrorists into their PA hideouts, the world (which never complains about the murder of innocent Israelis) condemns Israel for "attacking" the poor, down-trodden Palestinians. Palestinian propaganda, aided by world media, has done a masterful job of depicting tiny Israel as cruel Goliath and the surrounding Muslim enemies, with overwhelming numerical superiority, as little David, righteously standing up to the evil giant.

Alleged peace has brought devastating commercial consequences as well. Palestinians who owe money to Israelis no longer make their monthly payments, leaving the Israelis with no hope of ever collecting. The same is true of millions of dollars in debts owed to Israeli businesses and industry that had been selling to Palestinians on credit. "Lawyer Amnon Zichroni, who represents the PA in Israel, has bluntly told Israeli creditors that 'their chances of recovery are virtually non-existent.'"[9]

And so it is with thieves and hoodlums, who can now steal cars, deal drugs, burglarize and rob with abandon, knowing it is just a few steps to a safe haven within PA territory, where the Israeli police can neither follow nor trace them.[10]

THE TOUTED "PEACE PROCESS"

While Israel's leaders negotiate "peace" with Syria, Katyusha rockets fired by Hizballah terrorists, backed and protected by Syria, rain down upon Galilee. Syrian Defense Minister Mustafa Tlass has called Israel "a burden to the U.S. and the rest of the world."[11] Yet until the recent increase in suicide bombings by terrorists and escalation of hostilities, Israel's leaders had kept the faith for years, continuing to believe that peace could somehow be established with those whose implacable hatred seeks only her annihilation, as Islam requires. The recent attacks upon New York and the Pentagon have been the final proof that negotiating with terrorists is tantamount to suicide.

In the Fall of 1995, just before departing for the Washington Summit, on Jordanian TV Arafat reassured Arabs that the 1974 PLO Plan of Phases (pretend peace to establish a foothold inside Israel from which to launch her final destruction) was right on track. Numerous public speeches by Arafat since the inception of the "peace process" continued to openly call for Israel's destruction. A number of sources offer videos with footage of Arafat and his spokesmen and Islamic clerics over the last twenty years stating clearly in Arabic to Muslim audiences that all of the "peace" negotiations are aimed at one thing: the ultimate destruction of Israel. Article 19 of the PLO Charter couldn't be any clearer: "The establishment of the State of Israel is null and void, regardless of the passage of time." But the Western world's media and political and religious leaders deliberately close their eyes and ears to the obvious truth and dream up new "peace plans," as though that were what the Arabs really wanted.

In contrast to most of his colleagues around the world, Mortimer Zuckerman, editor-in-chief of *U.S. News & World Report*, is not afraid to state the facts. While European and UN leaders were still praising Arafat as a man of peace, worthy of the Nobel Prize he had received, Zuckerman wrote plainly: "The man's [Arafat's] duplicity is the stuff of legend. Dennis Ross, the former U.S. envoy to the Middle East, wrote, 'I've never met an Arab leader who trusts Arafat.... Almost all Arab leaders have stories about how he misled or betrayed them."[12]

Kuwait learned the hard way when Arafat, whom they had propped up with hundreds of millions of dollars, betrayed them by giving Saddam Hussein the vital intelligence for his 1990 invasion of that country. Arafat was sure Hussein would prevail even against the United States and wanted to be on the good side of the victor, not the victims. Yet the West continued to support Arafat financially as it forced Israel to treat him like an honest leader in a mutual effort for peace.

THE RE-MADE ARAFAT

A number of Arafat's diatribes vowing Israel's destruction were put together on a video by then Chairman of the House Foreign Relations Committee Ben Gilman (Republican, New York), who announced he would present the Arafat tapes to the world in a press conference on September 21, 1995. No one from the media was interested! Even more incredible, Israel's Ambassador to the U.S., Itamar Rabinovich, pleaded with Gilman not to air the tapes—it might hinder the "peace process"![13]

And how did this vaunted "peace process" begin? It is an incredible story of the pressure of world opinion forcing Israel into acceptance of Arafat and the PLO, in spite of the fact that they were in exile in Tunisia, and the PLO Charter plainly denied Israel's existence and called for its annihilation—as it still does. No fiction writer could have expected any audience to believe such a scenario—but it happened. Jeff Jacoby explains it in the Boston Globe as well as anyone could:

> In 1993, following secret negotiations in Oslo, [Israel] embarked on a "peace process" designed to elevate Arafat and the PLO to heights of power, wealth, and respect they had never before known. In exchange for Arafat's written promise of peace—"the PLO renounces the use of terrorism and other acts of violence"—Israel agreed to forget the PLO's long history of mass murder and to treat it as the legitimate representative of the Palestinians. The deal was sealed at the White House on Sept. 13, 1993, when Prime Minister Yitzhak Rabin gave Arafat his hand and affirmed his new status as Israel's partner in peace.
>
> What followed was unprecedented in the history of statecraft. Arafat and thousands of PLO killers, now reconstituted as the "Palestinian Authority," entered Gaza and the West Bank in triumph. In short order, Israel transferred virtually every Arab city and town in the territories to Arafat's control. It allowed

the Palestinian Authority to assume full administrative power over the Palestinian people. It not only agreed to the creation of an armed Palestinian Authority militia, it supplied the authority with weapons. It began paying Arafat a multimillion-dollar monthly allowance and lobbied internationally for additional financial support. It permitted the Palestinian Authority to build an airport, operate radio and television networks, and deal with other countries as a sovereign power.[14]

Netanyahu writes, "My party and I were virtually isolated in our warning that Arafat would not keep his word.... We were widely castigated as enemies of peace.... Our argument was that handing Gaza over to Arafat would immediately create a lush terrorist haven...." Of course, Netanyahu was right.

1. From diary entry of Henry (Chips) Cannon, September 28, 1938.

2. http://www.geocities.com/onemansmind/hr/hitler/Hitler05.html.

3. http://www.stormfront.org/books/mein_kampf/mkv1ch11.html.

4. G. Kepel, *The Prophet and Pharaoh* (London: Al-Saqi Books, 1985), 112-113.

5. Joan Peters, *From Time Immemorial: The Origins of the Arab-Jewish Conflict Over Palestine* (New York: J. KAP Publishing U.S.A., 1984), 314.

6. Ezekiel 13:10,16.

7. Article XII, 2.

8. Article XVIII.

9. *The Jerusalem Post International Edition*, Week Ending January 6, 1996, p. 10.

10. Ibid.

11. *The Jerusalem Post International Edition*, Week Ending January 6, 1996, p. 1.

12. *U.S. News & World Report*, July 8, 2002.

13. *The Jerusalem Post International Edition*, Week Ending November 25, 1995, p. 30.

14. http://www.science.co.il/Arab-Israeli-conflict/Articles/Jacoby-2002-04-04.asp.

10—DELUSIONS AND DESTINY

THE WEST WAS THRILLED when President Jimmy Carter, on March 26, 1979, hosted the signing of what had been dreamed of for decades—a genuine Middle East peace treaty. This would be the first ever signed between Israel and a Muslim nation. Carter had brought together soon-to-be-assassinated Egyptian President Anwar Sadat and Israeli Prime Minister Menachim Begin by talking Israel into "giving back" the Sinai to Egypt, even though it had never belonged to her. The four-thousand-year-old title deed, signed by the God of the Bible, had described the Promised Land as "from the river of Egypt unto the great river, the river Euphrates."[1]

Sadat was not entering into this agreement out of any love for Jews or Israel but to gain prestige in the Arab world by taking a huge chunk of territory away from Israel without firing a shot. In September of 1953, there had been rumors that Hitler was still alive. "The official Egyptian regime-controlled weekly, *Al Mussawar*, asked prominent Egyptians the following question: 'If you wanted to send Hitler a personal letter, what would you write to him?'" One of those questioned was Colonel Anwar el-Sadat. Here is part of what he said in an open letter to Hitler: "My dear Hitler, I congratulate you from the bottom of my heart. Even if you appear to have been defeated, in reality you are the victor."[2]

As a professing Christian, Carter felt a sense of destiny. Surely history would remember him as the president who at last brought peace to the Middle East. To make the event even more memorable, in his televised speech at the formal signing of the agreement in the White House, Carter wanted to quote one verse about peace from the Qur'an and one from the Bible. There are more than four hundred such verses in the Bible, but Carter's speech writers had to search the Qur'an long and hard before finding at last the *lone verse* about peace. There are 114 Surahs (chapters) in the Qur'an. The verse they found was in Surah 8, verse 61. Had the speech writers been well acquainted with Islam and the Qur'an they might not have given this verse to the President—but it was the only one available.

Enthusiastically, Carter declared to the watching world: "In the Qur'an, we read, 'But if the enemy incline towards peace, do thou also incline towards peace and trust in God.'[3] So let us now lay aside war.... We pray God...that these dreams will come true."

Islam's "dream," however, as we have seen, is not what Carter and Israel imagined. The verse says "Allah," not "God," and Allah hates Jews and has decreed their destruction—not a likely foundation for peace with Israel! Furthermore, Surah 8 is titled, "Spoils of War" and is all about fighting and pillaging to spread Islam throughout the entire world. For example, verse 65 says, "O Prophet, exhort the believers to fight...." Verse 67 says, "It is not for any Prophet to have captives until he hath made slaughter in the land." All Carter needed was an umbrella in hand to perfect his impersonation of Chamberlain.

The *only* peace Islam offers is to those vanquished in *jihad* who surrender to Muslim warriors and acknowledge Allah as the only God and Muhammad as his prophet. No Muslim leader in the world can go against Muhammad's example set in the A.D. 628 Treaty of Hudaybiya to which we have referred. Therefore, as soon as he had signed the Oslo Accords in 1993, Arafat immediately began to apologize in Arabic to Muslims around the world, explaining that he was only following Muhammad's example, entering into a *hudna* to deceive Israel and ultimately to destroy her. He did not want to suffer the fate of Sadat, who had been assassinated by the Muslim Brotherhood for daring to make peace with Israel.

HOW DID ISRAEL GET HERE?

How did Israel come to the place where an enemy that is determined to annihilate her is looked upon as her "partner for peace"? The painful "peace process" has been going on for nearly thirty years. It began when Sadat finally realized that attacking Israel in war after war was getting the Arabs nowhere. He made an unprecedented visit to Jerusalem on November 19-21, 1977—the first by an Arab head of state to Israel. He addressed the Israeli Knesset and was named "Man of the Year for 1977" by *Time Magazine.* Peace negotiations were begun between Israel and Egypt. When they deadlocked in mid-1978, Sadat and Israel Prime Minister Menachem Begin accepted President Carter's invitation to a U.S./Israeli/ Egyptian summit meeting at the Presidential retreat, Camp David (in Maryland), on September 5, 1978.

Twelve days of intensive negotiations resulted in the agreement referred to above, supposedly based on UN resolutions 242 and 338. Arafat and Begin shared the 1978 Nobel Peace Prize for their historic agreements. It was to set an example for any other neighbors willing to negotiate with Israel. To reach the "agreement," Carter bribed Sadat with Israel's military secrets (also given to Saudi Arabia at the same time). Egypt came out of Camp David with a huge monetary reward and Israel's military secrets. All Israel had was a worthless piece of paper that violated the Qur'an and everything Islam stands for and would never be honored by any other Muslims. It was a bad exchange!

On October 14, 1988, Arafat (the worst mass murderer of modern times other than Hitler, Stalin, and Mao) in a letter to Israel's Prime Minister, condemned all forms of terrorism and recognized Israel's right to exist. Never mind that he didn't mean it—this deceitful pledge created a delusion that changed everything for the Middle East.

Imagine Osama bin Laden brought to court and found guilty of his many murders. Admitting his guilt, he declares to the court, "From now on, scout's honor, I promise to be a good boy. No more terrorism for me!" Duly impressed by bin Laden's forthrightness, the judge, jury, attorneys, and spectators give him a standing ovation, and the judge says, "We'll give you the Nobel Prize and make you a world ambassador for peace!"

That incredible scenario is no more absurd than Arafat's re-invention as an icon of peace. Indeed, it was childishly simple: he vowed to reform, and—presto!—his heinous crimes of four decades were as though they had never been. Under pressure from the world, Israel made the huge mistake of accepting this master terrorist as its "partner for peace." Without a vote from the Palestinians themselves, the PLO—a terrorist organization (and one that hadn't even been created by Palestinians)—was recognized as the official representative of the Palestinians and given UN status as a Non-Government Organization (NGO). The Madrid Peace Conference of October 1991 followed, bringing together delegates from Israel, Syria, Jordan, and Lebanon, along with the PLO, that had now taken on the identity of the Palestinians. This led to secret PLO-Israeli talks in Oslo in January 1993 that culminated in what is now known as "the Oslo Accords."

In a letter to Israeli Prime Minister Rabin, September 9, 1993, Arafat said: "The PLO recognizes the right of...Israel to exist in peace and security...commits itself...to a peaceful resolution of the conflict between the two sides...renounces the use of terrorism and other acts of violence [and] affirms that those articles of the Palestinian Covenant which deny Israel's right to exist...are now inoperative and no longer valid [and] undertakes to submit to the Palestinian National Council for formal approval the necessary changes...." As we have already seen, lying is honorable for a Muslim if it succeeds in deceiving the enemy—and words have a different meaning. As Arafat often said, "'Peace,' for us, is the destruction of Israel."

As a reward for this transparent deceit, President Clinton naïvely promised to pay $500 million of U.S. taxpayers' money to the PLO and its agencies. In exchange, Arafat solemnly swore to comply with all terms of the Oslo Accords. As subsequent events have proved, he had no more intention of living up to that promise than Hitler had to keep any of his promises to Chamberlain. It was *déjà vu* once again. Arafat's ability to lie like Hitler and thereby get the foolishly trusting Israelis to make further concessions elevated him in the eyes of not only the Palestinians but the entire Arab world. After all, for them, Hitler ranks second only to Muhammad!

THE FRUIT OF THE OSLO ACCORDS

On September 13, 1993, Prime Minister Yitzhak Rabin and Yasser Arafat signed the Oslo "Declaration of Principles"—a mockery of the League of Nations' 1922 "Declaration of Principles"—and Israel officially recognized Arafat and the PLO. In fact, Arafat never kept one provision of this agreement and never intended to do so. He couldn't have kept it without betraying Islam. Immediately, over radio and television, as we have noted, to save himself from Sadat's fate, Arafat began apologizing in Arabic for Oslo, while reassuring Muslims of his true intent.

On May 4, 1994, in Cairo, Arafat and Rabin (who would be assassinated on November 4, 1995) signed the "Jericho First" Peace Accord, supposedly implementing Oslo. The whole "peace process" was an Islamic ploy by Arafat and will be no different under his successor and long-time terrorist partner, Mahmoud Abbas. Oslo required Arafat to remove from the PLO Charter the call for Israel's annihilation. In grand style he announced that the clause had been revoked. Yet in the same speech he praised terrorists and terrorist countries. It was a bald "hoax," as London's *Daily Telegraph*, May 2, 1996, declared. The clause had not and still has not been removed. And even if it were, that would change nothing. It is not the PLO Charter that determines Israel's extermination, but Islam itself, which the PLO (as good Muslims) must follow under pain of death.

So ecstatic that she was blind to the obvious truth, Rabin's widow exclaimed joyfully, "Tonight I can tell you that the Palestinian

National Council has revoked the clauses in its covenant that called for the destruction of Israel!" Rabin's successor, Prime Minister Shimon Peres, hailed this "most important historical development in our region in 100 years." On *Voice of Israel Radio* he exulted (evoking once again the haunting memory of Chamberlain), "Today we have ended the Israeli-Arab conflict—Utopia is coming!" What madness! He has eaten those ridiculously irrational words and gotten indigestion from them many times since.

Israeli leaders were willfully closing their eyes and ears to the frequent calls for an end to Israel, repeated many times throughout the "peace negotiations" by Arafat and other PLO leaders. Arafat's deputy, Abu Iyad, declared: "It is our right that we should have...an independent Palestinian state that will function as a base from which to liberate Jaffa, Akko and all of Palestine."[4] Instead of Utopia, the hell that Islam has created for Israel was only getting hotter. In the ten years prior to Oslo, about two hundred Israelis had been killed by terrorists, while in the ten years following, about twelve hundred were killed and more than five thousand wounded. This is *peace*? But Israel is always blamed.

U.S. News & World Report Editor-in-Chief, Mortimer B. Zuckerman, perceptively writes:

> Yasser Arafat may be dead, but Arafatism lives on. That is the crucial fact amid all the talk about resurrecting the road map to peace. Arafat's principal legacy is hate, his gift to the world a kind of terrorism whose techniques have been aped from Indonesia to Iraq. Arafat...used every platform—radio, TV, newspapers, the mosques, schools, even summer camps for kids—to inculcate a hatred of Jews, Israel, and the West.... The Palestinians who mobbed his coffin represented as much the hate he had fostered as grief.
>
> Yet even when he broke his promises the Clinton administration refused to hold him accountable while the hundreds of millions of dollars he received to improve life for Palestinians were diverted to support a terrorist network.... The fatal flaw of Oslo was that violations of Palestinian obligations provided the rationale not for rebuke but for more concessions.... If George Bush

[holds Palestinians accountable and] takes the long view, he could become not only a war president but a peace president too.[5]

ISLAM'S LEGACY OF DEATH—AND WESTERN BLINDNESS

On the very afternoon of the historic handshake with Yitzhak Rabin on the White House lawn, Arafat's name appeared near the top of a list of world terrorists released by a congressional committee. Al Gore had been one of nearly fifty Senators who had signed a petition in 1988 to have Arafat arrested and tried as the terrorist he was. Clinton and Gore later received him repeatedly as an honored statesman and good friend in the White House.

Thankfully, President Bush refused to deal with Arafat at all. In his condolences to the Palestinian people for Arafat's death on November 11, 2004, Bush carefully avoided honoring Arafat in any way. He referred to Arafat's death as "a significant moment in Palestinian history," and for "the period of transition that is ahead," urged "all in the region and throughout the world to join in helping make progress toward…the ultimate goal of peace."[6] What President Bush and the rest of the Western world still will not openly admit, however, is that Arafat's bloody career was based on Islam. Furthermore, Islam must and will continue to control the actions of Arafat's successors beginning with sixty-nine-year-old Abbas and whoever else may succeed him in days to come!

All nineteen of the 9/11/01 hijackers were Muslims—fifteen from Saudi Arabia, our supposed ally in the war against terrorism. We have traced their path and know that their evil was all done in the name and to the glory of Allah and Islam. They left behind records of the Islamic purification rituals they went through in preparation and the prayers they recited to Allah just before impact. Evidence gathered by the FBI shows that the Twin Towers were brought down in pursuit of world conquest for Allah and to obtain Islam's promised Paradise for the hijackers.

Yet immediately following 9/11, in a speech at the Islamic Center in Washington D.C., President Bush declared, "The face of terror is not the true face of Islam. Islam is peace." He reassured a joint session of Congress and the Senate and the people of the United States, "Terrorists practice a fringe form of Islamic extremism that has been rejected by Muslim clerics [and] perverts the peaceful teachings of Islam.... Its teachings are good and peaceful." Echoing the same politically correct delusion, Prime Minister Tony Blair declared, "This terrorist act has nothing to do with Islam." Colin Powell likewise said, "Leave Islam out of this. Islam is a peaceful religion." They couldn't possibly have been so ignorant of the horrible truth as to have believed the lie they were passing on to the public. Terrorists were greatly encouraged to persist in their murderous intent, having been given proof once again that they would be called peacemakers no matter what they did.

Amir Taheri, practicing Iranian Muslim and editor of the Paris-based *Politique Internationale*, warned that continuing to deny the undeniable responsibility of Islam itself in the September 11, 2001, attacks in order not to offend Muslims, "amounts to a whitewash." He added that such denials are "not only disingenuous but also a disservice to Muslims.... It is both dishonest and dangerous for Muslims to remain in a state of denial...."[7]

Yet President Bush insists, "The terrorists are traitors to their own faith, trying, in effect, to hijack Islam itself." If that is true, then Muhammad "hijacked" Islam thirteen centuries ago at its very start. But how could the founder and his immediate successors practice an extreme and illegitimate form of Islam? Who knew and lived Islam better than Muhammad himself?

In the *Wall Street Journal,* Eliot Cohen of Johns Hopkins School of Advanced International Studies reminded any world leaders who would listen that "an hour spent surfing the Web will give...the kind of insights [into Islam]...found during World War II by reading *Mein Kampf* or the writings of Lenin, Stalin or Mao. Nobody would like to think that a major world religion has a deeply aggressive and dangerous strain in it...but uttering uncomfortable and unpleasant truths...defines leadership." The major threat to Israel today—and to the world—is not from a few fanatics, as we have pointed out, but from devout Muslims. Indeed, from Islam itself!

WHAT ABOUT 1967?

One often hears the proposed solution to Middle East woes: "Just move the borders back to 1967. The Palestinians will be happy, and that will bring peace." It was in 1964, however, during those nineteen years from 1948 to 1967 when Jordan and Egypt held the West Bank and Gaza Strip (and could have created the "Palestinian State" had they so desired), that the Palestine Liberation Organization (PLO) was formed. Obviously, then, going back to the 1967 borders is not what the Arabs really want—though they would take it as a first stage toward the planned destruction of Israel. In fact, in 1967 they were so unhappy with the borders existing then (established by the war in 1948) that they were in the final stages of readiness to attack and annihilate Israel after nineteen years of preparation.

There is no special significance to 1967. The PLO charter declares that the very existence of Israel is illegitimate at any time. It says that the Jews are merely citizens of the countries where they happen to live all over the world, not entitled to a land of their own, and that the intention of the Arabs is to take all of Palestine for themselves and literally "exterminate" the Jews. The logo of the PLO shows Palestine as comprising the entire territory from the Mediterranean to the River Jordan. Israel isn't even a small part of the picture—it doesn't exist, as far as Islam is concerned, for reasons already explained.

On July 26, 1959, Egypt's president Gamal Abdel Nasser, who would found the PLO five years later in Cairo (Palestinian pawns in the camps had no part in its formation), boasted during a speech in Alexandria, "I announce from here, on behalf of the United Arab Republic people, that this time we will exterminate Israel." "This time" was a reminder that the 1948 and 1956 defeats at the hands of Israel would be avenged. Indeed, the Arabs had been planning that revenge from the very day the 1948 war had supposedly ended. In 1967, the average Muslim on the street referred to "the nineteen-year war," by which he meant that in obedience to Islam, there had never been "peace." As far as the Arabs were concerned, they were still involved in the same 1948 war through planning and preparation, until they were ready to annihilate Israel.

To Egypt's National Assembly, March 26, 1964, Nasser declared that the problem was "the very existence of Israel." On March 8, 1965, he boasted, "We shall enter [Palestine] with its soil saturated in blood." Shortly thereafter he declared, "We aim at...the eradication of Israel." After nineteen years preparing for this war, the Arab world was supremely confident that this time Israel would at last be overwhelmed and destroyed.

On May 16, 1967, Nasser ordered UN peace-keeping forces to leave the Sinai, showing the impotence of that organization to keep any peace. By May 18, Egyptian troops were massed in the Sinai on Israel's border, and Syrian troops had done the same on the Golan. The *Voice of the Arabs* radio program announced, "The sole method we shall apply against Israel is total war, which will result in the extermination of Zionist existence." On May 20 the Syrian Defense Minister boasted, "Our forces are now entirely ready...to explode the Zionist presence in the Arab homeland...to enter into a battle of annihilation." On May 22 Egypt closed the Straits of Tiran to all Israeli shipping, cutting off a major life line. It was an act of war. On May 27 Nasser threatened, "Our basic objective will be the destruction of Israel.... We will not accept any coexistence with Israel...."

On May 30, as self-assigned leader of the Arab world, Nasser confidently boasted, "The armies of Egypt, Jordan, Syria and Lebanon are poised on the borders of Israel...while standing behind us are the armies of Iraq, Algeria, Kuwait, Sudan and the whole Arab nation...the critical hour has arrived." Iraq's president thundered, "The existence of Israel is an error which must be rectified. This is our opportunity to wipe out the ignominy which has been with us since 1948. Our goal is clear—to wipe Israel off the map." Such was and still is their unwavering intent as required by Islam, and which they have never been ashamed to declare to the world.

WE WERE THERE!

My wife, Ruth, and I, together with our four children, ages eight to fifteen, were driving through Egypt at that time in our VW mini-bus, as eyewitnesses to Arab intentions. Early in June, on an Egyptian freighter from Alexandria to Beirut (at that time the "jewel of the Mediterranean," comparable to any European city), I sat in the lounge with wild-eyed, cheering Arabs around me, watching on TV the military buildup under Nasser and listening as he vowed repeatedly that Israel would be destroyed. We saw the confident exhilaration with which the Arab world was intoxicated, momentarily united behind Nasser in this common goal, certain that the time had come at last to exterminate the Jews. We were driving through Syria into Jordan when the Lord graciously redirected us north to Turkey. We crossed that border safely just before war broke out.

Instead of waiting passively until the enemies surrounding and threatening her decided in their time and way to begin the attack, Israel had no choice but to make a preemptive strike in self-defense. As friends should do, Israel told the U.S. of its plans and was promptly betrayed to the Arabs. The destruction of the Egyptian and Syrian air forces on the ground and the humiliating defeat of the Arab armies in what became known as the "Six-Day War" is history. It was just another fulfillment of inerrant biblical prophecy: "In that day will I make the governors of Judah like…a torch of fire in a sheaf; and they shall devour all the people round about…and Jerusalem shall be inhabited again…."[8]

On June 8, the morning of the fourth day of the war, the USS Liberty, a floating electronics vacuum, arrived off the Sinai coast. It began to sweep Israel, sucking in every Israeli military communication and relaying it all to the British Secret Service's giant electronic listening post on Cyprus, which had the capability of filtering, decoding, and analyzing the mass of electronics the Liberty was accumulating. This was then transmitted to the Arab armed forces, giving complete maps of every Israeli military movement in advance. With that help, the Arabs might have been able to use their overwhelming numerical superiority to turn the tide of the war. At least casualties on both sides would have been much larger.

The CIA had already been leaking secret Israeli information to the Jordanians, but what the Liberty was doing was carrying the diplomatic game too far. Israel had no choice except to sink this American ship, which she did forthwith. Of course, the media was filled with criticism for this heartless attack. No one believed Israel's excuse that the Liberty had been mistaken for a hostile Egyptian ship. Neither the U.S. nor Israel cared to tell the truth, so the criticism persists to this day.

Abba Eban, Israeli foreign minister, came the closest to telling the story, if one reads between the lines. He was in New York at the United Nations attempting to arrange a cease-fire. Although the Egyptians, in the months before the war, had gone on record repeatedly that they were going to attack Israel and would exterminate all the Israelis, they now self-righteously demanded that Israeli forces withdraw first. But when the Liberty was sunk, Eban reports that the Egyptian ambassador to the UN, El-Kony, was reduced to tears, having received a message from Cairo "to get a cease-fire as soon as possible."[9] This is not the only time the Americans have betrayed Israel, their only true ally in the Middle East. After all, unlike the Soviets in the days when they were the chief sponsors of the Arabs, the U.S. tries to play both sides.

Nasser never recovered from the blow to his ego and died of a heart attack in 1970. His successor, Anwar el-Sadat, is remembered for making "peace" with Israel. For that crime, while watching a military parade, he was assassinated by his own troops, who were members of the Muslim Brotherhood.

Israel's stunning victory aroused Jew hatred to new heights and made the Muslims all the more determined to annihilate her. In Aden, a rash of "murder, looting, renewed destruction to synagogues" was the result. When the British learned that the Arabs were "planning to massacre what remained of the Jewish community," they helped to evacuate them.[10] Coming under renewed attack, the Jewish community in Morocco began to head for Israel in earnest.

The murders of Libyan Jews that had followed the UN's partition of Palestine in 1947 were renewed after the Six-Day War, literally forcing the remaining Jews to escape for their lives. In 1970, President Qaddafy "confiscated Jewish owned property that the fleeing Libyan-born Jews had left behind."[11] It was the same everywhere, so that most Jews who still remained in Muslim countries got out with only the clothes on their backs. In Egypt, all Jewish men from sixteen to seventy years old were put in concentration camps when war broke out. When finally released to join their families in the exodus to Israel, they had to sign a paper that they were not being pushed out of Egypt and that they would never come back.[12]

WHAT ABOUT TODAY?

Calls for annihilation of Jews still resound throughout the Muslim world. For example, in a typical Friday sermon in Gaza's Zayed bin Sultan Al Nahyan mosque, October 14, 2000, the imam shouted: "Have no mercy on the Jews...kill them...and those Americans who...established Israel here, in the beating heart of the Arab world...."[13] That very day, two Israeli reservists innocently took a wrong turn into Ramallah and were literally torn apart by a frenzied mob—an event that was cheered when the grizzly details, including their murderers holding and waving their victims' entrails in bloody hands were shown on Palestinian TV. In like manner, Muslim mobs around the world danced for joy in the streets when New York's World Trade Center's twin towers came down. Does Islam dehumanize its followers?

Hamas leader Mahmoud al-Zahar succinctly expressed Islam's sentiment, "From our ideological point of view, it is not allowed to recognize that Israel controls one square meter of historic Palestine." Hamas is completely opposed to any move toward peace with Israel, because all such moves are fraught with danger that Muslims might, in the process, compromise and allow Jews to keep even the tiniest part of Palestine. The slogan of Hamas is, "Allah is the target, the prophet is its model, the Qur'an its constitution, jihad is the path and death for the sake of Allah is the loftiest of its wishes." A kindergarten that is run by Hamas has slogans on the wall such as, "The children of kindergarten are the holy martyrs of tomorrow." Hamas boasts, "Israel has nuclear bombs; we have human bombs."

In view of Islam's passion to destroy Israel, "peace" plans are a macabre joke! Even the moderate King Hussein of Jordan, the most friendly toward Israel of all Arab heads of state, told his countrymen on December 1, 1973: "After we perform our duty in liberating the West bank and Jerusalem, our national duty is to liberate all the Arab occupied territories." That is a euphemism for the annihilation of Israel. King Hussein died of cancer February 7, 1999, and was succeeded by his son, Abdullah II.

On September 4, 1999, in the Egyptian town of Sharm el-Sheikh, the PLO and Israel signed a Memorandum calling for full implementation of all prior agreements reached since September 1993. The agreement called for final status negotiations to be completed by September 13, 2000 in accord with United Nations resolutions 242 and 338. It allowed the Palestinians to have their own sea port on which construction was to begin October 1, 1999. The agreement was signed by Israel and the PLO and witnessed by representatives of the Arab Republic of Egypt, the Hashemite Kingdom of Jordan, and the United States.

Attempting to assist in the implementation of the Sharm el-Sheikh agreement, President Clinton invited Israeli Prime Minister Ehud Barak and Yasser Arafat to a summit meeting at Camp David, Maryland, on July 11, 2000. Under intense pressure from Clinton, in an effort to reach a final agreement, and with promises of American support and security guarantees, Prime Minister Barak offered far-reaching concessions that went beyond all the long-standing Israeli "red lines" set forth in prior negotiations, especially as regards Jerusalem. He offered to give up East Jerusalem, the Jordan Valley, about 98 percent of the West Bank, and all of Gaza—everything and then some that he possibly could. East Jerusalem would be the capital of the Palestinian state. All refugees would have the "right of return" to their own state. The West Bank and Gaza Strip would be connected by an overland highway with no Israeli checkpoints, and refugees would be compensated out of a $30 billion international fund.

The U.S. team called Barak's offer "courageous." In return, Arafat had to declare the "end of conflict" and agree that no further claims on Israel could be made in the future. Israelis were stunned at the sweeping concessions Barak offered, but Arafat rejected them out of hand. Indicating that he would not compromise on return of the 1948 refugees into Israel itself, or on full sovereignty over the Temple Mount, including the Western Wall so significant to Israelis, Arafat did not even deign to make a counteroffer. Instead, he went home on July 25, and at the first opportunity initiated the al-Aqsa intifada. Barak's disappointed comment was, "Israel was ready to reach agreement at a painful price but not at any price."

What else could Barak, the United States, or any rational person willing to face the truth have reasonably expected? This whole peace process has been a charade from the beginning—and continues to be. After all, Arafat and the entire Arab world had gone on record many times that nothing less would suffice than Israel's surrender of its entire land, leaving Israelis living as fifth-class citizens (*dhimmis*) under the "benevolent protection" of Muslim Palestinians. Islam itself would not allow Arafat to accept Barak's offer. Had he done so, he would have been assassinated like so many Muslim leaders before him.

INSIDE THE MUSLIM MIND

Loyalty to Islam means that Muslims can never forgive Americans for coming to Saudi Arabia and defiling its sacred soil with their pagan boots, even though they came at the urgent request of the Saudis to rescue them from Saddam Hussein's merciless aggression. They can never forget the humiliation of American tanks controlling the streets of Baghdad, the center of Islamic power for six hundred years—or forgive American and British troops for taking over Afghanistan, in spite of the fact that the order and safety they have brought is far preferable to the reign of terror by the Taliban and the constant fighting among local war lords. The latter are all Muslims, devout and even fanatical followers of this "religion of peace," as their ancestors have been for centuries, but there is no peace between them.

Islam does not bring peace. It never has and it never will. This is the simple fact of its very nature. No Muslim can point to even one example in history where Islam ever brought peace. There is no peace even among Muslims themselves anywhere in the world today.

The Muslim can never forget that in the glorious days of its early conquests, Islam ruled an empire from France to China, including *all of Palestine*. Islam does not allow any territory once controlled by Muslims ever to be relinquished. Thus, there can be no forgiveness for the "imperialists" who snatched this glorious empire from Muslims. Any knowledgeable Muslim understands that Islam is destined to recover that long-ago empire, must do so, and finally take over the entire world—and that every Muslim is a warrior in that cause.

This goal is justified by the apparently sincere but incredibly deluded belief that Islam is the best of religions and actually brings freedom to those under its rule. Even Ayatollah Khomeini, in spite of the brutal totalitarian Islamic rule he imposed in Iran, declared without any apparent sense of irony, "Islam is the religion of the strugglers who want right and justice, the religion of those demanding freedom and independence, and those who do not want the infidels to dominate believers." He accused the "imperialists" of lying about Islam by portraying it as a religion opposed to peace and freedom!

What can Muslims be thinking when they make such claims? No matter how irrational such statements may seem, we must take seriously those who make them. How the Western world assesses and responds to such claims, in this defining moment in history, is now the issue and will determine its future.

1. Genesis 15:18.
2. http://www.jtf.org/israel/israel.arab.moderates.part.one.htm.
3. Surah 8:61.
4. Kuwaiti paper, *Al-Sachrah*, January 6, 1987.
5. Mortimer B. Zuckerman, "A look at life after Arafat," *U.S. News & World Report*, November 29, 2004, 68.
6. http://www.usembassy.org.uk/bush307.html.
7. *The Wall Street Journal*, October 27, 2001.
8. Zechariah 12:6.
9. Abba Eban, *Personal Witness: Israel Through My Eyes* (London: Jonathan Cape, 1993), 422.
10. Sir Tom Hickinbotham, *Aden* (London: 1958), 87.
11. *The New York Times*, July 22, 1970.
12. Joan Peters, *From Time Immemorial: The Origins of the Arab-Jewish Conflict Over Palestine* (New York: J. KAP Publishing U.S.A., 1984), 98-115.
13. Mitchell G. Bard, *Myths and Facts: A Guide to the Arab Israeli Conflict* (American-Israeli Cooperative Enterprise, 2001), 195.

11—REBELLION AND JUDGMENT

PROPHECIES IN THE BIBLE refer often to "the last days," "the latter days," or "the latter times."[1] The first use of that phrase is found in Genesis 49:1, where Jacob declares to his sons: "Gather yourselves together, that I may tell you that which shall befall you in the last days." In addition to foretelling what will happen at that time, Jacob's prophecy clearly declares that in the "last days," Israel will still exist and be important in God's plans—a biblical teaching that many who call themselves Christians deny today.

Nor can Israel and its importance *as a nation*, as already noted, in possession of the entire Promised Land, *ever* cease. Repeatedly, the Bible declares that God gave the Promised Land to Israel by an "everlasting covenant."[2] God's integrity is tied to Israel, to her survival, ultimate restoration, and eternal blessing, as He has promised in His Word through His prophets. Therefore, as we've seen, if Satan could destroy her and thereby prevent this full restoration and ultimate blessing, he would have proved God to be a liar, removing any moral basis for God to punish him for his lies to mankind, including the lies with which he deceived Eve in the Garden of Eden. The Satanic goal of Israel's destruction is the only rational explanation for worldwide anti-Semitism, including Islam's determination to annihilate every Jew on earth.

Of the hundreds of prophecies about Israel, many can be fulfilled only in "the last days." For that reason, too, Israel cannot cease to exist, or many prophecies would be false. If even one prophecy were false, how could we trust anything else the Bible says? Incredibly, there are pastors and seminary professors who pick and choose what they believe of Scripture. In so doing, they are destroying the very foundation of the faith they profess.

What could be more foolish than for mere men to judge God? If the Bible is God's Word, it is *all* true; if not, then let's stop honoring it, the God who claims to have written it, and the Christ it tells us about, and let's honestly admit that Christianity is a blatant delusion.

The climax of all prophecy involves Jerusalem and occurs in what is referred to as "the day of the LORD," also called "that day." For example, "Behold, the day of the LORD cometh...I will gather all nations against Jerusalem to battle...."[3] The question is often asked, "Is the United States in Bible prophecy?" Yes. *All* nations (and that must include the United States) will join together under Antichrist in one massive attack upon Israel and Jerusalem at the end of the Great Tribulation. Christ will intervene to rescue His people, destroying Antichrist's armies and kingdom at Armageddon.

God says, "*I will* gather all nations." But isn't Satan the one who hates Israel and who will continue to attempt to destroy her to the very end? Doesn't he gather all nations against Israel under his false messiah, the Antichrist? How can God and Satan be working together? They cannot. God *uses* Satan and his followers, but He does not inspire Satan to evil—that is Satan's nature.

Nor does God even encourage, much less cause, anyone to seek to destroy Israel. He *allows* this hatred against Israel to be vented in order for the truth about the human heart to be revealed. He also allows it as part of His judgment upon Israel. That judgment is clearly spelled out in the prophecies given by Israel's own inspired prophets.

It was Israel that gave us the Bible and the Messiah. The Bible's attention is focused on Israel from beginning to end. The current

Middle East crisis is unfolding exactly as the Bible foretells. One cannot avoid the conclusion that the grand finale of "last days" prophecies is drawing very close, as we will see in the last chapter.

PROPHECY IS HISTORY RECORDED IN ADVANCE

The entire history of the Jewish people and of the nation of Israel is foretold by the Hebrew prophets under inspiration of the Holy Spirit. We have been able to look at only a small fraction of those amazing prophecies and the ongoing fulfillment-in-process of some of them today. When He brought the Israelites into their land, God warned that if they forsook Him for pagan gods, He would scatter them to the ends of the earth. They would be hated, persecuted, and killed like no other people. He would not, however, forsake them completely. A remnant would be preserved. In the last days He would bring them back into their own land again. At that time, God would make Jerusalem a cup of trembling to the neighbors surrounding her—and a crushing burden to the whole world. We have dealt briefly with these prophecies, which are clearly in the process of being fulfilled in our day.

How astonishing that "the people of God,"[4] in spite of all the miracles they had witnessed, would rebel against God, turn to idolatry and immorality (these two always go together), and as a result be cast out of their land in God's wrath! That fact, however, could not have been stated more plainly than in the many declarations concerning the future by Israel's own prophets. Such prophecies are given in specific detail and elaborated upon by many Hebrew prophets throughout the Bible.

The following prophecies are not the pronouncements of anti-Semites, but of God himself speaking through chosen men of God. And no one pronounced God's judgment upon rebellious Israel more severely than Moses, who led them out of Egypt and to the borders of the Promised Land. As they were about to enter Canaan, God warned them once again through this prophet, to whom He spoke "face to face, as a man speaketh unto his friend."[5] Nor can it be denied that all of the following has occurred exactly as God foretold:

> But it shall come to pass, if thou wilt not hearken unto the voice of the LORD thy God, to observe to do all his commandments and his statutes which I command thee this day; that all these curses shall come upon thee, and overtake thee….
>
> The Lord shall cause thee to be smitten before thine enemies: thou shalt go out one way against them, and flee seven ways before them: and shalt be removed into all the kingdoms of the earth…. And thou shalt become an astonishment, a proverb, and a byword, among all nations whither the Lord shall lead thee…. Moreover all these curses shall come upon thee, and shall pursue thee, and overtake thee, till thou be destroyed; because thou hearkenedst not unto the voice of the Lord thy God, to keep his commandments and his statutes which he commanded thee: And they shall be upon thee for a sign and for a wonder, and upon thy seed for ever…if thou wilt not observe to do all the words of this law that are written in this book, that thou mayest fear this glorious and fearful name, THE LORD THY GOD…ye shall be left few in number….
>
> And it shall come to pass, that as the Lord rejoiced over you to do you good, and to multiply you; so the Lord will rejoice over you to destroy you, and to bring you to nought; and ye shall be plucked from off the land whither thou goest to possess it. And the Lord shall scatter thee among all people, from the one end of the earth even unto the other…among these nations shalt thou find no ease…the Lord shall give thee there a trembling heart, and failing of eyes, and sorrow of mind: And thy life shall hang in doubt before thee; and thou shalt fear day and night, and shalt have none assurance of thy life: In the morning thou shalt say, Would God it were even! and at even thou shalt say, Would God it were morning! for the fear of thine heart wherewith thou shalt fear, and for the sight of thine eyes which thou shalt see.[6]

JUDGMENT CONTINUING TO THIS DAY

That theme of judgment pursuing a scattered people was taken up by many other Hebrew prophets, as God reiterated His warnings. The fulfillment of these judgments upon Israelites scattered everywhere is one more proof that they are the people of God to whom the Promised Land was given. No other people have experienced through history this continuing specific judgment. There are hundreds more such passages in Scripture. We can only cite short excerpts of a very few:

> If ye transgress, I will scatter you abroad among the nations....[7] I will cause them to be removed into all kingdoms of the earth....[8] I will sift the house of Israel among all nations, like as corn is sifted in a sieve....[9] Then shall they know that I am the LORD, when I have laid the land most desolate because of all their abominations....[10]
>
> And the LORD hath sent unto you all his servants the prophets, rising early and sending them; but ye have not hearkened, nor inclined your ear to hear. They said, Turn ye again now every one from his evil way, and from the evil of your doings.... Yet ye have not hearkened unto me, saith the LORD; that ye might provoke me to anger with the works of your hands to your own hurt.[11] As I live, saith the Lord GOD, I have no pleasure in the death of the wicked; but that the wicked turn from his way and live: turn ye, turn ye from your evil ways; for why will ye die, O house of Israel? [12]

In spite of the unbelief of most Jews around the world, there has always been a nucleus through the centuries who believed God's promises—and who even recognized and admitted that the dispersion of Jews all over the world was God's judgment because of their sin. Moses ben Maimon (Maimonides), the famous Jewish physician and philosopher, whose family had fled from Islamic persecution in Spain to, of all places, Fez (and who himself had to flee from Morocco later), wrote in his "Epistle to Yemen" in 1172:

> It is...one of the fundamental articles of the faith of Israel that the future redeemer of our people will...gather our nation, assemble our exiles, redeem us from our degradation....
>
> On account of the vast number of our sins, God has hurled us in the midst of this people, the Arabs, who have persecuted us severely...as Scripture has forewarned us.... Never did a nation molest, degrade, debase, and hate us as much as they....[13]

AN INCREDIBLE EVENT!

Both God's blessings and judgments upon Israel throughout her history reveal His character: He is loving, kind, faithful, and true, but He will not leave rebellion unpunished and He will not go back on His promises, whether for blessing or for punishment. Israel is a picture of all of mankind. Her history shows that God knows our weaknesses and is willing to pardon. But it also shows that, like Israel, we are all by nature stubborn rebels, proud, selfish, self-willed, determined to take our own way, and that God's love, mercy, and forgiveness must be tempered with His justice. From out of the fire of His presence that was blazing atop Mount Sinai, God thundered the Ten Commandments in a terrifyingly majestic voice that all Israel audibly heard—yet, incredibly, did not obey!

As they well might, the people trembled before this awesome display of God's presence and power. No fiction writer would have imagined, much less dared to write, the unbelievable scenario that Scripture tells us occurred next. One of the many evidences that the Bible is the true Word of God lies in the fact that in giving us man's history from the Garden of Eden through the flood and onward, it spells out the evil in the heart even of those whom God graciously blesses—and nowhere more clearly than at Mount Sinai.

Astonishing though it seems, in spite of this audible and visible proof of exactly who the true God was—the God of Abraham, Isaac, and Jacob, the God of Israel, who had delivered them miraculously from Egypt—they rebelled against Him. God had taken them through the Red Sea on dry ground, drowning the pursuing Egyptians behind them. He had led them with a pillar of cloud by day and a pillar of fire by night, and fed them daily with manna. Yet while Moses was on Mount Sinai receiving the law from God, the people below broke the very commandments that they had just heard audibly spoken in their ears out of the fire and lightning where Moses lingered above:

> And when the people saw that Moses delayed to come down [they said] unto Aaron...make us gods, which shall go before us....

And all the people brake off the golden earrings…in their ears, and brought them unto Aaron. And he…made it a molten calf: and they said, These be thy gods, O Israel, which brought thee up out of the land of Egypt. And…Aaron…built an altar before it [and] made proclamation…. To morrow is a feast to the LORD. And they rose up early on the morrow, and offered burnt offerings…and the people sat down to eat and to drink, and rose up to play.

And the LORD said unto Moses, Go, get thee down; for thy people [have] turned aside quickly out of the way which I commanded them: they have made them a molten calf, and have worshipped it, and have sacrificed thereunto….a stiffnecked people: Now therefore let me alone, that my wrath may wax hot against them, and that I may consume them: and I will make of thee a great nation.

And Moses besought the LORD his God…. Remember Abraham, Isaac, and Israel, thy servants, to whom thou swarest by thine own self, and saidst unto them…all this land that I have spoken of will I give unto your seed, and they shall inherit it for ever…. And Moses turned, and went down from the mount, and the two tables of the testimony were in his hand…the writing was the writing of God, graven upon the tables.[14]

God was testing Moses with the offer of having his descendants replace the twelve tribes of Israel. That was a great temptation— and Moses passed the test. He reminded God of His promises to Abraham, Isaac, and Jacob—promises that He must fulfill to maintain His integrity. If He failed to establish their descendants as a nation in the land He had promised to them, the other nations would say, with good reason, that He was not the true God.

The same holds true today. God must fulfill His promises of ultimately restoring Israel as a nation in her own land once more, never to be scattered again—or He is a liar and not God.

We well know the tragic story. When Moses returned to the camp of Israel and saw with his own eyes the idolatry and fornication that the people had fallen into at the very base of Sinai, he angrily smashed to the ground the tables of stone on which God had written His commandments. And why not? The people had already broken the law. What an incredible and yet instructive story, revealing each of our hearts!

GOD'S COMPASSIONATE LOVE—AND JUSTICE

It was in the midst of this awesome scene that Moses begged of God, "I beseech thee, show me thy glory."[15] The Mount was ablaze, the earth was quaking, and the people were being punished for this grievous, almost unbelievable sin. It was the perfect setting for God to thunder, "I will show you what a harsh judge I am!" Instead, He invited Moses to come once more up the Mount into His presence, where He would write the law on tables of stone again—the law that Israel had already broken.

In response to the request of Moses, God replied, "I will make all my goodness pass before thee."[16] Up on the mount once again, "the LORD passed by before him, and proclaimed,The Lord, The Lord God, merciful and gracious, longsuffering, and abundant in goodness and truth, keeping mercy for thousands, forgiving iniquity and transgression and sin, and that will by no means clear the guilty...."[17]

God seems to add "will by no means clear the guilty" almost reluctantly. Repeatedly the God of the Bible tells the Jews that He loves them: "The LORD thy God hath chosen thee to be a special people unto himself...because the LORD loved you...."[18] The Apostle John, inspired of the Holy Spirit, declares, "God is love."[19] He cannot *but* love not only Israel but all mankind, because love is His very essence.

Yet God is also perfectly just. He cannot "clear the guilty," for that would condone sin and corrupt His justice. The penalty He has pronounced must be paid. And, wonder of wonders, God would Himself come as a man to pay that penalty in full (as He alone could) so that all who would believe could righteously be forgiven.

Generation after generation, as they continued to rebel against Him, God sent His prophets to plead with His chosen people: "Come now, and let us reason together, saith the LORD: though your sins be as scarlet, they shall be as white as snow.... If ye be willing and obedient, ye shall eat the good of the [promised] land: but if ye refuse and rebel, ye shall be devoured with the sword: for the mouth of the LORD hath spoken it."[20] God did not want to punish His people (nor does He want to pour out His wrath upon this world), but He cannot condone evil. His pleadings with Israel came to an end at last—as they will with all mankind shortly. His holiness and righteousness required Him finally to punish Israel:

> I sent unto you all my servants the prophets, rising early and sending them, saying, Oh, do not this abominable thing that I hate. But they hearkened not, nor inclined their ear to turn from their wickedness.... Wherefore my fury and mine anger was poured forth.[21]

Sadly, in spite of God's pleadings for His people to return to Him with their whole heart, Israel has persisted to this day in idolatry and rebellion against Him and thus has missed the full blessing God graciously had promised to their forefathers. From the days of Moses to the present time, rebellious Israel has been under God's judgment. Nevertheless, Israel's full and final restoration (already in process) is assured, never to be under His judgment again—but only by God's grace, not by her merits. Scripture makes that fact clear:

> The LORD thy God hath chosen thee to be a special people unto himself, above all people that are upon the face of the earth... because the LORD loved you, and because he would keep the oath which he had sworn unto your fathers.... I do not this for your sakes, O house of Israel, but for mine holy name's sake, which ye have profaned among the heathen...be ashamed and confounded for your own ways, O house of Israel...."[22]

THE PROMISE OF THE MESSIAH

The entire world would be included in the mercy of God toward Israel. At the very beginning, when God told Abraham, "I will...curse him that curseth thee," He also declared, "in thee shall all families of the earth be blessed."[23] That amazing guarantee was repeated again to Abraham,[24] later to his son Isaac,[25] then to Jacob.[26] This promise, of course, could be fulfilled only through the Messiah, who would come to pay the full penalty for the sins of all mankind. "All families of the earth" could be forgiven and brought into unbroken fellowship with their Creator—if they were willing to accept salvation on His terms.

The Messiah would not suddenly appear on earth out of thin air. He required a genealogy of human ancestors in order to be a genuine man. He had to be God in order to be without sin and capable of paying the infinite penalty His own justice demanded for the sins of mankind. Yet He had to be a genuine flesh-and-blood man in order to pay the penalty on behalf of all mankind. God chose Abraham, and through him, Isaac, Jacob, and King David (and revealing His grace and forgiveness, even the harlot Rahab and Ruth the Moabitess), to be the ancestors of the Messiah. The Messiah had to be and is a Jew—another reason why God has a special place in His heart for Israel.

There is no escaping the prophecy of the great Hebrew prophet, Isaiah:

> For unto us a child is born [the baby born in Bethlehem], unto us a son is given [the eternal Son of God come as a man]: and the government shall be upon his shoulder [so this promised One is the Messiah]: and his name shall be called Wonderful, Counsellor, The mighty God, The everlasting Father [so God is a Father and has a Son whom He gives to be the Messiah, and they are one], the Prince of Peace [this is the one who will bring everlasting peace].[27]

To be God's chosen people is a great honor, but it holds responsibilities as well as blessings. That the Jews would be scattered all over the world, hated, persecuted, and killed was more than prophecy—it was God's judgment upon them for rebellion and for the worst rebellion of all: rejecting their Messiah. Yet through that rejection would come the salvation of the world. Many centuries after God's promise of the Messiah to Abraham, Isaac, and Jacob, Isaiah would not only foretell His coming as quoted above, but His rejection by His own people and, through that, the redemption of mankind:

> He is despised and rejected of men; a man of sorrows, and acquainted with grief: and we hid as it were our faces from

him…and we esteemed him not…. But he was wounded for our transgressions, he was bruised for our iniquities…with his stripes we are healed. All we like sheep have gone astray; we have turned every one to his own way; and the LORD hath laid on him the iniquity of us all….

Yet it pleased the LORD to bruise him; he hath put him to grief…mak[ing] his soul an offering for sin….[28]

RESTORATION PROMISED

In spite of their being under God's severe discipline for unbelief, and in spite of the prophesied fact that for centuries they would reject their Messiah, nevertheless, dozens of times in His Word Yahweh has promised to preserve the Jews from total destruction.[29] He would finally establish them back in their own land as an identifiable ethnic people with the Messiah reigning over them on the throne of His father David.[30] God's integrity is tied to the ultimate restoration of Israel to her own land, never to be displaced again:

> But fear not thou, O my servant Jacob, and be not dismayed, O Israel: for, behold, I will save…thy seed from the land of their captivity; and Jacob shall return, and be in rest and at ease, and none shall make him afraid. Fear thou not, O Jacob…I will make a full end of all the nations whither I have driven thee: but I will not make a full end of thee, but correct thee in measure; yet will I not leave thee wholly unpunished. [31]

We have been able to refer to only a small fraction of biblical prophecies concerning Israel. We have sufficiently documented, however, what is being fulfilled in our own day to show beyond doubt that everything that still remains for the future of what God has foretold for Israel, and for the world that opposes her, will yet take place exactly as foretold. God's promise that He would finally gather all Jews from around the world to establish them as a nation back in their own land as an identifiable ethnic people, with the Messiah reigning over them on the throne of His father David, is now in process and will yet be completely fulfilled.

Only since 1948 has God begun to restore Israel, and then only partially and with continued fierce opposition from the Muslim nations surrounding her and from the entire world as foretold. There can be no question that the following prophecies have begun to be fulfilled and will be completed in their prophesied time:

> I will…gather you out of all countries, and will bring you into your own land….[32] I will multiply them, and set my sanctuary in the midst of them for evermore.[33] Hear the word of the LORD, O ye nations, and declare it in the isles afar off, and say, He that scattered Israel will gather him, and keep him, as a shepherd doth his flock. For the LORD hath redeemed Jacob, and ransomed him from the hand of him that was stronger than he. Therefore they shall come and sing in the height of Zion, and shall flow together to the goodness of the LORD, for wheat, and for wine, and for oil, and for the young of the flock and of the herd: and their soul shall be as a watered garden; and they shall not sorrow any more at all…. For I will turn their mourning into joy, and will comfort them, and make them rejoice from their sorrow…and my people shall be satisfied with my goodness, saith the LORD.[34]
>
> As a shepherd seeketh out his flock…so will I seek out my sheep, and will deliver them out of all places where they have been scattered…and I will…gather them from the countries, and will bring them to their own land….[35]
>
> Behold I will gather them out of all countries whither I have driven them in mine anger…and I will bring them again unto this place, and I will cause them to dwell safely: and they shall be my people, and I will be their God…. And I will make an everlasting covenant with them, that I will not turn away from them…that they shall not depart from me…so will I bring upon them all the good that I have promised them.[36] And I will bring again the captivity of my people of Israel, and they shall build the waste cities, and inhabit them…and they shall no more be pulled up out of their land which I have given them, saith the LORD thy God.[37]

AN UNBIBLICAL, IRRATIONAL THEORY

There are Christians today who claim that these prophecies refer not to the last days in which we live but to Israel's deliverance under

Moses from Egypt. That this view is in error is made clear by the precise language of Scripture. Just the word *again* is enough to disprove that theory. The repeated phrase, "all places where they have been scattered," and, "all the countries whither I have driven them," clearly could not refer to the exodus from one country, Egypt. Nor could the future language employed in prophecies uttered many centuries after the exodus refer to that past event. What is the point of a "prophecy" that foretells events that have already occurred?

Nor could "they shall build the waste cities" describe Israel's first entrance under Joshua into the Promised Land, which at that time was "flowing with milk and honey"[38] and whose cities were prosperous and anything but lying in "waste." Nor could, "they shall no more be pulled up out of their land," describe the entrance into the land after the deliverance from Egypt, or these would be false prophecies in view of the Babylonian captivity and subsequent diasporas as well as the fact that the land lay barren for centuries before Israel's return, exactly as these prophecies also foretold. It is inescapable that the prophets foretold a *future and final* restoration of Israel, never to be removed again—and which could not take place without the return of the Messiah to reign on the throne of His father, David.

Unequivocal as these statements are, however, and in spite of the clarity of their language, they have not been believed by most Jews, either in the past or today, whether in Israel or worldwide. Nor have they been accepted at face value by the majority of professing Christians. The Roman Catholic Church rejects these promises because she claims to have replaced Israel. Most Calvinists take the "Reformed" position that Israel has been replaced, but by the Protestant church.

OPPOSITION OF MANY CHRISTIANS TO ISRAEL

We have seen from the scriptures cited above (and there are literally hundreds more like them) that God has promised a full and final restoration of Israel, both physically in relation to her land and spiritually in relation to God himself. Of that final restoration, Paul declares:

I say then, Have they stumbled that they should fall? God forbid:
but rather through their fall salvation is come unto the Gentiles,
for to provoke them to jealousy. Now if the fall of them be the
riches of the world, and the diminishing of them the riches of the
Gentiles; how much more their fulness…? For if the casting away
of them be the reconciling of the world, what shall the receiving
of them be, but life from the dead? [39]

It is astonishing how many who claim to be Christians apparently have no fear of the God of the Bible and of Israel. They are not
afraid to flaunt their denigration of Israel in the face of the Creator
of the universe, who 203 times calls Himself "the God of Israel" and
has declared that these are His people by an *everlasting* covenant.
Moses said, "For the LORD's portion is his people; Jacob is the lot of
his inheritance…he kept him as the apple of his eye."[40] Clearly, this
does not refer to Jews as individuals but to Israel as a nation—much
less does it refer to the church as Israel's replacement! Twice more
in Scripture is the nation of Israel affectionately referred to as "the
apple" of God's eye.[41]

Yet Calvinists and those who call themselves "Reformed" insist that
Israel has been replaced by the church. For example, in 2002 the faculty
of Calvinistic Knox Seminary in Fort Lauderdale, Florida (D. James
Kennedy, Founder, Chancellor, President, and Professor of Evangelism)
issued "An Open Letter to Evangelicals and Other Interested Parties:
The People of God, the Land of Israel, and the Impartiality of the
Gospel." This statement, which denied that the physical descendants
of Abraham, Isaac, and Jacob (i.e., the Jews) have any special blessings
or place in prophecy, much less any claim upon the land of Israel, was
initially signed by seventy-one prominent evangelical leaders, among
them R. C. Sproul and Michael S. Horton.

This document declares:

Section VI: The inheritance promises that God gave to
Abraham…do not apply to any particular ethnic group, but to
the church of Jesus Christ, the true Israel….

Section IX: The entitlement of any one ethnic or religious group
to territory in the Middle East called the "Holy Land" cannot

be supported by Scripture. In fact, the land promises specific to Israel in the Old Testament were fulfilled under Joshua.

Fulfilled under Joshua? Yet this refers to the church? Can they be serious? The church didn't even exist in Joshua's day!

The error of that statement should be plain to any serious student of the Bible. We have seen that the land was given to Abraham, Isaac, and Jacob, and their physical descendants by an "everlasting covenant." Certainly the "everlasting" possession of that land could not have been fulfilled under Joshua because he died at the age of 110—a far cry from "everlasting." The "land promises specific to Israel in the Old Testament" included prophecies that Israel would be cast out of the land for unbelief, but brought back into it in the last days. Surely neither the casting out nor restoration were fulfilled under Joshua.

Nor could the prophecies possibly have been fulfilled under Joshua that the Messiah would come to that land as a man to redeem Israel, that Israel would reject and crucify Him, or that Israel, having returned to her land after being scattered worldwide, would be attacked by all the nations of the world in the battle of Armageddon and that the Messiah would intervene to rescue her. Behold the power of prejudice against the Jews to blind Christian leaders to the plain teaching of God's Word!

ISRAEL MUST BE FULLY RESTORED

For Satan to be defeated, it is not enough for individual Jews to survive. Israel must exist as a nation in her own land: "Thus saith the LORD, which giveth the sun for a light by day, and the ordinances of the moon and of the stars for a light by night, which divideth the sea when the waves thereof roar...if those ordinances depart from before me...then the seed of Israel also shall cease from being a nation before me for ever."[42]

Many Jews worldwide reject the Bible and deny the existence of the God of Israel. Their Jewishness is purely cultural and traditional. As a consequence, they denounce what the world calls "Zionism."

Norman G. Finkelstein, already mentioned, is an example of such. He rejects the very existence of a nation called Israel "whose proprietorship would be Jewish."[43] Yet he has no problem with the fact that the "proprietorship" of Germany is German, of France is French, etc. He cannot allow there to be a Jewish state that would serve as the homeland for a people who were repeatedly thrown out of their land by aggressors and persecuted and killed all over the world for centuries! He argues that the very existence of a "historical homeland of the Jewish people" would render "the Jewish people 'alien' to every other state/territorial unit, thus sanctioning the claims of anti-Semitism."[44] It's apparently acceptable that everyone else, from American Indians to Finns to Zulus, claims a "historical homeland"—but not for Jews. He even supports Arab imperialism that claims the entire Middle East for the "great Arab nation" with no room in it for Israel to exist! He doesn't recognize that his anti-Israel position is inspired of another being in whom he doesn't believe—Satan.

This same opposition to Israel is firmly held by many who call themselves Christians. It is astonishing how many true believers who are clear on most of the Bible remain adamantly opposed to what the Bible declares so plainly about Israel being restored fully to her land in the last days. It could rightly be said that one's attitude toward Israel (which is by far the major subject of the Bible, taking up at least 70 percent of its pages) defines whether or not one is a truly biblical Christian. Almost every event in the Bible happened either to or in Israel.

The church is not a nation but is made up of people from every nation, and therefore could not have replaced Israel in prophecy. There is only one nation and one people—the Jews alone—to whom God ever gave a land and specific, perpetual promises concerning it.

Certainly, the Promised Land was never given to the church, nor did she ever occupy it as a "nation." The church was never, for her rebellion against God, cast out of a Promised Land. Nor was the church ever promised a return to be established again as a nation in that land. But all of that and more was prophesied of and fulfilled in Israel. The church is clearly not Israel—it never was nor ever could be!

A CLEAR DISTINCTION

God declares through Jeremiah that if a distinct nation known as Israel (which must comprise the physical descendants of the Israel that was established in the Promised Land under Joshua) no longer exists, there is no sun in the sky, the stars have vanished, and the whole natural order is destroyed! Yet there are not only Muslims and atheists but also many Jews and professing Christians who say that today's Israel has neither prophetic significance nor divine legitimacy. They are in direct opposition to God and to His Word. Indeed, they are denying the major prophetic proof God gives for His existence and that the Bible is His Word. They must either repent or be punished for their opposition to what the prophets have foretold.

Romans Chapters 9 and 10 make as clear a distinction between the church and the physical people known as Jews constituting the nation of Israel as could be made. Paul is willing to go to hell eternally if that would bring about the salvation of his "kinsmen according to the flesh: who are Israelites...of whom as concerning the flesh Christ came."[45] But one must be saved to be in the church—the church is composed only of saved people.

Moreover, there are Germans, French, Spanish, Australian aborigines, Zulus—in fact, people from every tribe and nation on earth in the church. How could this variety of races all be called "Israelites," the "kinsmen according to the flesh" of Paul and Christ? Impossible! He goes on to say that his "heart's desire and prayer to God for Israel is, that they might be saved."[46] Paul declared that Israel isn't saved. Then how could Israel be the church? This teaching turns the Bible inside out!

Indeed, so perverse is this teaching that many who espouse it claim that Christ's promise to return has already been fulfilled—that He came back in A.D. 70 in the person of the Roman armies to destroy Jerusalem and to punish the Jews for rejecting Him. Well, the dead were certainly not raised at that time, nor were the living caught up to meet Christ in the air and taken to heaven as the Scripture declares.[47] He is coming to rescue Israel, not to destroy her—and to rule the world from David's throne in Jerusalem.

Even more astonishing, some of those who teach the "Israel is now the church" doctrine even claim that we are in the Millennial reign of Christ. But the lion doesn't lie down with the lamb and eat straw like an ox[48] as Scripture foretells for the millennium; and it certainly could not be said that Satan is now locked up.[49] In fact, he still goes about "as a roaring lion seeking whom he may devour."[50]

Tragically, from the days of Moses to the present time, Israel has been under God's judgment, as her history proves—and will continue to be, though back in her land, until she repents and turns to the Lord. At the same time, however, she is under His protection, and woe to those who harm her! Jerusalem will continue to be "trodden down of the Gentiles until the times of the Gentiles be fulfilled."[51] In the final chapter we shall see when that judgment from God will end.

1. Numbers 24:14; Deuteronomy 4:30; 31:29; Isaiah 2:2; Hosea 3:5; Micah 4:1; Acts 2:17; 1 Timothy 4:1; 2 Timothy 3:1; James 5:3; 2 Peter 3:3, etc.
2. Genesis 17:7, 13, 19; 2 Samuel 23:5; 1 Chronicles 16:17; Psalm 105:8-11; Isaiah 55:3; 61:8, etc.
3. Zechariah 14:1-2.
4. Judges 20:2; Hebrews 11:25, etc.
5. Exodus 33:11; Deuteronomy 34:10, etc.
6. Deuteronomy 28:15-68.
7. Nehemiah 1:8.
8. Jeremiah 15:4.
9. Amos 9:9.
10. Ezekiel 33:29.
11. Jeremiah 25:4-5, 7.
12. Ezekiel 33:11.
13. Isadore Twersky, ed., *A Maimonides Reader* (New York, 1972), 456-457.
14. Exodus 32:1-14.
15. Exodus 33:18.
16. Exodus 33:19.
17. Exodus 34:6-7.
18. Deuteronomy 7:6-8.
19. 1 John 4:8, 16.
20. Isaiah 1:18-20.
21. Jeremiah 44:4-6.

22. Deuteronomy 7:6-8; Ezekiel 36:22, 32, etc.
23. Genesis 12:3.
24. Genesis 22:18.
25. Genesis 26:4.
26. Genesis 28:14.
27. Isaiah 9:6.
28. Isaiah 53:3-10.
29. Jeremiah 30:10-17; 46:27-28, etc.
30. Jeremiah 31; Ezekiel 34, 36, 37, etc.
31. Jeremiah 46:27-28.
32. Ezekiel 36:24.
33. Jeremiah 31; Ezek 34, 36, 37, etc.
34. Jeremiah 31:10-14.
35. Ezekiel 34:12-13.
36. Jeremiah 32:37-42.
37. Amos 9:14-15.
38. Exodus 3:8, 17; 13:5; Leviticus 20:24; Numbers 13:27; Deuteronomy 31:20; Joshua 5:6, etc.
39. Romans 11:11-15.
40. Deuteronomy 32:9-10.
41. Lamentations 2:18; Zechariah 2:8.
42. Jeremiah 31:35-36.
43. Norman G. Finkelstein, *Image and Reality of the Israel-Palestine Conflict* (London: Verso, 1995),10.
44. Ibid., 14.
45. Romans 9:3-5.
46. Romans 10:1.
47. 1 Corinthians 15:51-57; 1 Thessalonians 4:13-18.
48. Isaiah 11:1-9; 65:24-25.
49. Revelation 20:1-3, 7-9.
50. I Peter 5:8.
51. Luke 21:24; Romans 11:25.

12—SOME IMPORTANT DISTINCTIONS

IN THE BELIEF THAT ITS MEMBERS have replaced Israel as the people of God, the Roman Catholic Church has taken for Rome the titles that God gave to Jerusalem: city of God, eternal city, holy city. In 1904, the year of his death, Theodore Hertzl, founder of the modern Zionist movement, recorded in his diary that he had asked Pope Pius X for help in establishing the Jewish settlers back in their land. He records that the Pope replied, "We cannot prevent the Jews from returning, but we could never condone it."

In 1919, Cardinal Pietro Gaspari, Secretary of State for the Vatican, confessed, "The thing that frightens us the most is the creation of a Jewish State in Palestine." Why should the Roman Catholic Church be opposed to and even frightened at the prospect of the Jews returning to their own land in fulfillment of God's many promises to restore them? If this "only true Church" is that far out of touch with God and His Word in this regard, what other errors does it promote? We have considered that question in detail in other books, so will not repeat it here.[1] It is only its anti-Semitism that concerns us at the moment.

Before he became Pope Pius XII, Cardinal Eugenio Pacelli (at that time Papal Nuncio to Germany) had given Vatican money to

Hitler to help fund the Nazi Party. The 1933 Vatican Concordat that Pacelli negotiated with Hitler gave the Nazis a certain legitimacy and, in Hitler's words, was a great help in the "struggle against international Jews." Upon becoming Pope, Pacelli sent a condescending message to the Führer assuring him of the Vatican's good will. In part it said:

> To the Illustrious Herr Adolf Hitler, Fuehrer and Chancellor of the German Reich! We recall with great pleasure the many years we spent in Germany as Apostolic Nuncio, when we did all in our power to establish harmonious relations between Church and State. Now…how much more ardently do we pray to reach that goal….

Shouldn't the "Vicar of Christ" have more discernment than that? This was 1939, and Hitler's abuse of and intentions for the Jews had been fully exposed to the world. In January of that year Hitler had warned that the outbreak of war would result "in the extermination of the Jewish race." The Pope very well knew from cardinals, bishops, and priests in Germany, exactly what Hitler was doing and that he intended to exterminate them. That Pius XII would, in spite of such knowledge, direct such flattery to Hitler is therefore all the more damning.

A LONG HISTORY OF ROMAN CATHOLIC ANTI-SEMITISM

As we have seen, it is a Roman Catholic doctrine that neither the land of Israel nor the Jewish people are any longer of any special significance to "the God of Israel" because the Church has taken Israel's place. The Jews have been blamed for crucifying Christ, when in fact they had no such authority. It was the Romans who did so. What the Jews did was to reject Him as their king and demand that He be crucified—and thus He became the Savior of the world, dying for the sins of all. The vast majority of mankind still reject Him.

Having blamed the Jews for the crucifixion (without which no one could be saved), the Church treated them as worse than scum. The Council of Vienna (A.D. 1311) forbade all intercourse between

Roman Catholics and Jews. The Council of Zamora (1313) ruled that Jews must be kept in strict subjection and servitude. The Council of Basel (1431-33) instructed secular authorities to confine the Jews in separate quarters, compel them to wear a distinguishing badge (as would Hitler), and assure their attendance at sermons designed to convert them.

Pope Eugenius IV (1431-47) prohibited Jews from holding public office or inheriting property from Catholics and ordered confiscation of the property of any Italian Jew found reading Talmudic literature. The mistreatment, persecution and murder of Jews by the Roman Catholic Church throughout its history goes far beyond anything we can recite in this volume. There were, of course, some Catholics who were kind to Jews, but to do so endangered their own standing with the Church.

Some Jews were rescued during World War II by individual Roman Catholics, but not generally by the church. The authors of *Shoah* point out: "Even when the Church engaged in isolated rescue activities, the motive seems to have been to bring the rescued Jews into the bosom of Christianity [Catholicism]. Thousands of Jewish children were taken into monasteries, and after the war, many were not returned to their people and faith even after relatives pleaded for their release."[2]

Pope Benedict XIV (1740-58) had decreed that a Jewish child, though baptized against its own and its parents' will, was nevertheless a Roman Catholic. As only one of many examples, in 1851 a Catholic maid, without the Jewish parent's knowledge or consent, secretly baptized their baby son shortly after his birth. When the boy was seven years old, Pius IX ruled that he was a Roman Catholic and ordered the papal police to take the child from his parents and put him in a Catholic boarding school, never to return him to his family. The popes operated a House of Catechumens in Rome that managed to indoctrinate and baptize a number of Jews each year. Church officials complained that only the least intelligent and poorest Jews, dressed in rags, came voluntarily to be baptized, and only in order to escape the poverty and confinement of the ghetto.

A few popes (a very small minority) were friendly and at times even helpful to Jews: Gregory I, Alexander III, Gregory IX (though the founder of the Inquisition that swallowed up hundreds of thousands of Jews and non-Jews, far more of the latter), and Innocent IV. The vast majority of popes, however, persecuted the Jews—and that was the official stance of the Roman Catholic Church. Pope Urban II, who organized the First Crusade, promised instant entrance to heaven for those who died in that cause (hardly different from Islam's promise of Paradise for *jihad* martyrs). On the way to the Holy Land, the Crusaders slaughtered Jews (more than one thousand in the city of Worms alone in 1096), and when they took Jerusalem, they herded the Jews into the synagogue and set it ablaze. Urban II had told them to take that land—not to restore it to the Jews, to whom it belonged as the Bible so clearly declared, but to the Church as the new people of God.

Pope John Paul II made a show of "apologizing" for Roman Catholic past persecutions of Jews (without any mention of evangelical Christians, of whom far more perished at the hands of the Church than Jews). He always worded his statements very carefully, apologizing for "the misdeeds of the sons and daughters of the Church," but never admitting that it was the Roman Catholic Church itself, under the specific leadership of its popes, that perpetrated the evil. In fact, history shows that "for more than six centuries without a break, the papacy was the sworn enemy of elementary justice. Of eighty popes in a line from the thirteenth century on, not one of them disapproved of the theology and apparatus of the inquisition. On the contrary, one after another added his own cruel touches to the workings of this deadly machine."[3]

TRUE CHRISTIANS, VICTIMS LIKE THE JEWS

A Roman Catholic professor of Church history at Munich writes in the nineteenth century, "Both the initiation and the carrying out of this new principle [the Inquisition] must be ascribed to the popes alone...the long series of Papal ordinances on the Inquisition, ever increasing in severity and cruelty…runs on without a break…every pope improves upon the devices of his predecessor [which] contradicted the simplest principles of Christian justice…."[4] Another historian writes:

> From Rome and Madrid came the orders to rack and to kill…dungeons were filled as fast as they were emptied by the scaffold. Men and women were broken on the wheel, racked, dragged at horses' tails; their sight was extinguished, their tongues torn out by the roots…were starved, drowned, hanged, burned, killed in every slow and agonizing way that the malicious inventiveness of priests could devise…hooked by the middle of the body…then made to swing to and fro over a slow fire until entirely roasted… all was done under the authority of the holy father, the Pope.[5]

During the brief pontificate of Paul IV (1555-59) the population of Rome was decimated by almost half, with the Jews the main victims. He issued a landmark bull, *Cum nimis absurdum*, that returned Jews to their ghettos, forced them to sell their properties at huge losses, and reduced them to the status of slaves and rag merchants—the only item they were allowed to sell. Jews were not allowed even to travel outside the ghetto without permission from a high Church official. And yet, incredibly, the lie persisted that Jews were behind every evil and were plotting to take over the world. How they could do that from the confinement of their ghettos has never been explained.

Hitler was "well aware of the Catholic Church's long anti-Jewish record."[6] On April 26, 1933, justifying his planned extermination of the Jews, Hitler reminded Church representatives Bishop Berning and Monsignor Steinmann that "the Church for 1500 years had regarded the Jews as parasites, had banished them into ghettos, and had forbidden Christians [Catholics] to work for them…[and that] he, Hitler, merely intended to do more effectively what the Church had attempted…."[7] A French Jewish scholar, after careful research, argued that "without centuries of Christian [Roman Catholic] catechism [and] preaching…the Hitlerian teachings, propaganda and vituperation would not have been possible."[8] The authors of *Shoah* concluded the same:

Without Christianity [Roman Catholicism], the success of Nazism would not have been possible.... Were it not for the fact that dozens of generations in Europe had been imbued with religious hatred, the growth of racist hatred towards Jewry in modern times could not have taken place."[9]

These Jewish authors don't understand the distinction between Roman Catholics and true evangelical Christians. They imagine that everyone who claims to be a Christian really is, but that is not the case. Jesus was a Jew—the greatest in history. No true Christian would persecute his brethren, but would love them and desire for them every blessing God has promised in His Word.

We are born again into the family of God and become true Christians through believing the gospel, which is "the power of God unto salvation to every one that believeth [it]."[10] Roman Catholicism presents a false gospel: that being baptized as an infant delivers from sin's penalty and makes one a Christian; that Christ's sacrifice on the Cross was not sufficient to pay the penalty for sins even though He declared, "It is finished [*tetelestai*, i.e. paid in full]," and Catholic priests must therefore continue to offer Him in the form of a wafer in the sacrifice of the Mass on Catholic altars; that Christ's suffering for sin on the Cross was not enough to open the gates of heaven, but that one must personally suffer for one's sins in the flames of purgatory—a penalty from which the Church (for a fee) offers incremental deliverance by sacrificing "Christ" in more Masses but doesn't guarantee how many Masses are enough. According to Christ himself, those who believe this false gospel are not Christians, and Christianity should not be blamed for their misdeeds.

It is important for Jews to realize that the popes and the Roman Catholic Church slaughtered far more evangelicals than they did Jews. The "Edict of the Emperors Gratian, Valentinian II, and Theodosius I" of February 27, 380, established Roman Catholicism as the state religion and set the distinction between those who accepted Rome's false gospel and biblical Christians. In part, the edict declared:

We order those who follow this doctrine to receive the title of Catholic Christians, but others we judge to be mad and raving and worthy of incurring the disgrace of heretical teaching, nor are their assemblies to receive the name of churches. They are to be punished not only by Divine retribution but also by our own measures, which we have decided in accordance with Divine inspiration.[11]

In fact, what the Roman Catholic Church did to true Christians is far worse than what they did to Jews. Those who followed Christ and His Word were persecuted and killed by the millions for more than a thousand years before the Reformation, Martin Luther said, "We are not the first to declare the papacy to be the kingdom of Antichrist since for many years before us so many...have undertaken to express the same thing so clearly...." The true Christians were known under many names (Albigenses, Waldenses, Cathari, Bogomils, Huguenots, Hussites, etc.), were called heretics, and were tortured, drowned, burned at the stake, and otherwise martyred for their faith. These people were marked for extermination just as surely as Muslims have marked Jews. Pope Martin V (1417-31) commanded the King of Poland in 1429 (one hundred years before the Reformation) to exterminate the Hussites (sympathizers with the martyred Jan Hus): "Know that the interests of the Holy See, and those of your crown, make it a duty to exterminate the Hussites [who] dare proclaim principles of equality...that Christ came on earth to abolish slavery; they call the people to liberty.... Turn your forces against Bohemia; burn, massacre...nothing could be more agreeable to God, or more useful to the cause of kings, than the extermination of the Hussites."[12] As a result of many years of research, Henry H. Halley wrote sadly:

[The Albigenses] preached against...the claims of the Church of Rome; made great use of the Scriptures.... By 1167 they embraced possibly a majority of the population of South France.... In 1208 a crusade was ordered by Pope Innocent III; a bloody war of extermination followed, scarcely paralleled in history; town after town was put to the sword and the inhabitants murdered without distinction of age or sex...within 100 years the Albigenses were utterly rooted out.

> Between 1540 and 1570, no fewer than 900,000 Protestants were put to death in the Pope's war for the extermination of the Waldenses.... On the night of August 24, 1572, 70,000 Huguenots, including most of their leaders, were massacred [St. Bartholemew's massacre]. Some 200,000 more perished as martyrs...[and] 500,000 fled to Protestant countries.[13]

A RATS' NEST OF DECEPTION!

Much of the anti-Semitism to which we have referred, and which appears on the surface around the world, is only the tip of the iceberg. The most vicious and far-reaching anti-Semitism is that which has been exercised by governments, international corporations (especially oil companies), and religious institutions, both Protestant and Catholic. There are no moral principles or loyalties—the only motive for any partnerships is profit.

One week before his death of a cerebral hemorrhage on April 4, 1945, Franklin D. Roosevelt promised Ibn Saud that the U.S. would not assist the Jews against the Arabs. His successor, Harry S. Truman (who would shock the world three years later by recognizing Israel only minutes after its declaration of independence), realizing that his ministers were betraying him, began an investigation, which was stopped by Allen Dulles' threats of oil sources drying up. At the end of the war, Dulles managed to smuggle Nazi money back to his clients. Yet he became head of the CIA! Of course, the destruction of Israel was an integral part of the plans. One had to make a choice between helping Israel, or having plenty of oil—a choice that most didn't find difficult to make. The pressure against allowing the state of Israel to be formed was overwhelming, which makes the miracle of her birth all the more amazing.

To these international "chess players," Israel is at best a nuisance and at worst a liability that could be jettisoned at any time to assure the West of Arab oil and goodwill. The only hesitation is due to fear of what the Arabs would do if there were no Israeli buffer between them and the West. John Loftus and Mark Aarons deserve our thanks for their monumental book, which is the fruit of nearly two decades of digging into secret government files and interviewing hundreds of former spies. Its introduction is shocking:

> The major powers of the world have repeatedly planned covert operations to bring about the partial or total destruction of Israel. Long before there even was a Jewish state in Palestine, Western spies already were out to wreck the Zionist dream. The savage extent of the secret wars against the Jews will horrify the Western public. This chapter of espionage history, beginning in the 1920s, and continuing to the present day, had never been revealed before....
>
> No one is more despised around Washington than someone who insists on telling the truth and can back it up with good files.... In its undiluted form, truth is an acid.... The "old spies" keep their leaders' ugly secrets bottled up within them, and it hurts. You can see the pain of knowing what really happened burning inside them. Although they want to denounce these deceptions...they preserve with painful silence the lies told by their superiors.... Silence is what they get paid for [it] keeps the pension checks coming.... It does not matter whether we are talking about the savings and loan scandal, or the arms race, or the intelligence wars against Israel...our politicians have developed the cover-up into an art form....
>
> With respect to the Middle East, our governments do not want their own citizens to know that a covert double standard has applied to the Jews, so they have lied to us for half a century. You may not be convinced [that what this book declares] is true in all respects, but at least you may be convinced that much of what has hitherto been accepted history is either false or, at best, seriously deficient. Our only claim for this book is that it is an accurate account of how many spies view the West's conduct toward Israel. This is their story...a very different look at history....
>
> From the CIA's sabotage of Jimmy Carter's presidency, through the twelve long years of Presidents Reagan and Bush, the secret betrayal of Israel was the touchstone of the men who made their incredible profits from the Arabs.... If the "old spies" are right, the U.S. policy was lenient compared to that of the British, French, Japanese, Soviets, and Germans. In fact, all the great nations have treated the Jews as expendable...obstacles to the secure supply of Arab oil.[14]

England's King Edward VIII was pro-Nazi, the enemy of the Jews, and encouraged Hitler to seize Czechoslovakia. The FBI's J. Edgar Hoover wanted to have him arrested. John Foster Dulles, who would become Secretary of State, and his brother Allen, who would become head of the CIA, were anti-Israel and pro-Arab, pursuing the ambition of gaining a dominant position for their corporate clients with regard to Middle East oil. Standard Oil was run by Dulles' pal, John D. Rockefeller. In the 1930s, Allen Dulles established a financial network that included Nazi corporations, American oil companies, and Saudi Arabia. His team of American and British investors continued to do business with the Nazis all during the war.

Considering the worldwide opposition, the fact that Israel exists today is an absolutely astonishing miracle that testifies to God's intention to fulfill His promises to Abraham, Isaac, and Jacob. It is this miracle that provides the strongest assurance that we are indeed in the last of the last days and that the removal from earth to heaven of the church composed of all true believers in the Rapture is very near.

Many skeptics imagine that the instant mass disappearance of millions of true Christians in the event known as the Rapture is pure fantasy invented by weaklings who dream of escaping this world. Such skeptics need to consider very carefully the fact that the same Bible from which we have been quoting prophecies that have unerringly foretold the entire history of Israel and events being fulfilled in our day also foretells the Rapture. To be left behind could be serious indeed.

After World War II, with the full knowledge and blessing of American, French, and British intelligence, the Vatican ran an underground escape network known as the "Vatican Ratlines." Thousands of the worst Nazi war criminals were taken by this means to South America, mostly to Argentina and Paraguay.[15] Nazi scientists were smuggled into Egypt to help it build missiles and other weapons to be used against Israel. All of this was with the knowledge and blessing of major Western powers—including the United States—who were, in fact, taking their pick of the Nazis for their own scientific and political programs. Soviet intelligence, the best in the world at that time, penetrated the operation and sub-verted it for Stalin's purposes. Underlying everything on all sides was an anti-Israel bias that has pervaded world politics for centuries and is still rampant today behind the scenes, hidden to the public, and never reported in the media.

Some unbelieving Jews who survived the Holocaust "felt compelled to return to Judaism [because] their experience simply confirmed to them that there was no way to avoid Jewish destiny—that assimilation among the gentiles was ultimately impossible."[16]

ISRAEL'S TRUE FRIENDS: EVANGELICAL CHRISTIANS

Most evangelical Christians who believe in the Rapture of the church to heaven before Antichrist appears have always actively supported the restoration of the Jews to the Promised Land. They have been confident that it would eventually occur, even when from all earthly appearances it seemed impossible. They based their faith upon biblical prophecies that clearly foretold the rebirth of Israel in her own land in the last days. One of the early supporters of Israel was William E. Blackstone, a descendant of prominent eighteenth-century English jurist William Blackstone. From studying the Bible, he became convinced that the Jewish people would indeed be restored to their land and that this event would precede the return of Christ to earth, even though it seemed highly unlikely in his day.

In 1878, Blackstone produced a 96-page book titled, *Jesus Is Coming*, later enlarged to 256 pages. The book was translated into more than forty-two languages, including Hebrew and Yiddish. The Hebrew version, published in 1925, bore the title *Hofaat Ha-Mashiach Ha-Shin—The Second Appearance of the Messiah*. It has often been said that the simplest answer to the challenge "Why do you believe in God?" is just two words: "The Jew!" Blackstone repeatedly said, "If anyone desires to know our place in God's chronology...look at Israel." Here is a sample of his writings about God's Chosen People:

> But, perhaps you say: "I don't believe the Israelites are to be restored to Canaan, and Jerusalem rebuilt." Dear Reader! Have you read the declaration of Gods' word about it? Surely nothing is more plainly stated in the Scriptures.... We beg of you to read [the biblical passages] thoughtfully. Divest yourself of prejudice and preconceived notions, and let the Holy Spirit show you, from His word, the glorious future of God's chosen people, "who are beloved" (Romans 11:28), and dear unto Him as "the apple of His eye" (Zechariah 2:8).

In November of 1890, Blackstone convened a conference between Jews and Christians on "The Past, Present, and Future of Israel." That resulted in "The Blackstone Petition of 1891," later known as the "Blackstone Memorial." Signed by 413 outstanding Christian and Jewish leaders (including Supreme Court Chief Justice Melville W. Fuller; speaker of the House of Representatives, Thomas B. Reed; and Ohio Congressman William McKinley, who later became President), it concerned the mistreatment of Jews particularly in Russia and proposed an international conference aimed at restoring the land of Palestine to the covenant people Israel.

Blackstone presented the petition to President Benjamin Harrison on March 5, 1891. It requested the President and Secretary Blaine "to use their good offices and influence" with Czar Alexander III, Sultan Abdul Hamid II, Queen Victoria, and the other European rulers to convene an international conference that would sympathetically consider "the condition of the Israelites and their claims to Palestine as their ancient home...." Through the State Department, it was distributed to the principal nations of the world. Asking the question, "What shall be done for the Russian Jews?" the petition boldly and biblically proposed:

> Why not give Palestine back to them again? According to God's distribution of nations, it is their home, an inalienable possession, from which they were expelled by force.... Why shall not the powers which under the treaty of Berlin, in 1878, gave Bulgaria to the Bulgarians and Serbia to the Serbians now give Palestine back to the Jews?... Let us now restore them to the land of which they were so cruelly despoiled by our Roman ancestors.

Other evangelicals, such as Theodor Herzl's close friend, William H. Hechler, worked diligently to promote political Zionism as the ultimate solution to the Jewish question. Hechler tried to encourage heads of state (including the Turkish sultan, who at that time controlled Palestine as part of the Ottoman Empire) to support Herzl's proposals. Hechler accompanied Herzl to Palestine in 1898 to meet with Kaiser Wilhelm II. The active support of such Christian Zionists in many countries influenced political action and played an important role in the small steps taken by world powers even before UN resolution 181, which gave to Israel at least part of the land, though only a small fraction of what was rightfully hers.

Another outstanding American Christian businessman who worked for the rebirth of the State of Israel as a haven for Jews suffering in many lands was Carl Hermann Voss, referred to earlier. He was active in founding the American Christian Palestine Committee. Its membership eventually grew to twenty thousand leaders, among whom was Johns Hopkins University archaeologist William F. Albright. Voss lectured widely and persuasively and fought the U.S. State Department, which then, as now, was opposed to Israel. In his Balfour Day address on November 2, 1943, Voss argued in part:

> The Arabs today have…more than a million square miles…. The Jews have none. Out of the last war the Arabs gained freedom and independence for Iraq, Saudi Arabia and later Transjordan…. The Arabs are destined to make new great gains at the conclusion of this conflict [WWII], and [should] thank the Jewish soldiers…who laid down their lives to help repel Rommel when his tanks were thundering across Egypt. For the Arabs to permit a Jewish State in Palestine, "a tiny notch" in the vast Arab expanse, involves no sacrifice to the Arabs; on the contrary, it provides them with a progressive and democratic neighbor eager to create a joint future in which the hopes of both peoples may be realized. For the Jews to give up Palestine would be to invite a new calamity for a people whose great misfortune is its homelessness.[17]

On October 30, 1977, Billy Graham addressed the National Executive Council meeting of the American Jewish committee and called for the rededication of the United States to the existence and safety of Israel. At the Bicentennial Congress of Prophecy in Philadelphia the year before, a proclamation in support of Israel had been signed by eleven prominent fundamentalist evangelicals. It then quickly received seven thousand additional signatures and was presented to the ambassador of the State of Israel. Statements of support also appeared in full-page newspaper advertisements, several in *The New York Times.*

UNBELIEF OF JEWS AND PSEUDO-CHRISTIANS

Today, tragically, most Jews, including those living in Israel, do not accept the Bible as the infallible Word of God and therefore do not believe God's promises made to Abraham, Isaac, and Jacob. The glad expression, "Next year in Jerusalem," and even the solemn prayer, "Sound the great Shofar for our freedom...bring our exiles together and assemble us from the four corners of the earth...,"[18] has been repeated by Jews around the world for centuries, but far more often as a tradition than by conviction or desire. Consequently, they leave themselves with no better claim upon the land than the Arabs have—and at the mercy of world powers that voted them in and could just as well vote them out.

Even many of the Zionists didn't fully believe God's promises. That movement eventually split over whether to accept territory in Africa or elsewhere that some considered just as suitable, perhaps even better than Palestine. To settle anywhere except in the ancient land of Israel was finally rejected by the Seventh Zionist Congress in 1915.

Clearly, in addition to the fact that Allah is not the God of the Bible, another major point of difference between a Christian and a Muslim is Israel. Muslims would be only too happy to agree that the church has replaced Israel. If that is true, then who are those Jews living there? Muslims would find their mutual rejection of Israel a basis for unity with those who claim that those aren't really Jews in Israel but Khazars and that Jews as a people have vanished.

If so, then God is a liar, His Word is not reliable, and we can't believe what it says about the Messiah and salvation. Yet we know that the Bible is 100 percent accurate in all it says—and that fact can be proved from just the prophecies concerning Israel. Those who reject any part of the Bible as not true, and particularly what it says about Israel, have placed themselves in a position to believe the misinformation spread by Islam.

SWEET WORDS OF REBELLION

Incredible though it may seem, the vast majority of those who call themselves Christians pick and choose out of the Bible what they want to believe and reject the rest. We've already shown the irrationality of such an attitude, which reduces God's Word to what man wants to accept, pretends that man knows more than God, rejects any rebuke from God to man, and thus removes any hope of salvation. The very concept of the Jews as God's "chosen people," though stated clearly hundreds of times in unmistakable language in Scripture, is rejected as undemocratic, as though what God decrees must first be submitted to majority vote. Multiple errors are introduced as in the following:

> Only in a theology rooted in a God who loves all people can there be genuine reconciliation, justice and peace. Christians, Muslims and Jews, people of the three Abrahamic faiths, must reject a "God" who chooses one people against all others, for in this "God" lies the ultimate mandate for genocide.[19]

That statement may sound appealing, but its irrationality and unbiblical nature are obvious. Reconciliation must first of all be between man and God—and that can only come on God's terms. We don't negotiate with Him. The quote above is contained in a full-page article in the *National Catholic Reporter*, which, although viciously critical of Israelis, has not one word of rebuke for Islam's slaughter of millions of Jews, Christians, and pagans (and hundreds of thousands of Muslims by Muslims as well) through the centuries.

Islam is passed off as a religion of "justice and peace," when that is so manifestly not the case that we need not document its evils further.

That God loves all mankind does not contradict His choosing of Abraham, Isaac, and Jacob, from whom the Messiah would descend as a man. Indeed, it was precisely because of His love for all that the eternal Son of God came to this earth as a man—"For God so loved the world, that he gave his only begotten Son, that whosoever believeth in him should not perish, but have everlasting life."[20] For the Messiah to be a real man in order to represent mankind in paying the penalty for the sins of all, he had to have human ancestors. That Jesus was a Jew does not mean that they are superior to all others—they are simply God's chosen people through whom the Messiah would be born.

The Jews had to live somewhere. God gave them a definite land, and in that land are bound up people and events in fulfillment of definite prophecies that give us the absolute proof of the existence of this God, who loves all, and of the Messiah, who would be born into that land descended from these people, and who would be man's Savior. Reject these facts and you have rejected the only salvation God has for mankind and have declared yourself an incorrigible rebel without hope for eternity. Furthermore, to blind one's eyes to the distinct and important differences between Islam, Judaism, and Christianity is once again to reject God's salvation. It is rebellion of the rawest kind to call Islam an "Abrahamic faith"! In fact, it is the clearest rejection of the faith of Abraham that could be conceived!

"ISLAM AND CHRISTIANS JOIN HANDS"?

Muslims are busy duping the West through promoting alleged "solidarity and understanding" between Muslims and Christians. The latter seem unaware of or give no importance to the fact that such conferences could never take place in a Muslim country, where it is the death penalty for a Muslim to become a Christian. What "solidarity" is that?!

Typical was "Islam Awareness Week," organized by the Waikato Muslim Association in New Zealand's north island in mid-August 2004. The newspaper report on this event was titled, "Islam and Christians join hands" and declared enthusiastically, "Commonalities between Abrahamic Faiths: Islam and Christianity [any mention of Judaism or acknowledgement that Jews are the physical descendants of Abraham was oddly missing!] was the theme of a dialogue in the Hamilton City Council reception lounge [which] attracted...Members of Parliament, local dignitaries and church leaders.... Yahya Ibrahim, who has committed the Koran to memory, said there is more about Jesus than Mohammed in the Koran...."

Whether there is more about Jesus than about Muhammad in the Qur'an is questionable. But even if there were, it would be no cause for imagining that Islam and Christianity have anything in common. In fact, they have nothing. Apparently, it never occurred to the Christian participants to find out for themselves exactly what the Qur'an says about Jesus. They might have lost some of their enthusiasm and goodwill had they learned that the Qur'an denies the very heart of Christianity, including the deity of Christ, His death on the Cross for our sins, His resurrection, His indwelling life in the believer, His coming again in power and glory to reign over the world from David's Jewish throne, and much more. Such ignorance is both appalling and is, I fear, in many cases willful.

The article continued, "Waikato Interfaith Council Executive member Alan Leadley, said the evening was very positive...for Hamilton...a sign of hope and understanding.... 'I learned a lot about Islam Faith,' said Reverend Dennis Clow." On the contrary, he learned nothing factual about Islam. All he received was the misinformation the Muslims fed to the unsuspecting and willingly duped Christians. "I have discovered that there is a considerable overlap between Christianity and Islam," added Clow. [21]

In fact, there is no overlap at all. As we have amply demonstrated from the Qur'an and the Bible, even when Islam claims to be referring to Abraham, Moses, Christ, or other biblical personalities, they are all supposedly Muslims and seen in a contradictory light. At this "Islam

Awareness Week," where "Islam and Christians" would supposedly "join hands," the Muslims only told what they thought would gain good will. They held back the real truth about Islam, which would have revealed its contradiction of biblical Christianity on every point and its ultimate intention to kill all Jews and conquer the world. But such subterfuge is typical of ecumenical conferences of all kinds.

INEXCUSABLE, IF NOT DELIBERATE, DELUSION

The naïveté and willingness to be deceived was beyond comprehension but quite normal for such forums. Chamberlain would have felt right at home. Seemingly forgotten in the euphoria of new "understanding" (or overlooked in ignorance) was the fact that anyone who attempted to promote a comparable "Christian Awareness Week" in any Muslim country would be jailed or deported if he were a non-Muslim, and probably killed if he were a Muslim. The celebrated "overlap between Christianity and Islam" is not sufficient to eliminate the death penalty for Muslims who become Christians (or even want to give Christianity an honest examination), a law established by Muhammad himself and still practiced in Saudi Arabia and wherever else Islam is in charge. How can a Muslim gain any understanding of Christianity if he is unable to examine it openly for fear of incurring the death penalty?

For many, such empty-headed statements are not made out of ignorance but by those who, claiming to be the most knowledgeable, hate the Bible, the God of the Bible, and Israel, His chosen people. Anti-Israel ecumenical seminars and conferences (their "ecumenism" embraces everyone except Jews and evangelical Christians) are frequently in progress somewhere in the world. Typical was the Fifth International Conference of the Sabeel Ecumenical Palestinian Liberation Theology Center held at the Roman Catholic Pontifical Notre Dame Ecumenical Centre in Jerusalem on April 14-18, 2004. The theme of the conference was "Challenging Christian Zionism...." It featured the anti-Israel comments typical of liberal church leaders. An opening greeting was given by Archimandrite

Attalah Hanna of the Greek Orthodox Church (outspoken supporter of suicide bombers, who deliberately target innocent women and children). Hanna trashed the Bible and rejected all of God's promises to Israel.

The Dean of Te Rau Kahikatea Anglican Theological College in New Zealand, Convener of the Global Anglican Peace and Justice Network, described Christian Zionism (the biblical belief that God gave the land of Canaan to His chosen people descended from Abraham, Isaac, and Jacob) as a "manifest evil [an] insidious presence."

Canon Jonathan Geogh, Secretary for Ecumenism under Rowan Williams, the Archbishop of Canterbury, presented an address on Williams' behalf, distinguishing modern Israel from the Israel of the Bible, yet remarkably, without the anti-Israel rhetoric of the other speakers. Reverend Michael Prior, professor of Bible and Theology at St. Mary's College (University of Surrey), began his talk with, "The Bible is a very dangerous book. On its cover should be written, 'This is a dangerous book. Reading it may damage somebody else's health.'" He described the book of Exodus as a "con-job" full of myths and legends and called Joshua "the patron saint of ethnic cleansers...a continuous genocidist...."

Such professed Christians are only too happy, in defiance of God and His Word, to declare their "solidarity" with the enemies of the people of God, such as the Pakistani Muslim leader who, less than a month after 9/11, declared that "the life of one Muslim is worth the lives of all Americans." Along with other Muslim leaders, he called upon all Muslims around the world to join in a holy war against the United States.[22] Such peace! Yet when it comes to Israel, many Christian leaders are in virtual agreement. Muslims say Israel must be destroyed, while many Christians say Israel was *already* destroyed.

It is not difficult to see the entire world one day condemning Israel and attacking her to effect Hitler's "final solution to the Jewish problem." The secular world can justify its attitude because "Christians" say that those Jews in Israel are there illegally, and they're not God's Chosen People after all—that honor belongs to the church.

"CHRISTIAN" OPPOSITION TO ISRAEL

It is a matter of indisputable record that Pope Pius XII never spoke out publicly to rebuke Hitler for attempting to exterminate the Jews. Had he done so forcefully, and had he forbidden Roman Catholics (who were a large percentage of the German military, Gestapo, SS, etc.) to participate in the mistreatment and extermination of Jews under pain of excommunication (should murderers remain in good standing in the Church?), he might have saved millions from Hitler's ovens. His defenders claim that Pius XII worked against the Holocaust behind the scenes. The Nazi archives, however, have yielded no evidence whatsoever to support this assertion—and access to the Vatican archives is denied to truth seekers.

The Pope knew how to express himself forcefully when he wanted to—and he did so in opposition to the reestablishment of Israel in its own Promised Land. He both worked behind the scenes and openly to prevent Israel's restoration, to which he and his Church were adamantly opposed. On June 22, 1943, with the smoke of burning Jews hovering over Europe, the Pope wrote to President Roosevelt:

> It is true that at one time Palestine was inhabited by the Hebrew Race, but there is no axiom in history to substantiate the necessity of a people returning to a country they left nineteen centuries before. If a "Hebrew Home" is desired, it would not be too difficult to find a more fitting territory than Palestine. With an increase in the Jewish population there, grave, new international problems would arise.

Of course, there is "no axiom in history" that would require the Jews to return to their land (this is a unique event)—but there are hundreds of promises from God to that effect. How could the Pope, who claimed to be the representative of Christ on earth, the head of the true Church, have overlooked the hundreds of promises in God's Word that He would restore the Jews to their ancient land? Indeed, how could the Pope and his Church dare to defy God in this regard! As the war neared its end, the Pope pleaded with the

Allied Forces to deal leniently with Hitler and Mussolini. Both were Catholics to their deaths. Pius XII never excommunicated either of these master criminals and mass murderers.

Not only have Muslims and the Roman Catholic Church been opposed to the existence of Israel, but that has been true of many evangelicals as well, as we saw briefly in the last chapter. The unbiblical claim that the church has replaced the Jews as the people of God is a Roman Catholic doctrine from which some of the Reformers were never delivered. It has persisted among Reformed Churches, such as Presbyterian and some Baptists. In an effort to ruin her financially, Presbyterians, Lutherans, and the National Council of Churches have called for a boycott of companies that do business with Israel.

There are evangelicals today who deny any legitimacy to Israel because, as they say, "those Jews over there rebelled against God, rejected their Messiah, and are in that land in unbelief!" But the Bible declares that the scattered and persecuted Jews must return to their land in unbelief because it will be in that land that Israel will come to faith in Christ:

> And it shall come to pass in that day, that I will seek to destroy all the nations that come against Jerusalem. And I will pour upon the house of David, and upon the inhabitants of Jerusalem, the spirit of grace and of supplications: and they shall look upon me whom they have pierced, and they shall mourn for him, as one mourneth for his only son, and shall be in bitterness for him, as one that is in bitterness for his firstborn. In that day there shall be a fountain opened to the house of David and to the inhabitants of Jerusalem for sin and for uncleanness. [23]

If, after having returned to their ancient land, the Jews recognize and come to believe in their Messiah as the God of Israel, who has been "pierced" for their sins and has intervened to rescue them at Armageddon, then obviously they must have come *back* to the land in unbelief. This fact was recognized and preached more than one hundred years ago by such leading evangelicals as the great evangelist D. L. Moody and by James M. Gray, former dean and president of Moody Bible Institute. Gray declared that "the Jews will have returned to Jerusalem as yet in an unconverted state with reference to the Messiah before the Great Tribulation occurs."[24]

President Bush claims to be a Christian. Then how can he be the architect of a "road map to peace" that violates God's will for Israel and promises to bring God's judgment upon America and the world? Apparently, he can ignore Joel 3:2 rather easily and with remarkably good conscience. He has advisors who embrace Reformed theology and who teach that this verse no longer applies because Israel rejected Christ and has been cut off.

THE LAST WORDS OF MOSES

God will have the last word in all of this. The last words He spoke to Israel through Moses were words of comfort and assurance. In spite of her rebellion, God declared that He would not forsake her and would restore her to more and better blessings in the end than at the beginning. Specific prophecies are given for each of the twelve tribes of Israel— another proof that ten tribes would not be "lost."

Repentance and faith could have brought these blessings to Israel at any time in her history. Sadly, she continued in rebellion as she is today. The final words of Moses to Israel await their ultimate fulfillment in the last days. They end like this:

> The eternal God is thy refuge, and underneath are the everlasting arms: and he shall thrust out the enemy from before thee; and shall say, Destroy them.
>
> Israel then shall dwell in safety alone: the fountain of Jacob shall be upon a land of corn and wine; also his heavens shall drop down dew.
>
> Happy art thou, O Israel: who is like unto thee, O people saved by the LORD, the shield of thy help, and who is the sword of thy excellency! And thine enemies shall be found liars unto thee; and thou shalt tread upon their high places.[25]

Some of God's declarations ought to strike terror in the hearts of those who have made themselves His enemies by defying Him in His declared purposes for Israel. Before pronouncing God's last days' blessing upon Israel, Moses had a final word of warning from God for the nations that would oppose and oppress her:

> See now that I, even I, am he, and there is no god with me: I kill, and I make alive; I wound, and I heal: neither is there any that can deliver out of my hand. For I lift up my hand to heaven, and say, I live for ever. If I whet [sharpen] my glittering sword, and mine hand take hold on judgment; I will render vengeance to mine enemies, and will reward them that hate me. I will make mine arrows drunk with blood, and my sword shall devour flesh; and that with the blood of the slain and of the captives, from the beginning of revenges upon the enemy. Rejoice, O ye nations, with his people: for he will avenge the blood of his servants, and will render vengeance to his adversaries, and will be merciful unto his land, and to his people.[26]

The language is vivid and terrifying. God is sharpening His sword of judgment. There will be a false peace that will deceive Israel. Then all nations will attack to destroy her. With Israel on the brink of annihilation, and after two-thirds of all Jews on earth have been killed,[27] God will "make [His] arrows drunk with blood, and [His] sword shall devour [the] flesh" of His enemies. We will come to these events in the two final chapters.

1. Dave Hunt, *A Woman Rides the Beast: The Roman Catholic Church and the Last Days* (Eugene, OR: Harvest House Publishers, 1994); Dave Hunt, *Occult Invasion* (Eugene, OR: Harvest House, 1998).

2. Rabbi Nosson Scherman/Rabbi Meir Zlotowitz, General Editors, *Shoah* (Brooklyn, New York: Mesorah Publications, Ltd., 1990), 161.

3. Peter De Rosa, *Vicars of Christ: The Dark Side of the Papacy* (New York: Crown Publishers, Inc., 1988), 175-176.

4. J. H. Ignaz von Dollinger, *The Pope and the Council* (London: Roberts, 1869), 191-192.

5. E. M. MacDonald (preface), *A Short History of the Inquisition* (New York: The Truth Seekers Co., 1907), 202, 296.

6. Guenter Lewy, *The Catholic Church and Nazi Germany* (McGraw Hill, 1964), 274.

7. Ibid.

8. Jules Isaac, *Jesus et Israel* (Paris, 1948), 508.

9. Rabbi Nosson Scherman/Rabbi Meir Zlotowitz, General Editors, *Shoah* (Brooklyn, New York: Mesorah Publications, Ltd., 1990), 159.

10. Romans 1:16.

11. Sidney Z. Ehler, John B. Morral, trans. and eds., *Church and State Through the Centuries* (London, 1954), 7.

12. R. W. Thompson, *The Papacy and the Civil Power* (New York, 1876), 553.

13. Henry H. Halley, *Pocket Bible Handbook* (Chicago, 1944), 608-13.

14. John Loftus and Mark Aarons, *The Secret War Against the Jews: How Western Espionage Betrayed the Jewish People* (New York: St. Martin's Press, 1994), Introduction, 1-14.

15. See Dave Hunt, *A Woman Rides the Beast: The Roman Catholic Church and the Last Days* (Eugene, OR: Harvest House Publishers, 1994), 265-328; also Mark Aarons and John Loftus, *Unholy Trinity: How the Vatican's Nazi Networks Betrayed Western Intelligence to the Soviets* (New York: St Martin's Press, 1991); and Mark Aarons and John Loftus, *The Secret War Against the Jews: How Western Espionage Betrayed the Jewish People* (New York: St. Martin's Press, 1994).

16. *Shoah*, 271.

17. Quoted in David A. Rausch, *The Middle East Maze: Israel and Her Neighbors* (Chicago: Moody Press, 1991), 73-74.

18. Daily Prayer Book, *Ha-Siddur Ha-Shalem* (New York, 1949).

19. Rosemary Radford Ruether, "Jewish settlers as pushy 'chosen people' – Christian Peacemakers have thankless task," *National Catholic Reporter*, April 26, 1996, 12.

20. John 3:16.

21. *Waikato Times*, August 16, 2004, 11.

22. CNN, October 3, 2001.

23. Zechariah 12:9-10; 13:1.

24. Rausch, *Middle East*, 63, 65.

25. Deuteronomy 33:27-29.

26. Deuteronomy 32:39-43.

27. Zechariah 13:8-9.

13—GOD OFFERS SALVATION

As important as the Middle East conflict is, its significance is only temporary. No matter what happens, we will all be gone in a few years, just as Arafat, one of the major players in this drama, has already left this earth. The PLO and Israeli conflict is the least of his concerns now. That fact calls our attention to the necessity of preparing for a death that looms ever over our heads and from which no one can escape.

Clearly, where we will spend eternity when we leave this earth and all of its possessions and ambitions behind ought to be our primary focus. And it is on this very point, the most important of all, that we find the greatest difference between the uncertain hope of the Muslim, who can't be sure of his destiny, and the Christian, who has absolute confidence that he will be eternally with Christ in heaven. Such is the beauty and promise of the gospel of Jesus Christ—and it is based upon many infallible proofs given to us in prophecy and verified by history. God offers salvation to all who will believe on Christ by their own free choice based upon all the evidence. No one is forced into anything. The true God wants our hearts.

Some Muslims have expressed surprise and anger that their religion is being linked with terrorism—a violent form of coercion to intimidate the otherwise unwilling to submit to Islam. But there is no denying the fact that the overwhelming majority of terrorist acts in the world (especially suicide bombings) are perpetrated in the name of Islam, to the glory of Allah. The Muslim Council of Britain has urged imams across that country to change this image by asking Friday worshipers to cooperate with police in their anti-terror investigations and efforts. In 2004, the Turkish government ordered the mosques in that nation to deliver an anti-terrorism message as authorities pieced together evidence to determine who was behind a string of suicide bombings (a trademark of Islam) that killed fifty-seven people and wounded hundreds more. There is a growing movement within mosques in the United States to remind worshipers that Islam does not condone unlawful acts.[1]

That terminology, however, is misleading. What counts with the Muslim is that Islamic terrorists are obeying Allah and Muhammad and are thus not lawbreakers, no matter what the laws are in their country of residence. That they are murderers of innocent women and children according to man's laws is of no concern. They are not looked down upon as lawbreakers but admired as heroic martyrs in Islam's *jihad* against the world of unbelievers. There are, however serious conflicts of opinion when the terrorism is by one faction of Islam against another faction.

Surprising to most Westerners, who imagine that non-Muslims are the only targets of Islamic terrorism, is the fact that most terrorist acts are by Muslims against Muslims. We have seen that being played out in Iraq, where by far the greatest number of terrorists' victims are not coalition troops but Muslim civilians. News from Iraq is reported worldwide, but the many terrorist bombings in other Muslim countries are largely unheard of in the West. Consider one example out of hundreds that could be given: the October 1, 2004, suicide bombing during Friday prayers at the Masjid Zanabiya Shi'ite mosque in Sialkot, Eastern Pakistan. About thirty worshipers were killed and more than one hundred wounded. The victims are looked upon by Shi'ites as *shaheeds* (a martyr in *jihad*) assured of immediate entrance into Paradise. Yet the suicide bomber, a Sunni Muslim, imagined that by killing them he would gain instant entrance to Paradise for himself. Of course, the Shi'ite clerics said he went directly to hell.[2]

Who is right? This is a serious question!

TERRORISM IS ENDEMIC TO ISLAM

As we have documented repeatedly, terrorism has always been an integral part of Islam as taught by Muhammad and practiced by him and his successors for more than thirteen hundred years. The fact cannot be denied that many mosques are training and support centers for terrorists. In some of them, even in the West, terrorism is openly preached, as it is in every mosque in Muslim countries. We have already seen that this is not extremism but true Islam as Muhammad established it and as his successors practiced it for centuries, all the way from France to China. Today, terrorism is a worldwide phenomenon perpetrated in the name of Allah to advance by intimidation the cause of Islam—or a particular brand of it, depending upon the Islamic faction involved.

Of course, all Muslims of every faction are united in their hatred of Israel and the West. On September 30, 2003, the Israeli army captured Hamas propaganda materials at al-'Ein mosque in al-Bireh. The material included posters commemorating *sha-heeds* who were suicide bombers attacking Israel. Other material was dedicated to terrorists held in custody. Laudatory posters were also found proclaiming the bravery and virtue of those who carried out suicide bombing attacks on September 9, 2003, near the cities of Ramla and Jerusalem and elsewhere.[3] In the mosque were also militant Islamic manifestoes attacking Israel, the Jewish people, the United States, and the entire Western world. Remember the statement issued on September 11, 2001, in *Al-Hayat Al-Jadida*, the official PA newspaper, "Suicide bombers of today…are the salt of the earth…the noblest people among us."

The IDF found a Hamas operative rolled up in a prayer rug in the Abd al-Nasser mosque in Ramallah. Ahmad Odeh, another wanted Hamas terrorist, was discovered hiding in the Zeid mosque near the entrance to the city of Tulkarm on the West Bank. He shot at Israeli troops, who returned fire and killed him.

Many mosques in the West, including some in America, have been associated with terrorist cells. In February of 2004, Representative Peter King (R) of New York, a member of the House Select Committee on Homeland Security, claimed that 85 percent of mosques have extremist leadership and that "no Muslims [in America] are cooperating" with law enforcement in the war on terror. The FBI's raid of the Masjid As-Salam ("House of Peace") in Albany, N.Y., in August 2004, has led to indictments against the mosque's imam and another member caught in a government sting on charges of money laundering and promoting terrorism.[4] These are but a few of the examples that could be given.

Again, the mistake is being made of calling true Muslims "extremists." Was Muhammad an "extremist"? That would be absurd. How can the founder of Islam be an extremist? Surely of all Muslims, he would be the exemplification of true Islam if ever there was one! Yet Muhammad plundered and murdered in the name of Allah to the glory of Islam. This refusal to face the fact that Islam itself is the enemy is costing us dearly.

A RELIGION OF DEATH

Fallujah, Iraq's "holy city" of more than one hundred mosques and the largest Sunni city west of Baghdad, sheltered so many terrorists (acting for Islam and to the glory of Allah) and was such a center from which terrorist attacks were launched, that the U.S. and Iraqi military had to take the city, house by house. In the process, they captured or killed hundreds of terrorists. The military operation captured at least fifteen portable surface-to-air missiles capable of shooting down aircraft, dozens of mortar tubes, and sophisticated anti-tank weapons among hundreds of weapons caches, many of them in mosques. One out of every two mosques in Fallujah was used for hiding fighters and/or weapons.[5] This practice is only to be expected in Islam, because it recognizes no distinction between religion and state.

The place of one's burial is extremely important to a Muslim's hope for the next life. Najaf, another of Iraq's "holy cities," this one Shi'ite, has a booming business entirely devoted to corpses. Here is located the tomb of Ali, cousin and son-in-law of Muhammad. His murder by rival Sunni Muslims near Kufa some thirteen hundred years ago gave birth to the Shi'ite movement. Near Ali's mausoleum is the largest graveyard in the world, with more than 1.8 million tombs. Why so many? Amir Taheri, editor of a Muslim publication, explains:

> For the world's 150 million Muslim Shias, Najaf is the ideal burial place. Proximity to Ali is supposed to improve chances of avoiding Gehenna, the abode of the fallen, according to the Koran. [*Improve chances?* What hope is that?] Believers spend a lifetime's savings to have their corpses transported to Najaf for burial close to Ali's mausoleum. Five generations of my family are buried there thanks to a tradition that began in the 17th century. [What does this have to do with justice and truth? It sounds like Catholicism!]
>
> Death is at the centre of life here. Tens of thousands of grave-diggers, undertakers, masters of funeral ceremonies, tomb watchers, givers of prayers for the dead, intercessors, Koran reciters, mediums for communication with the departed, and so on make up the bulk of the workforce.
>
> While Najaf's chief import is corpses, its major export is mullahs. The city hosts the most eminent of Shia seminaries which, at the height of its theological boom in the 1950s, boasted 124 madrassahs with 40,000 trainee mullahs. All the grand ayatollahs of the past 150 years either studied or taught there.[6]

Muhammad's son-in-law, Ali, is to the Shi'ite what Catholic "saints" are to their devotees. However, neither praying to a Catholic saint nor being buried near Ali's remains will ever pay the penalty for sin. Not even earthly justice—and certainly not God's—works that way. Certainly, being buried in the same tomb with Ali would not help. Muslims are all being deceived! How can God remain just and holy and yet forgive sins? This is the issue. The Bible is clear, and it rings true to the conscience: God can only forgive those who have accepted the full payment Christ made for their sins. "The blood of

Jesus Christ [shed in His death on our behalf] cleanseth us from all sin." Inspired of the Holy Spirit, Paul declared:

> But now the righteousness of God without the law is manifested, being witnessed by the law and the prophets; Even the righteousness of God…by faith of Jesus Christ unto…them that believe: for there is no difference: For all have sinned, and come short of the glory of God; Being justified freely by his grace through the redemption that is in Christ Jesus…for the remission of sins that are past, through the forbearance of God…that he might be just, and the justifier of him which believeth in Jesus.[7]

For the *jihad* "martyr," it is his own blood—not Christ's blood—that pays for sin. He is not washed or dressed but buried just as he died. His blood will thus presumably testify to Allah that he is worthy of entering Paradise because he sacrificed his life to kill others, sending them to hell. Every conscience is repelled by such perversion! Israel does not return the mutilated bodies to their Muslim families because that would give occasion for parading the remains and arousing even more fanaticism at the funeral. Israel, however, claims that it gives each of them a proper Muslim burial.

SUPPOSED WAYS TO PARADISE

Islam has one thing in common with every other religion, which separates all religions from true Christianity: attempting to appease God with works and sacrifices—and for a Muslim, even giving up one's own life to gain Paradise. Whatever happens, it is up to the individual Muslim to live a good enough life and to make amends for any misdeeds in order to be acceptable to Allah. But Allah changes his mind and decides to send some to hell regardless of what they may think or do. In this respect Islam, like Calvinism, puts a great deal of emphasis upon predestination, with nothing the individual Muslim or Calvinist can do about it.

Likewise Catholicism, while claiming to be a Christian religion, denies the sufficiency of the sacrifice of Christ on the Cross for sins and like Islam is a religion of appeasement through good works and sacraments. In addition to Christ's suffering for us, Catholics must be purged of their sins by suffering after death in the flames of purgatory. Biblical Christianity rejects such ideas. Because of the work of redemption, which Christ finished on the Cross, good works are of no value for salvation but are offered to God in love and gratitude for the salvation He has given us freely by His grace and mercy.

Of all terrorists, suicide bombers are the most difficult to detect and stop. There are literally millions of young men and boys in training in Iraq, Pakistan, Iran, Saudi Arabia, and other Muslim countries to become suicide bombers. In Iran alone, in just one appeal, ten thousand were signed up for suicide missions in Iraq, where thousands of foreign fighters have infiltrated to confront the coalition and Iraqi troops. For many, this is a lifetime ambition. The greater the number of innocent people the bomber kills, the greater the reward from Allah. The families of a successful *shaheed* (i.e., who kills others in his suicide) will receive a large monetary reward, once paid by Saddam Hussein, but now by the Saudi royal family and from contributions collected from Saudi citizens.

The *shaheed* is promised instant entrance into Paradise, where the rivers run with wine (forbidden to the Muslim in this life), the tables are laden with every delicacy the palate could desire, and at least seventy-two, and perhaps hundreds or even thousands of dark-eyed *houris* await his pleasure. He is promised the appetite and strength of one hundred men for food, drink, and sex.

For most Muslims, martyrdom is the one sure way to Paradise—but Paradise is not sure even then. Abu Bakr, Muhammad's first successor, received from Muhammad his personal promise of Paradise without martyrdom. Yet we quote him in Chapter Seven declaring that he feared that he might be "the first one to enter [hell fire]." He was afraid that even if he had one foot inside Paradise, Allah might shove him out. Can a suicide bomber, then, really be certain of his destiny when Abu Bakr was not? And on whose authority, if Abu Bakr didn't accept Muhammad's?

The disastrous fact is that the first thing the *jihad* "martyr" discovers after his suicide is that he is not in heaven but in hell and that instead of being rewarded, he is being punished for the murders and mayhem he caused in this final act of his life. What a tragedy that so many are being deceived in this way.

What "god" rewards murderers with heaven? The conscience God has given each person cries out in protest! Those under this immoral delusion are victims as well as those they murder. The fact that the United Nations, world leaders, and billions of citizens around the world do not rise up in outrage against this barbaric practice is as clear an indictment of the world of our day as was the thunderous silence in the face of the Holocaust in Nazi times!

JUSTICE MUST BE SATISFIED

Let us think clearly for a moment. How can one's sins, committed over a lifetime, be expunged by one final sin of mass murder? What court of law would accept that? The murderer would, in fact, be sentenced to death for this additional crime. And imagine the hundreds of thousands of trusting Muslims who pay dearly to be buried as close to Ali's tomb as possible under the delusion that they will thereby gain some greater measure of mercy from Allah. Amir Taheri is an intelligent man. Can he really believe that his family's sins have been forgiven because of their being buried in the vicinity of Ali's remains? What "justice" is that?

Nor is this the only deadly delusion that grips Muslims. We have noted that only by killing every Jew on earth can Muslims bring to pass the "last day." And what is its significance? This is when one's deeds will supposedly be weighed by Allah in the balance, and if the good outweighs the bad, then one is admitted to Paradise without being a *jihad* martyr.

Every conscience rejects such reasoning. What judge would excuse the guilty party from paying a speeding ticket because he or she had driven more within the speed limit than exceeding it? Or what judge would declare innocent a man who had committed five murders, because he had once saved the lives of six (or even one hundred) people from drowning or from a burning building?

To the person who promises never to break the law again if the judge will let him off this time, the judge would surely reply, "If you never break the law again, you are only doing what the law requires. You don't get extra credit for that with which to pay the penalty for past or future sins."

THE PENALTY MUST BE PAID IN FULL

The human race, individually and collectively, is guilty of rebellion against God. Living by its own rules and for its own ends, mankind is collectively defying the Creator of the universe! That rebellion will not go unpunished.

God pronounced eternal death (i.e., separation from Him in pain and sorrow) as the penalty for breaking His law in even the smallest way. In fact, there is no "small" breach of the law. To break the law in any respect is rebellion against God. That mankind would act selfishly rather than for God was inevitable. Obviously, then, God needed to have a means of forgiving and restoring man. But to forgive man without the penalty being paid would make God a partner with him in his sin.

Conscience teaches every man that it is wrong to lie, steal, murder, commit adultery, to fornicate, to covet what belongs to someone else, to be proud, self-serving, etc.[8] Man also knows that justice demands a penalty for breaking God's laws. We can't buy God off. He doesn't negotiate with us or work out any special deals. His perfect, holy justice must be satisfied. The penalty must be paid. Yet God loves every person deeply enough to find a way to forgive man righteously. The only way was for God himself to come to this earth as a man and pay that penalty for the entire human race—which He did in Jesus Christ:

> For God so loved the world, that he gave his only begotten Son, that whosoever believeth in him should not perish, but have everlasting life. For God sent not his Son into the world to condemn the world; but that the world through him might be saved.[9]
>
> He that believeth on the son hath everlasting life: and he that believeth not the Son shall not see life; but the wrath of God abideth on him.[10]

Christianity is separated from every religion in the world by an impassable gulf—and the difference rings true to the conscience. All religions propose that man do good works, engage in ritual, make sacrifices, or do something to somehow appease God; the Bible teaches that it is a matter of justice, not of appeasement. The penalty must be paid in full. God's justice and the penalty for breaking His law are infinite because God is infinite, and thus God is the only one who can pay it—which He did in Christ. All man can do is accept the substitutionary death of Christ in His enduring the full penalty for the sins of all mankind, and thereby be forgiven. This is good news that every Christian is obliged to share with the world, persuasively, in love and reason—and without being dissuaded from doing so by threats or force.

INTIMIDATION OF CHRISTIANS BY MUSLIMS

What a tragedy that the Muslim knows nothing of the assurance of sins forgiven through Christ's payment of the full penalty in his place. And that tragedy is exacerbated by the reluctance of Christians to tell that good news to Muslims for fear of retaliation. Mark A. Gabriel (a pseudonym for obvious reasons) was a staunch Muslim and professor of Islamic history at Al-Azhar University in Cairo, Egypt, the most authoritative center of Islamic thought in the world. Here is part of his story:

> I could see Christians wherever I went in my country [but] not one Christian person tried to talk to me about his Jesus Christ...except the wonderful pharmacist who gave me the Bible.... Fundamentalists tried to burn down her pharmacy, and she ultimately left Egypt and went to Canada. Christians living in Egypt...are persecuted by the Muslim fundamentalist groups. So they have decided to live quietly and to distance themselves as much as possible from the more than 50 million Muslims living in the country who need to hear about Jesus Christ. This Christian society lives under great fear, and they actually refuse to witness to Muslims.
>
> I was required to spend one year in the Egyptian military. I shared a room with one other soldier, who happened to be a Christian.... I questioned him constantly about his faith. I asked

him how he could believe in…the Trinity…how he could believe that God has a son. "Does God have a wife?" I mocked. All these concepts were blasphemous according to Islam. Whenever I questioned him, he refused to answer. He would say to me, "Let us just be friends. Leave religion to God, please…." He was very fearful of me and of the Muslims in our military group…this was one of the most difficult years in his life.

After I met the Lord Jesus Christ, I remembered this man… sorry for how he allowed the spirit of fear to control his life… [and how he] refused to share the true Jesus Christ with others…. When I went back to the Christian pharmacist who had given me the Bible and declared my faith in Jesus Christ…she arranged to go with me to meet the leader of an Egyptian church. She hoped this man would…baptize me [and] help me in biblical study and receive me as a new member…. We sat down together in his office, and he basically told me, "My son, you can go back to your home. We do not need to add a number to our congregation. And if you go home, we will not lose any number of our congregation. We are not interested." Later [he told] my pharmacist friend that he didn't want other Muslims to hear that he had opened up his church to a [former] Muslim because he was afraid they would come and burn down the building.[11]

Yet Christ commanded His early disciples (and every Christian today is included) to "go ye into all the world, and preach the gospel to every creature."[12] Millions of Muslims have come to the West so that we cannot excuse ourselves by saying that we aren't able to go to them. They have come to us. True Christians must in love and compassion and without fear share the good news of the gospel of the Lord Jesus Christ with Muslims and Jews and with the whole world. The greatest challenge we face is how to bring this message of God's love not only to Muslims in the West, but to those remaining in their own countries.

This author has prayed for many years that the Islamic Curtain, which is more vicious and impenetrable than the Iron or Bamboo Curtains ever were, could somehow be brought down. The Muslim world desperately needs to hear the good news of salvation through Christ's payment for their sins. They need to have the opportunity to make a free choice without intimidation. For that to become possible, some major changes would have to take place. At this time, even to question Islam, or to consider alternate beliefs (much less to turn away from Islam to another religion), would bring persecution and even death. This is the frightening situation even for those living in Muslim communities within the Western world. The long arm of zealous enforcers can reach anywhere.

SOME HOPEFUL SIGNS

The first indication that events are moving in a better direction has been an awakening on the part of some Western leaders and certain segments of the media to the truth about Islam—and, what is most important, the courage to express it. For months after 9/11, the lie that Islam is peace was sounded by almost every public voice in the West. Honesty, however, cannot forever turn a blind eye to the truth. Eventually, the realization can no longer be stifled that those responsible for the vast majority of terrorism in the world today (and it is spreading like a virus) are devout Muslims—and the terrorism they inflict upon the world is for the purpose of spreading Islam by bringing all mankind into submission to Allah and Muhammad as his prophet.

Consequently, there has been a growing boldness not only to speak out against terror but also to expose its connection to Islam itself. One of the leaders in this new honesty, as we have noted, has been Mortimer B. Zuckerman, Editor-in-Chief of *U.S. News & World Report*. In mid-2004, in an editorial titled, "Looking evil right in the eye," he wrote:

> The grotesque cruelties...leave no doubt about the enemy we're up against. News of their horrific abductions and beheadings fly around the globe on...technologies, in their twisted minds, invented by the infidel.... The masked cowards pose with their helpless captives while presenting demands they know cannot, and will not, be met. Their purpose is manipulation: to increase the pain of the victim's family and friends; to force western governments to moderate their opposition to the terrorist networks; to panic foreigners into leaving Muslim lands.... We are in their way as these misguided men

seek to restore a new unified Muslim umma (community) ruled by a new Caliphate, governed by Islamic law, and organized to wage jihad against the rest of the world.

As for the Muslim world, which has bred this plague, it will have to decide who is the enemy…[it can't] have it both ways, the indulgence of deriding the West while tolerating the evil in their midst. It is outrageous that…Saudi Arabia, home to 15 of the 19 September 11 murderers, has done virtually nothing to clean up its colleges of intolerance. We must persuade the Muslim regimes to condemn this new barbarism—before it consumes them, too.[13]

There are hopeful signs within the Muslim community as well. A growing number not only of intellectuals but also of Islamic clergy are expressing increasing embarrassment and displeasure at the deeds of those they refer to as "Islamic extremists." By their definition, however, as we have documented, Islam's founding prophet, Muhammad himself, would have to be labeled an extremist and even a terrorist. So would most of his followers over the past thirteen hundred years—but we needn't press Muslim leaders to admit the obvious. That admission will come with time, and with it, we can hope and pray, a new willingness to engage in open discussion without the sword of Islam poised over the necks of those who may decide on the basis of the facts to leave this destructive religion for a new life.

There has been an attempt to root out "extremist" ideas from some Muslim public schools. "On September 5, 2004, Crown Prince Abdullah bin Abd Al-ʿAziz told senior education officials: 'Watch your teachers. We want to serve the religion and the homeland, not terrorism.…' Saudi Education Minister Muhammad Ahmad Al-Rashid said…'the Education Minister will in no way accept a teacher who holds misguided views that influence the younger generation' and that 'any element implementing an extremist policy will be uprooted from the education system.'" There's the mislabel "extremist" again, betraying the unwillingness to admit the horrible truth.

"Tabouk District Governor Prince Fahd bin Sultan said in a September 12, 2004, speech to members of the Tabouk Educational Council: 'It is unacceptable for one of us to disseminate extremism, fanaticism, terrorism, and apostasy. We must not allow anyone who identifies with the group holding a dangerous and deviant view to [remain] among us....' The Mecca Education Administration organized information campaigns in all the city's schools, with the aim of 'increasing awareness regarding the danger of terrorism and the extremist view, and [for encouraging] the middle path in Islam.'"[14] Although there is still an unwillingness to admit the truth about Islam, which is being swept under the rug of "extremism," at least some steps, no matter how small and groping, are being made in the right direction, for which the world can be thankful.

We have shown that terrorism is endemic to Islam, and that more Muslims than non-Muslims have died at the hands of other Muslims. We see this happening today in Iraq, where most of the victims of terrorism are not foreigners or coalition troops, but Iraqi citizens. Sunni and Shi'ite alike are slaughtering one another, most often through suicide missions. The fact that democratic elections were carried out in Iraq for the first time in its history, in spite of fierce terrorist attempts to prevent anyone from going to the polls, is a very encouraging sign. Bush pulled it off, confounding the multitude of doomsayers. In the process, terrorism revealed itself as the enemy of freedom in its ugliest and most brutal form—and the opposition of Islam itself to freedom is being exposed. Eyes are opening to the naked truth. Hopeful changes must follow.

AN AWAKENING IN THE MUSLIM WORLD?

Some of the lies that have been used to justify suicide bombings are being exposed by Muslim leaders themselves who oppose such tactics. One of the first to speak out was Hamza Yusuf, who declared that the obligation of opposing terrorists falls upon "Muslims to root them out. And I think it is a jihad now for the Muslims in the Muslim countries to rid themselves of this element."[15]

"Several Arab columnists have recently published articles critical of the [common excuse] that the main motivation behind terrorism is poverty or despair. They instead cite the role of cultural and religious factors in motivating terrorism, and particularly the incitement by sheikhs who encourage young men to conduct terror operations." For years, and not only in Palestinian territory but throughout the Muslim world, to be a suicide bomber has been held up to millions of Muslim youths from their earliest childhood as the loftiest ideal. That scam is now being openly and widely attacked by Muslim leaders with new vigor.

For example, Saudi columnist Muhammad Mahfouz courageously wrote recently in the *Saudi Gazette*, "The phenomenon of terrorism and violence we are facing [is] carried out by a group of brain-washed youth influenced by glamorous slogans.... In my opinion,...[any] delay in fighting this ideological cultural battle against terrorism will drag our country into the abyss of instability.... Our determination will pave the way for successfully dismantling the ideological and cultural structure that offers fertile ground for the proliferation of this phenomenon.[16]

Mohammed Sayed Tantawi, the Grand Sheikh of the Al-Azhar mosque of Cairo, recognized as the highest authority in Sunni Islam, declared at a conference in Kuala Lumpur, Malaysia, that extremist Islamic groups had appropriated Islam and its notion of *jihad*, or holy struggle, for their own ends. Another Islamic scholar, Dr. Muqtedar Kahn, in a scathing open letter dated February 12, 2003, addressed to Osama bin Laden, boldly declared: "I would rather live in America under Ashcroft and Bush at their worst, than in any 'Islamic state' established by ignorant, intolerant and murderous punks like you and Mullah Omar at their best." Another prominent Islamic scholar, Dr. Youssef Al-Qaradawi, openly condemned Al Qaeda for killing innocent civilians and for their bombing of a centuries-old Jewish synagogue on the Tunisian island of Djerba in April 2002.[17]

Swimming with this new tide, United Arab Emirates' writer, Abdallah Rashid, in the *Al-Itihad* daily, wrote: "The socio-economic situation of most of the terrorists who participate in the criminal operations around the world is very good.... Interrogations by the Iraqi authorities of terrorists arrested during raids and searches... revealed that most of the Saudi youth and some of the [youth] from the Gulf who went to Iraq to join the Al-Qaeda terrorist groups come from families that are not poor and from a social environment that does not suffer from economic problems…. The reason for the involvement of the Arab Muslim youth in such criminal and despicable acts…is the terrifying brainwashing…at the hands of 'religious clerics' [who] nourish the Muslim youth with…hostility, hatred and resentment towards…members of other divine religions…. They incite others to…fight 'the atheists and Christian infidels,' as they put it, while not one of them volunteers to go himself…as a model and an example to others…."[18] (Yet all of Christ's disciples—except Judas—died as martyrs.) Another Saudi columnist, Abdallah Nasser Al-Fawzan, pointed out the same hypocrisy of these rabble-rousing imams in the Saudi daily, *Al-Watan*, with the perceptive and embarrassing title, "Why Don't the Sheikhs Who Encourage the Youth to Fight Jihad Do So Themselves?" He appealed to the youths who were aspiring to martyrdom in *jihad* to think carefully for themselves:

> If there is a worthy deed that endangers one's life, but guarantees paradise, like Jihad for the sake of Allah, are we to suppose that young teenagers in the early stages of life should aspire to carry it out? Or should it rather be the elderly, nearing death…to aspire to end their lives through an honorable deed that will guarantee them paradise…?
>
> A youth traveled to another country in order to kill a man accused of atheism, in order to get closer to Allah…and thus reach paradise. Fate had it that the [intended victim] was the first one to meet the youth in a café [and] welcomed him. They had a friendly talk, and got to like one another…. When the youth mentioned him by name, the man was startled and asked, "Why are you inquiring about this man?" The youth said that the man was an evil atheist, and he intended to kill him to get closer to Allah and to reach paradise. Amazed, the man asked the youth, "How are you so certain that this man is an atheist deserving of death, and that killing him will bring you to paradise?" The youth responded, "Some sheikhs told me so." The man said, "Why don't these sheikhs aspire to reach paradise themselves, and why are they giving up for your sake carrying out this honorable deed which brings one to paradise?" The youth was embarrassed and said, "I don't know."

Today, the same question that the man asked the paradise-seeking youth could be addressed to the youth who blow themselves up…in order to reach paradise…influenced by the Fatwas…and instructions of men who have gained their trust…. These people who hold sway over the minds of the youth have deceived them into thinking that what they are doing is an act of Jihad that will bring them to paradise….

Oh youth…who seek paradise, where are your sheikhs [when it comes to] this honorable deed…? Why are your sheikhs shirking [Jihad] and not participating in your "honorable" mission?"[19]

Such articles as these being published in popular magazines and newspapers in Muslim countries are bound to have an effect. And as Muslims begin to rethink some of the dogma they have been taught in the mosques and public schools, perhaps they will also begin to question why converts must be threatened with death in order to force them into Islam, and why that same threat of death is necessary to prevent a mass exodus from this religion, and why any religion should be violent at all. If there is the possibility of thinking for oneself, simple logic would denounce a religion that kills in order to maintain itself—and any god who rewards murderers with paradise.

1. http://www.foxnews.com/story/0,2933,103872,00.html.
2. http://www.shaheedfoundation.org/foundationnews.asp?Id=292&Type=News.
3. http://www.intelligence.org.il/eng/sib/mpa_11_03/alein_12_03.htm.
4. *The Christian Science Monitor*, August 12, 2004.
5. *USA TODAY*, November 29, 2004, 1A.
6. Amir Taheri, *Times*, August 28, 2004, http://www.benadorassociates.com/article/6890.
7. Romans 3:21-26.
8. Romans 2:14-16.
9. John 3:16-17.
10. John 3:36.
11. Mark A Gabriel, Ph.D., *Islam and Terrorism: What the Qur'an really teaches about Christianity, violence and the goals of the Islamic jihad* (Lake Mary, FL: Charisma House, 2002), 188-190.
12. Mark 16:15.
13. Mortimer B. Zuckerman, Editor-in-Chief, "Looking evil right in the eye," *U.S. News & World Report*, July 19-26, 2004, 84.
14. memri@memri.org, "Public Debate in Saudi Arabia on Extremism in the School System," Special Dispatch – Saudi Arabia/Reform, January 5, 2005.
15. CBS's *60 Minutes*, September 30, 2001.
16. "Arab Columnists," memri@memri.org.
17. BBC News, 11 July, 2003.
18. "Arab Columnists," memri@memri.org.
19. *Al-Watan* (Saudi Arabia), January 1, 2005.

14—THE WORLD NEEDS A MESSIAH

Read (handwritten)

THE MIDDLE EAST CONFLICT between Israel and her Arab neighbors, a conflict that more and more pits this tiny nation against the entire world, is only symptomatic of the battle against God that rages in the human heart—and that includes Jews and Gentiles, Muslims, and non-Muslims. There is a passion within each of us to do our own thing, to live for ourselves, to command our own destiny. But we did not bring ourselves into existence, and that simple fact proves from the very beginning of life to its end in death that we are not in control of ourselves and our destiny. The first step toward reality is to admit this simple truth. Until we do so, we are only deceiving ourselves with grandiose delusions.

Mankind did not create planet earth, much less the universe of which it is a minute part. We did not evolve by chance. Each one of us begins life as a single cell the size of a period at the end of this sentence. How does that cell know how to build an integrated body composed of trillions of cells of many different kinds? And how does each of those trillions of cells know how to operate the multitude of incredibly complex chemical nano-machines of which it is composed? The construction and operating instructions for the entire body are written in words encoded on the DNA on every cell. We call this "information."

All information is nonphysical (though it may be communicated in physical form), proving that its source (the mind of God or of man, made in His image) is nonphysical also. Clearly, the nonphysical mind continues to exist and think after the death of the body, making heaven or hell conscious experiences. This spirit being living inside the temporary body is responsible to the Creator for thoughts, choices, and actions.

Einstein acknowledged that matter cannot arrange itself into information and thus cannot think. It is, therefore, not the physical brain that originates thoughts, but the nonphysical mind, or spirit. Matter can only express information that has been impressed upon it. In today's world, information can be communicated by many means: the human voice, audio or video cassette, radio waves, television, diskettes, CDs, DVDs, etc. Printed books are the most common way. Never does the means of communication originate the information. Information points beyond itself to a purposeful intelligence, which conceived of the thoughts and expressed them in some communicable form.

DNA is a means of communicating information to the cells. If the information in DNA the size of a pinhead were put into print, it would take a stack of books *five hundred times* the distance from earth to the moon to contain it. Obviously the "intelligence" that put that information on the DNA of untold "zillions" of cells is beyond any human capacity. Only God could have done so. As long as the cells of the body follow the DNA, they are healthy. Some cells do not follow the DNA. We call that cancer, and it must be destroyed for the patient to survive.

WE HAVE ALL BROKEN GOD'S RULES

Man is like a cancer on this earth, refusing to follow God's instructions for life: His law, which He has impressed in every human conscience. Those who adopt the belief that we are the product of chance are denying their Creator and have thus ruled out any purpose or meaning to life. They have decided to make up their own rules for life. They can't do that for the cells in their bodies, or for the physical universe around them, but insist that they can for their souls and spirits. That decision, of course, puts them in conflict with others who think the same way and want to make up their own rules as well.

One can't even play a game without rules. If each of the players makes up his own rules, there is no game. Chaos results. Who is to make the rules for the "game of life"? That is the question! *Someone* must be in charge. Thus the history of mankind is all about wars between nations, between rival factions within the nations, between families, and between husbands and wives, between parents and children, and between brothers and sisters—and religions—to see who could make the rules that everyone else must follow.

Those who want no rules have themselves made a rule that there are not to be rules—and they expect everyone else to obey that dictum. Those who say that there are no absolutes insist upon "*absolutely no absolutes!*" The anarchist himself has a goal in life—to live by his own rules. Buddha proposed that the problem underlying all of the problems and unhappiness that besets the human race was "desire." He set about to deliver himself from desire and thereby to reach nirvana. But to escape desire became his all-consuming desire.

The problem between man and God is a matter of justice. We have broken God's laws. God cannot pardon us justly without compromising His integrity—unless the penalty He has pronounced is paid in full. Only God could pay that penalty. We needed God to come to this earth as a man in order to pay that penalty for mankind. We have seen that this was the promise God made to Israel. The world needs Him to be its Messiah, or Savior. There have been (and still are today) a number of men who claimed that identity for themselves. We need not list them all, because the requirements are so stringent that only One could possibly qualify.

HOW MANY CANDIDATES FOR MESSIAH?

The Bible, and it alone, contains literally hundreds of prophecies concerning a coming Messiah—prophecies that are so definite that His identity would be established beyond any question. These prophecies are found throughout the Old Testament, uttered by different prophets who never knew one another, yet there is no contradiction between them on the specific details. He would be born of a virgin in Bethlehem, do miracles, be hailed as the Messiah, be betrayed for thirty pieces of silver that would be cast down in the temple and used to purchase a field for burying strangers, be rejected by His own people, and be crucified, rising from the dead the third day. This author and many others have documented these and other messianic prophesies in detail elsewhere.

If anyone fulfilled all of these prophecies, that would be absolute proof both of the supernatural validity of the prophecies and that He was the prophesied Messiah. This would be the only reliable identification. From the list of criteria in the paragraph above, one Person immediately stands out, and He alone, as having fulfilled them all. But even though Jesus Christ qualifies as the Messiah from all of the above, who is to say that some other person may not come along and meet all of these criteria also next year or one hundred or even one thousand years in the future? That theoretical possibility is easily eliminated.

The prophet Daniel presents a definitive prophecy that had to be fulfilled on a certain date two thousand years ago. He was told by the angel Gabriel, "Seventy weeks are determined upon thy people [the Jews] and upon thy holy city [Jerusalem], to finish the transgression, and to make an end of sins, and to make reconciliation for iniquity, and to bring in everlasting righteousness, and to seal up the vision and prophecy, and to anoint the most Holy [i.e., to complete all the Messianic prophecies]."[1] The Hebrew actually says "seventy sevens." These are known as "Daniel's seventy weeks." These are not weeks of days but weeks of years. Both this author and others have established that fact so thoroughly in other writings that we won't do so again here.

The very day on which the Messiah would present Himself to Israel was foretold: "Know therefore and understand, that from the going forth of the commandment to restore and to build Jerusalem [not to be confused with rebuilding of the Temple, which would already have been finished] unto the Messiah the Prince shall be seven weeks, and threescore and two weeks...."[2]

Thus it would be 7 plus 62, or 69, sevens (i.e., 483 years) after the command to rebuild Jerusalem that Messiah would ride into Jerusalem and be hailed as Israel's King: "Rejoice greatly, O daughter of Zion; shout, O daughter of Jerusalem: behold, thy King cometh unto thee: he is just, and having salvation; lowly, and riding upon...the foal of an ass."[3]

THE VERY DAY FORETOLD

In fact, the Bible dates the very day that the true Messiah would be hailed upon entering Jerusalem, and then be crucified! Nehemiah declares that reconstruction of Jerusalem was authorized in "the twentieth year of Artaxerxes the king."[4] The rule of Artaxerxes Longimanus, under whom Nehemiah served, began in 465 B.C. and the twentieth year of his reign would be in 445 B.C. Thus the Messiah was to ride into Jerusalem 483 years later, or in A.D. 32. (In verifying this, don't forget that the Hebrew and Babylonian calendars were 360 days, and don't forget leap year.) Today, those few Jews who believe in a Messiah are still waiting for Him to appear.

Yet according to her own prophets, it is nearly two thousand years too late for Him to come—the first time. Israel will know at His Second Coming that He is the One they rejected the first time He came.

Jesus of Nazareth rode into Jerusalem on the very day and on the very animal foretold and was spontaneously hailed as the Messiah by crowds lining the road, also as foretold. When the Pharisees told Him to rebuke His disciples for calling Him the Messiah, Christ reminded them that this was the very day the Messiah was to ride into Jerusalem and that therefore, if no one else hailed Him, the very stones would cry out:

> And when he was come nigh, even now at the descent of the mount of Olives, the whole multitude of the disciples began to

rejoice and praise God with a loud voice for all the mighty works that they had seen; Saying, Blessed be the King that cometh in the name of the Lord: peace in heaven, and glory in the highest. And some of the Pharisees from among the multitude said unto him, Master, rebuke thy disciples. And he answered and said unto them, I tell you that, if these should hold their peace, the stones would immediately cry out.[5]

Israel at that time longed for a warrior Messiah who would lead an army to deliver her from her Roman oppressors. Yet, incredibly, in fulfillment of prophecy, Jerusalem hailed as her Messiah a meek and humble man riding on the wobbly-legged colt of an ass! He would not offer her deliverance from the Romans but salvation through paying the penalty for their sins. That was an offer that did not interest Israel. Instead, acting for the rest of mankind, they would join with the Romans to crucify Him—exactly as the prophets had foretold. Hear Paul's indictment:

For they that dwell at Jerusalem, and their rulers, because they knew him not, nor yet the voices of the prophets which are read every sabbath day, they have fulfilled them in condemning him.

Beware therefore, lest that come upon you, which is spoken of in the prophets; Behold, ye despisers, and wonder, and perish: for I work a work in your days, a work which ye shall in no wise believe….[6]

In a seemingly impossible twist, Daniel declared that the Messiah, having just been received with great joy into Jerusalem, would be killed: "[Then] shall Messiah be cut off [i.e., killed], but not for himself [i.e., for the sins of the world]."[7] As a result of this rejection, "the city [of Jerusalem] and the sanctuary [temple]" would be destroyed by "the people of the prince that shall come [i.e., the false prince, or Antichrist]."[8]

The crucifixion of the Messiah was prophesied centuries before that torturous means of execution was even known on earth. Nor is crucifixion officially practiced any more. Those who follow Antichrist as the Messiah will have to deliberately ignore the obvious fact that he was never crucified nor did he rise from the dead.

How many candidates meet the prophetic criteria and thus qualify as Messiah? There are literally no competitors! Only Jesus of Nazareth rode into Jerusalem on that exact day, was hailed as the Messiah, and four days later rejected by those who had just welcomed Him, crucified as the prophets foretold, and then rose from the dead after three days.

MORE IRREFUTABLE EVIDENCE

In Chapter Eleven, we also saw that the Messiah would be God himself come to earth as a man through a virgin birth,[9] that He would be rejected by His own people and be crucified.[10] His death would be in fulfillment of the Passover and Levitical sacrifices in payment of man's sins—then He would rise from the dead the third day. King David foretold His crucifixion:

> …[All] my bones are out of joint…they pierced my hands and my feet…. They part my garments among them, and cast lots upon my vesture…. All the ends of the world shall remember and turn unto the LORD….[11]

It was foretold that Messiah's crucifiers would do to Him what was never done, and would not do to Him what was always done in crucifixion. The major purpose of crucifixion was to exact a slow torture upon the victim. Only when he had suffered long enough would his legs be broken to prevent him from supporting himself, and, unable to breathe, he would die. He would never be prematurely killed by thrusting a spear into his side, for that would end the intended excruciating agony.

But Scripture said of the Passover lamb, a type of the Messiah, "neither shall ye break a bone thereof."[12] David prophesied of the Messiah, "He [God] keepeth all his bones: not one of them is broken."[13] The Hebrew word in David's prophecy quoted above, "they pierced my hands and my feet," is *aryeh*, descriptive of what occurs in crucifixion. Referring to His Second Coming to rescue Israel at Armageddon, however, Yahweh, the God of Israel, declares: "and they shall look upon me whom they have pierced."[14] The Hebrew word here is *dawkar*, appropriate for the piercing of a spear. John records, "But one of the soldiers with a spear pierced his side, and…he [John] that saw it bare record…that ye might believe."[15]

There was no need to use the spear. Christ was already dead, a fact that Pilate found hard to believe.[16] Jesus had said, "No man taketh it [my life] from me, but I lay it down of myself. I have power to lay it down, and I have power to take it again."[17] Why did the soldier use the spear? Perhaps he acted in angry frustration that they had been cheated from watching this man's full agony. Crucified with Him, the thieves were still alive, but he was dead already. He had not died from weakness, but had shouted in triumph, "It is finished [the payment for our sins]!" The Greek word He used was *tetelestai*. It meant, "Paid in full," and was marked in that day on invoices and promissory notes when totally paid: "And when Jesus had cried with a loud voice, he said, Father, into thy hands I commend my spirit: and having said thus, he gave up the ghost."[18]

These prophecies and the biblical record of their fulfillment are unacceptable to most Jews and non-Jews alike. Muslims reject them because they are specifically denied in the Qur'an: "They slew him not nor crucified, but it appeared so unto them…they slew him not for certain. But Allah took him up unto Himself."[19] We reject the Qur'an's contradiction of the Bible and accept what the Bible says because it is backed by numerous prophecies and eyewitness accounts of their fulfillment.

THE CRUX OF THE CONFLICT

At the very heart of the gospel of Jesus Christ, and proving it to be true, are the numerous prophecies concerning Israel, her land, and her Messiah. Christ's genealogy, first advent, Second Coming, and future reign on earth are intertwined with Israel. Muslims cannot accept the forgiveness offered by the true God, because the Qur'an denies that Jesus died for the sins of the world and was resurrected. Moreover, at the very heart of Islam is a determination to destroy Israel, which, if it could be accomplished, would prove the Bible false, including its promise of the Messiah. There is no compromise in this conflict between Christianity and Islam, between Yahweh and Allah. To "dialogue" over mutually exclusive and hopelessly irreconcilable teachings in order to arrive at an ecumenical "understanding" would be absurd and a denial of both.

Imams worldwide preach that victory over Israel, and Islam's promised conquest of the world, will not come until Muslims return to the submissive practice of the fundamentals of their faith in full obedience to Muhammad and the Qur'an. Heeding this call, there has been a marked rise in a return to fundamentalist Islam in the last few decades. Complicating the controversy is the fact that Islam's Dome of the Rock sits on the very site of past Jewish temples. Most Israelis, whether religious or secular, are as determined to see the Temple rebuilt as the Muslims are to prevent it—even to the point of denying that a Jewish temple was ever there! The Bible declares that it will indeed be rebuilt.

Will the Dome of the Rock be moved? If so, why and how?

Though the idea was unknown in Islam's early centuries, Muslims today claim that the Dome of the Rock marks the sacred site to which Muhammad went on Buraq, his magic beast (a creature that was a cross between an ass and a mule) during his Night Journey (*Isra'*) from the Al-Haram mosque in Mecca to Al-Aqsa [literally, the most distant mosque]. From there, by Muhammad's own account, Gabriel lifted him to heaven, where he met, conversed with, and was honored as the final prophet by Adam, Abraham, Joseph, Moses, Jesus, and other biblical greats (all of them Muslims, according to Muhammad). There were, however, no witnesses to this important event, so we have only the word of Muhammad— and it conflicts with what the Bible teaches and what we know to be true both from prophecies fulfilled and eyewitnesses.

In contrast to Muhammad's alleged but unwitnessed ascension to heaven, the eleven apostles (Judas, the twelfth and false disciple, had "hanged himself")[20] all witnessed Christ's ascension from Mount Olivet to heaven after His resurrection.[21] As for His resurrection, this foundational belief of all true Christians (for which there were more than five hundred witnesses other than the apostles [22]) is vehemently denied by Islam.[23] Paul logically argues that "if Christ be not risen, then is our preaching vain, and your faith is also vain. Yea, and we are found false witnesses of God; because we have testified of God that he raised up Christ…. And if Christ be not raised…ye are yet in your sins [and those who died trusting] in Christ are perished. If in this life only we have hope in Christ, we are of all men most miserable."[24]

In further contrast to Muhammad's successors, who fought among themselves, killed one another, and spread Islam by the sword, Christ's disciples all died at the hands of others as true martyrs who did not take the life of a single person with them. And they died not only as martyrs out of devotion to Christ but as witnesses to the life, miracles, sinless character, death, and resurrection of Christ. No one is fool enough to die for what he knows is a lie. The fact that none of the disciples saved his own life by promising his executioners that he would expose the miracles and resurrection as lies is proof of the validity of their testimony—testimony that would stand up in any court of law.

Neither Islam nor any other religion has even one such witness to its validity. Christianity is opposed not only by Islam but by all of the world's religions. There is a choice that every person must make. We pray that Muslims will have the courage to face the truth and make this choice on the basis of the evidence, not emotion. In the case of Muslims, the choice is between a cult of death and despair, and the gospel of life and joy eternal.

THE TRUTH ABOUT THE DOME OF THE ROCK

Here is a simple test of the truth of two opposing beliefs. Surah 17:1 is the only verse in the Qur'an that mentions Al-Aqsa, which means "the most distant place of worship [i.e., mosque]." There is nothing in this verse, however, that even suggests Jerusalem as the destination of the Night Journey by Muhammad. That idea was not introduced until later. Most damaging to this theory is the fact that Surah 17:1 was not among the verses from the Qur'an originally inscribed in Arabic inside the dome. It was added as an afterthought only recently. That fact is sufficient proof that this structure was not built with Muhammad's alleged Night Journey in mind.

Mecca had been captured by Abd Allah Ibn az-Zubayr, who proclaimed himself Caliph. Unable to approach Mecca himself, Abd al-Malik, who also claimed to be Caliph, built the Dome of the Rock to entice devout Muslims to make the *hajj* to it rather than to the Ka'aba in Mecca. When Malik recaptured Mecca in 692, he abandoned the Dome. This bit of history shows why the present location of the Dome of the Rock on Temple Mount is not the impossible obstacle to rebuilding the temple that some imagine it to be.

The Egyptian Ministry of Culture recently published an interpretation of Surah 17:1 that turns the focus from Jerusalem back to Medina: "This text tells us that Allah took His prophet from the Al-Haram [sacred] mosque [in Mecca] to the Al-Aqsa Mosque.... But in Palestine during that time, there existed no mosque that could have been the mosque 'most distant' from the Al-Haram Mosque.... [T]he Night Journey (*Isra'*) was not to Palestine; rather, it was to Medina. It began at the Al-Haram Mosque...and the journey ended at the mosque of As'ad ibn Zurara...in Medina.... The details of the journey of the *Hijra* [Muhammad's escape by night from Mecca to Medina] are the very same details of the Night Journey (*Isra'*), because the Night Journey [of Surah 17:1] is indeed the secret *Hijra*."[25]

Declarations such as that from authoritative Muslim sources would make it easy for the Antichrist to order the Dome of the Rock to be moved to Medina. With the Temple Mount cleared of this rival structure, Antichrist would then order the Jewish temple to be rebuilt—and command peace between Muslims and Jews and over the entire earth. Israel would imagine that Antichrist was the Messiah she had been awaiting, inasmuch as the only two criteria (neither of them biblical) that most Jews have for recognizing the Messiah are: 1) He will rebuild the temple; and 2) He will bring "peace on earth." Israel as a whole will not suspect (until it is too late) that this imposter intends to put his own image in the temple—but those who read and believe the Bible would know.

GOD'S INTEGRITY IS AT STAKE

The everlasting covenant by which God gave Israel the Promised Land includes David's heir ruling an eternal kingdom on his reestablished throne over the twelve tribes of Israel and the entire world from Jerusalem.[26] Nor is it any less clear that this One, as we have seen, must be "The mighty God, The everlasting Father" if He is to be "The Prince of Peace" and reign forever over the world from David's throne.[27] That fact, however, is unpalatable to Jews and Gentiles alike who want the Messiah to be a good man who sets an example for us to follow, but surely not God come as a man, much less that the depths of man's sin will be revealed in his crucifying the Creator. The Qur'an, while admitting that Jesus was without sin, specifically denies that He is either God or the Son of God.

In spite of Israel's rejection of her Messiah, and the years of unbelief and rebellion against Him, God will not go back on His Word to Abraham, Isaac, and Jacob. Christians who deny that the Jews are still the people of God or with any special significance are denying God's Word. Those who deny God's promises of the full and final restoration of Israel to her land are denying to God the glory that is His in keeping His Word to Abraham, Isaac, and Israel. Did He not say, "I AM... the LORD God of your fathers, the God of Abraham, the God of Isaac, and the God of Jacob...this is my name for ever, and this is my memorial unto all generations"?[28]

The nations of the world are openly defying what God has plainly and repeatedly declared in His Word concerning the land that He gave to Israel by an everlasting covenant. In rejecting Israel, they are rejecting the Messiah and the salvation that He alone could bring and that God offers to all who will believe on Him. They will bear the consequences of this defiance. We turn to that in the final chapter.

A CHOICE TO MAKE

"God is love" (1 John 4:8), but He is also just. Love cannot condone rebellion against the Creator. Only because the Messiah paid the penalty in full can God justly forgive anyone. In denying that Jesus is God and that He died for our sins, both Jew and Muslim (like most of the rest of mankind) reject man's only hope.

Muslims, like everyone else, ought to have the freedom to consider the facts of life, death, and salvation carefully without fear that they will be killed if they decide for their own reasons to abandon Islam. Yet that right is not allowed under Islam. The United Nations condones Islam's destruction of the very human rights that it claims to uphold—and honors Muslim member nations that deny these rights. This attitude is also a rebellion against the very conscience God has given every man.

The real issue is whether or not the Bible is God's infallible Word. If it isn't, then nothing has any meaning, the universe happened by chance, and all mankind, along with it, are headed for oblivion. One day it will all be as though it had never been, and nothing we have said or done will have been of any significance. But if the Bible is the Word of the Creator of this universe (we have sufficiently proved that to be true through a multitude of prophecies fulfilled), then the United Nations, United States, European Union, Russia, and entire world (including the Muslim world and Israel) are all heading for judgment from God.

Deny that the God of the Bible exists, the One who has proved Himself with hundreds of prophecies fulfilled, then indeed there is no hope. If the God of Abraham, Isaac, and Jacob is not the true God, we are left without purpose or meaning to life. To deny that God chose a man named Abraham through whom He would bring mankind back to Himself; to deny the true history of this chosen people and the land given to them, to which the Messiah came as prophesied and to which He will return to rule the world; to deny the hundreds of prophecies fulfilled in Jesus Christ alone—is to deny the only hope for mankind. The choice is open to all—but it must be a free choice.

In the final analysis, the battle over Israel is a battle for the souls and destiny of mankind. If Islam and the nations siding with her should accomplish their goal of destroying Israel, then mankind is eternally lost. This is how serious this battle is! If the God of the

Bible, whose integrity is tied to Israel's ultimate restoration and blessing, has not told the truth about His chosen people and their destiny, then how could we believe His promises concerning Christ's payment for our souls' salvation? And no other "God" offers a solution based upon justice.

There is a choice to make. "Choose you this day whom ye will serve."[29] And do not forget God's command to "Pray for the peace of Jerusalem."[30]

---

1. Daniel 9:24.
2. Daniel 9:25.
3. Zechariah 9:9.
4. Nehemiah 2:1-8.
5. Luke 19:37-40.
6. Acts 13:27, 40-41.
7. Daniel 9:26.
8. Daniel 9:26.
9. Isaiah 9:6-7.
10. Isaiah 53:1-12.
11. Psalm 22:14-18, 27.
12. Exodus 12:46.
13. Psalm 34:20.
14. Zechariah 12:10.
15. John 19:34-35.
16. Mark 15:44.
17. John 10:18.
18. Luke 23:46.
19. Surah 4:157-158.
20. Matthew 27:5.
21. Acts 1:9-13.
22. 1 Corinthians 15:6.
23. See Surah 4:157-158.
24. 1 Corinthians 15:14-19.
25. Ahmad Muhammad 'Arafa, *Al-Qahira* (Egypt), August 3, 2003.

26. 2 Samuel 7:4-17.
27. Isaiah 9:6-7.
28. Exodus 3:15.
29. Joshua 24:15.
30. Psalm 122:6.

15—DESTRUCTION FROM THE ALMIGHTY

IN THE INEVITABLE ATTACK against her, as prophesied, from all the world's armed forces united under Antichrist, Israel will not go down to destruction without using its ultimate weapons. The Israeli Defense Forces (IDF) can deliver atomic missiles with multi-warheads from submarines. Israel has learned the hard way that it cannot rely solely upon the United States—and certainly not upon the UN. Continually being betrayed by her supposed friends, Israel was literally forced for her survival to develop atomic bombs and delivery systems. At the time that these were developed, Nixon was receiving Nazis as honored guests in the White House, and Asian fascists were allied with Arabs in working for the destruction of Israel. Something had to be done to assure her survival, and Israel had to do it alone.

Though unnecessary in the present dispute with Palestinian Arabs, atomic weapons will almost certainly be called upon when the armies of all nations attack Israel during Armageddon. This war is clearly foretold in Scripture and will in all likelihood involve the first nuclear exchange in history, unless the Lord intervenes to prevent it.

Since they were last defeated thirty years ago in the Yom Kippur War of 1973, Muslim nations have spent billions of dollars for the latest military equipment, with top priority for missiles carrying a variety of deadly warheads. In self-defense, the Israelis (in cooperation with American technology and more than half-funded by the U.S.) have developed the most sophisticated operational missile defense system in the world: the Arrow 2. It includes its own reconnaissance satellite and radar warning system and is superior to America's Patriot missile defense system, but is integrated with some improved Patriot batteries deployed in Israel. One Arrow mobile launcher can handle up to fourteen intercepts simultaneously, fire thirty-six shots before reloading, and reach a maximum altitude of sixty-two miles, which is three times higher than the Patriot. The latter has a new completely revamped generation, the PAC-3, but not yet deployed. The United States is hurriedly trying to make up for the time it lost on its defense during the Clinton administration.

ONLY A MATTER OF TIME

Since Israel withdrew from southern Lebanon, the terrorist group Hizballah (Party of Allah), with Syria's blessing, has deployed some thirteen thousand missiles along the Israeli border. Thirteen thousand missiles! The Arrow is practically useless against these low-level, short-range rockets, most of them Katyushas. The PLO has also smuggled missiles into the West Bank and deployed them along the new defense barrier route ordered by Israel's High Court. These new missiles could easily target Ben Gurion international airport and even the northern outskirts of Tel Aviv.

Jointly developed with the United States, the best defense against these low-level weapons is Israel's Theater High Energy Laser (THEL), which is capable of intercepting and destroying incoming artillery shells. How operational this system is at this time is unknown.

As President Bush has been saying for some time, Iran is presently the most dangerous of Israel's neighbors. It has been displaying in military parades missiles suited for nuclear warheads capable of reaching Israel and Europe. On December 28, 2004, during a speech at Qom University, General Qassem Shabani boasted, "At present we have…nuclear capabilities [to use] in the event of war against America…." Yet, at the same time, Iran vociferously denies that it even has a nuclear program and accuses Bush of lies.

Of course, Israel is the primary target of Iran's weapons. When an Egyptian soldier, Suleiman Khater, killed five Israeli tourists in the Sinai, Iran "declared him a hero, named a street after him, and set aside a day honoring him."[1] They hope to create many more such heroes by leading the Arab world in the determined destruction of Israel.

On January 20, 2005, Vice President Dick Cheney said, "You look around the world at potential trouble spots, and Iran is right at the top of the list." Skeptical that Iran is bargaining in good faith concerning its nuclear weapons program, President Bush refused to rule out war with this largely Shi'ite Muslim nation.

We know that Iran, though it speaks out of both sides of its mouth, doesn't yet have nuclear weapons. If they had, the Israelis would have destroyed their installations as they did Iraq's in 1981. This they must and will do. Although denying that they are specifically intended for Iran's subterranean nuclear installations, the United States has supplied Israel with deep-penetration "bunker-busting" super bombs. As with Saddam Hussein's nuclear complex, Israel cannot wait for the United Nations or the United States to take action—she will destroy them before they can be used against her.

The whole world knows that not only Iran's weapons but those of all of Israel's neighbors are intended for her destruction. Having learned their lesson from previous defeats at the hands of Israel, however, it is unlikely that the Arabs will act independently. They will join a coordinated, worldwide attack upon Israel in the not-too-distant future—an attack that the Bible calls "Armageddon," which will be led by the Antichrist. This final and greatest attempt by Satan to wipe out all Jews is the inevitable result of the fact that to save himself, he must prove God to be a liar.

ANTICHRIST, SECULAR AND RELIGIOUS RULER OF THE WORLD

The Bible foretells a coming world ruler, whom it calls the Antichrist: "And in the latter time...a king of fierce countenance, and understanding dark sentences, shall stand up. And his power shall be mighty, but not by his own power: and he shall destroy...the mighty and the holy people [2]...ye have heard that antichrist shall come."[3] He will bring peace to the Middle East and to the entire world, which is a major reason why Israel will accept him—but it will turn out to be a false peace. When Christ came the first time, He warned Israel that in rejecting Him, they would open themselves to a later acceptance of Antichrist as Messiah: "I am come in my Father's name, and ye receive me not: if another shall come in his own name, him ye will receive."[4]

Confusion is created by the word "Antichrist." It seems to imply that this "man of sin"[5] will declare himself openly to be opposed to Christ. On the contrary, "anti" is a Greek prefix with two meanings: "opposed to," or "against"; but also, "in the place of," or "a substitute for." In fact, he will pretend to be *the* Christ. All of Satan's power, no longer restrained after the Rapture of the church to heaven, will manifest through him:

> And then shall that Wicked [one] be revealed...whose coming is after the working of Satan with all power and signs and lying wonders. And with all deceivableness of unrighteousness in them that perish; because they received not the love of the truth, that they might be saved. And for this cause God shall send them strong delusion, that they should believe a lie: That they all might be damned who believed not the truth, but had pleasure in unrighteousness.[6]

Israel will be without excuse. Nor will there be any excuse for the rest of the world that will follow Antichrist as world leader. There are hundreds of prophecies concerning the Messiah so that He could be definitely identified when He came and thereby prevent anyone from being deceived by a counterfeit. But in contrast to Christ, whom the world continues to reject, this is the man the world will look up to and want to follow. Indeed, he will not only be followed because no one can oppose his power, but he will be worshiped:

> And they worshipped…the beast [Antichrist], saying…who is able to make war with him? And…power was given him over all kindreds, and tongues, and nations. And all that dwell upon the earth shall worship him, whose names are not written in the book of life of the Lamb slain from the foundation of the world.[7]

ANTICHRIST AND THE REBUILT TEMPLE

Unquestionably, the Temple will be rebuilt on its ancient site. This is the clear teaching of Scripture. Daniel declares that the Antichrist will enforce upon the world a seven-year "covenant" that will entail the rebuilding of the temple and re-institution of animal sacrifices: "…and in the midst of the week [i.e., final seven-year period marking 'Daniel's seventieth week'] he shall cause the sacrifice and the oblation to cease."[8] He could hardly cause sacrifices to cease that hadn't been resumed, and sacrifices could only be offered in the Temple, so it must have been rebuilt at this time.

Antichrist will control the world, force everyone to accept the rebuilding of the Jewish Temple, and pose as Israel's friend and protector. In reality, however, he is planning to put his image in the Temple and will demand to be worshiped as God by all mankind. And indeed, "all that dwell upon the earth shall worship him, whose names are not written in the book of life of the Lamb slain from the foundation of the world. If any man have an ear, let him hear."[9]

Many Christians enjoy speculating about Antichrist's possible identity and when he will appear. It is wasted effort. He can only be "revealed in his time."[10] That phrase clearly indicates that no one can *discover* the identity of Antichrist; it must be *revealed*—and that will not occur except at a special *time*. Paul tells us that the Antichrist, pretending to be God, will sit "in the temple of God, showing himself that he is God"[11]—further proof that the temple will indeed be rebuilt.

In spite of the many prophecies concerning Antichrist setting up a kingdom that Christ will destroy at His Second Coming, there are professing Christians who reject the Rapture and are convinced that the church must take over the schools, media, government, and entire world. They teach that the church must set up the kingdom of God on earth, and only then will Christ return—not to take them to heaven but to rule the kingdom they have established in His name. They warn those who think they will be taken to heaven in the Rapture before Antichrist comes that they would not be prepared to face him and could be deceived into thinking he is Christ.

The answer to that error is simple: those who are waiting for Christ to catch them up to meet Him in the air and to take them to heaven could never be deceived into accepting a "Christ" who meets them with his and their feet planted on earth. Tragically, those who deny the Rapture and are working to establish an earthly kingdom to present to Christ will find that they have been working for Antichrist. His kingdom must be established first, because only after Christ has destroyed that kingdom will He sit on David's throne to rule the world:

> And then shall that Wicked [i.e., antichrist] be revealed, whom the Lord shall consume with the spirit of his mouth, and shall destroy with the brightness of his coming: Even him whose coming is after the working of Satan with all power and signs and lying wonders. And with all deceivableness of unrighteousness in them that perish; because they received not the love of the truth, that they might be saved....[12]

A GLIMPSE OF THINGS TO COME

God gave Nebuchadnezzar, emperor of Babylon and the first man in history who could be called a "world ruler," a vision of the four world empires that would exist in the history of mankind. The vision took the form of a huge image of a man with a "head of fine gold...breast and arms of silver, his belly and his thighs of brass, his legs of iron, and his feet part of iron and part of clay." Daniel first revealed to Nebuchadnezzar the dream that he had forgotten, then by inspiration of God interpreted it for him:

> Thou, O king, art a king of kings…thou art this head of gold.
> And after thee shall arise another kingdom [Medo-Persian] infe-
> rior to thee, and another third kingdom of brass [Greek], which
> shall bear rule over all the earth. And the fourth kingdom shall be
> strong as iron [Roman]…. And whereas thou sawest the feet and
> toes, part of potters' clay, and part of iron, the kingdom shall be
> divided; but there shall be in it the strength of iron….[13]

As the image foretold (by its two legs), the Roman empire
was divided into two parts—politically and militarily—when
its emperor, Constantine, established Constantinople (today's
Istanbul) as his new imperial capital, leaving the Bishop of Rome
in charge in the West. Politically and militarily it deteriorated but
was held together religiously by the world Church of its day, the
Roman Catholic Church. It was divided religiously in 1054 when,
in a dispute over who should be in charge of the Church, Pope
Leo IX in Rome excommunicated Michael Cerularius, Patriarch
of Constantinople, dividing Roman Catholicism in the West from
Orthodoxy in the East, a division that exists to this day.

What about the other great kingdoms: the Ming and other dynas-
ties in China, Genghis Khan's far ranging empire, the vast Mayan
and Aztec kingdoms of Central and South America, the Muslim rule
we have referred to from France to China? They did not succeed one
another, were all destroyed, and none of them will rise again. The
ten toes of the image indicate a revival of the Roman Empire, which
was divided but never destroyed, and has lain dormant for centuries.
The ten toes, Daniel explains, are "ten kings" who can only arise in
the last days because their destruction very clearly comes from the
Messiah in the process of setting up His kingdom:

> And in the days of these kings shall the God of heaven set up a
> kingdom, which shall never be destroyed ["Of the increase of his
> government and peace there shall be no end." – Isaiah 9:7]…: it
> shall break in pieces and consume all these kingdoms, and it shall
> stand for ever.
>
> Thou sawest…a stone was cut out without hands, which
> smote the image upon his feet…and brake them to pieces.
> Then…the iron, the clay, the brass, the silver, and the gold…

became like the chaff of the summer threshingfloors; and the wind carried them away…and the stone that smote the image… filled the whole earth.[14]

The Antichrist will be so powerful that he will unite and deceive the entire world with a false peace that will eventually explode into Armageddon. Israel and the world would not be deceived if they paid attention to biblical prophecies. But they have turned their backs upon God and His Word. The problem is so simple: one Person is missing from today's halls of government. He has been put out of America's education system. He is locked out of the United Nations. He is deliberately excluded from all Middle East peace negotiations. Across any agreements that may be made must be written in bold, bleeding letters: THEY HAVE FORGOTTEN GOD! In a frightening warning, the Bible declares: "The wicked shall be turned into hell, and all the nations that forget God."[15]

THE COMING WORLD GOVERNMENT AND RELIGION

It is only a matter of time until, as the Bible declares, the entire world will be united both politically and religiously under Antichrist. Multinational corporations have put the entire international structure in place. The remarkable prophecy in Revelation 13 of one evil man controlling mankind with a number could not have come true without today's technology. To past generations, it didn't make sense. There is no question that we are moving in the direction of a cashless society, and there are many sound reasons why personal business will be transacted through a computer chip just under the skin in the forehead or in the hand, as Scripture implies.[16]

Christ foretold today's weapons of mass destruction (WMD) when He declared, "And except those days should be shortened, there should no flesh be saved…."[17] There was no danger of all flesh being wiped out with bows, arrows, swords, and spears during the destruction of Jerusalem in A.D. 70—nor even with the most powerful conventional weapons at any time prior to the 1940s. This prophecy could refer only to current WMDs (a recent term), which proves false the claim of some that Nero was the Antichrist and that everything Christ spoke of in Matthew 24 was fulfilled at that time. Those who teach this Preterist/Reconstructionist view even dare to say that Christ returned in the person of the Roman armies to destroy Israel, and therefore His promise to the church, "I will come again," was fulfilled then.

Christ, however, had very clearly said, "I will come again, *and receive you unto myself; that where I am, there ye may be also.*"[18] The coming of the Roman armies was a judgment upon Israel, but it certainly did not fulfill Christ's promise of coming for those who believe in Him to take them to His Father's "house [of] many mansions" in heaven.[19] Christ did not take anyone alive to heaven in A.D. 70. That promise can only still be future—the promise of the Rapture.

THE KEY TO THE PUZZLE

It will take more than mere technology, however, to unite Muslims and Communists and the whole world (Saudi Arabia, North Korea, all the Russian republics and China, for example) in one religion under one man whom all will worship. The Bible gives the secret in an event called the "Rapture." Christ told His disciples that He was going to His Father's house to prepare an eternal abode for them, and added: "I will come again, and receive you unto myself; that where I am, there ye may be also."[20] That is a straightforward promise of miraculously and instantly transporting from this world to heaven those who believe in Him.

The Apostle Paul describes what could only be the same catching away of believers from earth to heaven. Christ himself comes, bringing with Him from heaven the souls and spirits of those who had died believing in Him as their Savior, to be reunited with their resurrected bodies. The living are transformed and all are caught up together with Christ into heaven:

> For the Lord himself shall descend from heaven with a shout, with the voice of the archangel, and with the trump of God: and the dead in Christ shall rise first: Then we which are alive and remain shall be caught up together with them in the clouds, to meet the Lord in the air: and so shall we ever be with the Lord. [21]
>
> Behold, I show you a mystery; We shall not all sleep [i.e., die] but we shall all be changed, In a moment, in the twinkling of an eye, at the last trump: for the trumpet shall sound, and the dead shall be raised incorruptible, and we shall be changed. For this corruptible must put on incorruption, and this mortal must put on immortality. [22]

We don't know how many true Christians there are on earth. There may be more than 100 million. For even half that many individuals to suddenly vanish would terrify those left behind far beyond anything we could imagine. The fearsome questions on everyone's mind would be, "Where did they go? Who took them? Why didn't they take me? Are they coming back to get me, too?"

The United Nations and governments of every nation would be meeting in emergency session. No one would believe that this event was the Rapture. Those who "refused to receive the love of the truth" will be given "a strong delusion, that they should believe a lie: that they all might be damned who believed not the truth...."[23] In the midst of this chaos, a man steps forward who knows where the missing have been taken and promises to recover them. Perhaps he says they have been snatched by some space-traveling rogue civilization and taken to a slave planet and he is negotiating to recover them.

Whatever explanation he offers, the entire world realizes that it is facing a common enemy capable of snatching people at will from earth. Driven by desperation, the world unites behind the one man who seems to hold the only hope for survival. Furthermore, he comes with "the working of Satan with all power and signs and lying wonders, and with all deceivableness of unrighteousness in them that perish...."[24]

We are told that "the dragon [Satan] gave him his power, and his seat [as world ruler], and great authority." The world will not know this fact, but it wouldn't matter if they did. They will be ready at that time to follow Satan himself. Indeed, the whole world will worship "the dragon which gave power unto the beast [Antichrist]."[25]

SATAN IN CONTROL

Without any Christians left on earth to influence society, evil will take over to an extent that is beyond present imagination. Those not raptured who never heard the gospel of Christ will be given the opportunity to believe. Many will receive Christ, reject Antichrist, and be put to death for their new-found faith. They will be resurrected at Christ's Second Coming at the end of the Great Tribulation. John sees it all in the vision he has been given:

> I saw under the altar the souls of them that were slain for the word of God, and for the testimony which they held: And they cried with a loud voice, saying, How long, O Lord, holy and true, dost thou not judge and avenge our blood on them that dwell on the earth? And...it was said unto them, that they should rest yet for a little season, until their...brethren, that should be killed as they were, should be fulfilled.[26]
>
> These are they which came out of great tribulation, and have washed their robes, and made them white in the blood of the Lamb.[27]
>
> And they overcame him by the blood of the Lamb, and by the word of their testimony; and they loved not their lives unto the death.[28]
>
> And I saw the souls of them that were beheaded for the witness of Jesus, and for the word of God, and which had not worshipped the beast, neither his image, neither had received his mark upon their foreheads, or in their hands; and they lived [i.e., were resurrected] and reigned with Christ a thousand years. But the rest of the dead [who had not believed in Christ but had followed the Antichrist] lived not again until the thousand years were finished.[29]

Following and worshiping Antichrist, the world will be in complete rebellion and God will begin to execute judgment upon the rampant evil. Christ foretold this period of time with these words: "For then shall be great tribulation, such as was not since the beginning of the world to this time, no, nor ever shall be."[30] The Book of Revelation gives the details of God's wrath being poured out upon this earth. It will be a terrifying time for earth's inhabitants, yet they will not back down from their defiance of the Creator: "[They] blasphemed the God of heaven because of their pains and their sores, and repented not of their deeds."[31]

TWO-THIRDS OF ALL JEWS WORLDWIDE KILLED

When God judged the gods of Egypt with the plagues recorded in the Book of Exodus, even though most Israelites were not serving Him, the land of Goshen where Israel lived was spared from the worst of them.[32] It seems logical and biblical that the small part of "Palestine" occupied by Israel could very well be spared from most if not all of the plagues that this world will suffer at the hands of God during the Great Tribulation. The land of Israel (though following Antichrist like the rest of the world), will be the only safe place for a Jew to inhabit. That distinction would anger the rest of the nations and raise speculation about some "secret weapon" Israel might be aiming at her enemies. During the Middle Ages, when Jewish communities escaped the plague because they followed the sanitation laws of Moses, they were accused of putting a curse on the Gentile communities, which then launched pogroms against the Jews. So her escape from God's wrath poured out upon earth would only add to the world's hatred of Israel.

Most Jews are still living outside of Israel. The fact that Israel is escaping the judgment being suffered elsewhere would surely cause many Jews to attempt to return to the Promised Land. Yet Scripture is clear, without telling us how it happens, that two-thirds of all Jews on earth will be slain.[33] The Bible describes this as "the time of Jacob's trouble; but he shall be saved out of it."[34]

The history of Israel, as we have seen, is a history of unbelief and rebellion. No matter how much evidence God has given to them (delivered from Egypt, the Red Sea opening for them and drowning the pursuing Egyptians, God speaking with an audible voice from Mount Sinai, water from a rock, manna from the sky for food, etc.), they have persistently rebelled against Him and continued largely in rebellion for centuries. God is finally going to prove Himself to Israel beyond any doubt, breaking their hard, stubborn hearts. The one-third who are still alive will all repent and believe when they see Him intervene to rescue them from the world's attacking armies.

Mankind is proud and rebellious. God is going to reveal Himself in terrifying demonstration of His power to the entire world. The Great Tribulation will reach its climax in an event called Armageddon. Though it has been exploited in Hollywood movies and sensational books, the Bible foretells Armageddon, and the Bible has proved itself true. Of course, most of the world will not believe until the events are upon them, and even then they will shake their fists at God. The description of God's wrath poured out upon this earth is dreadful.

FALSE PEACE, THEN DESTRUCTION

Many prophecies in the Old Testament have two applications. There was a fulfillment near at hand and one that was deferred to the last days. Here are the words of two different Hebrew prophets who never knew one another. They each referred to a destruction that came in their day; but their separate prophecies also agreed concerning a destruction from the Lord that would be worldwide and that was not fulfilled at that time but could only come in the last days:

> Howl ye; for the day of the LORD is at hand; it shall come as a destruction from the Almighty. Therefore shall all hands be faint, and every man's heart shall melt: And they shall be afraid: pangs and sorrows shall take hold of them; they shall be in pain as a woman that travaileth: they shall be amazed one at another; their faces shall be as flames. Behold, the day of the LORD cometh, cruel both with wrath and fierce anger, to lay the land desolate: and he shall destroy the sinners thereof out of it.
>
> For the stars of heaven and the constellations thereof shall not give their light: the sun shall be darkened in his going forth, and the moon shall not cause her light to shine. And I will punish the world for their evil, and the wicked for their iniquity; and

I will cause the arrogancy of the proud to cease, and will lay low the haughtiness of the terrible. I will make a man more precious than fine gold; even a man than the golden wedge of Ophir. Therefore I will shake the heavens, and the earth shall remove out of her place, in the wrath of the LORD of hosts, and in the day of his fierce anger. [35]

Alas for the day! for the day of the LORD is at hand, and as a destruction from the Almighty shall it come.[36]

Two of the most electrifying prophecies in the Bible are found in Ezekiel Chapters 38 and 39. They concern a people who are attacked by the armies of the world and are rescued by God's intervention. Their identity and the delusion that has overtaken them are clear. They "dwell safely…without walls…bars nor gates…[a] people that are gathered out of the nations…."[37] This can only be Israel, a people that have been scattered among the nations and have come back to their own land. They mistakenly feel secure from any possible enemies, having believed Antichrist's promise and guarantee of their safety.

We can thus say on the authority of God's Word that the wall and fence Israel is erecting to protect her from terrorists will be removed by Israel's own initiative. Israel will have been deceived by Antichrist with a false peace that is intended to destroy her, but he himself will be destroyed by Christ. Of this one, who pretends to be the true Messiah, we are told: "He shall magnify himself in his heart, and by peace shall destroy many: he shall also stand up against the Prince of princes [Christ]; but he shall be broken without hand."[38]

Israel has shown a naïve eagerness to believe any promise of "peace" and has often been deceived. Arafat deceived Israel times without number, and now Israel seems willing to be deceived by Mahmoud Abbas, Arafat's successor as Palestinian Authority Chairman via the January 9, 2005, election. Israel's Labor Party leader, Shimon Peres, enthusiastically described Abbas as "A moderate man…. Let's give him a chance."[39] Presumably, it is his "moderation" that causes him to deny the Holocaust and to call Israel (in his campaign speeches) "the Zionist enemy."

In contrast to Arafat, with whom he would not negotiate nor receive into the White House, President Bush has opened his arms to Abbas and welcomed him to Washington. Yet everything that Bush found objectionable in Arafat is echoed in Abbas. He was Arafat's partner in terrorism even before 1965 when he and Arafat co-founded Fatah, the PLO's largest terrorist arm, with the blood of thousands of victims on its hands. Within Fatah is the Al-Aqsa Martyrs Brigade, one of the most vicious terrorist organizations. As though to welcome their co-founder's elevation to head of the PLO and Palestinian Authority and to show that nothing had changed with the death of Arafat, four days after the "election" of Abbas, a group of terrorists from the Al-Aqsa Martyrs Brigade of Fatah stormed an Israeli base at the "Karni" Gaza crossing, killing five Israelis.[40] During his campaign speeches, Abbas had the flag of the Al-Aqsa Martyrs Brigade slung around his neck, showing his sympathy and identity with them.

Abbas campaigned in Jenin with members of al-Aqsa Martyrs Brigade. Before the elections, Abbas met in Damascus "with some of the region's most implacable terror groups, including Hamas [and] Islamic Jihad…. Abbas' 'foreign minister,' Nabil Sha'ath, declared that between the Palestinian Authority and the other groups, 'there are no differences over the objectives [i.e., destruction of Israel]."[41]

Israel is desperate for peace. After sixty years of war, she would agree to almost anything. The Antichrist will not only "guarantee" peace, but will command the rebuilding of the Temple. It will be an offer which Israel, in her unbelief and rejection of Christ, will not be able to resist.

EZEKIEL CHAPTERS 38 AND 39

The majority of Christians do not believe that Ezekiel 38 and 39 describe Armageddon but instead refer to some lesser war. Most Bible commentators interpret this passage as a preliminary attack by Russia and Muslim nations (either just before the Great Tribulation or in the midst of it) against Israel, during which they will be destroyed miraculously by God. The destruction described is so complete, however, that it would be unimaginable for anyone ever to attack Israel again. Who would dare to do so?

Referring to Antichrist and the armies of the world attacking Israel with him, God says, "I will bring thee against my land, that the heathen may know me [and] my fury shall come up in my face…."[42] Clearly this is a special event in which God has a climactic purpose. The description of what will happen at Armageddon is terrifying. The language could not possibly refer to a preliminary war, but to the grand finale!

God declares, "Surely in that day there shall be a great shaking in the land of Israel; so that the fishes of the sea, and the fowls of the heaven, and the beasts of the field, and all creeping things…and all the men that are upon the face of the earth, shall shake at my presence, and the mountains shall be thrown down…and I will be known in the eyes of many nations, and they shall know that I am the LORD" (Ezekiel 38:19-23).

God himself is coming to this earth and everything—animate and inanimate, and every person—will tremble like leaves on a tree, shaking in a violent storm! What the Bible describes as "judgment from the Almighty" is going to fall upon those who have attacked Israel. The invading armies will be miraculously and totally destroyed by Jesus Christ, whom Israel will at last recognize as the Messiah who was "pierced" for their sins: "They shall look upon me [says the God of Israel] whom they have pierced."[43] In the throes of this cataclysm, God will prove Himself to all creation as Sovereign. Clearly, what is being described could not be a preliminary war. This can only be Armageddon itself.

ARMAGEDDON!

The language in Ezekiel 38 is apocalyptic. This war will be Satan's most vicious attempt to destroy Israel (and mankind made in the image of God). Antichrist will lead the armies of the entire world against Jerusalem. The Messiah will intervene to rescue Israel and mankind and to stop the weapons of mass destruction from wiping out the human race—weapons that have been launched against Israel (not only atomic but chemical and biological), and hers launched in retaliation. Antichrist and his armies will be destroyed. Otherwise, as Christ warned, "there should no flesh be saved."[44]

As we have seen, God has two purposes at Armageddon: He is going to demonstrate His power by punishing the world in righteousness; and He will prove Himself to His people the Jews worldwide, breaking their stubborn hearts once and for all. Thereafter they will never rebel against Him again. This is the Day of the Lord referred to in Chapter Eleven—the day of Israel's redemption:

> If I whet my glittering sword, and mine hand take hold on judgment; I will render vengeance to mine enemies, and will reward them that hate me. I will make mine arrows drunk with blood, and my sword shall devour flesh....[45] For, behold, the LORD will...render his anger with fury, and his rebuke with flames of fire. For by fire and by his sword will the LORD plead with all flesh: and the slain of the LORD shall be many.... For I know their works and their thoughts: it shall come, that I will gather all nations and tongues; and they shall come, and see my glory.[46]
>
> Therefore prophesy thou against them all these words, and say unto them, The LORD shall roar from on high, and utter his voice from his holy habitation; he shall mightily roar upon his habitation; he shall give a shout, as they that tread the grapes, against all the inhabitants of the earth. A noise shall come even to the ends of the earth; for the LORD hath a controversy with the nations, he will plead with all flesh; he will give them that are wicked to the sword, saith the LORD. Thus saith the LORD of hosts, Behold, evil shall go forth from nation to nation, and a great whirlwind shall be raised up from the coasts of the earth. And the slain of the LORD shall be at that day from one end of the earth even unto the other end of the earth: they shall not be lamented, neither gathered, nor buried; they shall be dung upon the ground.[47]

There are many other similar prophecies. Some of the language is derisive. Man's rebellion is described: "The kings of the earth set themselves, and the rulers take counsel together, against the LORD, and against his anointed, saying, Let us break their bands asunder, and cast away their cords from us."[48] The scene turns to heaven: "He that sitteth in the heavens shall laugh: the LORD shall have them in derision."[49]

This prophetic Psalm is about Jerusalem, the Messiah who will rule there, man's opposition to God's will, and God's punishment because of this rebellion. God has warned the world, "Kiss the Son, lest he be angry, and ye perish from the way, when his wrath is kindled but a little. Blessed are all they that put their trust in him" (Psalm 2:12). But mankind as a whole refuses to bow the knee to the Creator and blunders on to judgment.

The architects of the road map to peace (and the world that supports it, including Muslim nations and Israel) have two choices. Either they repent of their opposition to God's promises to Israel and accept His forgiveness on His terms—or they remain in defiance and go willingly and knowingly to judgment. God is finalizing the fulfillment of prophecy in our day. He has made Jerusalem a cup of trembling to her neighbors and a burdensome stone to the entire world. And exactly as He said, He is also going to bring all nations against Israel to punish them there. That this is the way the world is going seems indisputable.

SALVATION OF ISRAEL

There are no chapter divisions in the original manuscripts. Ezekiel 39 is a continuation of chapter 38. Again the language is clear: "So will I make my holy name known in the midst of my people Israel; and I will not let them pollute my holy name any more…the house of Israel shall know that I am the LORD their God from that day and forward."[50] The language here, as earlier, could not apply to some preliminary event, but only to the climax of God's dealings with the world and with Israel.

Israel has obviously been driven to repentance and is transformed, never to be in God's disfavor again: "Neither will I hide my face any more from them: for I have poured out my spirit upon the house of Israel, saith the Lord GOD."[51] Only Armageddon could have brought Israel to her knees and caused every Jew left alive on earth to cry out in humble submission to the Messiah.

God declares: "Then shall they know that I am the LORD their God, which caused them to be led into captivity among the heathen: but I have gathered them unto their own land, and have left none of them any more there."[52] Not one Jew will be left anywhere on earth outside of Israel; all will have been miraculously brought back to the Promised Land. This can only be what Christ refers to in Matthew 24—the final gathering of every physical descendant of Abraham-Isaac-Jacob left on earth back to Israel for the Messiah's millennial reign at His Second Coming to rescue Israel in the midst of Armageddon: "They shall see the Son of man coming in the clouds of heaven with power and great glory. And he shall send his angels with a great sound of a trumpet, and they shall gather together [back to Israel] his elect from the four winds...."[53]

HOW MUCH TIME TO JUDGMENT DAY?

President Bush has Christian friends and advisors who tell him that Israel has been replaced by the church and therefore, that Joel 3:2, which pronounces judgment upon those who divide the land, no longer applies. To maintain that idea, hundreds of biblical prophecies that foretell a final restoration of Israel in her land would have to be denied or spiritualized. Consider only one of those prophecies:

> I will do better unto you than at your beginnings: and ye shall know that I am the LORD...I will take you from among the heathen, and gather you out of all countries, and will bring you into your own land.... A new heart also will I give you, and a new spirit will I put within you...so shall the waste cities be filled with flocks of men: and they shall know that I am the LORD.[54]

How far in the future are these prophesied events? Isaiah's prophecies end with Israel restored to her land and the Messiah reigning in peace over the entire world. We seem to be experiencing right now the very things Isaiah foretold that would lead up to the final restoration. The language is riveting:

> Who hath heard such a thing? who hath seen such things? Shall the earth be made to bring forth in one day? or shall a nation be born at once? for as soon as Zion travailed, she brought forth her children. Shall I bring to the birth, and not cause to bring forth? saith the LORD: shall I cause to bring forth, and shut the womb? saith thy God. Rejoice ye with Jerusalem, and be glad with her, all ye that love her: rejoice for joy with her, all ye that mourn for her....[55]

Surely a nation "born in a day" can refer only to the rebirth of Israel in 1948. It was an event unprecedented in the history of mankind. And as Isaiah describes, it was also a birth that was not completed in a moment. It has been in process for the last century and has come to a climax in the last fifty-seven years. God is causing "to bring forth," the womb is open, but Israel will not be fully birthed until she possesses all of the territory that God gave to her as described in Genesis 15:18-21. That miraculous birth still being in process, God will not "shut the womb." This process cannot go on much longer.

As soon as Zion travailed she brought forth her children. The greatest travail in Zion's history was without doubt the Holocaust. Had it not been for that horror and the momentary twinge of conscience among the nations of the world, the United Nations would never have voted for partition of Palestine, giving Israel a legitimacy that the Arabs still deny and that bit by bit the "peace process" has been taking back.

There are eyewitness reports that many Jews went to their deaths in Nazi gas chambers singing psalms of faith in God. Surely in their distress many must have believed in God's promise of the Messiah and understood what it meant to them personally for eternity. No doubt many cried out to the God of Abraham, Isaac, and Jacob and found mercy according to His promise: "For whosoever shall call upon the name of the Lord shall be saved."[56]

Shall I bring to the birth, and not cause to bring forth?...shall I cause to bring forth, and shut the womb? This is language of assurance. We have come a long way in history. Israel has been brought to birth once again in her own land; she is surrounded by enemies who are all united to destroy her; the technology and weapons are at hand to fulfill prophecies that could not have been understood in prior generations. Many other prophecies are being fulfilled before our eyes. God is not going to shut it all down and wait a few more centuries. The time is at hand to bring fully to birth!

1. David Lamb, *The Arabs: Journeys Beyond the Mirage* (New York: Vintage Books, 1988), 87.
2. Daniel 8:23-24.
3. 1 John 2:18.
4. John 5:43.
5. 2 Thessalonians 2:3.
6. 2 Thessalonians 2:8-12.
7. Revelation 13:4-8.
8. Daniel 9:27.
9. Revelation 13:8-9.
10. 2 Thessalonians 2:6.
11. 2 Thessalonians 2:4.
12. 2 Thessalonians 2:8-10.
13. Daniel 2:31-43.
14. Daniel 2:34-35, 44.
15. Psalm 9:17.
16. Revelation 13:15-18.
17. Matthew 24:22.
18. John 14:3.
19. John 14:2.
20. John 14:3.
21. 1 Thessalonians 4:13-18.
22. 1 Corinthians 15:51-53.
23. 2 Thessalonians 2:10-12.
24. Ibid.
25. Revelation 13:4.
26. Revelation 6:9-11.
27. Revelation 7:14.
28. Revelation 12:11.
29. Revelation 20:4-5.
30. Matthew 24:21.
31. Revelation 16:11.
32. Exodus 8:22; 9:26.
33. Zechariah 13:8-9.
34. Jeremiah 30:7.
35. Isaiah 13:6-13.

36. Joel 1:15.
37. Ezekiel 38:11-12.
38. Daniel 8:25.
39. January 11, 2005 edition of http://www.csmonitor.com.
40. *USA TODAY*, January 14, 2005, 7A.
41. January 10, 2005, JewishWorldReview.com.
42. Ezekiel 38:16-18.
43. Zechariah 12:10.
44. Matthew 24:22.
45. Deuteronomy 32:41-42.
46. Isaiah 66:15-18.
47. Jeremiah 25:30-33.
48. Psalm 2:2-3.
49. Psalm 2:4.
50. Ezekiel 39:7, 22.
51. Ezekiel 39:29.
52. Ezekiel 39:28.
53. Matthew 24:30-31.
54. Ezekiel 36:11, 24, 26, 38.
55. Isaiah 66:8-10.
56. Romans 10:13.

APPENDIX A

"PEACE IN THE MIDDLE EAST"

SENATE FLOOR STATEMENT
BY U.S. SEN. JAMES M. INHOFE (R-OKLA)
MARCH 4, 2002

I WAS INTERESTED THE OTHER DAY when I heard that the de facto ruler, Saudi Arabian Crown Prince Abdullah, made a statement which was received by many in this country as if it were a statement of fact, as if it were something new, a concept for peace in the Middle East that no one had ever heard of before. I was kind of shocked that it was so well received by many people who had been down this road before. I suggest to you that what Crown Prince Abdullah talked about a few days ago was not new at all. He talked about the fact that under the Abdullah plan, Arabs would normalize relations with Israel in exchange for the Jewish state surrendering the territory it received after the 1967 Six-Day War as if that were something new. He went on to talk about other land that had been acquired and had been taken by Israel. I remember so well on December 4 when we covered all of this and the fact that there isn't anything new about the prospect of giving up land that is rightfully Israel's land in order to have peace. When it gets right down to it, the land doesn't make that much difference because Yasser Arafat and others don't recognize Israel's right to any of the land. They do not recognize Israel's right to exist.

I will discuss seven reasons, which I mentioned once before, why Israel is entitled to the land they have and that it should not be a part of the peace process. If this is something that Israel wants to do, it is their business to do it. But anyone who has tried to put the pressure on Israel to do this is wrong. We are going to be hit by skeptics who are going to say we will be attacked because of our support for Israel, and if we get out of the Middle East—that is us—all the problems will go away. That is just not true. If we withdraw, all of these problems will again come to our door. I have some observations to make about that. But I would like to reemphasize once again the seven reasons that Israel has the right to their land.

I. THE JEWS' RIGHT TO ISRAEL: ARCHAEOLOGICAL ARGUMENT

The first reason is that Israel has the right to the land because of all of the archaeological evidence. That is reason, No. 1. All the archaeological evidence supports it. Every time there is a dig in Israel, it does nothing but support the fact that Israelis have had a presence there for 3,000 years. They have been there for a long time. The coins, the cities, the pottery, the culture—there are other people, groups that are there, but there is no mistaking the fact that Israelis have been present in that land for 3,000 years. It predates any claims that other peoples in the regions may have. The ancient Philistines are extinct. Many other ancient peoples are extinct. They do not have the unbroken line to this date that the Israelis have. Even the Egyptians of today are not racial Egyptians of 2,000, 3,000 years ago. They are primarily an Arab people. The land is called Egypt, but they are not the same racial and ethnic stock as the old Egyptians of the ancient world. The first Israelis are in fact descended from the original Israelites. The first proof, then, is the archaeology.

II. THE JEWS' RIGHT TO ISRAEL: HISTORICAL ARGUMENT

The second proof of Israel's right to the land is the historic right. History supports it totally and completely. We know there has been an Israel up until the time of the Roman Empire. The Romans conquered the land. Israel had no homeland, although Jews were allowed to live there. They were driven from the land in two dispersions: One was in A.D. 70 and the other was in A.D. 135. But there was always a Jewish presence in the land. The Turks, who took over about 700 years ago and ruled the land up until about World War I, had control. Then the land was conquered by the British. The Turks entered World War I on the side of Germany. The British knew they had to do something to punish Turkey, and also to break up that empire that was going to be a part of the whole effort of Germany in World War I. So the British sent troops against the Turks in the Holy Land.

One of the generals who was leading the British armies was a man named Allenby. Allenby was a Bible-believing Christian. He carried a Bible with him everywhere he went and he knew the significance of Jerusalem. The night before the attack against Jerusalem to drive out the Turks, Allenby prayed that God would allow him to capture the city without doing damage to the holy places. That day, Allenby sent World War I biplanes over the city of Jerusalem to do a reconnaissance mission. You have to understand that the Turks had at that time never seen an airplane. So there they were, flying around. They looked in the sky and saw these fascinating inventions and did not know what they were, and they were terrified by them. Then they were told they were going to be opposed by a man named Allenby the next day, which means, in their language, "man sent from God" or "prophet from God." They dared not fight against a prophet from God, so the next morning, when Allenby went to take Jerusalem, he went in and captured it without firing a single shot.

The British Government was grateful to Jewish people around the world, particularly to one Jewish chemist who helped them manufacture niter. Niter is an ingredient that was used in nitroglycerin which was sent over from the New World. But they did not have a way of getting it to England. The German U-boats were shooting on the boats, so most of the niter they were trying to import to make nitroglycerin was at the bottom of the ocean. But a man named Weitzman, a Jewish chemist, discovered a way to make it from materials that existed in England. As a result, they were able to continue that supply.

The British at that time said they were going to give the Jewish people a homeland. That is all a part of history. It is all written down in history. They were gratified that the Jewish people, the bankers, came through and helped finance the war. The homeland that Britain said it would set aside consisted of all of what is now Israel and all of what was then the nation of Jordan—the whole thing. That was what Britain promised to give the Jews in 1917. In the beginning, there was some Arab support for this action. There was not a huge Arab population in the land at that time, and there is a reason for that. The land was not able to sustain a large population of people. It just did not have the development it needed to handle those people, and the land was not really wanted by anybody. Nobody really wanted this land. It was considered to be worthless land.

I want the Presiding Officer to hear what Mark Twain said. And, of course, you may have read "Huckleberry Finn" and "Tom Sawyer." Mark Twain—Samuel Clemens—took a tour of Palestine in 1867. This is how he described that land. We are talking about Israel now. He said: "A desolate country whose soil is rich enough but is given over wholly to weeds. A silent, mournful expanse. We never saw a human being on the whole route. There was hardly a tree or a shrub anywhere. Even the olive and the cactus, those fast friends of a worthless soil, had almost deserted the country."

Where was this great Palestinian nation? It did not exist. It was not there. Palestinians were not there. Palestine was a region named by the Romans, but at that time it was under the control of Turkey, and there was no large mass of people there because the land would not support them.

This is the report that the Palestinian Royal Commission, created by the British, made. It quotes an account of the conditions on the coastal plain along the Mediterranean Sea in 1913. This is the

Palestinian Royal Commission. They said: "The road leading from Gaza to the north was only a summer track, suitable for transport by camels or carts. No orange groves, orchards or vineyards were to be seen until one reached the Yavnev village. Houses were mud. Schools did not exist. The western part toward the sea was almost a desert. The villages in this area were few and thinly populated. Many villages were deserted by their inhabitants." That was 1913.

The French author Voltaire described Palestine as "a hopeless, dreary place." In short, under the Turks the land suffered from neglect and low population. That is a historic fact. The nation became populated by both Jews and Arabs because the land came to prosper when Jews came back and began to reclaim it. Historically, they began to reclaim it. If there had never been any archaeological evidence to support the rights of the Israelis to the territory, it is also important to recognize that other nations in the area have no longstanding claim to the country either. Did you know that Saudi Arabia was not created until 1913, Lebanon until 1920? Iraq did not exist as a nation until 1932, Syria until1941; the borders of Jordan were established in 1946 and Kuwait in 1961. Any of these nations that would say Israel is only a recent arrival would have to deny their own rights as recent arrivals as well. They did not exist as countries. They were all under the control of the Turks.

III. THE JEWS' RIGHT TO ISRAEL: PRACTICAL ARGUMENT

Historically, Israel gained its independence in 1948. The third reason that land belongs to Israel is the practical value of the Israelis being there. Israel today is a modern marvel of agriculture. Israel is able to bring more food out of a desert environment than any other country in the world. The Arab nations ought to make Israel their friend and import technology from Israel that would allow all the Middle East, not just Israel, to become an exporter of food. Israel has unarguable success in its agriculture.

IV. THE JEWS' RIGHT TO ISRAEL: HUMANITARIAN ARGUMENT

The fourth reason I believe Israel has the right to the land is on the grounds of humanitarian concern. You see, there were 6 million Jews slaughtered in Europe in World War II. The persecution against the Jews had been very strong in Russia since the advent of communism. It was against them even before then under the Czars. These people have a right to their homeland. If we are not going to allow them a homeland in the Middle East, then where? What other nation on Earth is going to cede territory, is going to give up land? They are not asking for a great deal. The whole nation of Israel would fit into my home State of Oklahoma seven times. It would fit into the Presiding Officer's State of Georgia seven times. They are not asking for a great deal. The whole nation of Israel is very small. It is a nation that, up until the time that claims started coming in, was not desired by anybody.

V. THE JEWS' RIGHT TO ISRAEL: STRATEGIC ARGUMENT

The fifth reason Israel ought to have their land is that she is a strategic ally of the United States. Whether we realize it or not, Israel is a detriment, an impediment, to certain groups hostile to democracies and hostile to what we believe in, hostile to that which makes us the greatest nation in the history of the world. They have kept them from taking complete control of the Middle East. If it were not for Israel, they would overrun the region. They are our strategic ally. It is good to know we have a friend in the Middle East on whom we can count. They vote with us in the United Nations more than England, more than Canada, more than France, more than Germany—more than any other country in the world.

VI. THE JEWS' RIGHT TO ISRAEL: DEFENSE ARGUMENT

The sixth reason is that Israel is a roadblock to terrorism. The war we are now facing is not against a sovereign nation; it is against a group of terrorists who are very fluid, moving from one country to another. They are almost invisible. That is whom we are fighting against today. We need every ally we can get. If we do not stop terrorism in the Middle East, it will be on our shores. We have said this again and again and again, and it is true. One of the reasons I believe the spiritual door was opened for an attack against the United States of America is that the policy of our Government has been to ask the Israelis, and demand it with pressure, not to retaliate in a significant way against the terrorist strikes that have been launched against them.

Since its independence in 1948, Israel has fought four wars: The war in 1948 and 1949—that was the war for independence—the war in 1956, the Sinai campaign; the Six-Day War in 1967; and in 1973, the Yom Kippur War, the holiest day of the year, and that was with Egypt and Syria. You have to understand that in all four cases, Israel was attacked. They were not the aggressor. Some people may argue that this was not true because they went in first in 1956, but they knew at that time that Egypt was building a huge military to become the aggressor. Israel, in fact, was not the aggressor and has not been the aggressor in any of the four wars. Also, they won all four wars against impossible odds. They are great warriors. They consider a level playing field being outnumbered 2 to1. There were 39 Scud missiles that landed on Israeli soil during the gulf war. Our President asked Israel not to respond. In order to have the Arab nations on board, we asked Israel not to participate in the war. They showed tremendous restraint and did not. Now we have asked them to stand back and not do anything over these last several attacks. We have criticized them. We have criticized them in our media. Local people in television and radio often criticize Israel, not knowing the true facts. We need to be informed.

I was so thrilled when I heard a reporter pose a question to our Secretary of State, Colin Powell. He said: Mr. Powell, the United States has advocated a policy of restraint in the Middle East. We have discouraged Israel from retaliation again and again and again because we've said it leads to continued escalation—that it escalates the violence.

Are we going to follow that preaching ourselves? Mr. Powell indicated we would strike back. In other words, we can tell Israel not to do it, but when it hits us, we are going to do something.

But all that changed in December when the Israelis went into the Gaza with gunships and into the West Bank with F-16s. With the exception of last May, the Israelis had not used F-16s since the 1967 6-Day War. And I am so proud of them because we have to stop terrorism. It is not going to go away. If Israel were driven into the sea tomorrow, if every Jew in the Middle East were killed, terrorism would not end. You know that in your heart. Terrorism would continue. It is not just a matter of Israel in the Middle East. It is the heart of the very people who are perpetrating this stuff. Should they be successful in overrunning Israel—which they won't be—but should they be, it would not be enough. They will never be satisfied.

VII. THE JEWS' RIGHT TO ISRAEL: DIVINE ARGUMENT

No. 7, I believe very strongly that we ought to support Israel; that it has a right to the land. This is the most important reason: Because God said so. As I said a minute ago, look it up in the book of Genesis. It is right up there on the desk. In Genesis 13:14-17, the Bible says: The Lord said to Abram, "Lift up now your eyes, and look from the place where you are northward, and southward, and eastward and westward: for all the land which you see, to you will I give it, and to your seed forever.... Arise, walk through the land in the length of it and in the breadth of it; for I will give it to thee." That is God talking. The Bible says that Abram removed his tent and came and dwelt in the plain of Mamre, which is in Hebron, and built there an altar before the Lord. Hebron is in the West Bank. It is at this place where God appeared to Abram and said, "I am giving you this land,"—the West Bank. This is not a political battle at all. It is a contest over whether or not the word of God is true.

The seven reasons, I am convinced, clearly establish that Israel has a right to the land. Eight years ago on the lawn of the White House, Yitzhak Rabin shook hands with PLO Chairman Yasser

Arafat. It was a historic occasion. It was a tragic occasion. At that time, the official policy of the Government of Israel began to be, "Let us appease the terrorists. Let us begin to trade the land for peace." This process continued unabated up until last year. Here in our own Nation, at Camp David, in the summer of 2000, then Prime Minister of Israel Ehud Barak offered the most generous concessions to Yasser Arafat that had ever been laid on the table. He offered him more than 90 percent of all the West Bank territory, sovereign control of it. There were some parts he did not want to offer, but in exchange for that he said he would give up land in Israel proper that the PLO had not even asked for. And he also did the unthinkable. He even spoke of dividing Jerusalem and allowing the Palestinians to have their capital there in the East. Yasser Arafat stormed out of the meeting. Why did he storm out of the meeting? Everything he had said he wanted was offered there. It was put into his hands. Why did he storm out of the meeting?

A couple of months later, there began to be riots, terrorism. The riots began when now Prime Minister Ariel Sharon went to the Temple Mount. And this was used as the thing that lit the fire and that caused the explosion. Did you know that Sharon did not go unannounced and that he contacted the Islamic authorities before he went and secured their permission and had permission to be there? It was no surprise. The response was very carefully calculated. They knew the world would not pay attention to the details. They would portray this in the Arab world as an attack upon the holy mosque. They would portray it as an attack upon that mosque and use it as an excuse to riot. Over the last eight years, during this time of the peace process, where the Israeli public has pressured its leaders to give up land for peace because they are tired of fighting, there has been increased terror. In fact, it has been greater in the last eight years than any other time in Israel's history. Showing restraint and giving in has not produced any kind of peace. It is so much so that today the leftist peace movement in Israel does not exist because the people feel they were deceived. They did offer a hand of peace, and it was not taken. That is why the politics of Israel have changed drastically over the past twelve months. The Israelis have come to see that, "No matter what we do, these people do not want to deal with us.... They want to destroy us." That is why even yet today the stationery of the PLO still has upon it the map of the entire state of Israel, not just the tiny little part they call the West Bank that they want. They want it all.

We have to get out of this mind set that somehow you can buy peace in the Middle East by giving little plots of land. It has not worked before when it has been offered. These seven reasons show why Israel is entitled to that land.

The unwavering loyalty we have received from our only consistent friend in the Middle East has got to be respected and appreciated by us. No longer should foreign policy in the Middle East be one of appeasement. As Hiram Mann said, "No man survives when freedom fails. The best men rot in filthy jails and those who cried 'appease, appease' are hanged by those they tried to please."

Islamic fundamentalist terrorism has now come to America. We have to use all of our friends, all of our assets, and all of our resources to defeat the satanic evil.

When Patrick Henry said, "We will not fight our battles alone. There is a just God who reigns over the destiny of nations who will raise up friends who will fight our battles with us," he was talking about all our friends, including Israel. And that is what is happening, as of yesterday and I thank God for that. Israel is now in the battle by our side.

That is what is happening. As of last December, Israel is now in the battle by our side, and I thank God for that. It is time for our policy of appeasement in the Middle East and appeasement to the terrorists to be over. With our partners, our victory must and will be absolute victory.

http://inhofe.senate.gov
http://dunamai.com/articles/Israel/absolute_victory.html

APPENDIX B

HAMAS AND HIZZONER

By John Perazzo
FrontPageMagazine.com | March 5, 2003

It probably wouldn't fly too well if the mayor of our nation's largest city appointed, to a panel responsible for enforcing anti-discrimination laws, a member of a militant, white supremacist group ideologically sympathetic to the notion that our country should return—by any means necessary—to the days of Jim Crow. Surely political leaders and civil rights activists from coast to coast would clamber to find microphones and news cameras before which they could righteously thunder their disapproval of such an appointment; undoubtedly the national media would be all over such a story. It seems, however, that organizations composed of nonwhite, "politically correct" bigots do not ignite a similar passion in the breasts of our society's masters of moral preening. What else could explain the dearth of attention given to New York Mayor Michael Bloomberg's recent appointment of Omar Mohammedi, general counsel to the New York chapter of the Council on

American-Islamic Relations (CAIR), to his city's Human Rights Commission?

As Middle East scholar Daniel Pipes points out, the Washington-based CAIR, founded in 1994, "presents itself as just another civil-rights group"—cultivating an image of moderation that enables it to garner "sizable donations, invitations to the White House, respectful media citations, and a serious hearing by corporations." The organization's goal, CAIR spokesman Ibrahim Hooper says benignly, is to promote "interest and understanding among the general public with regards to Islam and Muslims in North America."

But the reality is something not nearly so benevolent, and Americans ought to become aware of it. CAIR is a direct outgrowth of the Islamic Association of Palestine (IAP). According to Oliver Revell, the FBI's former associate director of Counter Intelligence Operations, the IAP "is an organization that has directly supported [the Palestinian terror group] Hamas' military goals. It is a front organization for Hamas that engages in propaganda for Islamic militants. It has produced videotapes that are very hate-filled, full of vehement propaganda." Such roots can hardly be considered "moderate," and as we examine CAIR more closely, what we see only gets uglier.

CAIR's founder and executive director, Nihad Awad, was the IAP's public relations director with a long history of extremism. Awad openly praised Iran's notorious Ayatollah Khomeini. He blasted the trial and conviction of the 1993 World Trade Center bombers—against whom the evidence of guilt was overwhelming—as "a travesty of justice." At a 1994 Barry University forum, he candidly stated, "I am in support of the Hamas movement."

The IAP's current president, Rafeeq Jaber, was a founding director of CAIR. Mohammed Nimer, who directs CAIR's Research Center, was on the board of the United Association for Studies and Research, which is the strategic arm of Hamas in the US and was founded by Hamas operative Mousa Abu Marzook. The aforementioned Ibrahim Hooper, CAIR's Director of Communications, lso workedfor the IAP. To this day, he refuses to publicly denounce

Osama bin Laden. He euphemistically ascribed the 1998 bombings of two American embassies in Africa to a "misunderstanding of both sides." He dismisses the Sudanese Islamic government's enslavement and torture of millions of black Christians and animists during the past two decades—to say nothing of its slaughter of some two million more—as mere "inter-tribal hostage-taking." He makes no secret of his desire to see America one day become a Muslim country. "I wouldn't want to create the impression that I wouldn't like the government of the United States to be Islamic sometime in the future," he told the Minneapolis Star Tribune. "But I'm not going to do anything violent to promote that. I'm going to do it through education."

Such sentiments echo those of CAIR chairman Omar M. Ahmad, who in July 1998 told a crowd of California Muslims, "Islam isn't in America to be equal to any other faith, but to become dominant. The Koran . . . should be the highest authority in America, and Islam the only accepted religion on earth." In a similar vein, CAIR board member Imam Siraj Wahaj calls for replacing the American government with a caliphate, and warns that America will crumble unless it "accepts the Islamic agenda." Wahaj, it should be noted, served as a character witness for Sheik Omar Abdel Rahman, the Muslim cleric convicted for his role in the 1993 World Trade Center bombing; the same cleric who was busy devising plans to blow up American landmarks, buildings, and bridges; the same cleric whose conviction CAIR called a "hate crime" against Muslims. And even though Wahaj was listed as an un-indicted co-conspirator in Rahman's case, CAIR now permits him to sit on its advisory board, deeming him "one of the most respected Muslim leaders in America."

With regard to the war on terror, CAIR's anti-American loyalties are all too clear. In October 1998, for instance, the group demanded the removal of a Los Angeles billboard that dubbed Osama bin Laden "the sworn enemy," complaining that such a caption was "offensive to Muslims." In the wake of 9/11, CAIR actually denied bin Laden's culpability, a position from which it would not budge until three months after the attacks, by which time the evidence against al-Qaeda's linchpin was irrefutable. The Website for CAIR's New York chapter—with which Mayor Bloomberg's appointee Omar Mohammedi has been affiliated—openly doubted that Islamic hijackers were responsible for the attacks, speculating that either the Bush administration or Israel orchestrated the nightmare.

CAIR has been the mouthpiece of some of the vilest anti-Semitism imaginable. For example, the organization co-sponsored a 1998 Brooklyn College rally at which a militant Egyptian Islamist led the attendees in chanting, "No to the Jews, descendents of the apes." Hussam Ayloush, who heads CAIR's Los Angeles office, contemptuously refers to Israelis as "Zionazis."

Over the years, a good portion of CAIR's funding came from a group called the Holy Land Foundation for Relief and Development (HLF). Yet when President Bush closed the HLF in December 2001 upon learning that it was raising money to support Hamas terror attacks, CAIR reacted with its characteristic petulance and indifference to American interests. Calling Bush's move "unjust" and "disturbing," the group circulated a petition exhorting the government to unfreeze HLF assets—charging that "there has been a shift from a war on terrorism to an attack on Islam."

CAIR'S recently published 2002 Civil Rights Report reads much like virtually all other "civil rights" reports that are preordained to "discover" that the purportedly victimized groups in question are suffering unimaginable pain. It details "incidents and experiences of anti-Muslim violence, stereotyping, discrimination, and harassment" allegedly spawned by the "epidemic" of "Islamophobic backlash that occurred following the September 11 terrorist attacks." According to the report, "Muslims in the United States are more apprehensive than ever about discrimination and intolerance." From passenger profiling at airports, to crackdowns on visa violators, to the closing of terrorist-linked Muslim charities like the HLF, to the Patriot Act's provisions (which, incidentally, made possible the recent crucial arrest of Khalid Sheikh Mohammed)—all of these measures, according to CAIR, constitute proof that "discrimination is now part of daily life for American Muslims."

Predictably, CAIR says nothing about the remarkable prosperity of Muslims in America, who in fact constitute the most affluent Muslim society on earth. As Daniel Pipes reported in November 2000, American Muslims "boast among the highest rates of education of any group in the country (a whopping 52 percent appear to hold graduate degrees), and this translates into a pattern of prestigious and remunerative employment." Muslim Americans' median household income of about $69,000 stands well above the national average.

All in all, CAIR's dual agenda is abundantly clear: (A) to depict the United States as a snake pit of "Islamophobes," wherein Muslims must fend for their very lives at every moment; and (B) to promote the hateful aspirations of our nation's deadliest enemies, radical Islamic terrorists. Does it make any sense, then, for the mayor presiding over the very city where the Twin Towers once stood, to appoint an important figure of such an organization to a Human Rights position in city government? Some might consider it an abomination.

GLOSSARY

Allah – Contraction of Al-ilah (al is "the," ilah is "god"), meaning the chief among some 360 idols in the Ka'aba, located in Mecca. Moon god worshiped by pagan Arab tribes long before Muhammad was born.

Al-Qaeda – Terrorist group that brought down the World Trade center in New York September 11, 2001, headed by Osama bin Laden and Dr. Abu Musab al-Zarkawi,

Anti-Semitism – Irrational and Satanic hatred of all Jews, fulfilling Bible prophecy.

Arabs – Semitic people group that claims direct descent from Ishmael, Abraham's firstborn son, and thus exclusive right to the Promised Land given by God to Abraham.

Calvinist – Christian who claims to adhere to the "Reformed faith" of John Calvin as true Christianity. Teaches that God has predestined some for heaven (Christ died only for them) and the rest for eternal damnation—and that the church has replaced Israel. Includes most Presbyterians and many Baptists and Independents.

Christian – One who believes in Jesus Christ as Savior of the world through His death on the Cross for mankind's sins, and His burial and resurrection as revealed in the Bible.

Dhimmi – A fifth-class citizen (only a Christian or Jew) heavily oppressed and humiliated under "protective" Muslim rule. All others, looked upon as pagans, must either convert or be killed.

Evangelical – Bible-believing, born-again Christian who follows the Word of God without compromise and obeys the command to preach the gospel everywhere and to everyone.

God of the Bible – The Creator of the universe, as revealed in the Bible, who exists outside of time, not part of the universe, as three persons, separate and distinct, yet one God.

God of Israel – The God of the Bible, called the "God of Israel" 203 times in Scripture.

Hadith – Sayings and deeds of Muhammad as reported by his closest companions. Considered to be as authoritative as the Qur'an, which cannot be understood without it.

Hajj – Pilgrimage to the Ka'aba in Mecca and participation in the pagan rituals involved. One of the Five Pillars of Islam and required of a Muslim at least once in a lifetime.

Hamas – Islamic, anti-Israel/Jew terrorist organization responsible for multiple suicide bombings and other terrorist attacks against Israel.

Hijrah – Muhammad's night flight from Mecca to Yathrib about A.D. 622. Muslim calendar of 30-day months dates from that time and is shown as A.H., meaning Anno Hijrah, in the year of the Hijrah, just as A.D. means Anno Domini, in the year of our Lord.

Hizballah – Terrorist organization. Name means "Party of Allah." Based in Damascus. Responsible for many attacks upon Israeli civilians, leaving thousands dead and wounded.

Holocaust – The Nazi-planned and efficiently executed murder of about 6 million Jews, mostly in death camps designed and operated for that purpose.

Islam – Seventh-century Arab religion founded by Muhammad, now with about 1.3 billion followers. Basically a carry-over of pagan practices involving the hajj and feast of Ramadan that had been followed by Arab tribes for centuries before Muhammad was born. Includes belief that Allah (formerly the chief idol in the Ka'aba) was the only god and must be worshiped by all peoples under pain of death, and that any who become Muslims and then convert to another religion are to be beheaded.

Israel – Land that the God of the Bible, the God of Israel, gave to Abraham and his heirs as an everlasting inheritance. Known then as the land of Canaan, occupied by Canaanites, who, because of their evil, were killed or expelled by the Israelites, under God's command. Thereafter known as Israel until the Romans renamed it Provincia Syria-Palestina in A.D. 135.

Jihad – Holy War commanded in the Qur'an to be fought perpetually against all peoples until all the world submits to Allah as the only God and to Muhammad as his messenger.

Hudaybiya, Treaty of – A 10-year cease fire between Muhammad and Mecca in A.D. 628 (A.H. 6). Established the law of war and peace in Islam that no Muslim may violate today: no peace with non-Muslims, a cease-fire only, cannot be longer than 10 years. Purpose is to deceive while gaining strength to conquer the enemy.

Hudna – Arabic name for the 10-year cease fire Muslims may enter into with the enemy.

Intifada – Uprising of Palestinians against Israel instituted by Arafat in December 1987. Periodic false charges of alleged Israeli atrocities providing occasion for new flare-ups of violence. "Intifada" came to be associated with any violent Palestinian uprising. Al-Aqsa Intifada in 2000 protested Ariel Sharon simply visiting temple mount.

Ka'aba – Temple in Mecca containing about 360 idols and center of pagan worship of Arabs for centuries before Muhammad was born. Muhammad destroyed all idols, but kept the Ka'aba, its sacred stones, and rituals as central to Islam. Ka'aba today is surrounded by a mosque built around it.

Messiah – The promised redeemer of Israel foretold in numerous prophecies so He could be identified beyond question. All were fulfilled in the life, death, and resurrection of Jesus of Nazareth. Fulfilled prophecies were basis of the gospel preached by the early church and still are today.

Muslim – A follower of Muhammad, Allah, and the religion of Islam.

Palestine – Name given to land of Israel by Romans in A.D. 135, and still used by most of world today. Is actually the land of Israel and will be restored by the Messiah to theJews, "from the river of Egypt unto the great river, the river Euphrates" (Genesis 15:18-21).

Palestinian – A person living in "Palestine." Applied originally to Jews only, but now claimed by Arabs who call themselves Palestinians.

Passover – A feast involving a roast lamb, instituted by God the night Israel was miraculously delivered from Egypt. Kept annually by

Jews worldwide ever since by God's command as a memorial of this great event in Israel's history. Proof that those keeping it are the true heirs of Abraham.

Qiblah – Direction in which Muslims must kneel for their daily prayers. Briefly toward Jerusalem, but Muhammad changed to be toward the Ka'aba in Mecca.

Qur'an – Compilation by Uthman ibn Affan, third Caliph to succeed Muhammad, of revelations Muhammad allegedly received from Allah through the angel Gabriel—except for those parts which were lost or inaccurately remembered.

Ramadan – Islam's yearly dawn-to-sunset 30-day fast beginning with the first appearance of the moon in the ninth month of the Muslim lunar calendar, ending with the feast of Eid Fitr.

Sharia law – The strict adherence to the practice of Islam enforced upon Muslim and non-Muslim alike with the death penalty for those who refuse to submit. Must be imposed upon the entire world, allowing no separation between religious and political rule.

Shi'ite – Second largest sect among Muslims (about 150 million worldwide), the majority in both Iraq and Iran. Shi'ites believe that Ali ibn Abi Talib. (murdered in 661 in the mosque in Kufa and buried in Najaf, Iraq), Muhammad's cousin and son-in-law, should have been the first Caliph to succeed Muhammad, not the fourth of the "rightly guided Caliphs," and that his descendants are the only line of succession to Muhammad that should lead Islam today.

Suicide bomber – Muslim who secretes a bomb on his person and sets it off while among non-Muslims (especially Israelis) or members of a rival Muslim sect, believing that killing and wounding others at the cost of his own life qualifies as martyrdom in jihad and thus earns entrance into paradise. Has become widespread only within the last 50 years. Generally approved by Muslim authorities, though some reject it.

Sunni – Largest Islamic sect making up the vast majority of Muslims today. Accept hadith as authoritative, and accept the "rightly guided Caliphs" (except Ali whom they blame for Uthman's murder) as successors to Muhammad.

Trinity – Biblical teaching that the only true God and Creator of the universe exists in three persons, Father, Son, and Holy Spirit, distinct from each other, yet One God.

Yahweh – Name (I AM) of God as He revealed Himself to Moses at the burning bush (Exodus 3:13-16),. The self-existent One, without beginning or end and with neither need for nor dependence upon any other.

Zion – City of David (Jerusalem) and sometimes designating hill upon which it was built.

Zionism – Belief that the Promised Land given to Abraham and to his heirs belongs to the Jews, who have the right to return and to claim it as their own. Not an attempt by Jews to take over the world as some falsely claim.

SELECTED BIBLIOGRAPHY

Abraham, A. J., and George Haddad. *The Warriors of God*. Bristol, IN: Wyndham Hall Press, 1989.

Accad, Louad Elias. *Building Bridges: Christianity and Islam*. Colorado Springs: NavPress, 1997.

Arlen, Michael J. *Passage to Ararat*. n.p.: Ballantine Books, 1975.

Bard, Mitchell G. *Myths and Facts: A Guide to the Arab-Israeli Conflict*. Chevy Chase, MD: American-Israeli Cooperative Enterprise, 2001.

Bar-Illan, David, ed. *Jerusalem:The Truth* (A compilation of editorials by Executive Editor of *The Jerusalem Post*). Jerusalem: *The Jerusalem Post*, 1996.

Becker, Jill. *The PLO: The Rise and Fall of the Palestine Liberation Organization*. New York: St. Martin's Press, 1984.

Ben-Gad, Yitschak. *The Roadmap to Nowhere: A Layman's Guide to the Middle East Conflict*. Green Forest, AR: Balfour Books, 2004.

Bennett, Ramon. *Philistine: The Great Deception*. Jerusalem: Arm of Salvation, 1995.

SELECTED BIBLIOGRAPHY

Berenbaum, Michael. *The World Must Know: The History of the Holocaust as told in the United States Holocaust Museum*. New York: Little, Brown and Company, 1933.

Bergen, Peter L. *Holy War Inc.: Inside the Secret World of Osama bin Laden*. New York: The Free Press, 2001.

Bloom, Jonathan, and Sheila Blair. *Islam: A Thousand Years of Faith and Power*. New Haven: Yale University Press, 2002.

Bormans, Maurice, ed., Speight, R. Marston, trans. *Interreligious Documents: Guidelines for Dialogue between Christians and Muslims, Pontifical Council for Interreligious Dialogue*. New York: Paulist Press, 1981.

Braswell, George W., Jr. *Islam: Its Prophet, Peoples, Politics and Power*. Nashville: Broadman & Holman Publishers, 1996.

———. *What You Need to Know About Islam & Muslims*. Nashville: Broadman & Holman Publishers, 2000.

Bukay, David, ed. *Muhammad's Monsters: A Comprehensive Guide to Radical Islam for Western Audiences*. Green Forest, AR: Balfour Books, 2004.

Caner, Emir Fethi and Ergun Mehmet. *More Than a Prophet: An Insider's Response to Muslim Beliefs About Jesus & Christianity*. Grand Rapids, MI: Kregel Publications, 2003.

———. *Unveiling Islam: An Insider's Look at Muslim Life and Beliefs*. Grand Rapids, MI: Kregel Publications, 2002.

Carroll, James. *Constantine's Sword: The Church And The Jews*. Boston: Houghton Mifflin Company, 2001.

Chamish, Barry. *Traitors and Carpetbaggers in the Promised Land: A Journal of Israel's Betrayal*. Oklahoma City: Hearthstone Publishing, 1997.

Chouraqui, Andre. *Between East and West: A History of the Jews of North Africa*, Philadelphia: Jewish Publication Society of North America, 1968.

Chomsky, Noam. *Fateful Triangle: The United States, Israel & The Palestinians*. Cambridge: South End Press, 1999.

Demy, Timothy and Gary P. Stewart. *In the Name of God: Understanding the Mindset of Terrorism*. Eugene, OR: Harvest House Publishers, 2002.

De Rosa, Peter. *Vicars of Christ: The Dark Side of the Papacy*. New York: Crown Publishers, Inc., 1988.

Dershowitz, Alan. *The Case for Israel*. Hoboken, NJ: John Wiley & Sons, Inc., 2003.

Diprose, Ronald E. *Israel in the development of Christian thought*. Rome: Instituto Biblico Evangelico Italiano, 2000.

Durant, Will. *The Story of Civilization*, vol. VI, *The Reformation*. New York: Simon and Schuster, 1950.

Eban, Abba. *My People: The Story of the Jews*. New York: Random House, 1968.

———. *Personal Witness: Israel Through My Eyes*. London: Jonathan Cape, 1993.

Ehler, Sidney Z. and John B. Morral, trans. and eds. *Church and State Through the Centuries*. London, 1954.

Fallaci, Oriana. *The Rage And The Pride*. New York: Rizzoli, 2002.

Findley, Paul. *Silent No More—Confronting America's False Images of Islam*. Beltsville, MD: Amana Publications, 2001.

Finkelstein, Norman G. *Image and Reality of the Israel-Palestine Conflict*. London: Verso, 1995.

———. *The Holocaust Industry: Reflections on the Exploitation of Jewish Suffering*. London: Verso, 2001.

Fregosi, Paul. *Jihad in the West: Muslim Conquests From the 7th to the 21st Centuries*. Amherst, NY: Prometheus Books, 1998.

Freudmann, Lillian C. *Antisemitism in the New Testament*. New York: University Press of America, 1994.

Fromkin, David. *A Peace to End All Peace: The Fall of the Ottoman Empire and the Creation of the Modern Middle East*. New York: Henry Holt and Company, 1989.

Gabriel, Mark A. *Islam and Terrorism: What the Qur'an really teaches about Christianity, violence and the goals of the Islamic jihad*. Lake Mary, FL: Charisma House, 2002.

Gazit, Shlomo and Zeev Eytan. *The Middle East Military Balance: 1993-1994*. Jerusalem: Jaffee Center for Strategic Studies, 1994.

Gilbert, Martin. *Israel: A History.* New York: William Morrow and Company, Inc., 1998.

———. *The Holocaust: A History of the Jews of Europe During the Second World War.* New York: Henry Holt and Company, Inc., 1985.

Gold, Dore. *Hatred's Kingdom: How Saudi Arabia Supports the New Global Terrorism.* Washington, D.C.: Regnery Publishing, Inc., 2003.

Goldhagen, Daniel Jonah. *A Moral Reckoning: The Role of the Catholic Church in the Holocaust and its Unfulfilled Duty of Repair.* New York: Alfred A. Knopf, 2002.

———. *Hitler's Willing Executioners: Ordinary Germans and the Holocaust.* New York: Alfred A. Knopf, 1996.

Halley, Henry H. *Pocket Bible Handbook.* Chicago, 1944.

Hickinbotham, Sir Tom. *Aden.* London: 1958.

Hirschberg, H.Z. *A History of the Jews in North Africa.* Leiden, Netherlands: 1974.

Horton, George. *The Blight of Asia: An Account of the Systematic Extermination of Christian Populations by Mohammedans and of the Culpability of Certain Great Powers; with the True Story of the Burning of Smyrna.* Indianapolis: Bobbs-Merrill Company, 1926.

Hunt, Dave. *A Woman Rides the Beast: The Roman Catholic Church and the Last Days.* Eugene, OR: Harvest House Publishers, 1994.

———. *Occult Invasion.* Eugene, OR: Harvest House, 1998.

Isaac, Jules. *Jesus et Israel.* Paris: 1948.

Ishaq, Ibn. *The Life of Muhammad.* tr. Guillaume. N.p.: 1967.

Jiryis, Sabri. *Al Nahor.* Beirut: 1975.

John Paul II. *On Jews and Judaism, 1979-1986.* Washington, D.C.: United States Catholic Conference, Inc., 1987.

Katz, Arthur. *The Holocaust–Where was God?* Laporte, MN: 1998.

Katz, Samuel. *Battleground: Fact and Fantasy in Palestine.* New York: Bantam Books, 1973.

Kaufman, Myron. *The Coming Destruction of Israel.* New York: The American Library Inc., 1970.

Kepel, G. *The Prophet and Pharaoh.* London: Al-Saqi Books, 1985.

Kertzer, David I. *The Popes Against the Jews: The Vatican's Role in the Rise of Modern Anti-Semitism.* New York: Alfred A. Knopf, 2001.

Khadduri, Majid. *War and Peace in the Law of Islam.* Baltimore: The Johns Hopkins Press, 1962.

Kierman, Thomas. *Yasir Arafat.* London: Sphere Books, 1976.

Klinov, I., ed. *Israel Reborn.* Tel Aviv: Israel Publishing Co., Ltd., 1951.

Laffin, John. *The PLO Connections.* London: Transworld, 1982.

Lamb, David. *The Arabs: Journeys Beyond the Mirage.* New York: Vintage Books, 1988.

Lane, Edward William. *Manners and Customs of the Modern Egyptians 1833-1835.* London: 1890.

Lawrence, Gunther. *Three Million More?* Garden City, NY: Doubleday & Company, Inc.,1970.

Lewis, Bernard, ed. *A Middle East Mosaic: Fragments of Life, Letters and History.* New York: Random House, 2000.

Lewy, Guenter. *The Catholic Church and Nazi Germany.* N.p.: McGraw Hill, 1964.

Livingstone, Neil C., and David Halevy. *Inside the PLO: Covert Units, Secret Funds, and the War Against Israel and the United States.* New York: William Morrow and Company, Inc., 1990.

Loftus, John and Mark Aarons. *The Secret War Against the Jews: How Western Espionage Betrayed the Jewish People.* New York: St. Martin's Press, 1994.

———. *Unholy Trinity: How the Vatican's Nazis Networks Betrayed Western Intelligence to the Soviets.* New York: St. Martin's Press, 1991.

MacDonald, E. M. (preface). *A Short History of the Inquisition*. New York: The Truth Seekers Co., 1907.

Ma'oz, Moshe. *The Image of the Jew in Official Arab Literature and Communications Media*. Hebrew University of Jerusalem, 1976.

Marshall, Paul with Lela Gilbert. *Their Blood Cries Out: The Worldwide Tragedy of Modern Christians Who Are Dying for Their Faith*. Dallas: Word Publishing, 1997.

McQuaid, Elwood. *The Zion Connection: Evangelical Christians and the Jewish Community...Destroying the Myths, Forging an Alliance*. Eugene, OR: Harvest House Publishers, 1996.

Mikhail, Labib. *Islam: Muhammad and the Koran: A Documented Analysis*. Springfield, VA: Blessed Hope Ministry, 2002.

Mitchell, Edwin and Jody. *The Two-Headed Dragon of Africa*. Santa Fe, NM: Josiah Publishing, 1991.

Mordecai, Victor. *Is Fanatic Islam A Global Threat?* Taylors, SC: 1997.

Moshay, G.J.O. *Who Is This Allah?* Gerrards Cross, UK: Dorchester House Publications, 1995.

Musk, Bill A. *Touching the Soul of Islam*. Crowborough, England: Monarch Publications, 1995.

Netanyahu, Benjamin. *A Durable Peace: Israel and its Place Among the Nations*. New York: Warner Books, 2000.

———. *A Place Among the Nations: Israel and the World*. New York: Bantam Books, 1993.

———. *Fighting Terrorism: How Democracies Can Defeat the International Terrorist Network*. New York: Farrar, Straus and Giroux, 2001.

Ostrovsky, Victor, and Claire Hoy. *By Way of Deception: The Making and Unmaking of a Mossad Officer*. New York: St. Martin's Press, 1990.

Peters, Joan. *From Time Immemorial: The Origins of the Arab-Jewish Conflict Over Palestine*. New York: J. KAP Publishing U.S.A., 1984.

Phillips, McCandlish. *The Bible, the Supernatural, and the Jews*. Minneapolis: Bethany Fellowship, Inc., 1970.

Pipes, Daniel. *Militant Islam Reaches America*. New York: W. W. Norton & Company, 2002.

Poston, Larry A., with Carl F. Ellis, Jr. *The Changing Face of Islam in America*. Camp Hill, PA: Horizon Books, 2000.

Price, Randall. *Unholy War: America, Israel and Radical Islam, the Truth Behind the Headlines*. Eugene, OR: Harvest House Publishers, 2001.

Rausch, David A. *The Middle East Maze: Israel and Her Neighbors*. Chicago: Moody Press, 1991.

Rosenwasser, Penny. *Voices from a "Promised Land": Palestinian & Israeli Peace Activists Speak Their Hearts*. Willimantic, CT: Curbstone Press, 1992.

Runciman, S. *A History of the Crusades*. Cambridge, 1954.

Schafi, Abd El. *Behind the Veil: Unmasking Islam*. N.p.: 2000.

Schechtman, Joseph B. *The Mufti and the Fuehrer: The Rise and Fall of Haj Amin el-Husseini*. New York: Thomas Yoseloff, Publisher, 1965.

Scherman, Rabbi Nosson and Rabbi Meir Zlotowitz, Gen. Eds. *Shoah: A Jewish perspective on tragedy in the context of the Holocaust*. New York: Mesorah Publications, Ltd., 1990.

Schwartz, Leo W., ed. *Great Ages and Ideas of the Jewish People*. New York: Random House, 1956.

Shorrosh, Anis, with James and Marti Hefley. *The Liberated Palestinian: The Anis Shorrosh story*. Dallas: Acclaimed Books, n.d.

Simon, Merrill. *Jerry Falwell and the Jews*. Middle Village, NY: Jonathan David Publishers, Inc., 1984.

Tal, Eliyahu. *Whose Jerusalem?* Tel Aviv: International Forum for a United Jerusalem, 1994.

Thompson, R. W. *The Papacy and the Civil Power*. New York, 1876.

Trifkovic, Serge. *The Sword of the Prophet: Islam, history, theology, impact on the world*. Boston: Regina Orthodox Press, Inc., 2002.

Tsoukalas, Steven. *The Nation of Islam: Understanding the "Black Muslims."* Phillipsburg, NJ: P&R Publishing, 2001.

Twersky. Isadore, ed. *A Maimonides Reader*. New York: 1972.

von Dollinger, J. H. Ignaz. *The Pope and the Council*. London: Roberts, 1869.

Warraq, Ibn. *Why I Am Not a Muslim*. Amherst, NY: Prometheus Books, 1995.

Wiesel, Elie. *Night*. New York: Bantam Books, 1982.

Wurmser, Meyrav. *The Schools of Ba'athism: a Study of Syrian Textbooks*. MEMRI, 2000.

Ye'or, Bat. *The Decline of Eastern Christianity under Islam: From Jihad to Dhimmitude*. London: Associated University Presses, 1996.

———. *The Dhimmi: Jews and Christians under Islam*. London: Associated University Presses, 1985.

INDEX

A

Abba Eban: 224, 229

Abd al-Malik: built Dome of the Rock, 18, 156, 303; suppression of Christianity by, 101; Mecca retaken by, 156

Abraham/Abram: Arabs claim descent from through Ishmael, but are mixed race, 76-77; believes God's promises, 50; burial of, 53-54; Friend of God, 45; Hebron becomes his home in Canaan, 50-51; God of, 52; God's everlasting covenant with re Promised Land, 45, 50-52, 74; Islam's false claims concerning, 74, 125, 129-30, 267, 301; Islam wrongfully claims Arabs are his heirs, 59, 129-30; Islam's wrongful association of with Mecca and Ka'aba, 51, 125; Jews rightful heirs of, 60-65, 327; Messiah his heir, 45, 240, 266; sons of, 49

Abraham, Isaac, and Jacob: God of, 52, 92, 236, 260, 264, 269, 304-5, 328; believed in by Israeli military, 92; God's covenant with/promises to, 92, 237, 239-40, 244-45, 264, 304-5, 328; Messiah descends from, 45, 240, 266, 327

Abu Bakr, first Caliph to succeed Muhammad: can't trust Allah for Paradise, 152-53, 281; father of Aisha, Muhammad's favorite wife, 130, 154; Muhammad's first successor and father-in-law, 137; refuses to compile Qur'an, 130; rejects Ali's demand for share in Muhammad's property, 155; Wars of Apostasy led by, 137, 151

Abu Mazen (Mahmoud Abbas): admits not Israel but Arabs made "Palestinians" flee in 1948 war, 98-99; Arafat's long-time partner in terrorism and successor,

D

E

F

G

Human rights: egregious violators of Human Rights are members, never corrected, 43, 305; Islamic "human rights," the shameful record, 148-51; Israel barred from membership, often condemned by, 28, 43; Muslims in West use Western freedoms to destroy democracy, 161-62, 168; need to pressure Muslim nations to grant basic human rights, 188-90; personal freedom as in West is repugnant to Islam, 147-48, 168; refusal of Arab nations to recognize human rights of Jewish refugees, 106; Saudi anti-American material in mosques in America, 146; UN Commission on Human Rights, 28, 43; UN Universal Declaration of Human Rights signed by violators, 147; Universal Islamic Declaration of Human Rights (sharia), 147-48; West overlooks, excuses human rights violations by Muslim nations, 170-72

Hussein, King of Jordan: British paratroops called to protect him from Iraq and Egypt, 150; destruction of Israel intended by, 226; drives PLO our of Jordan, 179-80; two of his best armored brigades sent to fight against Israel in 1973 war, 9; given by British, Transjordan/Jordan, destroys everything Jewish, 11, 88; admits it was Arabs who created "Palestinian refugees" and exploit them, 98

Hussein, Saddam: 28, 31-32, 121; intelligence for invasion of Kuwait given to him by Arafat, 208; invaded Iran, 155; invaded Kuwait and intended to take over all of the Gulf states, 121; murdered thousands of own citizens, 178; paid bounty to families of suicide bombers, 281; rained Scud missiles on Israel, cheered as hero for doing so, 179

I

Iftaar: feast of: 129

Ilah: generic word for god in Arabic: 134

Immigration: British attempt to stop Jewish immigration into "Palestine," 87; of Muslims to West, 29, 161-62, 191-92

Inquisition: 254, 273

Intifada: 119, 146, 199

International Conference on the Prophet Muhammad and his Message: London 1980, 147

Iran: anti-Semitism officially declared, 27; atrocities committed by against own citizens, 178, 228; backs largest political party in Iraq, United Iraq Alliance (UIA), 144-45; Jews fled from in 1948, 103; largest Shi'ite nation, 155; most dangerous enemy of Israel in Middle East, 310-11; nuclear missiles in arsenal (it says) can reach America, 311; nuclear program will be destroyed by Israel if bomb achieved, 311; plotted overthrow of other Muslim nations, 150; Sharia imposed there but not strictly enforced, 144; suicide bombers recruited by the thousands in, 281; voted for UN Universal Declaration of Human Rights, but violates continually, 168, 228; War with Iraq (1980-1988), 155

Iraq: bombarded Israel with Scud missiles during Gulf War 1991, 179; democracy voted in—will it work?, 144-45, 176; foreign terrorists infiltrating, 90; invasion of Jordan threatened by in past, 150; Jews fled from in 1948, 103; Jews persecuted and murdered in, 31; Muslim leaders from present special Qur'an to John Paul II, 51; objects to UN partition of Palestine in 1947, swears annihilation of Jews, 89; Shi'ite world center, 155-56; victims of terrorism are mostly Iraqis, not foreign troops, 288; voted for UN Universal Declaration of Human Rights, but violated continually, 168; Zionism was a capital crime in, 27

Irgun Zvai Leumi: Israeli underground extremist splinter group, 87

Isaac: Abraham's second born son, by Sarah his wife, 49; all of his descendants alive on earth at Second Coming will believe in Christ, 327; buried in Hebron in cave of Machpelah, 54; God of Abraham is God of Isaac, not of Ishmael, 52, 92, 236, 260, 269, 305, 328; his descendants, not Ishmael's, meet all the criteria of inheritance, 61-63; lived and died in Canaan, not "Palestine," 74-75; offered on altar by Abraham in ultimate tests of his faith, 53, 128; only son recognized by God, 53; promise given directly from God to him, never to Ishmael, 64, 130, 239, 264, 304; Qur'an agrees that Isaac was born after Ishmael, 51; son promised by God to Abraham who would be heir, 52-53

Ishmael/Ishmaelites: Abraham's firstborn son, by Hagar, his wife Sarah's maid, 49, 51; Arab claims that he is the true heir of Abraham, 52, 53, 60, 76, 84, 130; descendants never lived in Canaan, 64; nomadic, intermarried, 61; Ka'aba falsely claimed to have been built by him and Abraham, 125; not a Canaanite or "Palestinian," 76-77; offered on altar by Abraham (Islam falsely claims), 128

Islam: admits God of Israel is the true God and Promised Land belongs to Jews, 60; advocates pretending peace to gain advantage, 7; apostasy punished by death, 137-40; believing not necessary for forced conversion into, 154, 173-74; claims that Abraham and Ishmael built the Ka'aba, 51; claims inheritance through Ishmael, 52-53; culture of hatred created by, 146, 186-87; killing a Jew assures entrance into Paradise, 31; history of vicious oppression and slaughter, 100-105, 149-59, 178, 219-20; human rights universally recognized are rejected as a danger to it, 82, 106, 147-48, 170-72; its deity and rituals inherited from Arab paganism, 113-15, 123-24, 127-29, 133-35; its true practice modeled in Saudi Arabia, 142-44, 146; most anti-Semitic, anti-Christian religion ever known, 30-34, 42, 82, 100-104, 106, 147-48, 158-59, 170-72, 213-14, 225, 235, 266-68, 300; most dangerous and egregious lie that it is a religion of peace, 7, 12-13, 181-87, 191-92, 204-5, 209-10, 213-18, 228, 273; murder and oppression required by admitted by Muslims, 117-18; must conquer entire world, 167; presents a false Jesus called "Isa," 83-84, 266-68; prevents integration of followers into non-Islamic society, 176-77; proven false

J

have long preached return of to their own land, 7, 261-264; God of is only true God, 135; God's chosen people, ancestors of the Messiah, 266; inherit Promised Land through Isaac and Jacob, 53-54; irrational hatred of, as Bible foretold, is worldwide, 25-41, 43-44; Islam's vicious record of hatred, persecution, and slaughter of, 30-34, 42, 82, 56-58, 89-94, 100-104, 106, 119-20, 147-48, 158-59, 170-72, 213-14, 225, 235, 266-68, 300; killing of assures Muslim entrance into Paradise, 31; many Christians deny any special place in God's plans for today, 45; Martin Luther opposed to, 24; Muslims taught to hate, 14, 141-42; numerous biblical prophecies that they would be scattered to all nations, hated, persecuted as no other people, 23; persecuted and killed in Muslim countries for 1300 years, 30-34; restoration promised, 241-42, 245-46; Roman Catholic Church's false view of, 24; returning to their land in unbelief, 271; that were ever a nation denied by PLO, 17; unbelief and rebellion of is unbelievable, 236-37; unbelief of most worldwide, 235; under God's judgment because of rebellion and unbelief, 233-35, 240-41; viciously treated by Roman Catholic Church, 252-58, 255

Jihad: commanded by Allah in Qur'an, a virtue, 118-19; dying as martyr in is highest honor, 182-83, 276; Paradise promised to such, 119, 141, 152, 171, 182, 254, 276, 280-82, "Islamic Jihad," terrorist movement, 13, 123, 323; Muslim media raising questions as to why leaders don't aspire to martyrdom, 290-91; perpetual commanded until all world submits to Islam, 174; "World Islamic Front for Jihad Against Jews and Crusaders," 189-90; would exterminate all Jews, 99, 142; youth incited to by religious leaders who promise Paradise, 290-91

Jordan (formerly Transjordan): armistice (Hudna) signed with Israel April 3, 1949, 74; army called Arab Legion, created and led by British, 91; attacks and terrorism against by other Muslim nations, 150; captured East Jerusalem and West Bank including Hebron in 1948, 57; created by British in 1946 out of land promised to Jews, 11, 88; peace treaty with Israel in 1994, 105; put "Palestinian refugees" in camps instead of integrating into normal life, 69-73, 99; shelter given to PLO, had to drive them out, 179-80; Six-day War of 1967 joined other Muslim nations against Israel, 222-23; State TV broadcast Arafat's diatribes against Israel, 208; Temple mount turned over to king of by General Moshe Dayan, 17; textbooks teach annihilation of Israel, 183

Joseph's tomb: destruction of by Palestinians, 70

Joshua: called "ethnic cleanser...genocidist" by "Christians," 269; claim by Christian leaders that all promises to Israel fulfilled under Joshua, 244-45; "Palestinian refugees" claim descent from inhabitants who pre-dated, 73

K

Ka'aba: attacked and burned by Muslims, then restored, 156, 303; built by Abraham and Ishmael says the Qur'an, 51; "first sanctuary...where Abraham

L

M

Machpelah, cave of: 53-54

Mahmoud Abbas. *See* Abu Mazen

Madrid: peace conference initiated there in 1991, 206, 216; train bombing in 2004, 175

Maimonides: 235, 248

Malcolm X: 132

Marshall, Secretary of State George C.: opposes Israel, 92

Martel, Prince Charles of France: and battle of Tours, 175

Martyrs: at hands of Roman Catholic Church, 257-58

Muslim suicide bombers: Arab youths seduced to become, 290; eager to be "martyred" for Allah to gain Paradise, 171; hundreds trained by Hamas, 16; most honored heroes among Muslims, 16; pros and cons in Islamic teachings, 281-83; "unshakable conviction" in virtue of is foundation of terrorism, 177-78

Marwan, Asma bint: 116

Massacres: Aden's Jewish community rescued by British from being massacred by Muslims in 1948, 224; alleged, falsely, at Jenin, 199-200; of Armenians, 159-60; of Muslims, 206; by Roman Catholic Church, 257-58

Mecca: goal of the hajj, 123-24; holiest city to Muslims, 18; Ka'aba located there, 51; Muhammad's birthplace, 113; non-Muslims may not approach, 125; Quraish tribe controlled, 113-15

Muslim Brotherhood: assassinates Anwar Sadat, 150, 214-15, 224; hatred of and lies against Jews, 205

Media: distorted coverage of Middle East by, 26, 55, 104, 200, 204; eager to paint Israel in worst possible light, 199-200, 207, 224; Jewish refugees that fled Muslim lands ignored by, 103; not free in Muslim countries, 143; of Muslim countries particularly dishonest, 186, 207; truth about Islam being denied by, 33, 159; truth finally being told by some, 172, 286; world media willingly closes eyes to truth and passes on lies, 207-9, 261

Median (Yathrib): flight to from Mecca known as Hijrah, begins Muslim calendar, 115; founded by Jews as Yathrib, all killed, name changed to Medina, 120; home of one faction of Muslims (Umayyads) that fought others, 155; night journey (Isra') of Muhammad was to Medina, not Jerusalem, 303; one of Islam's holiest cities, burial place of Muhammad, 79

O

oil: America betrayed Israel for, 9; Arab nations refuse to use their huge income from to help "Palestinian" refugees, 105, 107, 109; Britain betrays Jews for oil, 11, 88-89; gives clout to Muslims, 15, 19, 188; Saudi profits from paying for construction of and support for many mosques in the West, 174; slaughter of non-Muslims in Southern Sudan largely because of, 147; influence of used as club by Allen Dulles, 258, 260

Olympic games: 181

Osama bin Laden: 81, 145, 189, 216, 289

Oslo Accords: 70, 79, 214, 216-17

Ottoman Empire: 263

P

Pacelli, Cardinal Eugenio (became Pope Pius XII): 251-52

Pakistan: 29, 109, 118, 150, 168, 176, 190, 276, 281

Palestine: annihilation of Israel called "liberation of ," 10; Arab leaders denied designation as, 76; Arabs not there until 7th-century Muslim invasion of, 56; belongs solely to Arabs says Islam, 12-14, 60, 69, 185, 218, 222, 225, 228; Britain betrays mandate of, 11, 37, 87-88; Israel may not have one square meter of, 225; Israel only sovereign nation that ever existed there, 62; no such place or people, 50; partitioned by UN, 18, 89, 328; persecution of Jews in, 30-31, 34; Pope Pius XII's letter to Roosevelt opposing return of Jews to, 39; Promised land was not, but was Canaan, 50; Qur'an doesn't mention it once, 60; Roman Catholic Church historically opposed to Jew's presence there, 251, 270-71

Palestine Liberation Organization (PLO): agents of work for British secret service, 121; claims Hebron and Jerusalem not Israeli cities but "Palestinian," 20, 54; claimed Jerusalem as its headquarters, ousted by Israelis, 79; claims never was a Jewish temple and controls temple mount, 15, 17; driven out of Jordan into Lebanon, 150; founded by Nasser in 1964, Arafat became chairman in 1969, 81; Fatah, largest terrorist arm of co-founded by Arafat and Mahmoud Abbas and backed latter in election, 323; French police intimidated by, 187; funded by Saudi government, 145; in spite of its treachery, Israel continued to turn over territory to, 72, 73; Lebanon became base for terrorism with Syrian sponsorship, 180; logo shows "Palestine" without Israel, 14, 221; media of world eagerly passes on its lies against Israel and doesn't want to hear the truth, 200, 209; pretended peaceful intentions and was accepted by Israel and UN as leader for peace, 216-18; repeatedly denies Israel's right to exist, 82, 171, 221, 209, 221, 226; outrage that ought to be at its deeds and threats lacking in

Promised Land: Arabs could not possibly be descended from original inhabitants of, 77; was Canaan, not "Palestine," 51; evangelical Christians have always supported Israel's full restoration to, 261-64; Pope Pius XII objected to Israel's restoration to, 270; fullness of promises concerning not fulfilled under Joshua, 242-46, nor in the church, 247-48; not one Jew left outside of at Second Coming of Christ, 327; God's judgment sternly declared at borders of, 233; Holocaust survivors driven back by British within sight of, 88; 4,000-year-old title deed signed by God himself gives size of, 213; Islam claims for Arabs as descendants of Ishmael, the firstborn, 52; Israel must retain possession of it all, 231; judgment pronounced by God after bringing Israel into, 23; Messiah must rule over Israel restored to, 304; proof that the son of promise is not Ishmael but Israel is given many times in Scripture, 53, 61-65, 233-35; Qur'an agrees that it was given to Israel, 59-60; return to by Jews accelerated for good reason during reign of Antichrist, 320; twelve tribes there to the very end, 44

prophecy/prophecies, biblical: amazing foretelling of today's weapons of mass destruction (WMDs), 316-317; anti-Semitism another specific fulfillment of, 12-15, 23-42; exclusion of Israel from UN committees, Red Cross, etc. another specific fulfillment of, 42-43; concerning Messiah unmistakably point to Jesus Christ, 240-41, 296-300; Ezekiel's concerning Israel's leaders promising peace when is no peace apropos to our day, 206; God is finalizing fulfillment of in our day, 326; many re Israel can only be fulfilled in "last days," 5, 231-32; provides full proof of God, the Bible, Christ, and that Israelis are the chosen people who inherit the land, 5, 62-63, 275; specific prophecies fulfilled in Israel's modern defeat of Arab attackers, 8-10, 223, 246, and in Holocaust, 91, and in rebirth of as nation, 42-42, and precise concerning Jerusalem, 6-7, 17-19; return from diaspora among all nations not fulfilled under Joshua as falsely claimed by some, 243-45

"Protestant B": 121

Protocols of the Learned Elders of Zion: 183, 203

Q

Qaddafi, Muammar: 10, 147, 151, 181

Qur'an: Allah of hates Jews and Israel, 7; calls Christians and Jews "people of the book," 30, 59; calls for Islamic take-over of entire world by force, 167, 178-80, 182, 184-85; declares Promised Land belongs to Jews, 60, 51; completely anti-Christian, 129; denies Christ died on Cross, 300-301; encourages murder of non-Muslims, 117-18, 138; executed for expressing lack of respect for, 101, 117-18; false claims about Ka'aba, 125; final unchangeable authority, 204; Israel's survival proves it false, 12-13, 42; Jerusalem not mentioned once, and demeaned as wrong qiblah, 5, 79, 302; Jesus is "Isa" in and not the Jesus of Bible, 83-84, 267, 304; Muhammad had doubts about its source of inspiration, 114; offers no assurance of Paradise, 152-53; only "peace" offered is surrender

but overlooked by United States, 170, 174, 179, 182; part of a secret network of oil interests working with the Nazis during WWII and put together by the Dulles brothers and John D. Rockefeller, 260; sword appropriately displayed on flag of, 126; textbooks promote jihad against non-Muslims, and do not recognize Israel's existence, 69, 182-84; state visit by Vatican official to, 135; violates every day human rights it promised to uphold as member of UN, 146-47; visit to by Malcolm X led to his assassination, 132; will be united with rest of world under Antichrist, 317; young men training to be suicide bombers in, 281;

schools, Muslim: all teach that every Jew must be killed, 12; Iraq a school for training terrorists, 176; textbooks promote jihad against non-Muslims, and do not recognize Israel's existence, 69, 182-84

Schroeder, Captain Gustav: of SS St. Louis, 36-37

Schuller, Robert: 132-33

second coming of Christ: 297, 299-300, 313, 319, 327

Shafarevich, Igor R., anti-Semitic leading Russian mathematician, 28-29

Sharia: 126, 144-45, 147, 161, 172, 177

Sharm el-Sheikh Agreement: 226

Sharon, Prime Minister Ariel: 184, 343

Shi'ite/Shi'ites: 51, 144, 155, 276, 279, 288, 311

Shukairy, Ahmed: 76

Sinai: 62, 213, 222-23, 236-37, 311, 320

Sissalem, Dr. Issam, University of Gaza, Holocaust denier: 34

Smyrna, destruction of: 159, 165

Soviets: 8, 224, 259, 274

SS St. Louis, German ocean liner carrying refugees from Nazi Germany: 36-37

Stalin, Joseph: 27, 32, 172, 215, 220

Sudan: 43, 144, 147-48, 163-64, 170, 177, 205, 222

Suicide bombers: can't explain away as extremists, 174; children encouraged to become, 182; defense of as normal to Islam, 117; Israel criticized for forcefully defending itself against, 202; justified by lies about Israeli atrocities passed on willingly by Western media, 199; most honored heroes in PLO territory, 16-17, 277; millions in training to for missions as, 281; no certainty even in Islam of Paradise for, 152, 281; openly supported by some "Christian" leaders, 269; praised by Muzammil Siddiqi, past president of Islamic Society of North

America, 126; President Bush calls them "homicide bombers," 16; wedding announcements for, 16

Sunni/Sunnis: 51, 126, 155, 277-79, 288-89

Syria: Armistice (Hudna) with Israel, July 20,1949, 74; desperate for farm workers for years but would not take Palestinian refugees, 103-9; Europeans consider Israel a greater threat to peace than, 26; gave its blessing and help to Arafat when he fled Jordan to Lebanon, 180; haven for Haj Amin when he fled Palestine in 1941, 31; headquarters of Hizballah, which backs and protects it, 79, 207; home for some Palestine refugee camps, 69; Jewish population went from 30,000 to about 100 when Jews fled in 1948, 103; major role in Yom Kippur sneak attack against Israel in 1973, 8-9; Muslim invading army conquered it in A.D. 640, 153; persecution and slaughter of Jews in, 119-20; route for Arab Liberation Army infiltrating Israel beginning in January 1948, 91; signed UN Declaration of Human Rights in 1945 and violates it every day, 168; slaughter of up to 25,000 Syrian civilians in destruction of Hama by Hafez Assad, 151, 178; textbooks call for annihilation of Israel, 182-83; UN delegate of walked out and threatened annihilation of Israel in retaliation against 1947 partition recognizing Israel's existence, 89

T

Taliban: 140, 144, 168, 179, 181, 227

Tamerlane: Muslim leader (typical of many) who slaughtered hundreds of thousands from Palestine to India in the 15th century: 158

Tel Aviv: 19, 21, 84, 310

temple/temple mount: Arab and Muslim sources in past verifying that Jewish temple was there, 18; controlled by PLO, 15; Dome of the Rock not an impossible barrier to rebuilding, 303; full sovereignty over demanded by Palestinians, 227; Israelis determined to see it rebuilt, 301; Israel refused to allow Arafat to be buried on, 82; largest mosque in world under construction while attempting to destroy any evidence of Jewish presence in past, 17; Romans attempted in A.D. 132 to build temple to Jupiter on this site, 75

Ten "lost tribes": 44-45

Terrorism/terrorists: Arafat, most vicious and successful in history, 179-81, 209-10; billions in funding for comes from Saudi Arabia, 145-46; early example set by Haj Amin, 58, 149-50, 205-6; endemic to Islam, 119, 138, 219, 275-76, 277-78, but it is being whitewashed, 122, 219-220; example of and rules for set by Muhammad and Qur'an, 117-19; ignored by critics (even Jewish) who blame Israel for existing, 96; Mahmoud Abbas, Arafat's successor, deeply involved in, 323; most honored heroes among Muslims, 16-17, 205-10, 277; reconstruction funds diverted into by Arafat, 107, 218; pagan

U

V

W

ALSO BY DAVE HUNT

THE GOD MAKERS
—*Ed Decker & Dave Hunt*

Mormons claim to follow the same God and the same Jesus as Christians. They also state that their gospel comes from the Bible. But are they telling the truth? One of the most powerful books to penetrate the veil of secrecy surrounding the rituals and doctrines of the Mormon Church, this eye-opening exposé has been updated to reveal the current inner workings and beliefs of Mormonism. Harvest House Publishers, 292 pages.

ISBN: 1-56507-717-2 • TBC: B04023

DEATH OF A GURU:
A REMARKABLE TRUE STORY OF ONE MAN'S SEARCH FOR TRUTH
—*Rabi R. Maharaj with Dave Hunt*

Rabi R. Maharaj was descended from a long line of Brahmin priests and gurus and trained as a Yogi. He meditated for many hours each day, but gradually disillusionment set in. He describes vividly and honestly Hindu life and customs, tracing his difficult search for meaning and his struggle to choose between Hinduism and Christ. At a time when eastern mysticism, religion, and philosophy fascinate many in the West, Maharaj offers fresh and important insights from the perspective of his own experience. Harvest House Publishers, 208 pages.

ISBN: 0-89081-434-1 • TBC: B04341

THE SEDUCTION OF CHRISTIANITY: SPIRITUAL DISCERNMENT IN THE LAST DAYS
—*Dave Hunt & T. A. McMahon*

The Bible clearly states that a great Apostasy must occur before Christ's Second Coming. Today Christians are being deceived by a new worldview more subtle and more seductive than anything the world has ever experienced. Scripture declares that this seduction will not appear as a frontal assault or oppression of our religious beliefs; instead, it will come as the latest "fashionable philosophies" offering to make us happier, healthier, better educated, even more spiritual. As the first bestselling book to sound the alarm of false teaching in the church, this ground-breaking classic volume still sounds a clear call to every believer to choose between the Original and the counterfeit. As delusions and deceptions continue to grow, this book will guide you in the truth of God's Word. Harvest House Publishers, 239 pages.

ISBN: 0-89081-441-4 • TBC: B04414

IN DEFENSE OF THE FAITH:
BIBLICAL ANSWERS TO CHALLENGING QUESTIONS
—*Dave Hunt*

Why does God allow suffering and evil? What about all the "contradictions" in the Bible? Are some people predestined to go to hell? This book tackles the tough issues that Christians and non-Christians alike wonder about today, including why a merciful God would punish people who have never heard of Christ, how to answer attacks against God's existence and the Bible, and how to tell the difference between God's workings and Satan's. Harvest House, 347 pages.

ISBN: 1-56507-495-5 • TBC: B04955

THE NONNEGOTIABLE GOSPEL
—*Dave Hunt*

A must for the Berean soul-winner's repertory, this evangelistic booklet reveals the gem of the gospel in every clear-cut facet. Refines and condenses what Dave has written for believers to use as a witnessing tool for anyone desiring a precise Bible definition of the gospel. The Berean Call, 48 pages.

ISBN: 1-928660-01-0 • TBC: B45645

BATTLE FOR THE MIND
–*Dave Hunt*

Positive thinking is usually better than negative thinking and can sometimes help a great deal, but it has its limitations. To deny those commonsense limitations and to believe that the mind can create its own universe is to step into the occult where the demons who foster this belief will eventually destroy the soul. Unfortunately, increasing millions in the West are accepting this mystical philosophy, forgetting that it is the very thing which has brought many deplorable conditions wherever it has been practiced. The Berean Call, 48 pages.

ISBN: 1-928660-09-6 • TBC: B45650

DEBATING CALVINISM: FIVE POINTS, TWO VIEWS
—*Dave Hunt & James White*

Is God free to love anyone He wants? Do you have any choice in your own salvation? "This book deserves to be read carefully by anyone interested in the true nature of God." —Tim LaHaye, co-author of the Left Behind series. Calvinism has been a topic of intense discussion for centuries. In this lively debate, two passionate thinkers take opposite sides, providing valuable responses to the most frequently asked questions about Calvinism. Only you can decide where you stand on questions that determine how you think about your salvation.

ISBN: 1-590522-73-7 • TBC: B05000

WHEN WILL JESUS COME?
COMPELLING EVIDENCE FOR THE SOON RETURN OF CHRIST
—*Dave Hunt*

Jesus has promised to return for His bride, the church. But when will that be? In this updated revision of How Close Are We?, Dave takes us on a journey through the Old and New Testaments as he explains prophecy after prophecy showing that we are indeed in the last of the last days. In the process, Dave compellingly shows that Scripture illuminates the truth that Jesus will return two times, and that His next appearance—the "rapture" of His church—will occur without any warning. The question is, are you ready? Harvest House Publishers, 251 pages.

ISBN: 0-7369-1248-7 • TBC: B03137

COUNTDOWN TO THE SECOND COMING:
A CHRONOLOGY OF PROPHETIC EARTH EVENTS HAPPENING NOW
—*Dave Hunt*

At last, a book that presents in a concise manner the events leading up to the return of Christ. Dave Hunt, in his characteristic direct style, answers questions such as, Who is the Antichrist? How will he be recognized? How are current events indicators that we really are in the last of the last days? Using Scripture and up-to-date information, Dave draws the exciting conclusion that, indeed, time is short. This book instructs, encourages, warns, and strengthens, urging readers to "walk circumspectly, not as fools, but as wise, redeeming the time, because the days are evil" (Ephesians 5:15-16). The Berean Call, new paperback edition, 96 pages.

ISBN: 1-928660-19-3

A WOMAN RIDES THE BEAST: THE ROMAN CATHOLIC CHURCH AND THE LAST DAYS
—*Dave Hunt*

In Revelation 17, the Apostle John describes in great detail the characteristics of a false church that will be the partner of the Antichrist. Was he describing the Roman Catholic Church? To answer that question, Dave has spent years gathering historical documentation (primarily Catholic sources) providing information not generally available. Harvest House, 549 pages.

ISBN: 1-56507-199-9 • TBC: B01999

OCCULT INVASION: THE SUBTLE SEDUCTION OF THE WORLD AND CHURCH
—*Dave Hunt*

Occult beliefs march freely across America today powerfully influencing our children, our society, our government, and even our churches. The deadly impact of Satan's dominion is seen in the rise of teen suicide, the increase in violence, and the immorality that pervades our society. Noted cult expert Dave Hunt reveals: how Satan's lies are being taught behind the academic respectability of science; how demonic activities are presented as the path to enlightenment through "alien" contacts and paranormal experiences; how pagan religions are being promoted through ecology and "we are one" philosophies; and how evil is being reinvented as good by psychology and the legal system. Harvest House Publishers, 647 pages.

ISBN: 1-56507-269-3 • TBC: B02693

WHAT LOVE IS THIS? CALVINISM'S MISREPRESENTATION OF GOD
—*Dave Hunt*

Most of those who regard themselves as Calvinists are largely unaware of what John Calvin and his early followers of the sixteenth and seventeenth centuries actually believed and practiced. Nor do they fully understand what most of today's leading Calvinists believe. Multitudes who believe they understand Calvinism will be shocked to discover its Roman Catholic roots and Calvin's grossly un-Christian behavior as the "Protestant Pope" of Geneva, Switzerland. It is our prayer that this book will enable readers to examine more carefully the vital issues involved and to follow God's Holy Word and not man. The Berean Call, 576 pages.

ISBN: 1-928660-12-6 • TBC: B03000

SEEKING & FINDING GOD: IN SEARCH OF THE TRUE FAITH
—*Dave Hunt*

It is astonishing how many millions of otherwise seemingly intelligent people are willing to risk their eternal destiny upon less evidence then they would require for buying a car—yet the belief of so many, particularly in the area of religion, has no rational foundation. With compelling proofs, this book demonstrates that the issue of where one will spend eternity is not a matter of preference. In fact, there is overwhelming evidence that we are eternal beings who will spend eternity somewhere. But where will it be? And how can we know? The Berean Call, 160 pages.

ISBN:1-928660-23-1 • TBC: B04425

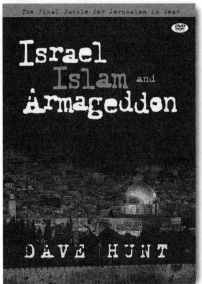